THE COMPLETE 101 COLLECTION

THE
COMPLETE

101

COLLECTION

JOHN C. MAXWELL

HARPERCOLLINS
LEADERSHIP

AN IMPRINT OF HARPERCOLLINS

Published by HarperCollins Leadership, an imprint of HarperCollins Focus LLC.

Published in association with Yates & Yates, www.yates2.com

Portions of this book have been previously published in *The 17 Essential Qualities
of a Team Player, The 17 Indisputable Laws of Teamwork, The 21 Indispensable Qualities
of a Leader, The 21 Irrefutable Laws of Leadership, The 360° Leader, Becoming a Person
of Influence, Developing the Leaders Around You, Developing the Leader within You,
Failing Forward, Your Road Map for Success, The Winning Attitude, Winning with
People, Talent Is Never Enough,* and *Leadership Gold.*

ISBN: 978-0-7180-2209-9 (TP)
ISBN: 978-1-4002-0395-6 (HC)
ISBN: 978-1-4002-8108-4

Printed in the United States of America
19 20 21 22 LSC 16 15 14 13 12

CONTENTS

PREFACE

I've been passionate about personal growth for most of my life. In fact, I've created and pursued a plan for growth every year for the last forty years! People say that wisdom comes with age. I don't believe that's true. Sometimes age comes alone. I wouldn't have achieved any of my dreams had I not been dedicated to continual improvement. If you want to grow and become the best person you can be, you've got to be intentional about it.

At the same time, life is busy and complex. Most people run out of day long before their to-do list is done. And trying to get to the bottom line in just about any area of life can be a challenge. Did you know that more new information has been produced in the last thirty years than in the previous five thousand? A single weekday edition of *The New York Times* contains more information than most people in seventeenth-century England were likely to encounter in their lifetime.

That's why we've developed this series of 101 books. We've cherry-picked the essentials in subjects such as leadership, attitude, relationships, teamwork, and mentoring and put them into a format that is easy to read.

And now for the first time, we've combined all six of the 101 books in one volume.

In many of my larger books, I go into my subject in great depth. I do that because I believe it is often the best way to add value to people. But the 101 series is different. Each 101 book is an introduction to a subject, not the "advanced course." I believe these concentrated versions will help you on your way to significant growth in specific areas of your life.

I hope you enjoy this volume, and I pray that it serves you well as you seek to improve your life and achieve your dreams.

ATTITUDE

101

WHAT EVERY LEADER NEEDS TO KNOW

Published in Nashville, Tennessee, by Thomas Nelson. Thomas Nelson
is a registered trademark of Thomas Nelson, Inc.

Published in association with Yates & Yates, www.yates2.com

Thomas Nelson, Inc., titles may be purchased in bulk for educational,
business, fund-raising, or sales promotional use. For information,
please e-mail SpecialMarkets@ThomasNelson.com.

Unless otherwise noted, Scripture quotations are from
THE NEW KING JAMES VERSION of the Bible. © 1979,
1980, 1982, Thomas Nelson, Inc., Publishers.

Scripture quotations noted NIV are from the HOLY BIBLE: NEW
INTERNATIONAL VERSION®. © 1973, 1978, 1984 by International Bible Society.
Used by permission of Zondervan Publishing House. All rights reserved.

Portions of this book were previously published in *The Winning Attitude, Failing Forward, Your Roadmap
for Success, The 17 Indisputable Laws of Teamwork,* and *The 21 Irrefutable Laws of Leadership.*

Library of Congress Cataloging-in-Publication Data

Maxwell, John C., 1947–
Attitude 101 / John C. Maxwell.
p. cm.
ISBN 978-0-7852-6350-0
1. Success—Psychological aspects. 2. Attitude (Psychology). I. Title.
BF637.S8 M3415 2002
153.8'5—dc21
2002011491

Contents

PART I

THE IMPACT
OF ATTITUDE

I

How Does Attitude Impact Leadership?

Attitude is always a "player" on your team.

Growing up, I loved basketball. It all started for me in the fourth grade when I saw a high school basketball game for the first time. I was captivated. After that, I could usually be found practicing my shooting and playing pickup games on my small court at home.

By the time I got to high school, I had become a pretty good player. I started on the junior varsity team as a freshman, and when I was a sophomore, our JV team had a 15-3 record, which was better than that of the varsity. We were proud of our performance—maybe a little too proud.

The next year, critics who followed high school basketball in Ohio thought our team had a chance to win the state championship in our division. I guess they looked at the players who would return as seniors from the previous year's varsity team, saw the talent that would be moving up from the JV, and figured we would be a powerhouse. And we did have a lot of talent. How many high school teams in the late 1960s could say that all but a couple of players on the team could dunk the ball? But the season turned out far different from everyone's expectations.

FROM BAD TO WORSE

From the beginning of the season, the team suffered problems. There were two of us juniors on the varsity who had the talent to start for the team: John Thomas, who was the team's best rebounder, and me, the best shooting guard. We thought playing time should be based strictly on ability, and we figured we deserved our place on the team. The seniors, who had taken a backseat to the previous year's seniors, thought we should be made to pay our dues and wait on the bench.

What began as a rivalry between the JV and varsity the year before turned into a war between the juniors and the seniors. When we scrimmaged at practice, it was the juniors against the seniors. In games the seniors wouldn't pass to the juniors and vice versa. The battles became so fierce that before long, the juniors and the seniors wouldn't even work together on the court during games. Our coach, Don Neff, had to platoon us. The seniors would start, and when a substitution became necessary, he'd put not one but five juniors in the game. We became two teams on one roster.

I don't remember exactly who started the rivalry that split our team, but I do remember that John Thomas and I embraced it early on. I've always been a leader, and I did my share of influencing other team members. Unfortunately, I have to confess that I led the juniors in the wrong direction.

What started as a bad attitude in one or two players made a mess of the situation for everyone. By the time we were in the thick of our schedule, even the players who didn't want to take part in the rivalry were affected. The season was a disaster. In the end, we finished with a mediocre record and never came close to reaching our potential. It just goes to show you, rotten attitudes ruin a team.

TALENT IS NOT ENOUGH

From my high school basketball experience I learned that talent is not enough to bring success to a team. Of course, you need talent. My friend

Lou Holtz, the outstanding college football coach, observed, "You've got to have great athletes to win . . . You can't win without good athletes, but you can lose with them." But it also takes much more than talented people to win.

My high school teammates were loaded with talent, and if that were enough, we could have been state champions. But we were also loaded with rotten attitudes. You know which won the battle between talent and attitude in the end. Perhaps that is why to this day I understand the importance of a positive attitude and have placed such a strong emphasis on it for myself, for my children as they were growing up, and for the teams I lead.

Years ago I wrote something about attitude for my book *The Winning Attitude*. I'd like to share it with you:

> Attitude . . .
> It is the "advance man" of our true selves.
> Its roots are inward but its fruit is outward.
> It is our best friend or our worst enemy.
> It is more honest and more consistent than our words.
> It is an outward look based on past experiences.
> It is a thing which draws people to us or repels them.
> It is never content until it is expressed.
> It is the librarian of our past.
> It is the speaker of our present.
> It is the prophet of our future.[1]

Good attitudes among players do not guarantee a team's success, but bad attitudes guarantee its failure. The following five truths about attitudes clarify how they affect teamwork and a leader's team:

1. Attitudes Have the Power to Lift Up or Tear Down a Team

In *The Winner's Edge* Denis Waitley stated, "The real leaders in business, in the professional community, in education, in government, and in the home also seem to draw upon a special cutting edge that separates them from the rest of society. The winner's edge is not in a gifted birth, in a high IQ, or in talent. The winner's edge is in the attitude, not aptitude."[2]

Unfortunately, I think too many people resist that notion. They want to believe that talent alone (or talent with experience) is enough. But plenty of talented teams out there never amount to anything because of the attitudes of their players.

Various attitudes may impact a team made up of highly talented players:

Abilities	+	Attitudes	=	Result
Great Talent	+	Rotten Attitudes	=	Bad Team
Great Talent	+	Bad Attitudes	=	Average Team
Great Talent	+	Average Attitudes	=	Good Team
Great Talent	+	Good Attitudes	=	Great Team

If you want outstanding results, you need good people with great talent and awesome attitudes. When attitudes go up, so does the potential of the team. When attitudes go down, the potential of the team goes with it.

2. AN ATTITUDE COMPOUNDS WHEN EXPOSED TO OTHERS

Several things on a team are not contagious: talent, experience, and willingness to practice. But you can be sure of one thing: attitude is catching. When someone on the team is teachable and his humility is rewarded by improvement, others are more likely to display similar characteristics. When a leader is upbeat in the face of discouraging circumstances, others admire that quality and want to be like her. When a team member displays a strong work ethic and begins to have a positive impact, others imitate him. People become inspired by their peers. People have a tendency to adopt the attitudes of those they spend time with—to pick up on their mind-sets, beliefs, and approaches to challenges.

The story of Roger Bannister is an inspiring example of the way attitudes often "compound." During the first half of the twentieth century, many sports experts believed that no runner could run a mile in less than four minutes. And for a long time they were right. But then on May 6, 1954, British runner and university student Roger Bannister ran a mile in 3 minutes 59.4 seconds during a meet in Oxford. Less than two months later, another runner, Australian John Landy, also broke the four-minute barrier. Then suddenly dozens and then hundreds of others broke it. Why? Because the best runners' attitudes changed. They began to adopt the mind-sets and beliefs of their peers.

Bannister's attitude and actions compounded when exposed to others. His attitude spread. Today, every world-class runner who competes at that distance can run a mile in less than four minutes. Attitudes are contagious!

3. BAD ATTITUDES COMPOUND FASTER THAN GOOD ONES

There's only one thing more contagious than a good attitude—a bad attitude. For some reason many people think it's chic to be negative. I suspect that they think it makes them appear smart or important. But the truth is that a negative attitude hurts rather than helps the person who has it. And it also hurts the people around him.

To see how quickly and easily an attitude or mind-set can spread, just think about this story from Norman Cousins: Once during a football game, a doctor at the first aid station treated five people for what he suspected might be food poisoning. He soon discovered that all five people had bought drinks from a particular concession stand at the stadium.

The physician requested that the announcer advise people in the stadium to avoid buying drinks from the particular vendor because of the possibility of food poisoning. Before long, more than two hundred people complained of food poisoning symptoms. Nearly half the people's symptoms were so severe that they were taken to the hospital.

The story doesn't end there, however. After a little more detective work, it was discovered that the five original victims had eaten tainted potato salad from one particular deli on the way to the game. When the other "sufferers" found out that the drinks in the stadium were safe, they experienced miraculous recoveries. That just goes to show you, an attitude spreads very quickly.

4. ATTITUDES ARE SUBJECTIVE, SO IDENTIFYING A WRONG ONE CAN BE DIFFICULT

Have you ever interacted with someone for the first time and suspected that his attitude was poor, yet you were unable to put your finger on exactly what was wrong? I believe many people have that experience.

ATTITUDE IS REALLY ABOUT HOW A PERSON IS. THAT OVERFLOWS INTO HOW HE ACTS.

The reason people doubt their observations about others' attitudes is that attitudes are subjective. Someone with a bad attitude may not do anything illegal or unethical, yet his attitude may be ruining the team just the same.

People always project on the outside how they feel on the inside. Attitude is really about how a person is. That overflows into how he acts. Allow me to share with you common rotten attitudes that ruin a team so that you can recognize them for what they are when you see them.

An inability to admit wrongdoing. Have you ever spent time with people who never admit they're wrong? It's painful. Nobody's perfect, but someone who thinks he is does not make an ideal teammate. His wrong attitude will always create conflict.

Failing to forgive. It's said that Clara Barton, the founder of modern nursing, was once encouraged to bemoan a cruel act inflicted on her years earlier, but Barton wouldn't take the bait.

"Don't you remember the wrong that was done to you?" the friend goaded.

"No," answered Barton, "I distinctly remember forgetting that."

Holding a grudge is never positive or appropriate. And when unforgiveness occurs between teammates, it's certain to hurt the team.

Petty jealousy. An attitude that really works against people is the desire for equality that feeds petty jealousy. For some reason the people with this attitude believe that every person deserves equal treatment, regardless of talent, performance, or impact. Yet nothing could be farther from the truth. Each of us is created uniquely and performs differently, and as a result, we should be treated as such.

The disease of me. In his book *The Winner Within*, highly successful NBA coach Pat Riley writes about the "disease of me." He says of team members who have it, "They develop an overpowering belief in their own importance. Their actions virtually shout the claim, 'I'm the one.'" Riley asserts that the disease always has the same inevitable result: "The Defeat of Us."[3]

A critical spirit. Fred and Martha were driving home after a church service. "Fred," Martha asked, "did you notice that the pastor's sermon was kind of weak today?"

"No, not really," answered Fred.

"Well, did you hear that the choir was flat?"

"No, I didn't," he responded.

"Well, you certainly must have noticed that young couple and their children right in front of us, with all the noise and commotion they made the whole service!"

"I'm sorry, dear, but no, I didn't."

Finally in disgust Martha said, "Honestly, Fred, I don't know why you even bother to go to church."

When someone on the team has a critical spirit, everybody knows it because everyone on the team can do no right.

A desire to hog all the credit. Another bad attitude that hurts the team is similar to the "disease of me." But where the person with that disease may simmer in the background and create dissension, the credit hog continually steps into the spotlight to take a bow—whether he has earned it or not. His attitude is opposite that of NBA Hall of Fame center Bill Russell, who said of his time on the court, "The most important measure of how good a game I played was how much better I'd made my teammates play."

Certainly there are other negative attitudes that I haven't named, but my intention isn't to list every bad attitude—just some of the most common ones. In a word, most bad attitudes are the result of selfishness. If one of your teammates puts others down, sabotages teamwork, or makes himself out to be more important than the team, then you can be sure that you've encountered someone with a bad attitude.

5. ROTTEN ATTITUDES, LEFT ALONE, RUIN EVERYTHING

Bad attitudes must be addressed. You can be sure that they will always cause dissension, resentment, combativeness, and division on a team. And they will never go away on their own if they are left unaddressed. They will simply fester and ruin a team—along with its chances of reaching its potential.

Because people with bad attitudes are so difficult to deal with and because attitudes seem so subjective, you may doubt your gut reaction when you encounter someone with a bad attitude. After all, if it's only your opinion that he has a rotten attitude, then you have no right to address it, right? Not if you care about the team. Rotten attitudes ruin a team. That is always true. If you leave a bad apple in a barrel of good apples, you will always end up with a barrel of rotten apples. Attitudes always impact a leader's effectiveness.

President Thomas Jefferson remarked, "Nothing can stop the man with the right mental attitude from achieving his goal; nothing on earth can help the man with the wrong mental attitude." If you care about your team and you are committed to helping all of the players, you can't ignore a bad attitude.

Dealing with a person whose attitude is bad can be a very tricky thing. Before you try to address the issue, you would benefit from a closer look at attitudes and how they affect an individual.

How Does Attitude Impact an Individual?

Your attitude and your potential go hand in hand.

What is attitude? How do you put your finger on it? Well, attitude is an inward feeling expressed by behavior. That is why an attitude can be seen without a word being said. Haven't we all noticed "the pout" of the sulker, or the "jutted jaw" of the determined? Of all the things we wear, our expression is the most important.

Sometimes our attitude can be masked outwardly and others who see us are fooled. But usually the cover-ups will not last long. There is that constant struggle as the attitude tries to wiggle its way out.

My father enjoys telling the story of the four-year-old who had one of those trouble-filled days. After reprimanding him, his mother finally said to him, "Son, you go over to that chair and sit on it now!" The little lad went to the chair, sat down, and said, "Mommy, I'm sitting on the outside, but I'm standing up on the inside."

Psychologist/philosopher James Allen stated, "A person cannot travel within and stand still without." Soon what is happening within us will affect what is happening without. A hardened attitude is a dreaded disease.

It causes a closed mind and a dark future. When our attitude is positive and conducive to growth, the mind expands and the progress begins.

ATTITUDE DETERMINES SUCCESS OR FAILURE

While leading a conference in South Carolina, I tried the following experiment. I asked the audience, "What word describes what will determine our happiness, acceptance, peace, and success?" The audience began to express words such as *job, education, money, time*. Finally someone said *attitude*. Such an important area of their lives was a second thought. Our attitude is the primary force that will determine whether we succeed or fail.

For some, attitude presents a difficulty in every opportunity; for others it presents an opportunity in every difficulty. Some climb with a positive attitude, while others fall with a negative perspective. The very fact that the attitude "makes some" while "breaking others" is significant enough for us to explore its importance. Here are seven axioms about attitude to help you better understand how it impacts a person's life:

ATTITUDE AXIOM #1: OUR ATTITUDE DETERMINES OUR APPROACH TO LIFE

Our attitude tells us what we expect from life. Like an airplane, if our "nose" is pointed up, we are taking off; if it is pointed down, we may be headed for a crash.

One of my favorite stories is about a grandpa and grandma who visited their grandchildren. Each afternoon Grandpa would lie down for a nap. One day, as a practical joke, the kids decided to put Limburger cheese in his mustache. Quite soon he awoke sniffing. "Why, this room stinks," he exclaimed as he got up and went out into the kitchen. He wasn't there long until he decided that the kitchen smelled, too, so he walked outdoors for a breath of fresh air. Much to Grandpa's surprise, the open air brought no relief, and he proclaimed, "The whole world stinks!"

How true that is to life! When we carry "Limburger cheese" in our attitudes, the whole world smells bad. We are individually responsible for our view of life. That truth has been known for ages and is contained in Scripture: "For whatever a man sows, that he will also reap."[1] Our attitude toward and action in life help determine what happens to us.

It would be impossible to estimate the number of jobs lost, the number of promotions missed, the number of sales not made, and the number of marriages ruined by poor attitudes. But almost daily we witness jobs that are held but hated and marriages that are tolerated but unhappy, all because people are waiting for others, or the world, to change instead of realizing that they are responsible for their own behavior.

Attitude Axiom #2: Our Attitude Determines Our Relationships with People

All of life is impacted by your relationships with people, yet establishing relationships is difficult. You can't get along with some people, and you can't make it without them. That's why it is essential to build proper relationships with others in our crowded world.

The Stanford Research Institute says that the money you make in any endeavor is determined only 12.5 percent by knowledge and 87.5 percent by your ability to deal with people.

87.5% people knowledge + 12.5% product knowledge = Success

That is why Teddy Roosevelt said, "The most important single ingredient to the formula of success is knowing how to get along with people." And why John D. Rockefeller said, "I will pay more for the ability to deal with people than any other ability under the sun."

When the attitude we possess places others first and we see people as important, then our perspective will reflect their viewpoint, not ours. Until we walk in the other person's shoes and see life through another's eyes, we will be like the man who angrily jumped out of his car after a collision with another car. "Why don't you people watch where you're driving?" he shouted wildly. "You're the fourth car I've hit today!"

Usually the person who rises within an organization has a good attitude. The promotions did not give that individual an outstanding attitude, but an outstanding attitude resulted in promotions.

ATTITUDE AXIOM #3: OFTEN OUR ATTITUDE IS THE ONLY DIFFERENCE BETWEEN SUCCESS AND FAILURE

History's greatest achievements have been made by men who excelled only slightly over the masses of others in their fields. This could be called the principle of the slight edge. Many times that slight difference was attitude. The former Israeli Prime Minister Golda Meir underlined this truth in one of her interviews. She said, "All my country has is spirit. We don't have petroleum dollars. We don't have mines of great wealth in the ground. We don't have the support of a worldwide public opinion that looks favorably on us. All Israel has is the spirit of its people. And if the people lose their spirit, even the United States of America cannot save us."

Certainly aptitude is important to our success in life. Yet success or failure in any undertaking is caused more by mental attitude than by mere mental capacities. I remember times when Margaret, my wife, would come home from teaching school frustrated because of modern education's emphasis on aptitude instead of attitude. She wanted the kids to be tested on A.Q. (attitude quotient) instead of just the I.Q. (intelligence quotient). She would talk of kids whose I.Q. was high yet their performance was low. There were others whose I.Q. was low but their performance was high.

As a parent, I hope my children have excellent minds and outstanding attitudes. But if I had to choose an "either-or" situation, without hesitation I would want their A.Q. to be high.

A Yale University president some years ago gave similar advice to a former president of Ohio State: "Always be kind to your A and B students. Someday one of them will return to your campus as a good professor. And also be kind to your C students. Someday one of them will return and build a two-million-dollar science laboratory."

There is very little difference in people, but that little difference makes a big difference. The little difference is attitude. The big difference is whether it is positive or negative.

Attitude Axiom #4: Our Attitude at the Beginning of a Task Will Affect Its Outcome More Than Anything Else

Coaches understand the importance of their teams' having the right attitude before facing a tough opponent. Surgeons want to see their patients mentally prepared before going into surgery. Job-seekers know that their prospective employer is looking for more than just skills when they apply for work. Public speakers want a conducive atmosphere before they communicate to their audience. Why? Because the right attitude in the beginning ensures success at the end. You are acquainted with the saying, "All's well that ends well." An equal truth is, "All's well that begins well."

Most projects fail or succeed before they begin. A young mountain climber and an experienced guide were ascending a high peak in the Sierras. Early one morning the young climber was suddenly awakened by a tremendous cracking sound. He was convinced that the end of the world had come. The guide responded, "It's not the end of the world, just the dawning of a new day." As the sun rose, it was merely hitting the ice and causing it to melt.

Many times we have been guilty of viewing our future challenges as the sunset of life rather than the sunrise of a bright new opportunity.

For instance, there's the story of two shoe salesmen who were sent to an island to sell shoes. The first salesman, upon arrival, was shocked to realize that no one wore shoes. Immediately he sent a telegram to his home office in Chicago saying, "Will return home tomorrow. No one wears shoes."

The second salesman was thrilled by the same realization. Immediately he wired the home office in Chicago saying, "Please send me 10,000 shoes. Everyone here needs them."

Attitude Axiom #5: Our Attitude Can Turn Our Problems into Blessings

In *Awake, My Heart,* J. Sidlow Baxter wrote, "What is the difference between an obstacle and an opportunity? Our attitude toward it. Every opportunity has a difficulty and every difficulty has an opportunity."[2]

When confronted with a difficult situation, a person with an outstanding attitude makes the best of it while he gets the worst of it. Life can be likened to a grindstone. Whether it grinds you down or polishes you depends upon what you are made of.

While attending a conference of young leaders, I heard this statement: "No society has ever developed tough men during times of peace." Adversity is prosperity to those who possess a great attitude. Kites rise against, not with, the wind. When the adverse wind of criticism blows, allow it to be to you what the blast of wind is to the kite—a force against it that lifts it higher. A kite would not fly unless it had the controlling tension of the string to tie it down. It is equally true in life. Consider the following successes that were accomplished through a positive attitude.

WHEN CONFRONTED WITH A DIFFICULT SITUATION,
A PERSON WITH AN OUTSTANDING ATTITUDE MAKES THE
BEST OF IT WHILE HE GETS THE WORST OF IT.

When Napoleon's school companions made sport of him because of his humble origin and poverty, he devoted himself entirely to his books. Quickly rising above his classmates in scholarship, he commanded their respect. Soon he was regarded as the brightest in the class.

Few people knew Abraham Lincoln until the great weight of the Civil War showed his character.

Robinson Crusoe was written in prison. John Bunyan wrote *Pilgrim's Progress* in the Bedford jail. Sir Walter Raleigh wrote *The History of the World* during a thirteen-year imprisonment. Luther translated the Bible while confined in the castle of Wartburg. For ten years Dante, author of

The Divine Comedy, worked in exile and under the sentence of death. Beethoven was almost totally deaf and burdened with sorrow when he produced his greatest works.

When God wants to educate someone, He does not send him to the school of graces but to the school of necessities. Great leaders emerge when crises occur. In the lives of people who achieve, we read repeatedly of terrible troubles that forced them to rise above the commonplace. Not only do they find the answers, but they also discover a tremendous power within themselves. Like a groundswell far out in the ocean, this force within explodes into a mighty wave when circumstances seem to overcome. Then out steps the athlete, the author, the statesman, the scientist, or the businessman. David Sarnoff said, "There is plenty of security in the cemetery; I long for opportunity."

ATTITUDE AXIOM #6: OUR ATTITUDE CAN GIVE US AN UNCOMMONLY POSITIVE PERSPECTIVE

An uncommonly positive perspective is able to help us accomplish some uncommon goals. I have keenly observed the different approaches and results achieved by a positive thinker and by a person filled with fear and apprehension. For example, in ancient Israel when Goliath came up against the Hebrews, the soldiers all thought, *He's so big we can never kill him.* David looked at the same giant and thought, *He's so big I can't miss.*

George Sweeting, former president of Moody Bible Institute, tells a story about a Scotsman who was an extremely hard worker and expected all the men under him to be the same. His men would tease him, "Scotty, don't you know that Rome wasn't built in a day?" "Yes," he would answer, "I know that. But I wasn't foreman on that job."

Individuals whose attitudes cause them to approach life from an entirely positive perspective are not always understood. They are what some would call a "no-limit people." In other words, they don't accept the normal limitations of life as most people do. They are unwilling to accept "the accepted" just because it is accepted. Their response to self-limiting conditions will probably be "why?" instead of "okay." Certainly, they have limitations. Their gifts are not so plentiful that they cannot fail. But they are determined to walk to the very edge of their potential and the potential of their goals before accepting defeat.

They are like bumblebees. According to a theory of aerodynamics, as demonstrated through the wind tunnel tests, the bumblebee should be unable to fly. Because of the size, weight, and shape of its body in relationship to the total wing span, flying is scientifically impossible. The bumblebee, being ignorant of scientific theory, goes ahead and flies anyway and makes honey every day.

The future not only looks bright when the attitude is right, but also the present is much more enjoyable. The positive person understands that the journey of success is as enjoyable as the destination. Asked which of his works he would select as his masterpiece, architect Frank Lloyd Wright, at the age of eighty-three, replied, "My next one."

A friend of mine in Ohio drove eighteen-wheelers for an interstate trucking company. Knowing the hundreds of miles he logged weekly, I once asked him how he kept from getting extremely tired. "It's all in your attitude," he replied. "Some drivers 'go to work' in the morning, but I 'go for a ride in the country.'" That kind of positive perspective gives him the "edge" on life.

ATTITUDE AXIOM #7: YOUR ATTITUDE IS NOT AUTOMATICALLY GOOD BECAUSE YOU ARE A RELIGIOUS PERSON

It is noteworthy that the seven deadly sins—pride, covetousness, lust, envy, anger, gluttony, and sloth—are all matters of attitude, inner spirit, and motives. Sadly, many people of faith carry with them inner-spirit problems. They are like the elder brother contained in the parable of the prodigal son, thinking that they do everything right. While the younger brother left home to live a wild life, the elder brother chose to stay home with his father. He wasn't going to spend *his* time sowing wild oats! Yet when the younger brother returned home, some of the elder brother's wrong attitudes began to surface.

First was a feeling of self-importance. The elder brother was out in the field doing what he ought to do, but he got mad when the party began at home—his father would never let him have one for himself!

That was followed by a feeling of self-pity. The elder brother said, "Look! For so many years I have been serving you, and you have never thrown a party for me. But when your son who wasted all of your money comes home, you give him a big celebration."[3]

Often people overlook the true meaning of the story of the prodigal son. They forget that there are not one but two prodigals. The younger brother is guilty of the sins of the flesh, whereas the elder brother is guilty of the sins of the spirit. His problem is his attitude. At the end of the parable, it is the elder brother—the second prodigal—who is outside the father's house.

And that is a good lesson for all of us to remember. A poor attitude will take us places we don't want to go. Sometimes it can even take you completely out of the game. On the other hand, a good attitude puts you in the place of greatest potential.

Perhaps you're not sure if your attitude is where it ought to be. Or maybe you are leading someone whose attitude isn't as positive as it could be. How do you address that? First, you need to know how a person's attitude is formed. That's the subject of the next chapter.

PART II

THE FORMATION OF ATTITUDE

3

WHAT SHAPES A PERSON'S ATTITUDE?

A lot goes into an attitude—but a lot more comes out of it!

Attitudes aren't shaped in a vacuum. People are born with certain characteristics, and those impact their attitudes. But many other factors play an even greater role in people's lives and in the formation of their attitudes. While these factors continually impact people, in general, they make the greatest impression during the following times of life:

STAGES	FACTORS
PRE-BIRTH:	Inherent personality/temperament
BIRTH:	Environment
AGES 1–6:	Word expression
	Adult acceptance/affirmation
AGES 6–10:	Self-image
	Exposure to new experiences
AGES 11–21:	Peers, physical appearance
AGES 21–61:	Marriage, family, job, success
	Adjustments, assessment of life

PERSONALITY—WHO I AM

All people are born as distinct individuals. Even two children with the same parents, same environment, and same training are totally different from each other. These differences contribute to the "spice of life" we all enjoy. Like tract homes that all look alike, if we all had similar personalities, our journey through life would certainly be boring.

GENERALLY, PEOPLE WITH CERTAIN TEMPERAMENTS DEVELOP SPECIFIC ATTITUDES COMMON TO THAT TEMPERAMENT.

I love the story of two men out fishing together who began discussing their wives. One said, "If all men were like me, they would all want to be married to my wife." The other man quickly replied, "If they were all like me, none of them would want to be married to her."

A set of attitudes accompanies each personality type. Generally, people with certain temperaments develop specific attitudes common to that temperament. A few years ago, Tim LaHaye, coauthor of the popular "Left Behind" novels, lectured and wrote about the four basic temperaments. Through observation, I have noticed that a person with what he calls a *choleric* personality often exhibits attitudes of perseverance and aggressiveness. A *sanguine* person is generally positive and looks on the bright side of life. An introspective *melancholy* individual can be negative at times, while a *phlegmatic* is prone to say, "Easy come, easy go." Every individual's personality is composed of a mixture of these temperaments, and there are exceptions to these generalizations. However, a temperament ordinarily follows a track that can be identified by tracing a person's attitudes.

ENVIRONMENT—WHAT'S AROUND ME

I believe that environment is a greater controlling factor in our attitude development than our personality or other inherited traits. Before my wife, Margaret, and I began our family, we decided to adopt our children. We wanted to give a child who might not normally have the benefit of a loving faith-filled home an opportunity to live in that environment. Although our children may not physically resemble us, they certainly have been molded by the environment in which we have reared them.

The environment of early childhood develops a person's "belief system." Children continually pick up priorities, attitudes, interests, and philosophies from their environment. It is a fact that what I really believe affects my attitude! However, the things I believe may not be true. What I believe may not be healthy. It may even hurt others and destroy me. Yet an attitude is reinforced by a belief—whether it is right or wrong.

Environment is the first influencer of our belief system. Therefore the foundation of an attitude is laid in the environment to which we were born. Environment becomes even more significant when we realize that the beginning attitudes are the most difficult to change.

Word Expression—What I Hear

You've undoubtedly heard the old saying: "Sticks and stones may break my bones, but names will never hurt me." Don't you believe that! In fact, after the bruises have disappeared and the physical pain is gone, the inward pain of hurtful words remains.

Years ago when I was leading a church, during one of our staff meetings I asked the pastors, secretaries, and custodians to raise their hands if they could remember a childhood experience that hurt deeply because of someone's words. Everyone raised his hand. One pastor recalled the time when he sat in a reading circle at school. (Do you remember how intimidating those sessions were?) When his time came to read, he mispronounced the word *photography*. He read it photo-graphy instead of pho-tog-ra-phy. The teacher corrected him and the class laughed. He still remembers . . . forty years later. One positive result of that experience was his desire from that moment on to pronounce words correctly. Today one of the reasons he excels as a speaker is because of that determination.

ADULT ACCEPTANCE/AFFIRMATION—
WHAT I FEEL

Often when I am speaking to leaders, I tell them about the importance of accepting and affirming the ones they are leading. The truth is, people don't care how much you know until they know how much you care!

Think back to your school days. Who was your favorite teacher? Now think of why. Probably your warmest memories are of someone who accepted and affirmed you. We seldom remember what our teacher said to us, but we do remember how they loved us. Long before we understand teaching, we reach out for understanding. Long after we have forgotten the teachings, we remember the feeling of acceptance or rejection.

PEOPLE DON'T CARE HOW MUCH YOU KNOW
UNTIL THEY KNOW HOW MUCH YOU CARE.

Many times I have asked people if they enjoyed their pastor's sermon the previous week. After a positive response I ask, "What was his subject?" Seventy-five percent of the time they cannot give me the sermon title. They do not remember the exact subject, but they do remember the atmosphere and attitude in which it was delivered.

My favorite Sunday school teachers from my childhood are beautiful examples of this truth. First came Katie, my second grade teacher. When I was sick and missed her class, she would come and visit me on Monday. She would ask how I was feeling and give me a five-cent trinket that was worth a million dollars to me. Katie would say, "Johnny, I always teach better when you are in the class. When you come next Sunday morning, would you raise your hand so I can see you are in attendance? Then I will teach better."

I can still remember raising my hand and watching Katie smile at me from the front of the class. I also remember other kids raising their hands on Sundays when Katie began to teach and her class grew rapidly. That year, the Sunday school superintendent wanted to split the class and start a new one across the hall. He asked for volunteers for the new class and no one raised his hand. Why? No kid wanted to go with a new teacher and miss Katie's continual demonstration of love.

Another teacher I remember is Glen Leatherwood. He taught all the junior high school boys in the church where I grew up. Did you ever teach a group of ten-wiggles-per-minute boys? Usually those teachers go straight from teaching that class to their heavenly reward! But not Glen. He taught junior high boys for another thirty years. The twelve months I spent in his class made a profound impact on my faith and my life's work.

I was also privileged to grow up in a very affirming family. I never questioned my parents' love and acceptance. They continually affirmed their love through actions and words. When our children were growing up, Margaret and I tried to create that same environment for them. I believe that our kids saw or sensed our acceptance and affirmation at least thirty times a day. Today I'd say our grandchildren get almost twice as much. That's not too much! Have you ever been told too many times that you are important, loved, and appreciated? Remember, people don't care how much you know until they know how much you care.

SELF-IMAGE—HOW I SEE MYSELF

It is impossible to perform consistently in a manner inconsistent with the way we see ourselves. In other words, we usually act in direct response to our self-image. Nothing is more difficult to accomplish than changing outward actions without changing inward feelings.

One of the best ways to improve those inward feelings is to put some "success" under your belt. My daughter Elizabeth has a tendency to be shy and wants to hold back on new experiences. But once she has warmed up to a situation, it's "full steam ahead." When she was in first grade, her school had a candy bar sale. Each child was given thirty candy bars and was challenged to sell every one of them. When I picked up Elizabeth from school she was holding her "challenge" and needed some positive encouragement. It was time for a sales meeting with my new salesgirl.

All the way home I taught her how to sell candy bars. I surrounded each teaching point with a half dozen "You can do it—your smile will win them over—I believe in you" phrases. By the end of our fifteen-minute drive, the young lady sitting beside me had become a charming, committed saleslady. Off she went to the neighborhood with little brother Joel eating one of the candy bars and declaring that it was truly the best he had ever devoured.

At the end of the day, all thirty bars had been sold and Elizabeth was feeling great. I will never forget the words she prayed as I tucked her into bed that night: "O God, thanks for the candy sale at school. It's great. O Lord, help make me a winner! Amen."

Elizabeth's prayer reflects the heart's desire of every person. We all want to be winners. Sure enough, Elizabeth came home the next day with another box of candy bars. Now the big test! She'd exhausted the supply of friendly neighbors, and she was thrust into the cruel world of the unknown buyer. Elizabeth admitted fear as we went to a shopping center to sell our wares. Again I offered encouragement, a few more selling tips, more encouragement, the right location, more encouragement. And she did it. The experience amounted to two days of selling, two sold-out performances, two happy people, and one boosted self-image.

How we see ourselves reflects how others see us. If we like ourselves, it increases the odds that others will like us. Self-image sets the parameters for the construction of our attitudes. We act in response to how we see ourselves. We will never go beyond the boundaries that stake out our true feelings about ourselves. Those "new territories" can be explored only when our self-image is strong enough to give us permission to go there.

EXPOSURE TO NEW EXPERIENCES— OPPORTUNITIES FOR GROWTH

French philosopher François Voltaire likened life to a game of cards. Each player must accept the cards dealt to him. But once those cards are in the hand, he alone decides how to play them to win the game.

We always have a number of opportunities in our hand, and we must decide whether to take a risk and act on them. Nothing in life causes more stress, yet at the same time provides more opportunity for growth, than new experiences.

If you are a parent, you will find it impossible to shield your children from new experiences that might be negative. So it is essential to prepare positive encounters that will build self-image and confidence. Both positive and negative experiences can be used as tools in preparing children for life.

Children need continual reassurance and praise when their new experiences are less than positive. In fact, the worse the experience, the more encouragement they need. But sometimes we become discouraged when they are discouraged. This is a good formula to adopt:

New experiences + teaching applications x love = growth.

ASSOCIATION WITH PEERS—
WHO INFLUENCES ME

What others indicate about their perceptions of us affects how we perceive ourselves. Usually we respond to the expectations of others. This truth becomes evident to parents when their children go to school. No longer can parents control their children's environment.

My parents understood that others could exercise a sizable amount of control over their sons' behavior, so they were determined to watch and control our peer relationships as much as possible. Their strategy: Provide a climate in the Maxwell home that was appealing to their two boys' friends. This meant sacrificing their finances and time. They provided us with a shuffleboard game, Ping-Pong table, pool table, pinball machine, chemistry set, basketball court, and all the sports equipment imaginable. We also had a mother who was spectator, referee, counselor, arbitrator, and fan.

And the kids came, often twenty to twenty-five at a time. All sizes, shapes, and colors. Everyone had fun and my parents observed our friends. Sometimes, after the gang had gone, my parents would ask about one of our friends. They would openly discuss his language or attitudes and encourage us not to act or think that way. I realize now that most of my major decisions as a young boy were influenced by my parents' teaching and observation of my associations.

Casey Stengel, who was a successful manager of the New York Yankees baseball team, understood the power of associations on a ballplayer's attitude. He gave Billy Martin some advice when he was a rookie manager. Martin recalled, "Casey said there would be fifteen players on your team who will run through a wall for you, five who will hate you, and five who are undecided. When you make out your rooming list, always room your losers together. Never room a good guy with a loser. Those losers who stay together will blame the manager for everything, but it won't spread if you keep them isolated."

Charles "Tremendous" Jones, author of *Life Is Tremendous*, says, "What you will become in five years will be determined by what you read and who you associate with." That's good for all of us to remember.

PHYSICAL APPEARANCE—
HOW WE LOOK TO OTHERS

Our looks play an important part in the construction of our attitude. Incredible pressure is placed upon people to possess the "in look," which seems to be the standard of acceptance. The next time you're watching television, notice how much the commercials emphasize looks. Notice the percentage of ads dealing with clothing, diet, exercise, and overall physical attractiveness. Hollywood says, "Blandness is out and beauty is in." This influences our perception of our worth.

What can make it even more difficult is the realization that others also judge our worth by our appearance. Recently, I read a business article that stated, "Our physical attractiveness helps determine our income." For example, the research reported in that article showed the discrepancies between the salaries of men 6'2" and 5'10". The taller men consistently received higher salaries. Like it or not, physical appearance (and one's perception of it) impacts a person's attitude.

MARRIAGE, FAMILY, AND JOB— OUR SECURITY AND STATUS

New influences begin affecting our attitude as we approach our mid-twenties. It is during this time that most people start a career. They also often get married. That means another person influences our perspective.

When I speak on attitudes, I always emphasize the need to surround ourselves with positive people. One of the saddest comments that I often receive comes from someone who tells me their marriage partner is negative and doesn't want to change. To a certain extent, when the negative mate does not want to change, the positive one is imprisoned by negativism. In such situations I advise the couple to remember their spouse as the person they loved in their courtship days. Their marriage will improve if each other's weaknesses are not emphasized. But many end up in divorce court because the strengths are ignored. The partners go from expecting the best to expecting the worst, from building on strengths to focusing on weaknesses.

All of the factors I've mentioned go into the "mix" of attitude. They have impacted who you are and those whom you lead. But remember this: Whether you are eleven, forty-two, or sixty-five, your attitude toward life is *still* under construction. It's never too late for a person to change his attitude. And that's the subject of the next chapter.

4

CAN AN ATTITUDE BE CHANGED?

*The key to having a good attitude
is the willingness to change.*

We are either the masters or the victims of our attitudes. It is a matter of personal choice. Who we are today is the result of choices we made yesterday. Tomorrow we will become what we choose today. To change means to choose to change.

I'm told that in northern Canada there are just two seasons: winter and July. When the back roads begin to thaw, they become muddy. Vehicles going into the backwoods country leave deep ruts that become frozen when cold weather returns. For those entering remote areas during the winter months, there are signs that read, "Driver, please choose carefully which rut you drive in, because you'll be in it for the next twenty miles."

Some people seem to feel stuck in their current attitudes, like a car in a twenty-mile rut. However, attitude is not permanent. If you're not happy with yours, know that you can change it. If someone you lead has a bad attitude, then you can help them to change—but only if they truly *want* to change. Anyone can become the kind of positive person for whom life is a joy and every day is filled with potential if they genuinely desire to.

If you want to have a great attitude, then make the following choices:

CHOICE #1: EVALUATE YOUR PRESENT ATTITUDE

The process begins with knowing where you're starting from. Evaluating your present attitude will take some time. If possible, try to separate yourself from your attitude. The goal of this exercise is not to see the "bad you" but a "bad attitude" that keeps you from being a more fulfilled person. You can make key changes only when you identify the problem.

When he sees a logjam, the professional logger climbs a tall tree and locates a key log, blows that log free, and lets the stream do the rest. An amateur would start at the edge of the jam and move all the logs, eventually moving the key log. Obviously, both methods will get the logs moving, but the professional does his work more quickly and effectively.

To find the key "logs" in your attitude, use the following evaluation process (and write your answers in a journal or someplace where you can later refer back to them):

Identify Problem Feelings: What attitudes make you feel the most negative about yourself? Usually feelings can be sensed before the problem is clarified.

Identify Problem Behavior: What attitudes cause you the most problems when dealing with others?

Identify Problem Thinking: We are the sum of our thoughts. "As a man thinks within himself, so he is."[1] What thoughts consistently control your mind? Although this is the beginning step in correcting attitude problems, these are not as easy to identify as the first two.

Clarify Truth: In order to know how to change, you need to examine your feelings in light of truth. If you are a person of faith, then use the Scriptures. What do they tell you about how your attitude should be?

Secure Commitment: At this stage, "What must I do to change?" turns into "I must change." Remember, the choice to change is the one decision that must be made, and only you can make it.

Plan and Carry Out Your Choice: Act on your decision immediately and repeatedly.

CHOICE #2: REALIZE THAT FAITH IS STRONGER THAN FEAR

The only thing that will guarantee the success of a difficult or doubtful undertaking is faith from the beginning that you can do it. Philosopher William James said, "The greatest discovery of my generation is that people can alter their lives by altering their attitudes of mind." Change depends on your frame of mind. Believe that you can change. Ask your friends and colleagues to encourage you at every opportunity. And if you are a person of faith, ask for God's help. He knows your problems, and He is willing and able to help you overcome them.

CHOICE #3: WRITE A STATEMENT OF PURPOSE

When I was a boy, my father decided to build a basketball court for my brother and me. He made a cement driveway, put a backboard on the garage, and was just getting ready to put up the basket when he was called away on an emergency. He promised to put up the hoop as soon as he returned. *No problem,* I thought. *I have a brand-new Spalding ball and a new cement driveway on which to dribble it.* For a few minutes I bounced the ball on the cement. Soon that became boring, so I took the ball and threw it up against the backboard—once. I let the ball run off the court and didn't pick it up again until Dad returned to put up the rim. Why? It's no fun playing basketball without a goal. The joy is in having something to aim for.

In order to have fun and direction in changing your attitude, you must establish a clearly stated goal. This goal should be as specific as possible, written out and signed, with a time frame attached to it. The purpose statement should be placed in a visible spot where you see it several times a day to give you reinforcement.

You will attain this goal if each day you do three things:

1. Write specifically what you desire to accomplish each day.

The biblical story of David's encounter with Goliath is a fine illustration of faith and how it may overcome insurmountable odds with seemingly inadequate resources. But one thing perplexed me when I first began to study David's life. Why did he pick five stones for his sling on his way to encounter Goliath? The longer I pondered, the more perplexed I became. Why five stones? There was only one giant. Choosing five stones seemed to be a flaw in his faith. Did he think he was going to miss and that he would have four more chances? Some time later I was reading in 2 Samuel, and I got the answer. Goliath had four sons, so that means there were five giants. In David's reckoning, there was one stone per giant! Now that is what I mean about being specific in our faith.

What are the giants you must slay to make your attitude what it needs to be? What resources will you need? Don't be overcome with frustration when you see the problems. Take one giant at a time. Military strategists teach their armies to fight one front at a time. Settle which attitude you want to tackle at this time. Write it down. As you successfully begin to win battles, write them down. And spend time reading about past victories because it will encourage you.

2. Verbalize to an encouraging friend what you want to accomplish each day.

Belief is inward conviction; faith is outward action. You will receive both encouragement and accountability by verbalizing your intentions. One of the ways people resolve a conflict is to verbalize it to themselves or someone else. This practice is also vital in reaching your desired attitudes.

I know successful salesmen who repeat this phrase out loud fifty times each morning and fifty times each evening: "I can do it." Continually saying positive statements helps them believe in themselves and causes them to act on that belief. Start this process by changing your vocabulary. Here are some suggestions:

ELIMINATE THESE WORDS COMPLETELY	MAKE THESE WORDS A PART OF YOUR VOCABULARY
1. I can't	1. I can
2. If	2. I will
3. Doubt	3. Expect the best
4. I don't think	4. I know
5. I don't have the time	5. I will make the time
6. Maybe	6. Positively
7. I'm afraid of	7. I am confident
8. I don't believe	8. I do believe
9. (minimize) I	9. (promote) You
10. It's impossible	10. All things are possible

3. TAKE ACTION ON YOUR GOAL EACH DAY.

The difference between a wise man and a foolish one is his response to what he already knows: A wise man follows up on what he hears while a foolish man knows but does not act. To change, you must take action. And while you're at it, do something positive for someone else too. Nothing improves a person's outlook like unselfish service to someone with a greater need than their own.

CHOICE #4: HAVE THE DESIRE TO CHANGE

No choice will determine the success of your attitude change more than desiring to change. When all else fails, desire alone can keep you heading in the right direction. Many people have climbed over insurmountable obstacles to make themselves better when they realized that change is possible if they want it badly enough. Let me illustrate.

While hopping about one day, a frog happened to slip into a very large pothole along a country road. All of his attempts at jumping out were in vain. Soon a rabbit came upon the frog trapped in the hole and offered to help him out. He, too, failed. After various animals from the forest made three or four gallant attempts to help the poor frog out, they finally gave up. "We'll go back and get you some food," they said. "It looks like you're going to be here a while." However, not long after they took off to get food, they heard the frog hopping along after them. They couldn't believe it! "We thought you couldn't get out!" they exclaimed. "Oh, I couldn't," replied the frog. "But you see, there was a big truck coming right at me, and I had to."

FALL IN LOVE WITH THE CHALLENGE OF CHANGE AND WATCH THE DESIRE TO CHANGE GROW.

It is when we "have to get out of the potholes of life" that we change. As long as we have acceptable options, we will not change. The truth is that most people are more comfortable with old problems than new solutions. They respond to their needs for a turnaround in life like the Duke of Cambridge, who once said, "Any change, at any time, for any reason, is to be deplored." People who believe that nothing should ever be done for the first time never see anything done.

People can change, and that is the greatest motivation of all. Nothing sparks the fires of desire more than the sudden realization that you do not have to stay the same. Fall in love with the challenge of change and watch the desire to change grow. That's what happened to Aleida Huissen, seventy-eight, of Rotterdam, Netherlands. She had been a smoker for fifty years, and for fifty years she tried to give up the habit. But she was unsuccessful. Then Leo Jensen, seventy-nine, proposed marriage and refused to go through with the wedding until Aleida gave up smoking. Aleida says, "Willpower never was enough to get me off the habit. Love did it."

My life is dedicated to helping others reach their potential. I suggest that you follow the advice of Mark Twain, who said, "Take your mind out every now and then and dance on it. It is getting all caked up." It was his way of saying, "Get out of that rut." Too many times we settle into a set way of thinking and accept limitations that need not be placed upon us. Embrace change, and it will change you.

CHOICE #5: LIVE ONE DAY AT A TIME

Any person can fight the battle for just one day. It is only when you and I add the burdens of those two awful eternities, yesterday and tomorrow, that we tremble. It is not the experiences of today that drive people to distraction; it is the remorse or bitterness for something that happened yesterday and the dread of what tomorrow may bring. Let us therefore live but one day at a time—today!

CHOICE #6: CHANGE YOUR THOUGHT PATTERNS

That which holds our attention determines our actions. We are where we are and what we are because of the dominating thoughts that occupy our minds. Take a look at this syllogism. It emphasizes the power of our thought life:

Major premise: We can control our thoughts.
Minor premise: Our feelings come from our thoughts.
Conclusion: We can control our feelings by learning to change how
    we think.

It is that simple. Our feelings come from our thoughts. Therefore, we can change them by changing our thought patterns.

Our thought life, not our circumstances, determines our happiness. Often I see people who are convinced that they will be happy when they attain a certain goal. When they reach the goal, many times they do not find the fulfillment they anticipated. The secret to staying on an even keel?

Fill your mind with good thoughts. The apostle Paul advised, "Whatever things are true, whatever things are noble . . . whatever things are of good report, if there is any virtue and if there is anything praiseworthy—meditate on these things."[2] He understood that the things that hold our attention determine our action.

Choice #7: Develop Good Habits

An attitude is nothing more than a habit of thought. The process for developing habits—good or bad—is the same. It is as easy to form the habit of succeeding as it is to succumb to the habit of failure.

Habits aren't instincts; they're acquired actions or reactions. They don't just happen; they are caused. Once the original cause of a habit is determined, it is within your power to accept or reject it. Most people allow their habits to control them. When those habits are hurtful, they negatively impact their attitudes.

The following steps will assist you in changing bad habits into good ones:

Step #1: List your bad habits.
Step #2: What was the original cause?
Step #3: What are the supporting causes?
Step #4: Determine a positive habit to replace the bad one.
Step #5: Think about the good habit, its benefits and results.
Step #6: Take action to develop this habit.
Step #7: Daily act upon this habit for reinforcement.
Step #8: Reward yourself by noting one of the benefits from your good habit.

Choice #8—Continually Choose to Have a Right Attitude

Once you make the choice to possess a good attitude, the work has only just begun. After that comes a life of continually deciding to grow and maintaining the right outlook. Attitudes have a tendency to revert back to their original patterns if they are not carefully guarded and cultivated.

As you work to improve your attitude or to help the attitude of someone you lead, recognize that there are three stages of change where a person must deliberately choose the right attitude:

Early Stage: The first few days are always the most difficult. Old habits are hard to break. You must continually be on guard mentally to take the right action.

Middle Stage: The moment good habits begin to take root, options open that bring on new challenges. During this stage, new habits will form that can be good or bad. The good news is that the more right choices and habits you develop, the more likely other good habits will be formed.

Later Stage: In the later stage, complacency is the enemy. We all know someone (perhaps us) who lost weight only to fall back into old eating habits and gain it back. Don't let down your guard until the change is complete. And even then, be vigilant and make sure you don't fall into old negative habits.

You are the only one who can determine what you will think and how you will act. And that means you can make your attitude what you want it to be. But even if you succeed and become a positive person, that won't shield you from negative experiences. How does a positive person deal with obstacles and remain upbeat? To find the answer to that question, read the next chapter.

5

CAN OBSTACLES ACTUALLY
ENHANCE AN ATTITUDE?

*The greatest battle you wage against failure occurs
on the inside, not the outside.*

Working artists David Bayles and Ted Orland tell a story about an art teacher who did an experiment with his grading system for two groups of students. It is a parable on the benefits of failure. Here is what happened:

> The ceramics teacher announced on opening day that he was dividing the class into two groups. All those on the left side of the studio, he said, would be graded solely on the quantity of work they produced, all those on the right solely on its quality. His procedure was simple: on the final day of class he would bring in his bathroom scale and weigh the work of the "quantity" group: fifty pounds of pots rated an "A," forty pounds a "B," and so on. Those being graded on "quality," however, needed to produce only one pot— albeit a perfect one—to get an "A." Well, come grading time a curious fact emerged: the works of the highest quality were all produced

by the group being graded for quantity. It seems that while the "quantity" group was busily churning out piles of work—and learning from their mistakes—the "quality" group had sat theorizing about perfection, and in the end had little more to show for their efforts than grandiose theories and a pile of dead clay.[1]

It doesn't matter whether your objectives are in the area of art, business, ministry, sports, or relationships. The only way you can get ahead is to fail early, fail often, and fail forward.

TAKE THE JOURNEY

I teach leadership to thousands of people each year at numerous conferences. And one of my greatest concerns is always that some people will go home from the event and nothing will change in their lives. They enjoy the "show" but fail to implement any of the ideas that were presented to them. I tell people continually: We overestimate the event and underestimate the process. Every dream that anyone has achieved came because of dedication to a process. (That's one of the reasons I write books and create audio programs—so that people can engage in the ongoing process of growth.)

People naturally tend toward inertia. That's why self-improvement is such a struggle. But that's also the reason that adversity lies at the heart of every success. The process of achievement comes through repeated failures and the constant struggle to climb to a higher level.

IN ORDER TO ACHIEVE YOUR DREAMS,
YOU MUST EMBRACE ADVERSITY AND MAKE FAILURE A
REGULAR PART OF YOUR LIFE. IF YOU'RE NOT FAILING,
YOU'RE PROBABLY NOT REALLY MOVING FORWARD.

When it comes to facing failure, most people will grudgingly concede that any person must make it through some adversity in order to succeed.

They'll acknowledge that you have to experience the occasional setback to make progress. But I believe that success comes only if you take that thought one step further. In order to achieve your dreams, you must embrace adversity and make failure a regular part of your life. If you're not failing, you're probably not really moving forward.

THE BENEFITS OF ADVERSITY

Psychologist Dr. Joyce Brothers asserts, "The person interested in success has to learn to view failure as a healthy, inevitable part of the process of getting to the top." Adversity and the failure that often results from it should not only be expected in the process of succeeding; they need to be viewed as an absolutely critical part of it. In fact, the benefits of adversity are many. Take a look at some of the key reasons to embrace adversity and persevere through it:

1. ADVERSITY CREATES RESILIENCE

Nothing in life breeds resilience like adversity and failure. A study in *Time* magazine in the mid-1980s described the incredible resilience of a group of people who had lost their jobs three times because of plant closings. Psychologists expected them to be discouraged, but they were surprisingly optimistic. Their adversity had actually created an advantage. Because they had already lost a job and found a new one at least twice, they were better able to handle adversity than people who had worked for only one company and found themselves unemployed.

2. ADVERSITY DEVELOPS MATURITY

Adversity can make you better if you don't let it make you bitter. Why? Because it promotes wisdom and maturity. American novelist William Saroyan said, "Good people are good because they've come to wisdom through failure. We get very little wisdom from success, you know."

As the world continues to change at a faster and faster rate, maturity with flexibility becomes increasingly important. Those qualities come from weathering difficulties. Harvard business school professor John Kotter said, "I can imagine a group of executives 20 years ago discussing a candidate for a top job and saying, 'This guy had a big failure when he was 32.' Everyone else would say, 'Yep, yep, that's a bad sign.' I can imagine that same group considering a candidate today and saying, 'What worries me about this guy is that he's never failed.'"[2] The problems we face and overcome prepare us for future difficulties.

3. ADVERSITY PUSHES THE ENVELOPE OF ACCEPTED PERFORMANCE

Lloyd Ogilvie says that a friend of his, who was a circus performer in his youth, described his experience of learning to work on the trapeze as follows:

> Once you know that the net below will catch you, you stop worrying about falling. You actually learn to fall successfully! What that means is, you can concentrate on catching the trapeze swinging toward you, and not on falling, because repeated falls in the past have convinced you that the net is strong and reliable when you do fall . . . The result of falling and being caught by the net is a mysterious confidence and daring on the trapeze. You fall less. Each fall makes you able to risk more.[3]

Until a person learns from personal experience that he can live through adversity, he is reluctant to buck mindless tradition, push the envelope of organizational performance, or challenge himself to press his physical limits. Failure helps prompt people to rethink the status quo.

4. ADVERSITY PROVIDES GREATER OPPORTUNITIES

I believe that eliminating problems limits our potential. Just about every successful entrepreneur I've met has numerous stories of adversity and setbacks that opened doors to greater opportunity. For example, in 1978 Bernie Marcus, the son of a poor Russian cabinetmaker in Newark,

New Jersey, was fired from Handy Dan, a do-it-yourself hardware retailer. That prompted Marcus to team with Arthur Blank to start their own business. In 1979, they opened their first store in Atlanta, Georgia. It was called Home Depot. Today, Home Depot has more than 760 stores employing more than 157,000 people; they have expanded the business to include overseas operations, and each year they do more than $30 billion in sales.

I'm sure Bernie Marcus wasn't very happy about getting fired from his job back at Handy Dan. But if he hadn't been, who knows whether he would have achieved the success he has today.

5. ADVERSITY PROMPTS INNOVATION

Early in the twentieth century, a boy whose family had emigrated from Sweden to Illinois sent twenty-five cents to a publisher for a book on photography. What he received instead was a book on ventriloquism. What did he do? He adapted and learned ventriloquism. He was Edgar Bergen, and for over forty years he entertained audiences with the help of a wooden dummy named Charlie McCarthy.

The ability to innovate is at the heart of creativity—a vital component in success. University of Houston professor Jack Matson recognized that fact and developed a course that his students call "Failure 101." In it, Matson has students build mock-ups of products that no one would ever buy. His goal is to get students to equate failure with innovation instead of defeat. That way they will free themselves to try new things. "They learn to reload and get ready to shoot again," says Matson. If you want to succeed, you have to learn to make adjustments to the way you do things and try again. Adversity helps to develop that ability.

6. ADVERSITY BRINGS UNEXPECTED BENEFITS

The average person makes a mistake, and automatically thinks th' a failure. But some of the greatest stories of success can be fo' unexpected benefits of mistakes. For example, most peor' with the story of Edison and the phonograph: he ?

trying to invent something entirely different. But did you also know that Kellogg's Corn Flakes resulted when boiled wheat was left in a baking pan overnight? Or that Ivory soap floats because a batch was left in the mixer too long and had a large volume of air whipped into it? Or that Scott Towels were launched when a toilet paper machine put too many layers of tissue together?

"IN SCIENCE, MISTAKES ALWAYS PRECEDE THE TRUTH." —HORACE WALPOLE

Horace Walpole said that "in science, mistakes always precede the truth." That's what happened to German-Swiss chemist Christian Friedrich Schönbein. One day he was working in the kitchen—which his wife had strictly forbidden—and was experimenting with sulfuric and nitric acid. When he accidentally spilled some of the mixture on the kitchen table, he thought he was in trouble. (He knew he would experience "adversity" when his wife found out!) He hurriedly snatched up a cotton apron, wiped up the mess, and hung the apron by the fire to dry.

Suddenly there was a violent explosion. Evidently the cellulose in the cotton underwent a process called "nitration." Unwittingly, Schönbein had invented nitrocellulose—what came to be called smokeless gunpowder or gun-cotton. He went on to market his invention, which made him a lot of money.

7. ADVERSITY MOTIVATES

Years ago when Bear Bryant was coaching the University of Alabama's football team, the Crimson Tide was ahead by only six points in a game with less than two minutes remaining in the fourth quarter. Bryant sent his quarterback into the game with instructions to play it safe and run out the clock.

In the huddle, the quarterback said, "Coach says to play it safe, but that's what they're expecting. Let's give them a surprise." And with that, he called a pass play.

When the quarterback dropped back and threw the pass, the defending cornerback, who was a champion sprinter, intercepted the ball and headed for the end zone expecting to score a touchdown. The quarterback, who was not known as a good runner, took off after the cornerback and ran him down from behind, tackling him on the five-yard line. It saved the game.

After the clock ran out, the opposing coach approached Bear Bryant and said, "What's this business about your quarterback not being a runner? He ran down my speedster from behind!"

Bryant responded, "Your man was running for six points. My man was running for his life."

Nothing can motivate a person like adversity. Olympic diver Pat McCormick said, "I think failure is one of the great motivators. After my narrow loss in the 1948 trials, I knew how really good I could be. It was the defeat that focused all my concentration on my training and goals." McCormick went on to win two gold medals in the Olympics in London that year and another two in Helsinki four years later.

If you can step back from the negative circumstances you face in life, you will be able to discover that there are positive benefits to your negative experiences. That is almost always true; you simply have to be willing to look for them—and not take the adversity you are experiencing too personally.

So if you lose your job, think about the resilience you're developing. If you try something daring and survive, think about what you learned about yourself—and how it will help you take on new challenges. If a restaurant gets your order wrong, figure out if it's an opportunity to learn a new skill. And if you experience a train wreck in your career, think of the maturity it's developing in you. Besides, Bill Vaughan says, "In the game of life it's a good idea to have a few early losses, which relieves you of the pressure of trying to maintain an undefeated season." Always measure an obstacle next to the size of the dream you're pursuing. It's all in how you look at it. Try, and you can find the good in every bad experience.

WHAT COULD BE WORSE?

One of the most incredible stories of adversity overcome and success gained is that of Joseph of the ancient Hebrews. You may be familiar with the story. He was born the eleventh of twelve sons in a wealthy Middle Eastern family whose trade was raising livestock. As a teenager, Joseph alienated his brothers: First, he was his father's favorite, even though he was nearly the youngest. Second, he used to tell his father any time his brothers weren't doing their work properly with the sheep. And third, he made the mistake of telling his older brothers that one day he would be in charge of them. At first a group of his brothers wanted to kill him, but the eldest, Reuben, prevented them from doing that. So when Reuben wasn't around, the others sold him into slavery.

Joseph ended up in Egypt working in the house of the captain of the guard, a man named Potiphar. Because of his leadership and administrative skill, Joseph quickly rose in the ranks, and before long, he was running the entire household. He was making the best of a bad situation. But then things got worse. The wife of his master tried to persuade him to sleep with her. When he refused, she accused him of making advances toward her and got Potiphar to throw Joseph in prison.

FROM SLAVERY TO PRISON

At that point Joseph was in about as difficult a position as he could be. He was separated from his family. He was living away from home in a foreign land. He was a slave. And he was in prison. But again, he made the best of a tough situation. Before long, the warden of the prison put Joseph in charge of all the prisoners and all the prison's daily activities.

While in prison, Joseph got the chance to meet a fellow prisoner who had been an official from Pharaoh's court, the chief cupbearer. And Joseph was able to do him a favor by interpreting a dream the man had. When he saw that the official was grateful, Joseph made a request of him in return.

"When all goes well with you," Joseph asked, "remember me and show me kindness; mention me to Pharaoh and get me out of this prison. For I was forcibly carried off from the land of the Hebrews, and even here I have done nothing to deserve being put in a dungeon."[4]

Joseph had great hope a few days later when the official was returned to court and the good graces of the monarch. He expected any minute to receive word that Pharaoh was setting him free. But he waited. And waited. Two years passed before the cupbearer remembered Joseph, and he did so only because Pharaoh wanted someone to interpret one of his dreams.

FINALLY . . . THE PAYOFF

In the end, Joseph was able to interpret Pharaoh's dreams. And because the Hebrew showed such great wisdom, the Egyptian ruler put Joseph in charge of the entire kingdom. As the result of Joseph's leadership, planning, and system of food storage, when famine struck the Middle East seven years later, many thousands of people who otherwise would have died were able to survive—including Joseph's own family. When his brothers traveled to Egypt for relief from the famine—twenty years after selling him into slavery—they discovered that their brother Joseph was not only alive, but second in command of the most powerful kingdom in the world.

Few people would welcome the adversity of thirteen years in bondage as a slave and prisoner. But as far as we know, Joseph never gave up hope and never lost his perspective. Nor did he hold a grudge against his brothers. After their father died, he told them, "You intended to harm me, but God intended it for good to accomplish what is now being done, the saving of many lives."

Joseph found the positive benefits in his negative experiences. And if he can do it, so can we. To help you do that, you need to take the next step when it comes to attitude. You have to be able to deal positively with failure.

PART III

THE FUTURE WITH THE RIGHT ATTITUDE

6

WHAT IS FAILURE?

Every successful person is someone who failed,
yet never regarded himself as a failure.

I n an interview years ago David Brinkley asked advice columnist Ann
Landers what question she most frequently received from readers.
Her answer: "What's wrong with me?"

Landers's response reveals a lot about human nature. Many people
wrestle with feelings of failure, the most damaging being doubtful thoughts
about themselves. At the heart of those doubts and feelings is one central
question: Am I a failure? And that's a problem because I believe it's nearly
impossible for any person to believe he is a failure and succeed at the same
time. Instead, you have to meet failure with the right attitude and determine to fail forward.

It seems that advice columnists (such as the late Ann Landers) and
humor writers recognize that keeping a good attitude about yourself is
important to overcoming adversity and mistakes. The late Erma Bombeck,
who wrote a widely syndicated weekly humor column until a few weeks
before her death in 1996, had a firm grasp on what it meant to persevere
and fail forward without taking failure too personally.

FROM NEWSPAPER COPY GIRL TO
TIME MAGAZINE COVER GIRL

Erma Bombeck traveled a road that was filled with adversity, starting with her career. She was drawn to journalism early in life. Her first job was as a copy girl at the *Dayton Journal-Herald* when she was a teenager. But when she went off to college at Ohio University, a guidance counselor advised her, "Forget about writing." She refused. Later she transferred to the University of Dayton and in 1949 graduated with a degree in English. Soon afterward she began working as a writer—for the obituary column and the women's page.

That year adversity carried over into her personal life. When she got married, one of her deepest desires was to become a mother. But much to her dismay, her doctors told her she was incapable of having children. Did she give up and consider herself a failure? No, she and her husband explored the possibility of adoption, and then they adopted a daughter.

Two years later, a surprised Erma became pregnant. But even that brought her more difficulties. In four years she experienced four pregnancies, but only two of the babies survived.

In 1964 Erma was able to convince the editor of a small neighborhood newspaper, the *Kettering-Oakwood Times*, to let her write a weekly humor column. Despite the pitiful $3 per article she was paid, she kept writing. And that opened a door for her. The next year she was offered the opportunity to write a three-times-a-week column for her old employer, the *Dayton Journal-Herald*. By 1967 her column was syndicated and carried by more than nine hundred newspapers.

For slightly more than thirty years, Erma wrote her humor column. During that time she published fifteen books, was recognized as one of the twenty-five most influential women in America, appeared frequently on the television show *Good Morning America*, was featured on the cover of *Time* magazine, received innumerable honors (such as the American Cancer Society's Medal of Honor), and was awarded fifteen honorary degrees.

MORE THAN HER SHARE OF PROBLEMS

But during that span of time, Erma Bombeck also experienced incredible troubles and trials, including breast cancer, a mastectomy, and kidney failure. And she wasn't shy about sharing her perspective on her life experiences:

> I speak at college commencements, and I tell everyone I'm up there and they're down there, not because of my successes, but my failures. Then I proceed to spin all of them off—a comedy record album that sold two copies in Beirut . . . a sitcom that lasted about as long as a donut in our house . . . a Broadway play that never saw Broadway . . . book signings where I attracted two people: one who wanted directions to the restroom and the other who wanted to buy the desk.
>
> What you have to tell yourself is, "I'm not a failure. I failed at doing something." There's a big difference . . . Personally and career-wise, it's been a corduroy road. I've buried babies, lost parents, had cancer, and worried over kids. The trick is to put it all in perspective . . . and that's what I do for a living.[1]

That winning attitude kept Erma Bombeck down to earth. (She liked to refer to herself as "a former homeroom mother and obituary writer.") It also kept her going—and writing—through the disappointments, the pain, the surgeries, and the daily kidney dialysis until her death at age sixty-nine.

EVERY GENIUS COULD HAVE BEEN A "FAILURE"

Every successful person is someone who failed, yet never regarded himself as a failure. For example, Wolfgang Mozart, one of the geniuses of musical composition, was told by Emperor Ferdinand that his opera *The Marriage of Figaro* was "far too noisy" and contained "far too many notes." Artist

Vincent van Gogh, whose paintings now set records for the sums they bring at auction, sold only one painting in his lifetime. Thomas Edison, the most prolific inventor in history, was considered unteachable as a youngster. And Albert Einstein, the greatest thinker of our time, was told by a Munich schoolmaster that he would "never amount to much."

I think it's safe to say that all great achievers are given multiple reasons to believe they are failures. But in spite of that, they remain positive and they persevere. In the face of adversity, rejection, and failings, they continue believing in themselves and refuse to consider themselves failures. They choose to develop the right attitude about failure.

Failing Forward Is Not False Self-Esteem

I place high value on praising people, especially children. In fact, I believe that people live up to your level of expectation. But I also believe that you have to base your praise on truth. You don't make up nice things to say about others. Here's the approach I use to encourage and lead others:

> Value people.
> Praise effort.
> Reward performance.

I use that method with everyone. I even use a form of it with myself. When I'm working, I don't give myself a reward until after the job is finished. When I approach a task or project, I give it my very best, and no matter what the results are, I have a clear conscience. I have no problem sleeping at night. And no matter where I fail or how many mistakes I make, I don't let it devalue my worth as a person. As the saying goes, "God uses people who fail—'cause there aren't any other kind around."

It is possible to cultivate a positive attitude about yourself, no matter what circumstances you find yourself in or what kind of history you have.

SEVEN ABILITIES NEEDED TO FAIL FORWARD

Here are seven abilities of achievers that enable them to fail, not take it personally, and keep moving forward:

1. REJECT REJECTION

Author James Allen states, "A man is literally what he thinks, his character being the complete sum of all his thought." That's why it's important to make sure your thinking is on the right track.

People who don't give up keep trying because they don't base their self-worth on their performance. Instead, they have an internally based self-image. Rather than say, "I am a failure," they say, "I missed that one," or "I made a mistake."

Psychologist Martin E. Seligman believes we have two choices when we fail: we can internalize or externalize our failure. "People who blame themselves when they fail . . . think they are worthless, talentless, unlovable," says Seligman. "People who blame external events do not lose self-esteem when bad events strike."[2] To keep the right perspective, take responsibility for your actions, but don't take failure personally.

2. SEE FAILURE AS TEMPORARY

People who personalize failure see a problem as a hole they're permanently stuck in. But achievers see any predicament as temporary. For example, take the case of United States President Harry S. Truman. In 1922 he was thirty-eight years old, in debt, and out of work. In 1945 he was the most powerful leader of the free world, occupying the highest office in the land. If he had seen failure as permanent, he would have remained stuck and never would have kept trying and believing in his potential.

3. SEE FAILURES AS ISOLATED INCIDENTS

Author Leo Buscaglia once talked about his admiration for cooking expert Julia Child: "I just love her attitude. She says, 'Tonight we're going to make a soufflé!' And she beats this and whisks that, and she drops things on the floor . . . and does all these wonderful human things. Then she takes the soufflé and throws it in the oven and talks to you for a while. Finally, she says, 'Now it's ready!' But when she opens the oven, the soufflé just falls flat as a pancake. But does she panic or burst into tears? No! She smiles and says, 'Well, you can't win them all. Bon appetit!'"

When achievers fail, they see it as a momentary event, not a lifelong epidemic. It's not personal. If you want to succeed, don't let any single incident color your view of yourself.

4. KEEP EXPECTATIONS REALISTIC

The greater the feat you desire to achieve, the greater the mental preparation required for overcoming obstacles and persevering over the long haul. If you want to take a stroll in your neighborhood, you can reasonably expect to have few, if any, problems. But that's not the case if you intend to climb Mount Everest.

It takes time, effort, and the ability to overcome setbacks. You have to approach each day with reasonable expectations and not get your feelings hurt when everything doesn't turn out perfectly.

Something that happened on baseball's opening day in 1954 illustrates the point well. The Milwaukee Braves and the Cincinnati Reds played each other, and a rookie for each team made his major-league debut during that game. The rookie who played for the Reds hit four doubles and helped his team win with a score of 9-8. The rookie for the Braves went 0 for 5. The Reds player was Jim Greengrass, a name you probably haven't heard. The other guy, who didn't get a hit, might be more familiar to you. His name was Hank Aaron, the player who became the best home-run hitter in the history of baseball.

If Aaron's expectations for that first game had been unrealistic, who knows? He might have given up baseball. Surely he wasn't happy about his performance that day, but he didn't think of himself as a failure. He had worked too hard for too long. He wasn't about to give up easily.

5. FOCUS ON STRENGTHS

Another way achievers keep themselves from personalizing failure is by focusing on their strengths. Bob Butera, former president of the New Jersey Devils hockey team, was asked what makes a winner. He answered, "What distinguishes winners from losers is that winners concentrate at all times on what they can do, not on what they can't do. If a guy is a great shooter but not a great skater, we tell him to think only about the shot, the shot, the shot—never about some other guy outskating him. The idea is to remember your successes."

If a weakness is a matter of character, it needs much attention. Focus on it until you shore it up. Otherwise, the best bet for failing forward is developing and maximizing your strengths.

6. VARY APPROACHES TO ACHIEVEMENT

In *The Psychology of Achievement*, Brian Tracy writes about four millionaires who made their fortunes by age thirty-five. They were involved in an average of seventeen businesses before finding the one that took them to the top. They kept trying and changing until they found something that worked for them.

Achievers are willing to vary their approaches to problems. That's important in every walk of life, not just business. For example, if you're a fan of track-and-field events, you have undoubtedly enjoyed watching athletes compete in the high jump. I'm always amazed by the heights achieved by the men and women in that event. What's really interesting is that in the 1960s, the sport went through a major change in technique that allowed athletes to break the old records and push them up to new levels.

The person responsible for that change was Dick Fosbury. Where previous athletes used the straddle method to high jump, in which they went over the bar while facing it, with one arm and one leg leading, Fosbury developed a technique where he went over headfirst with his back to the bar. It was dubbed the Fosbury Flop.

Developing a new high-jump technique was one thing. Getting it accepted by others was another matter. Fosbury remarked, "I was told over and over again that I would never be successful, that I was not going to be competitive and the technique was simply not going to work. All I could do was shrug and say, 'We'll just have to see.'"

And people did see. Fosbury won the gold medal in the Mexico City Olympics in 1968, shattering the previous Olympic record and setting a new world record in the process. Since then, nearly all world-class high jumpers have used his technique. To achieve his goals, Fosbury varied his approach to high jumping, and he kept a positive attitude by not allowing others' comments to make him feel like a failure.

7. BOUNCE BACK

All achievers have in common the ability to bounce back after an error, mistake, or failure. Psychologist Simone Caruthers says, "Life is a series of outcomes. Sometimes the outcome is what you want. Great. Figure out what you did right. Sometimes the outcome is what you don't want. Great. Figure out what you did so you don't do it again."[3] The key to bouncing back is found in your attitude toward the outcome.

Achievers are able to keep moving forward no matter what happens. And that's made possible because they remember that failure does not make *them* failures. No one should take mistakes personally. That's the best way to pick yourself up after failure and continue with a positive attitude. Once you do that, you're ready for success, which happens to be the subject of the next chapter.

WHAT IS SUCCESS?

Attitude determines how far you can go
on the success journey.

D o you want to be successful? The problem for most people who want to be successful is *not* that they can't achieve success. The main obstacle for them is that they misunderstand success. They don't have the right *attitude* about it. Maltbie D. Babcock said, "One of the most common mistakes and one of the costliest is thinking that success is due to some genius, some magic, something or other which we do not possess."

What is success? What does it look like? Most people have a vague picture of what it means to be a successful person that looks something like this:

The wealth of Bill Gates,
the physique of Arnold Schwarzenegger,
(or Tyra Banks),
the intelligence of Albert Einstein,
the athletic ability of Michael Jordan,
the business prowess of Donald Trump,
the social grace and poise of Jackie Kennedy,

the imagination of Walt Disney, and
the heart of Mother Teresa.

That sounds absurd, but it's closer to the truth than we would like to
admit. Many of us picture success as looking like someone other than who
we are. That's the wrong way to think about it. If you tried to become just
like even one of these other people, you wouldn't be successful. You would
be a bad imitation of them, and you would eliminate the possibility of
becoming the person you were meant to be.

THE WRONG ATTITUDE ABOUT SUCCESS

Even if you avoid the trap of thinking that success means being like some
other person, you might still have a wrong attitude toward success. Many
people wrongly equate it with achievement of some sort, with arriving at
a destination or attaining a goal. Here are several of the most common
misconceptions about success:

WEALTH

Probably the most common misunderstanding about success is that
it's the same as having money. A lot of people believe that if they accu-
mulate wealth, they will be successful. But wealth doesn't eliminate current problems, and it introduces many new ones. If you don't believe
that, look at the lives of lottery winners. Wealth does not bring contentment or success.

A SPECIAL FEELING

Another common misconception is that people have achieved success
when they feel successful or happy. But trying to *feel* successful is probably
even more difficult than trying to become wealthy. The continual search
for happiness is a primary reason that so many people are miserable. If
you make happiness your goal, you are almost certainly destined to fail.
You will be on a continual roller coaster, changing from successful to

unsuccessful with every mood change. Life is uncertain, and emotions aren't stable. Happiness simply cannot be relied upon as a measure of success.

SPECIFIC AND WORTHWHILE POSSESSIONS

Think back to when you were a kid. Chances are that there was a time when you wanted something badly, and you believed that if you possessed that thing, it would make a significant difference in your life. When I was nine years old, it was a burgundy-and-silver Schwinn bicycle, which I received for Christmas. But I soon discovered that it didn't bring me the success or long-term contentment that I hoped for and expected.

That process has repeated itself in my life. I found that success didn't come when I became a starter on my high school basketball team, when I became the student body president in college, or when I bought my first house. It has never come as the result of possessing something I wanted. Possessions are at best a temporary fix. Success cannot be attained or measured that way.

POWER

Charles McElroy once joked, "Power is usually recognized as an excellent short-term antidepressant." That statement contains a lot of truth because power often gives the appearance of success, but even then, it's only temporary.

You've probably heard before the quote from English historian Lord Acton: "Power tends to corrupt and absolute power corrupts absolutely." Abraham Lincoln echoed that belief when he said, "Nearly all men can stand adversity, but if you want to test a man's character, give him power." Power really is a test of character. In the hands of a person of integrity, it is of tremendous benefit; in the hands of a tyrant, it causes terrible destruction. By itself, power is neither positive nor negative. And it is not the source of security or success. Besides, all dictators—even benevolent ones—eventually lose power.

ACHIEVEMENT

Many people have what I call "destination disease." They believe that if they can arrive somewhere—attain a position, accomplish a goal, or have a relationship with the right person—they will be successful. At one time I had a similar view of success. I defined it as the progressive realization of a predetermined worthwhile goal. But over time I realized that the definition fell short of the mark. Success isn't a list of goals to be checked off one after another. It's not reaching a destination. Success is a journey.

THE RIGHT ATTITUDE ABOUT SUCCESS

If success is a journey, how do you get started? What does it take to be successful? Two things are required: the right attitude toward success and the right principles for getting there. Once you redefine success as a journey, you can maintain the right attitude toward it. Then you're ready to start the process. The results may be as unique as each individual, but the process is the same for everyone. Here is my definition of success:

> *Success is . . .*
> *Knowing your purpose in life,*
> *Growing to reach your maximum potential, and*
> *Sowing seeds that benefit others.*

When you think of success in this way, you can see why it must be seen as a journey rather than a destination. No matter how long you live or what you decide to do in life, as long as you have the right attitude about it, you will never exhaust your capacity to grow toward your potential or run out of opportunities to help others. When you see success as a journey, you'll never have the problem of trying to "arrive" at an elusive final destination. And you'll never find yourself in a position where you have accomplished some final goal, only to discover that you're still unfulfilled and searching for something else to do.

To get a better handle on these aspects of success, let's take a look at each one of them:

KNOWING YOUR PURPOSE

Nothing can take the place of knowing your purpose. Millionaire industrialist Henry J. Kaiser, the founder of Kaiser Aluminum as well as the Kaiser-Permanente health care system, said, "The evidence is overwhelming that you cannot begin to achieve your best unless you set some aim in life." Or put another way, if you don't try actively to discover your purpose, you're likely to spend your life doing the wrong things.

I believe that God created every person for a purpose. According to psychologist Viktor Frankl, "Everyone has his own specific vocation or mission in life. Everyone must carry out a concrete assignment that demands fulfillment. Therein he cannot be replaced, nor can his life be repeated. Thus everyone's task is as unique as his specific opportunity to implement it." Each of us has a purpose for which we were created. Our responsibility—and our greatest joy—is to identify it.

Here are some questions to ask yourself to help you identify your purpose:

For what am I searching? All of us have a strong desire buried in our hearts, something that speaks to our deepest thoughts and feelings, something that sets our souls on fire. You only need to find it.

Why was I created? Each of us is different. Think about your unique mix of abilities, the resources available to you, your personal history, and the opportunities around you. If you objectively identify these factors and discover the desire of your heart, you will have done a lot toward discovering your purpose in life.

Do I believe in my potential? If you don't believe that you have potential, you will never try to reach it. You should take the advice of President Theodore Roosevelt, who said, "Do what you can, with what you have, where you are." If you do that with your eyes fixed on your life purpose, what else can be expected of you?

When do I start? The answer to that question is NOW.

GROWING TO YOUR POTENTIAL

Novelist H. G. Wells held that wealth, notoriety, place, and power are no measures of success whatsoever. The only true measure of success is the ratio between what we might have been and what we have become. In other words, success comes as the result of growing to our potential.

We have nearly limitless potential, yet too few ever try to reach it. Why? The answer lies in this: We can do *anything*, but we can't do *everything*. Many people let everyone around them decide their agenda in life. As a result, they never really dedicate themselves to *their* purpose in life. They become a jack-of-all-trades, master of none—rather than a jack-of-few-trades, focused on one.

If that describes you more than you'd like, you're probably ready to take steps to make a change. Here are four principles to put you on the road to growing toward your potential:

1. CONCENTRATE ON ONE MAIN GOAL.

Nobody ever reached her potential by scattering herself in twenty directions. Reaching your potential requires focus.

2. CONCENTRATE ON CONTINUAL IMPROVEMENT.

David D. Glass, chairman of the executive committee of the Wal-Mart board of directors, was once asked whom he admired most. His answer was Wal-Mart founder Sam Walton. He remarked, "There's never been a day in his life, since I've known him, that he didn't improve in some way." Commitment to continual improvement is the key to reaching your potential and to being successful.

3. FORGET THE PAST.

My friend Jack Hayford, pastor of Church on the Way in Van Nuys, California, commented, "The past is a dead issue, and we can't gain any momentum moving toward tomorrow if we are dragging the past behind us."

If you need inspiration, think of other people who overcame seemingly insurmountable obstacles, such as Booker T. Washington, Helen Keller, and Franklin Delano Roosevelt. Each of them overcame incredible odds to achieve great things. And remember, no matter what you've faced in the past, you have the *potential* to overcome it.

4. FOCUS ON THE FUTURE.

Baseball Hall of Famer Yogi Berra declared, "The future isn't what it used to be." Although that may be true, it's still the only place we have to go. Your potential lies ahead of you—whether you're eight, eighteen, forty-eight, or eighty. You still have room to improve yourself. You can become better tomorrow than you are today. As the Spanish proverb says, "He who does not look ahead remains behind."

SOWING SEEDS THAT BENEFIT OTHERS

When you know your purpose in life and are growing to reach your maximum potential, you're well on your way to being a success. But there is one more essential part of the success journey: helping others. Without that aspect, the journey can be a lonely and shallow experience.

It's been said that we make a living by what we get, but we make a life by what we give. Physician, theologian, and philosopher Albert Schweitzer stated it even more strongly: "The purpose of human life is to serve, and to show compassion and the will to help others." For him, the success journey led to Africa where he served people for many years.

For you, sowing seeds that benefit others probably won't mean traveling to another country to serve the poor—unless that is the purpose you were born to fulfill. (And if it is, you won't be satisfied until that's what you're doing.) However, if you're like most people, helping others is something you can do right here at home, whether it's spending more time with your family, developing an employee who shows potential, helping people in the community, or putting your desires on hold for the sake of your team at work. The key is to find your purpose and help others while you're pursuing it. Entertainer Danny Thomas insisted that "all of us are born for a reason, but all of us don't discover why. Success in life has nothing to do with what you gain in life or accomplish for yourself. It's what you do for others."

WE MAKE A LIVING BY WHAT WE GET,
BUT WE MAKE A LIFE BY WHAT WE GIVE.

Having the right view of success can help you keep a positive attitude about yourself and life, no matter what kind of circumstances you find yourself in. And if you can help the people you lead to adopt that same view of success, you can help them to always have hope and to become successful. Why? Because all people—regardless of talent level, education, or upbringing—are capable of knowing their purpose, growing to their maximum potential, and sowing seeds that benefit others. And helping people is what leadership is really all about.

But there's one more truth you need to know if you want to be a successful leader in the area of attitude. And you'll find that in the last chapter.

8

How Can a Leader Keep Climbing?

Leaders have to give up to go up.

Many people today want to climb up the corporate ladder because they believe that freedom and power are the prizes waiting at the top. What they don't realize is that the true nature of leadership is really sacrifice.

Most people will acknowledge that sacrifices are necessary fairly early in a leadership career. People give up many things in order to gain potential opportunities. For example, Tom Murphy began working for General Motors in 1937. But he almost refused the first position he was offered with the company because the one-hundred-dollar-a-month salary barely covered his expenses. Despite his misgivings, he took the job anyway, thinking the opportunity was worth the sacrifice. He was right. Murphy eventually became General Motors' chairman of the board.

Sacrifice is a constant in leadership. It is an ongoing process, not a one-time payment. It's an attitude that any successful leader must maintain. When I look back at my career, I recognize that there has always been a cost involved in moving forward. That's been true for me in the area of finances with every career change I've made since I was twenty-two years old. Any time you know that the step is right, don't hesitate to make a sacrifice.

YOU'VE GOT TO GIVE UP TO GO UP

Leaders who want to rise have to do more than take an occasional cut in pay. They have to give up their rights. As my friend Gerald Brooks says, "When you become a leader, you lose the right to think about yourself." For every person, the nature of the sacrifice may be different. Leaders give up to go up. That's true of every leader regardless of profession. Talk to any leader, and you will find that he has made repeated sacrifices. Usually, the higher that leader has climbed, the greater the sacrifices he has made.

THE HIGHER YOU GO, THE MORE YOU GIVE UP

Who is the most powerful leader in the world? I'd say it's the president of the United States. More than any other single person, his actions and words make an impact on people, not just in our country, but around the globe. Think about what he must give up to reach the office of president and then to hold that office. His time is no longer his own. He is scrutinized constantly. His family is under tremendous pressure. And as a matter of course, he must make decisions that can cost thousands of people their lives. Even after he leaves office, he will spend the rest of his life in the company of Secret Service agents who protect him from bodily harm.

The greater the leader, the more he must give up. Think about someone like Martin Luther King, Jr. His wife, Coretta Scott King, remarked in *My Life with Martin Luther King, Jr.*, "Day and night our phone would ring, and someone would pour out a string of obscene epithets . . . Frequently the calls ended with a threat to kill us if we didn't get out of town. But in spite of all the danger, the chaos of our private lives, I felt inspired, almost elated."

While pursuing his course of leadership during the civil rights movement, King was arrested and jailed on many occasions. He was stoned, stabbed, and physically attacked. His house was bombed. Yet his vision—and his influence—continued to increase. Ultimately, he sacrificed everything he had. But what he gave up he parted with willingly. In his last speech, delivered the night before his assassination in Memphis, he said,

> I don't know what will happen to me now. We've got some difficult days ahead. But it doesn't matter to me now. Because I've been to the mountaintop. I won't mind. Like anybody else, I would like to live a long life. Longevity has its place. But I'm not concerned about that now. I just want to do God's will. And He's allowed me to go up to the mountain. And I've looked over and I've seen the Promised Land. I may not get there with you, but I want you to know tonight that we, as a people, will get to the Promised Land. So I'm happy tonight . . . I'm not fearing any man. "Mine eyes have seen the glory of the coming of the Lord."[1]

The next day he paid the ultimate price of sacrifice. King's impact was profound. He influenced millions of people to peacefully stand up against a system and society that fought to exclude them.

THE HIGHER THE LEVEL OF LEADERSHIP YOU WANT
TO REACH, THE GREATER THE SACRIFICES
YOU WILL HAVE TO MAKE.

What successful people find to be true becomes even clearer to them when they become leaders. There is no success without an attitude of sacrifice. The higher the level of leadership you want to reach, the greater the sacrifices you will have to make. To go up, you have to give up. That is the true nature of leadership. That is the power of the right attitude.

SELF-IMPROVEMENT

101

WHAT EVERY LEADER NEEDS TO KNOW

Published in Nashville, Tennessee, by Thomas Nelson.
Thomas Nelson is a registered trademark of Thomas Nelson, Inc.

Published in association with Yates & Yates, www.yates2.com

Thomas Nelson, Inc., titles may be purchased in bulk for educational, business, fund-raising, or sales promotional use. For information, please e-mail SpecialMarkets@ThomasNelson.com.

Portions of this book have been previously published in *Your Road Map for Success, Talent is Never Enough, Developing the Leaders Around You, Failing Forward, The 360° Leader, Winning with People,* and *Leadership Gold* by John C. Maxwell.

Library of Congress Cataloging-in-Publication Data

Maxwell, John C., 1947–
Self-Improvement 101 : what every leader needs to know / John C. Maxwell.
p. cm.
ISBN 978-1-4002-8024-7
1. Leadership. 2. Self-actualization (Psychology) I. Title.
HD57.7.M39428 2009
658.4'092—dc22
2009028418

CONTENTS

PART I

LAYING A FOUNDATION FOR SELF-IMPROVEMENT

I

What Will It Take for Me to Improve?

Growth must be intentional—nobody improves by accident.

The poet Robert Browning wrote, "Why stay we on the earth except to grow?" Just about anyone would agree that growing is a good thing, but relatively few people dedicate themselves to the process. Why? Because it requires change, and most people are reluctant to change. But the truth is that without change, growth is impossible. Author Gail Sheehy asserted:

> If we don't change, we don't grow. If we don't grow, we are not really living. Growth demands a temporary surrender of security. It may mean a giving up of familiar but limiting patterns, safe but unrewarding work, values no longer believed in, relationships that have lost their meaning. As Dostoevsky put it, "taking a new step, uttering a new word, is what most people fear most." The real fear should be the opposite course.

I can't think of anything worse than living a stagnant life, devoid of change and improvement.

GROWTH IS A CHOICE

Most people fight against change, especially when it affects them personally. As novelist Leo Tolstoy said, "Everyone thinks of changing the world, but no one thinks of changing himself." The ironic thing is that change is inevitable. Everybody has to deal with it. On the other hand, growth is optional. You can choose to grow or fight it. But know this: people unwilling to grow will never reach their potential.

In one of his books, my friend Howard Hendricks asks the question, "How have you changed . . . lately? In the last week, let's say? Or the last month? The last year? Can you be *very specific*?" He knows how people tend to get into a rut when it comes to growth and change. Growth is a choice, a decision that can really make a difference in a person's life.

Most people don't realize that unsuccessful and successful people do not differ substantially in their abilities. They vary in their desires to reach their potential. And nothing is more effective when it comes to reaching potential than commitment to personal growth.

PRINCIPLES FOR SELF-IMPROVEMENT

Making the change from being an occasional learner to becoming someone dedicated to personal growth goes against the grain of the way most people live. If you asked one hundred people how many books they have read on their own since leaving school (college or high school), I bet only a handful would say they have read more than one or two books. If you asked how many listen to audio lessons and voluntarily attend conferences and seminars to grow personally, there would be even fewer. Most people celebrate when they receive their diplomas or degrees and say to themselves, "Thank goodness that's over. Just let me have a good job. I'm finished with studying." But such thinking doesn't take you any higher than average. If you want to be successful, you have to keep growing.

As someone who has dedicated his life to personal growth and development, I'd like to help you make the leap to becoming a dedicated self-developer. It's the way you need to go if you want to reach your potential. Besides that, it also has another benefit: it brings contentment. The happiest people I know are growing every day.

Take a look at the following eight principles. They'll help you develop into a person dedicated to personal growth:

1. Choose a Life of Growth

It's said that when Spanish composer-cellist Pablo Casals was in the final years of his life, a young reporter asked him, "Mr. Casals, you are ninety-five years old and the greatest cellist that ever lived. Why do you still practice six hours a day?"

What was Casals's answer? "Because I think I'm making progress." That's the kind of dedication to continual growth that you should have. The people who reach their potential, no matter what their profession or background, think in terms of improvement. If you think you can "hold your ground" and still make the success journey, you are mistaken. You need to have an attitude like that of General George Patton. It's said that he told his troops, "There is one thing I want you to remember. I don't want to get any messages saying we are holding our position. We are advancing constantly." Patton's motto was, "Always take the offensive. Never dig in."

The only way to improve the quality of your life is to improve yourself. If you want to grow your organization, you must grow a leader. If you want better children, you must become a better person. If you want others to treat you more kindly, you must develop better people skills. There is no sure way to make other people in your environment improve. The only thing you truly have the ability to improve is yourself. And the amazing thing is that when you do, everything else around you suddenly gets better. So the bottom line is that if you want to take the success journey, you must live a life of growth. And the only way you will grow is if you *choose* to grow.

2. START GROWING TODAY

Napoleon Hill said, "It's not what you are going to do, but it's what you are doing now that counts." Many un-successful people have what I call "someday sickness" because they could do some things to bring value to their lives right now. But they put them off and say they'll do them *someday*. Their motto is "One of these days." But as the old English proverb says, "*One* of these days means *none* of these days." The best way to ensure success is to start growing today. No matter where you may be starting from, don't be discouraged; everyone who got where he is started where he was.

Why do you need to determine to start growing today? There are several reasons:

- *Growth is not automatic.* In my book *Breakthrough Parenting*, I mention that you can be young only once, but you can be immature indefinitely.[1] That's because growth is not automatic. Just because you grow older doesn't mean you keep growing. That's how it is with some creatures, such as crustaceans. As a crab or a lobster ages, it grows and has to shed its shell. But that's not the trend for people. The road to the next level is uphill, and it takes effort to keep growing. The sooner you start, the closer to reaching your potential you'll be.

- *Growth today will provide a better tomorrow.* Everything you do today builds on what you did yesterday. And altogether, those things determine what will happen tomorrow. That's especially true in regard to growth. Oliver Wendell Holmes offered this insight: "Man's mind, once stretched by new ideas, never regains its original dimensions." Growth today is an investment for tomorrow.

- *Growth is your responsibility.* When you were a small child, your parents were responsible for you—even for your growth and education. But as an adult, you bear that responsibility entirely. If you don't make growth your responsibility, it will never happen.

There is no time like right now to get started. Recognize the importance that personal growth plays in success, and commit yourself to developing your potential today.

3. FOCUS ON SELF-DEVELOPMENT, NOT SELF-FULFILLMENT

There has been a change in focus over the last thirty years in the area of personal growth. Beginning in the late sixties and early seventies, people began talking about "finding themselves," meaning that they were searching for a way to become self-fulfilled. It's like making happiness a goal because self-fulfillment is about feeling good.

But self-development is different. Sure, much of the time it will make you feel good, but that's a by-product, not the goal. Self-development is a higher calling; it is the development of your potential so that you can attain the purpose for which you were created. There are times when that's fulfilling, but other times it's not. But no matter how it makes you feel, self-development always has one effect: It draws you toward your destiny. Rabbi Samuel M. Silver taught that "the greatest of all miracles is that we need not be tomorrow what we are today, but we can improve if we make use of the potential implanted in us by God."

4. NEVER STAY SATISFIED WITH CURRENT ACCOMPLISHMENTS

My friend Rick Warren says, "The greatest enemy of tomorrow's success is today's success." And he is right. Thinking that you have "arrived" when you accomplish a goal has the same effect as believing you know it all. It takes away your desire to learn. It's another characteristic of destination disease. But successful people don't sit back and rest on their laurels. They know that wins—like losses—are temporary, and they have to keep growing if they want to continue being successful. Charles Handy remarked, "It is one of the paradoxes of success that the things and ways which got you there are seldom those things that keep you there."

No matter how successful you are today, don't get complacent. Stay hungry. Sydney Harris insisted that "a winner knows how much he still has to learn, even when he is considered an expert by others; a loser wants to be considered an expert by others before he has learned enough to know how little he knows." Don't settle into a comfort zone, and don't let success go to your head. Enjoy your success briefly, and then move on to greater growth.

5. BE A CONTINUAL LEARNER

The best way to keep from becoming satisfied with your current achievements is to make yourself a continual learner. That kind of commitment may be rarer than you realize. For example, a study performed by the University of Michigan several years ago found that one-third of all physicians in the United States are so busy working that they're two years behind the breakthroughs in their own fields.[2]

If you want to be a continual learner and keep growing throughout your life, you'll have to carve out the time to do it. You'll have to do what you can wherever you are. As Henry Ford said, "It's been my observation that most successful people get ahead during the time other people waste."

That's one reason I carry books and magazines with me whenever I travel. During the downtimes, such as waiting for a connection in an airport, I can go through a stack of magazines, reading and cutting out articles. Or I can skim through a book, learning the major concepts and pulling out quotes I'll be able to use later. And when I'm in town, I maximize my learning time by continually listening to instructive tapes in the car.

Frank A. Clark stated, "Most of us must learn a great deal every day in order to keep ahead of what we forget." Learning something every day is the essence of being a continual learner. You must keep improving yourself, not only acquiring knowledge to replace what you forget or what's out-of-date, but building on what you learned yesterday.

6. DEVELOP A PLAN FOR GROWTH

The key to a life of continual learning and improvement lies in developing a specific plan for growth and following through with it. I recommend a plan that requires an hour a day, five days a week. I use that as the pattern because of a statement by Earl Nightingale, which says, "If a person will spend one hour a day on the same subject for five years, that person will be an expert on that subject." Isn't that an incredible promise? It shows how far we are capable of going when we have the discipline to make growth our daily practice. When I teach leadership conferences, I recommend the following growth plan to participants:

MONDAY: Spend one hour with a devotional to develop your spiritual life.

TUESDAY: Spend one hour listening to a leadership podcast or audio lesson.

WEDNESDAY: Spend one hour filing quotes and reflecting on the content of Tuesday's tape.

THURSDAY: Spend one hour reading a book on leadership.

FRIDAY: Spend half the hour reading the book and the other half filing and reflecting.

As you develop your plan for growth, start by identifying the three to five areas in which you desire to grow. Then look for useful materials—books, magazines, audiotapes, videos—and incorporate them into your plan. I recommend that you make it your goal to read twelve books and listen to fifty-two tapes (or read fifty-two articles) each year. Exactly how you go about it doesn't matter, but do it daily. That way you're more likely to follow through and get it done than if you periodically put it off and then try to catch up.

7. PAY THE PRICE

I mentioned before that self-fulfillment focuses on making a person happy, whereas self-development proposes to help a person reach potential. A trade-off of growth is that it is sometimes uncomfortable. It requires discipline. It takes time that you could spend on leisure activities. It costs money to buy materials. You have to face constant change and take risks. And sometimes it's just plain lonely. That's why many people stop growing when the price gets high.

But growth is always worth the price you pay because the alternative is a limited life with unfulfilled potential. Success takes effort, and you can't make the journey if you're sitting back waiting for life to come along and improve you. President Theodore Roosevelt boldly stated, "There has not yet been a person in our history who led a life of ease whose name is worth remembering." Those words were true when he spoke them almost a century ago, and they still apply today.

8. FIND A WAY TO APPLY WHAT YOU LEARN

Jim Rohn urged, "Don't let your learning lead to knowledge. Let your learning lead to action." The bottom line when it comes to personal development is action. If your life doesn't begin to change as a result of what you're learning, you're experiencing one of these problems: You're not giving your growth plan enough time and attention; you're focusing too much time on the wrong areas; or *you're not applying what you learn.*

Successful people develop positive daily habits that help them to grow and learn. One of the things I do to make sure I don't lose what I learn is file it. In my office I have more than twelve hundred files full of articles and information, and I have thousands upon thousands of quotes. But I also make an effort to apply information as soon as I learn it. I do that by asking myself these questions anytime I learn something new:

Where can I use it?
When can I use it?
Who else needs to know it?

These questions take my focus off simply acquiring knowledge and put it onto applying what I learn to my life. Try using them. I think they'll do the same for you.

Author and leadership expert Fred Smith made a statement that summarizes what committing to personal growth is really all about. He said:

> Something in human nature tempts us to stay where we're comfortable. We try to find a plateau, a resting place, where we have comfortable stress and adequate finances. Where we have comfortable associations with people, without the intimidation of meeting new people and entering strange situations.

Of course, all of us need to plateau for a time. We climb and then plateau for assimilation. But once we've assimilated what we've learned, we climb again. It's unfortunate when we've done our last climb. When we have made our last climb, we are old, whether forty or eighty.

Whatever you do, don't allow yourself to stay on a plateau. Commit yourself to climbing the mountain of personal potential—a little at a time—throughout your life. It's one journey you'll never regret having made. According to novelist George Eliot, "It is never too late to be what you might have become."

2

How Can I Grow In
My Career?

Be better tomorrow than you are today.

A turkey was chatting with a bull. "I would love to be able to get to the top of that tree," sighed the turkey, "but I haven't got the energy."

"Well," replied the bull, "why don't you nibble on some of my droppings? They're packed with nutrients."

The turkey pecked at a lump of dung and found that it actually gave him enough strength to reach the lowest branch of the tree. The next day, after eating some more dung, he reached the second branch. Finally after a fourth night, there he was proudly perched at the top of the tree. But he was promptly spotted by a hunter, who shot him down out of the tree.

The moral of the story: BS might get you to the top, but it won't keep you there.

How Growth Helps You Lead Up

I've met a lot of people who have destination disease. They think that they have "arrived" by obtaining a specific position or getting to a certain level in an organization. When they get to that desired place, they stop striving to grow or improve. What a waste of potential!

92

There's certainly nothing wrong with the desire to progress in your career, but never try to "arrive." Instead, intend your journey to be open-ended. Most people have no idea how far they can go in life. They aim way too low. I know I did when I first started out, but my life began changing when I stopped setting goals for *where* I wanted to be and started setting the course for *who* I wanted to be. I have discovered for others and me that the key to personal development is being more *growth* oriented than *goal* oriented.

There is no downside to making growth your goal. If you keep learning, you will be better tomorrow than you are today, and that can do so many things for you.

The Better You Are, the More People Listen

If you had an interest in cooking, with whom would you rather spend an hour—Mario Batali (chef, cookbook author, owner of Babbo Ristorante e Enoteca and other restaurants in New York City, and host of two shows on the Food Network) or your neighbor who loves to cook and actually does it "every once in a while"? Or if you were a leadership student, as I am, would you rather spend that hour with the president of the United States or with the person who runs the local convenience store? It's no contest. Why? Because you respect most and can learn best from the person with great competence and experience.

Competence is a key to credibility, and credibility is the key to influencing others. If people respect you, they will listen to you. President Abraham Lincoln said, "I don't think much of a man who is not wiser today than he was yesterday." By focusing on growth, you become wiser each day.

The Better You Are, the Greater Your Value Today

If you were to plant fruit and nut trees in your yard, when could you expect to start harvesting from them? Would you be surprised to learn that you had to wait years—three to seven years for fruit, five to fifteen years for nuts? If you want a tree to produce, first you have to let it grow. The more the tree has grown and has created strong roots that can sustain it, the more it can produce. The more it can produce, the greater its value.

People are not all that different. The more they grow, the more valuable they are because they can produce more. In fact, it's said that a tree keeps growing as long as it is living. I would love to live in such a way that the same could be said for me—"he kept growing until the day he died."

I love this quote from Elbert Hubbard: "If what you did yesterday still looks big to you, you haven't done much today." If you look back at past accomplishments, and they don't look small to you now, then you haven't grown very much since you completed them. If you look back at a job you did years ago, and you don't think you could do it better now, then you're not improving in that area of your life.

If you are not continually growing, then it is probably damaging your leadership ability. Warren Bennis and Bert Nanus, authors of *Leaders: The Strategies for Taking Charge*, said, "It is the capacity to develop and improve their skills that distinguishes leaders from followers."[1] If you're not moving forward as a learner, then you are moving backward as a leader.

THE BETTER YOU ARE, THE GREATER YOUR POTENTIAL FOR TOMORROW

Who are the hardest people to teach? The people who have never tried to learn. Getting them to accept a new idea is like trying to transplant a tomato plant into concrete. Even if you could get it to go into the ground, you know it isn't going to survive anyway. The more you learn and grow, the greater your capacity to keep learning. And that makes your potential greater and your value for tomorrow higher.

Indian reformer Mahatma Gandhi said, "The difference between what we do and what we are capable of doing would suffice to solve most of the world's problems." That is how great our potential is. All we have to do is keep fighting to learn more, grow more, become more.

One leader I interviewed for this book told me that when he was in his first job, his boss would sit him down after he made a mistake and talk it through with him. Every time before he left one of those meetings, his boss asked, "Did you learn something from this?" and he would ask him to explain. At the time, this young leader thought his boss was being pretty tough on him. But as he progressed through his career, he discovered that many of his successes could be traced back to practices he adopted as a result of those talks. It made a huge positive impact on him because it kept making him better.

If you want to influence the people who are ahead of you in the organization—and keep influencing them—then you need to keep getting better. An investment in your growth is an investment in your ability, your adaptability, and your promotability. No matter how much it costs you to keep growing and learning, the cost of doing nothing is greater.

How to Become Better Tomorrow

Founding father Ben Franklin said, "By improving yourself, the world is made better. Be not afraid of growing too slowly. Be afraid only of standing still. Forget your mistakes, but remember what they taught you." So how do you become better tomorrow? By becoming better today. The secret of your success can be found in your daily agenda. Here is what I suggest you do to keep growing and leading up:

1. Learn Your Craft Today

On a wall in the office of a huge tree farm hangs a sign. It says, "The best time to plant a tree is twenty-five years ago. The second best time is today." There is no time like the present to become an expert at your craft. Maybe you wish you had started earlier. Or maybe you wish you had found a better teacher or mentor years ago. None of that matters. Looking back and lamenting will not help you move forward.

A friend of the poet Longfellow asked the secret of his continued interest in life. Pointing to a nearby apple tree, Longfellow said, "The purpose of that apple tree is to grow a little new wood each year. That is what I plan to do." The friend would have found a similar sentiment in one of Longfellow's poems:

> *Not enjoyment and not sorrow*
> *Is our destined end or way;*
> *But to act that each tomorrow*
> *Find us further than today.*[2]

You may not be where you're supposed to be. You may not be what you want to be. You don't have to be what you used to be. And you don't have to ever arrive. You just need to learn to be the best you can be right now. As Napoleon Hill said, "You can't change where you started, but you can change the direction you are going. It's not what you are going to do, but it's what you are doing now that counts."

2. TALK YOUR CRAFT TODAY

Once you reach a degree of proficiency in your craft, then one of the best things you can do for yourself is talk your craft with others on the same and higher levels than you. Many people do this naturally. Guitarists talk about guitars. Parents talk about raising children. Golfers talk about golf. They do so because it's enjoyable, it fuels their passion, it teaches them new skills and insights, and it prepares them to take action.

Talking to peers is wonderful, but if you don't also make an effort to strategically talk your craft with those ahead of you in experience and skill, then you're really missing learning opportunities. Douglas Randlett meets regularly with a group of retired multimillionaires so that he can learn from them. Before he retired, Major League Baseball player Tony Gwynn was known to talk hitting with anybody who had knowledge about it. Every time he saw Ted Williams, they talked hitting.

I enjoy talking about leadership with good leaders all the time. In fact, I make it a point to schedule a learning lunch with someone I admire, at least six times a year. Before I go, I study up on them by reading their books, studying their lessons, listening to their speeches, or whatever else I need to do. My goal is to learn enough about them and their "sweet spot" to ask the right questions. If I do that, then I can learn from their strengths. But that's not my ultimate goal. My goal is to learn what I can transfer from their strength zones to mine. That's where my growth will come from—not from what they're doing. I have to apply what I learn to my situation.

The secret to a great interview is listening. It is the bridge between learning about them and learning about you. And that's your objective.

3. PRACTICE YOUR CRAFT TODAY

William Osler, the physician who wrote *The Principles and Practice of Medicine* in 1892, once told a group of medical students:

> Banish the future. Live only for the hour and its allotted work. Think not of the amount to be accomplished, the difficulties to be overcome, or the end to be attained, but set earnestly at the little task at your elbow, letting that be sufficient for the day; for surely our plain duty is, as Carlyle says, "Not to see what lies dimly at a distance, but to do what lies clearly at hand."

The only way to improve is to practice your craft until you know it inside and out. At first, you do what you know to do. The more you practice your craft, the more you know. But as you do more, you will also discover more about what you ought to do differently. At that point you have a decision to make: Will you do what you have always done, or will you try to do more of what you think you should do? The only way you improve is to get out of your comfort zone and try new things.

People often ask me, "How can I grow my business?" or, "How can I make my department better?" The answer is for you personally to grow.

The only way to grow your organization is to grow the leaders who run it. By making yourself better, you make others better. Retired General Electric CEO Jack Welch said, "Before you are a leader, success is all about growing yourself. When you become a leader, success is all about growing others."[3] And the time to start is today.

3

How Do I Maintain a
Teachable Attitude?

It's what you learn after you know it all that counts.

I f you are a highly talented person, you may have a tough time with
teachability. Why? Because talented people often think they know
it all. And that makes it difficult for them to continually expand their
talent. Teachability is not so much about competence and mental
capacity as it is about *attitude*. It is the desire to listen, learn, and
apply. It is the hunger to discover and grow. It is the willingness to
learn, unlearn, and relearn. I love the way Hall of Fame basketball
coach John Wooden states it: "It's what you learn after you know it all
that counts."

When I teach and mentor leaders, I remind them that if they stop
learning, they stop leading. But if they remain teachable and keep learning, they will be able to keep making an impact as leaders. Whatever
your talent happens to be—whether it's leadership, craftsmanship, entre-
preneurship, or something else—you will expand it if you keep expecting and striving to learn. Talented individuals with teachable attitudes
become talent-plus people.

TEACHABILITY TRUTHS

To make the most of your talent and remain teachable, consider the following truths about teaching:

1. NOTHING IS INTERESTING IF YOU ARE NOT INTERESTED

It's a shame when people allow themselves to get in a rut and never climb out. They often miss the best that life has to offer. In contrast, teachable people are fully engaged in life. They get excited about things. They are interested in discovery, discussion, application, and growth. There is a definite relationship between passion and potential.

German philosopher Goethe advised, "Never let a day pass without looking at some perfect work of art, hearing some great piece of music and reading, in part, some great book." The more engaged you are, the more interesting life will be. The more interested you are in exploring and learning, the greater your potential for growth.

2. SUCCESSFUL PEOPLE VIEW LEARNING DIFFERENTLY FROM THOSE WHO ARE UNSUCCESSFUL

After more than thirty-five years of teaching and training people, I've come to realize that successful people think differently from unsuccessful ones. That doesn't mean that unsuccessful people are unable to think the way successful people do. (In fact, I believe that just about anyone can retrain himself to think differently. That's why I wrote *Thinking for a Change*—to help people learn the thinking skills capable of making them more successful.) Those successful thinking patterns pertain to learning as well.

Teachable people are always open to new ideas and are willing to learn from anyone who has something to offer. American journalist Sydney J. Harris wrote, "A winner knows how much he still has to learn, even when he is considered an expert by others. A loser wants to be considered an expert by others, before he has learned enough to know how little he knows." It's all a matter of attitude.

It's truly remarkable how much a person has to learn before he realizes how little he knows. Back in 1992, I wrote a book called *Developing the Leader Within You*. At the time, I thought, *I've had some success at leadership. I'll write this book, and it will be my contribution to others on this important subject*. I then put *everything* I knew about leadership in that book. But that book was only the beginning. Writing it made me want to learn more about leadership, and my drive to learn went to another level. I searched out more books, lectures, people, and experiences to help me learn. Today, I've written a total of *eight* books on leadership. Am I finished with that topic? No. There are still things to learn—and to teach. My leadership world is expanding, and so am I. The world is vast, and we are so limited. There is much for us to learn—as long as we remain teachable.

3. Learning Is Meant to Be a Lifelong Pursuit

It's said that the Roman scholar Cato started to study Greek when he was more than eighty years old. When asked why he was tackling such a difficult task at his age, he replied, "It is the earliest age I have left." Unlike Cato, too many people regard learning as an event instead of a process. Someone told me that only one-third of all adults read an entire book after their last graduation. Why would that be? Because they view education as a period of life, not a way of life!

Learning is an activity that is not restricted by age. It doesn't matter if you're past eighty, like Cato, or haven't yet entered your teens. Author Julio Melara was only eleven years old when he began to acquire major life lessons that he has been able to carry with him into adulthood and to teach others. Here are some of the things he's learned, taken from his book *It Only Takes Everything You've Got!: Lessons for a Life of Success*.

Here is a list of all the jobs you will not find on my résumé but lessons that have lasted a lifetime:

- Started cutting grass for profit at age 11
  Lesson learned: It is important to give things a clean, professional look.

- Stock clerk at a local food store
  Lesson learned: Making sure that if I am going to sell something, the merchandise needs to be in stock.

- Dishwasher at local restaurant
  Lesson learned: Somebody always has to do the job no one else wants to do. Also, most people have a lot of food on their plates. (They do not finish what they start.)

- A janitor at an office building
  Lesson learned: The importance of cleanliness as it related to image.

- Fry and prep cook at a steak house
  Lesson learned: The importance of preparation and the impact of the right presentation.

- Construction helping hand (lug wood and supplies from one place to another)
  Lesson learned: I do not want to do this for the rest of my life.

- Sold newspaper subscription for daily paper
  Lesson learned: The job of rejection—had to knock on at least thirty doors before I ever sold one subscription.

- Shipping clerk at a plumbing supply house
  Lesson learned: Delivering your project or service on time is just as important as selling it.

- Breakfast cook at a twenty-four-hour restaurant stop
  Lesson learned: How to do fifteen things at once. Also learned about the weird things people like to eat on their eggs.

- Cleaned cars at detailing shop
  Lesson learned: The importance of details (washing vs. detailing).

You can pay $15 just to wash the outside of the car or $150 to clean the car inside and out and cover all the details. Details are a pain, but details are valuable.

- Shoe salesman at a retail store
  Lesson learned: To sell customers what they want and like. Also, learned to compliment people and be sincere.

- Busboy at a local diner
  Lesson learned: People enjoy being served with a smile and they love a clean table.

Every stage of life presents lessons to be learned. We can choose to be teachable and continue to learn them, or we can be closed-minded and stop growing. The decision is ours.

4. Pride Is the Number One Hindrance to Teachability

Author, trainer, and speaker Dave Anderson believes that the number one cause of management failure is pride. He wrote:

There are many reasons managers fail. For some, the organization outgrows them. Others don't change with the times . . . A few make poor character choices. They look good for a while but eventually discover they can't get out of their own way. Increasingly more keep the wrong people too long because they don't want to admit they made a mistake or have high turnover become a negative reflection on them. Some failures had brilliant past track records but start using their success as a license to build a fence around what they had rather than continue to risk and stretch to build it to even higher levels. But all these causes for management failure have their root in one common cause: pride. In simplest terms, pride is devastating . . . the pride that inflates your sense of self-worth and distorts your perspective of reality.

While envy is the deadly sin that comes from feelings of *inferiority*, the deadly sin of pride comes from feelings of *superiority*. It creates an arrogance of success, an inflated sense of self-worth accompanied by a distorted perspective of reality. Such an attitude leads to a loss of desire to learn and an unwillingness to change. It makes a person unteachable.

HOW TO TAKE YOUR TALENT TO THE NEXT LEVEL

If you want to expand your talent, you must become teachable. That is the pathway to growth. Futurist and author John Naisbitt believes that "the most important skill to acquire is learning how to learn." Here is what I suggest as you pursue teachability and become a talent-plus person:

1. LEARN TO LISTEN

The first step in teachability is learning to listen. American writer and philosopher Henry David Thoreau wrote, "It takes two to speak the truth—one to speak and one to hear." Being a good listener helps us to know people better, to learn what they have learned, and to show them that we value them as individuals.

As you go through each day, remember that you can't learn if you're always talking. As the old saying goes, "There's a reason you have one mouth but two ears." Listen to others, remain humble, and you will begin to learn things every day that can help you expand your talent.

2. UNDERSTAND THE LEARNING PROCESS

Here's how the learning typically works:

STEP 1: Act.
STEP 2: Look for your mistakes and evaluate.
STEP 3: Search for a way to do it better.
STEP 4: Go back to step 1.

Remember, the greatest enemy of learning is knowing, and the goal of all learning is action, not knowledge. If what you are doing does not in some way contribute to what you or others are doing in life, then question its value and be prepared to make changes.

3. Look for and Plan Teachable Moments

If you look for opportunities to learn in every situation, you will become a talent-plus person and expand your talent to its potential. But you can also take another step beyond that and actively seek out and plan teachable moments. You can do that by reading books, visiting places that will inspire you, attending events that will prompt you to pursue change, listening to lessons, and spending time with people who will stretch you and expose you to new experiences.

I've had the privilege to spend time with many remarkable people, and the natural reward has been the opportunity to learn. In my personal relationships, I've also gravitated toward people from whom I can learn. My closest friends are people who challenge my thinking—and often change it. They lift me up in many ways. And I've found that I often live out something stated by Spanish philosopher and writer Baltasar Gracian: "Make your friends your teachers and mingle the pleasures of conversation with the advantages of instruction." You can do the same. Cultivate friendships with people who challenge and add value to you, and try to do the same for them. It will change your life.

4. Make Your Teachable Moments Count

Even people who are strategic about seeking teachable moments can miss the whole point of the experience. I say this because for thirty years I've been a speaker at conferences and workshops—events that are designed to help people learn. But I've found that many people walk away from an event and do very little with what they heard after closing their notebooks. It would be like a jewelry designer going to a gem merchant to buy fine gems, placing them carefully into a case, and then putting that case on the shelf to collect dust. What's the value of acquiring the gems if they're never going to be used?

We tend to focus on learning events instead of the learning process. Because of this, I try to help people take action steps that will help them implement what they learn. I suggest that in their notes, they use a code to mark things that jump out at them:

T   indicates you need to some time thinking on that point.
C   indicates something you need to change.
☺   A smiley face means you are doing that thing particularly well.
A   indicates something you need to apply.
S   means you need to share that information with someone else.

After the conference I recommend that they create to-do lists based on what they marked, then schedule time to follow through.

5. ASK YOURSELF, "AM I REALLY TEACHABLE?"

I've said it before, but it bears repeating: all the good advice in the world won't help if you don't have a teachable spirit. To know whether you are *really* open to new ideas and new ways of doing things, answer the following questions:

1.   Am I open to other people's ideas?
2.   Do I listen more than I talk?
3.   Am I open to changing my opinion based on new information?
4.   Do I readily admit when I am wrong?
5.   Do I observe before acting on a situation?
6.   Do I ask questions?
7.   Am I willing to ask a question that will expose my ignorance?
8.   Am I open to doing things in a way I haven't done before?
9.   Am I willing to ask for directions?
10. Do I act defensive when criticized, or do I listen openly for the truth?

If you answered no to one or more of these questions, then you have room to grow in the area of teachability. You need to soften your attitude and learn humility, and remember the words of John Wooden: "Everything we know we learned from someone else!"

Thomas Edison was the guest of the governor of North Carolina when the politician complimented him on his creative genius.

"I am not a great inventor," countered Edison.

"But you have more than a thousand patents to your credit," the governor stated.

"Yes, but about the only invention I can really claim as absolutely original is the phonograph," Edison replied.

"I'm afraid I don't understand what you mean," the governor remarked.

"Well," explained Edison, "I guess I'm an awfully good sponge. I absorb ideas from every course I can, and put them to practical use. Then I improve them until they become of some value. The ideas which I use are mostly the ideas of other people who don't develop them themselves."

What a remarkable description of someone who used teachability to expand his talent! That is what a talent-plus person does. That is what all of us should strive to do.

4

WHAT ROLE DO OTHERS PLAY IN MY GROWTH?

What kind of attitude do you have when it comes to learning from others? All people fall into one of the categories described by the following statements:

NO ONE CAN TEACH ME ANYTHING—ARROGANT ATTITUDE

I think we sometimes assume that ignorance is the greatest enemy of teachability. However, that really has little to do with teachability. Haven't you known some highly educated and highly successful people who do not want to hear the suggestions or opinions of anyone else? Some people think they know it all! A person who creates a large, successful organization may think he can't learn from people who run a smaller one. A person who receives a doctorate can become unreceptive to instruction from anyone else because she is now considered an expert. Another person who is the most experienced in a company or department may not listen to the ideas of someone younger.

Such people don't realize how much they are hurting themselves. The reality is that no one is too old, too smart, or too successful to learn something new. The only thing that can come between a person and the ability to learn and improve is a bad attitude.

SOMEONE CAN TEACH ME EVERYTHING—NAIVE ATTITUDE

People who realize that they have room to grow often seek a mentor. That's usually a good thing. However, it's naive for individuals to think they can learn everything they need to know from just one person. People don't need a mentor—they need *many* mentors. I've learned so much from so many people. Les Stobbe taught me how to write. My brother, Larry, is my business mentor. I've learned a lot about communication from Andy Stanley. Tom Mullins models relationships for me. If I tried to include all the people who have taught me over the years, I'd fill page after page with names.

EVERYONE CAN TEACH ME SOMETHING—TEACHABLE ATTITUDE

The people who learn the most aren't necessarily the ones who spend time with the smartest people. They are the ones with a teachable attitude. Every person has something to share—a lesson learned, an observation, a life experience. We just need to be willing to listen. In fact, often people teach us things when they don't intend to do so. Ask any parents and you will find out that they learned things from their children—even when their kids were infants incapable of communicating a single word. The only time people can't teach us things is when we are unwilling to learn.

I'm not saying that every person you meet *will* teach you something. All I'm saying is that people have the potential to do so—if you'll let them.

HOW TO LEARN FROM OTHERS

If you have a teachable attitude—or you are willing to adopt one— you will be positioned well to learn from others. Then all you will need to do is take the following five steps:

1. MAKE LEARNING YOUR PASSION

Management expert Philip B. Crosby noted:

There is a theory of human behavior that says people subconsciously retard their own intellectual growth. They come to rely on clichés and habits. Once they reach the age of their own personal comfort with the world, they stop learning and their mind runs on idle for the rest of their days. They may progress organizationally, they may be ambitious and eager, and they may even work night and day. But they learn no more.[1]

That's sometimes the problem with people who received the *positions* they dreamed of or reached the *goals* they set for their organizations or earned the *degrees* they strived for. In their minds, they have reached their destinations. They get comfortable.

If you desire to keep growing, you cannot sit back in a comfort zone. You need to make learning your goal. Do that and you will never run out of gas mentally, and your motivation will be strong. And don't worry about having people to teach you. Greek philosopher Plato said, "When the pupil is ready, the teacher will appear."

2. VALUE PEOPLE

In 1976, I had been in my career for seven years, and I felt successful. In those days, churches were often judged by the success of their Sunday school programs, and the church I led had the fastest-growing program in the state of Ohio. And by then my church had grown to be the largest in my denomination. But I still wanted to learn. That year I signed up to attend a conference. There were three speakers that I wanted to hear. They were older, more successful, and more experienced than I was.

During the conference, one of the sessions was an idea exchange where anybody could talk. I figured it would be a waste of time, and I was going to skip it, but my curiosity got the best of me. It turned out to be a real eye-opener. Person after person shared what was working in his organization, and I sat there scribbling notes and jotting down ideas. It turned out that I learned more during that session than in all the others combined.

That surprised me, and later I realized why. Before that conference, I thought only older, more successful people could teach me anything. I had walked into that room placing very little value on the other people there. And that was a wrong attitude. People don't learn from people they don't value. I determined to change my thinking from that day forward.

3. DEVELOP RELATIONSHIPS WITH GROWTH POTENTIAL

It's true that everyone has *something* to teach us, but that doesn't mean anyone can teach us everything we want to learn. We need to find people who are especially likely to help us grow—experts in our field, creative thinkers who will stretch us mentally, achievers who will inspire us to go to the next level. Learning is often the reward for spending time with remarkable people. Who they are and what they know rub off. As Donald Clifton and Paula Nelson, authors of *Soar with Your Strengths*, observe, "Relationships help us define who we are and what we become."

4. IDENTIFY PEOPLE'S UNIQUENESS AND STRENGTHS

Philosopher-poet Ralph Waldo Emerson remarked, "I have never met a man who was not my superior in some particular." People grow best in their areas of strength—and can learn the most from another person's area of strength. For that reason, you can't be indiscriminate in choosing the people you seek out to teach you.

In the mid-1970s, I identified the top ten church leaders in the nation, and I tried to get an appointment for lunch with each of them. I even offered them one hundred dollars for an hour of their time—that was a half week's pay back then. Some were willing to meet me. Others weren't. I was extremely grateful to the ones who did.

My wife and I didn't have much money then, and these leaders lived all over the country, so we planned our vacations for several years around these visits. Why would I go to such lengths to meet these people? Because I was dying to learn the unique skills and strengths they possessed. The meetings made a huge difference in my life. And do you know what? Connection with great men and women continues to affect my life. Every month I try to meet with someone I admire and from whom I want to learn.

5. Ask Questions

The first year I was in college, I took a part-time job at a locker plant in Circleville, Ohio. It was a place where cows were slaughtered and the meat was stored in giant refrigerated lockers. My job was to haul freshly processed meat to the refrigeration areas and to retrieve orders of meat for customers.

Anytime I'm exposed to something new—and this was a new area for me—I try to learn about it. And the best way to learn is to watch and ask questions. I had been working for about two weeks when Pense, an old guy who had worked there for years, pulled me aside and said, "Son, let me tell you something. You ask too many questions. I've been working here for a long time. I kill cows. That's all I do—and that's all I'm gonna do. The more you know, the more they expect you to do." I had a hard time understanding why anybody *wouldn't* want to learn and grow. But obviously he was committed not to change.

Writer Johann Wolfgang von Goethe believed that "one ought, every day at least, to hear a little song, read a good poem, see a fine picture, and, if it were possible, to speak a few reasonable words." I would add that one ought to also ask questions to learn something new each day. The person who asks the right questions learns the most.

Choose a Mentor to Help You Grow

You must have the right attitude toward others in order to grow. But if you really want to maximize your progress, you need to take another step. You need to find a mentor who can model what you want to learn and help you grow. At first it doesn't have to be someone you know. Start by reading books, watching videos, and attending conferences. Read blogs. Then start looking for someone who can help you go to the next level.

Give careful thought to the people you follow because they will impact the course of your life. I have developed six questions to ask myself before picking a model to follow. Perhaps they will help you when choosing a mentor.

DOES MY MODEL'S LIFE DESERVE A FOLLOWING?

This question relates to quality of character. If the answer is not a clear yes, I have to be very careful. I will become like the people I follow, and I don't want models with flawed character.

DOES MY MODEL'S LIFE HAVE A FOLLOWING?

This question looks at credibility. It is possible to be the very first person to discover a leader worth following, but it doesn't happen very often. If the person has no following, he or she may not be worth following.

If my answer to either of the first two questions is no, I don't have to bother with the other four. I need to look for another model.

WHAT IS THE MAIN STRENGTH THAT INFLUENCES OTHERS TO FOLLOW MY MODEL?

What does the model have to offer me? What is his best? Also note that strong leaders have weaknesses as well as strengths. I don't want to inadvertently emulate the weaknesses.

DOES MY MODEL PRODUCE OTHER LEADERS?

The answer to this question will tell me whether the model's leadership priorities match mine in regard to developing new leaders.

IS MY MODEL'S STRENGTH REPRODUCIBLE IN MY LIFE?

If I can't reproduce his strength in my life, his modeling will not benefit me. For instance, if you admire Shaquille O'Neil's ability as a basketball center, but you're only 5 feet, 9 inches tall and weigh 170 pounds, you are not going to be able to reproduce his strengths. Find appropriate models . . . but strive for improvement. Don't be too quick to say that a strength is not reproducible. Most are. Don't limit your potential.

IF MY MODEL'S STRENGTH IS REPRODUCIBLE IN MY LIFE, WHAT STEPS MUST I TAKE TO DEVELOP AND DEMONSTRATE THAT STRENGTH?

You must develop a plan of action. If you only answer the questions and never implement a plan to develop those strengths in yourself, you are only performing an intellectual exercise.

The models we choose may or may not be accessible to us in a personal way. Some may be national figures, such as a president. Or they may be people from history. They can certainly benefit you, but not the way a personal mentor can.

GUIDELINES FOR MENTORING RELATIONSHIPS

When you find someone who can personally mentor you, use these guidelines to help develop a positive mentoring relationship with that person:

CLARIFY YOUR LEVEL OF EXPECTATIONS

Generally, the goal of mentoring is improvement, not perfection. Perhaps only a few people can be truly excellent—but all of us can become better.

ACCEPT A SUBORDINATE, LEARNING POSITION

Don't let ego get in the way of learning. Trying to impress the mentor with your knowledge or ability will set up a mental barrier between you. It will prevent you from receiving what he is giving. Be humble and patient.

RESPECT THE MENTOR, BUT DON'T IDOLIZE HIM

Respect allows us to accept what the mentor is teaching. But making the mentor an idol removes the ability to be objective and critical—faculties we need for adapting a mentor's knowledge and experience to ourselves. Learn from your mentor's weaknesses as well as strengths.

IMMEDIATELY PUT INTO EFFECT WHAT YOU ARE LEARNING

In the best mentoring relationships, what is learned comes quickly into focus. As soon as you learn something new, put it into practice or teach it to someone else. You will assimilate it more quickly if you do.

BE DISCIPLINED IN RELATING TO THE MENTOR

Arrange for ample and consistent time, select the subject matter in advance, and do your homework to make the sessions profitable.

REWARD YOUR MENTOR WITH YOUR OWN PROGRESS

If you show appreciation but make no progress, the mentor experiences failure. Your progress is his highest reward. Strive for growth, then communicate your progress.

DON'T THREATEN TO GIVE UP

Let your mentor know you have made a decision for progress and that you are a persistent person—a determined winner. Then he will know he is not wasting his time.

There is no substitute for your own personal growth. If you are not receiving and growing, you will not be able to give to the people you nurture and develop.

PART II

THE ONGOING PROCESS OF IMPROVEMENT

5

WHERE SHOULD I FOCUS MY TIME AND ENERGY?

To reach your potential, get in your strength zone.

Can you remember the first lesson you ever learned about leadership? I can. It came from my dad. He used to tell my brother, my sister, and me, "Find out what you do well and keep on doing it." That wasn't just casual advice. He and my mother made it their mission to help us discover our strengths and start developing them before we were old enough to leave home and go out on our own.

Dad also reinforced that advice by living it. One of his favorite sayings was "This one thing I do." He had an uncanny ability to remain focused within his areas of strength. That, coupled with his determination to finish what he started, served him well throughout his career and beyond. He stays in his strength zone. It is one of the reasons he has always been the greatest inspiration for my life.

SEARCHING FOR STRENGTHS

When I started my career, I was committed to finding my strength zone and working to stay in it. However, I was frustrated for my first few years working. Like many inexperienced leaders, I tried to do many different things to discover what I really could do well. In addition, people's expectations for what I would do and how I would lead did not always match my strengths. I think that is true for many young leaders just starting out.

My responsibilities and obligations sometimes required that I perform tasks for which I possessed neither talent nor skill. I was often ineffective as a result. It took me several years to sort all this out, find my strength zone, and recruit and develop other people to compensate for my weaknesses.

If you are a young leader and you are still uncertain about where your strengths lie, don't get discouraged. Try to be patient and keep working hard. If you persevere you will figure it out. Here's what I know: no matter if you're just starting out or if you are at the peak of your career, the more you work in your strength zone, the more successful you will be.

DEFINING PERSONAL SUCCESS

I've heard many definitions of success from many people over the years. In fact, I've embraced different definitions myself at different stages of my life. But in the last fifteen years, I have zeroed in on a definition that I think captures success no matter who people are or what they want to do. I believe success is

Knowing your purpose in life,
Growing to your maximum potential, and
Sowing seeds that benefit others.

If you are able to do those three things, you are successful. However, none of them is possible unless you find and stay in your strength zone.

I love the story of a group of neighborhood boys who built a tree house and formed their own club. When the grown-ups were told who had been selected for which office, they were astonished to hear that a four-year-old had been elected president.

"That boy must be a born leader," one dad observed. "How did it happen that all you bigger boys voted for him?"

"Well, you see, Dad," his son replied, "he can't very well be secretary because he doesn't know how to read or write. He couldn't be treasurer, because he can't count. He would never do for sergeant at arms because he's too little to throw anybody out. If we didn't choose him for anything, he'd feel bad. So we made him president."

Real life, of course, doesn't work that way. You don't become an effective leader by default. You must be intentional. And you must work from your strengths.

Whenever I mentor people and help them discover their purpose, I always encourage them to start the process by discovering their strengths, not exploring their shortcomings. Why? Because people's purpose in life is always connected to their giftedness. It always works that way. You are not called to do something that you have no talent for. You will discover your purpose by finding and remaining in your strength zone.

Similarly, you cannot grow to your maximum potential if you continually work outside of your strength zone. Improvement is always related to ability. The greater your natural ability, the greater your potential for improvement. I've known people who thought that reaching their potential would come from shoring up their weaknesses. But do you know what happens when you spend all your time working on your weaknesses and never developing your strengths? If you work really hard, you might claw your way all the way up to mediocrity! But you'll never get beyond it.

The final piece of the puzzle—living a life that benefits others—always depends upon us giving our best, not our worst. You can't change the world by giving only leftovers or by performing with mediocrity. Only your best will add value to others and lift them up.

FINDING YOUR OWN STRENGTH ZONE

British poet and lexicographer Samuel Johnson said, "Almost every man wastes part of his life in attempts to display qualities which he does not possess." If you have an image in your mind of what talents people are supposed to have, yet you do not possess them, then you will have a difficult time finding your true strengths. You need to discover and develop who *you* are. Here are a few suggestions to help you:

1. ASK, "WHAT AM I DOING WELL?"

People who reach their potential spend less time asking, "What am I doing right?" and more time asking, "What am I doing well?" The first is a moral question; the second is a talent question. You should always strive to do what's right. But doing what's right doesn't tell you anything about your talent.

2. GET SPECIFIC

When we consider our strengths, we tend to think too broadly. Peter Drucker, the father of modern management, wrote, "The great mystery isn't that people do things badly but that they occasionally do a few things well. The only thing that is universal is incompetence. Strength is always specific! Nobody ever commented, for example, that the great violinist Jascha Heifetz probably couldn't play the trumpet well." The more specific you can get about your strengths, the better the chance you can find your "sweet spot." Why be on the fringes of your strength zone when you have a chance to be right in the center?

3. LISTEN FOR WHAT OTHERS PRAISE

Many times we take our talents for granted. We think because we can do something well, anyone can. Often that's not true. How can you tell when you're overlooking a skill or talent? Listen to what others say. Your strengths will capture the attention of others and draw them to you. On the other hand, when you're working in areas of weakness, few people will show interest. If others are continually praising you in a particular area, start developing it.

4. Check Out the Competition

You don't want to spend all your time comparing yourself to others; that's not healthy. But you don't want to waste your time doing something that others do much better. Former GE CEO Jack Welch asserts, "If you don't have a competitive advantage, don't compete." People don't pay for average. If you don't have the talent to do something better than the competition, place your focus elsewhere.

To get a better picture of where you stand in relationship to the competition, you need to ask yourself the following questions:

- Are others doing what I am doing?
- Are they doing it well?
- Are they doing it better than I am?
- Can I become better than they are?
- If I do become better, what will be the result?
- If I don't become better, what will be the result?

The answer to the last question is: you lose. Why? Because your competition is working in their strength zone and you aren't! The point of asking yourself these questions is not for you to try to be like others. It's to help you see where you are different from others. Former all-star baseball catcher Jim Sundberg advised, "Discover your uniqueness, then discipline yourself to develop it." That's what I've tried to do. Many years ago I realized that one of my strengths was communicating. People have always been motivated when they hear me speak. After a while, many opportunities were given to me to speak at events with other motivational speakers. At first it was very intimidating because they were so good. But as I listened to them, the thing I kept asking myself was, "What can I do that will set me apart from them?" I felt it might not be possible for me to be better than they were, but it would be possible for me to be different. Over time I discovered and developed that difference. I would strive to be a motivational *teacher*, not just a motivation *speaker*. I wanted people not only to enjoy what I shared but to also be able to apply what I taught to their lives. For more than two decades, I have disciplined my life to develop that uniqueness. It's my niche—my strength zone.

TO BE A SUCCESSFUL LEADER, FIND AND DEVELOP THE STRENGTH ZONES OF YOUR PEOPLE

Whenever you see people who are successful in their work, you can rest assured that they are working in their strength zone. But that's not enough if you want to be successful as a leader. Good leaders help others find their strength zones and empower them to work in them. In fact, the best leaders are characterized by the ability to recognize the special abilities and limitations of others, and the capacity to fit their people into the jobs where they will do best.

Sadly, most people are not working in their areas of strength and therefore are not reaching their potential. The Gallup organization conducted research on 1.7 million people in the workplace. According to their findings, only 20 percent of employees feel that their strengths are in play every day in the work setting.[1] In my opinion, that is largely the fault of their leaders. They have failed to help their people find their strengths and place them in the organization where their strengths can be an asset to the company.

In her book *Hesselbein on Leadership*, Frances Hesselbein, the chairman of the board of governors of the Leader to Leader Institute founded by Peter F. Drucker, wrote, "Peter Drucker reminds us that organizations exist to make people's strengths effective and their weaknesses irrelevant. And this is the work of effective leaders. Drucker also tells us that there may be born leaders but there are far too few to depend on them."

If you desire to be an effective leader, you must develop the ability to develop people in their areas of strength. How do you do that?

STUDY AND KNOW THE PEOPLE ON YOUR TEAM

What are your people's strengths and weaknesses? Whom do they relate to on the team? Are they growing and do they have more growth potential in the area in which they're working? Is their attitude an asset or a liability? Do they love what they do and are they doing it well? These are questions that must be answered by the leader.

COMMUNICATE TO INDIVIDUALS HOW THEY FIT ON THE TEAM

What are the strengths that they bring to the table? Are there times their contribution will be especially valuable? How do they complement the other members of the team? What do they need from the other players that will complement their weaknesses? The more that people know how they fit on a team, the more they will desire to properly make the most of their fit and maximize their contribution.

COMMUNICATE TO ALL TEAM MEMBERS HOW EACH PLAYER FITS ON THE TEAM

It's obvious that you can't have a winning team without teamwork. However, not every leader takes steps to help team members work together. If you communicate to all the players how all the people fit together and what strengths they bring for their role, then teammates will value and respect one another.

EMPHASIZE COMPLETING ONE ANOTHER ABOVE COMPETING WITH ONE ANOTHER

Healthy competition between teammates is good. It presses them to do their best. But in the end, team members need to work together for the sake of the team, not only for themselves.

To some leaders, the idea of focusing almost entirely on strengths seems counterintuitive. Several years ago I was spending a day with leaders of several companies, and one of the subjects I addressed was the importance of staying in your strength zone. I repeatedly encouraged them not to work with their areas of weakness related to ability. During the Q&A session, a CEO pushed back against the idea. The example he used was that of Tiger Woods.

"When Tiger plays a bad round of golf," he observed, "he goes straight to the driving range and practices for hours. You see, John, he's working on his weaknesses."

"No," I replied, "he's working on his strengths. Tiger is the greatest golfer in the world. He's practicing golf shots. He's not practicing accounting or music or basketball. He is working on a weakness within his strength zone. That will always produce positive results."

Working on a weakness in your strength zone will always produce greater results than working on a strength in a weak area. I love golf, but if I practice golf shots, I will never greatly improve. Why? Because I'm an average golfer. Practice won't make perfect—it will make permanent! If I want to make progress, I need to keep working on my leadership and communication. Those are my strength zones.

Where are yours? If you're spending time in them, then you are making an investment in your success.

6

WHAT ROLE DOES
EXPERIENCE PLAY?

Experience plus honest self-examination leads to wisdom.

One of the most frustrating things for young leaders is having to wait to get their chance to shine. Leaders are naturally impatient, and I was no different. During the first ten years of my leadership, I heard a lot about the importance of experience. In my first position, people did not trust my judgment. They said I was too young and inexperienced. I was frustrated, but at the same time I understood their skepticism. I was only twenty-two years old.

After I led for a couple of years, people began to take notice of me. They saw that I had some ability. In my third year as a leader, a larger church considered me for their top leadership post. The position would have meant more prestige and better pay. But I soon found out that they had decided on an older, experienced leader. Once again, though disappointed, I understood.

At age twenty-five, I was nominated to become a member of my district's board. I was excited to be on the ballot. People my age were not usually considered for such a position. The election was close, but I lost to a well-respected veteran of our denomination.

"Don't worry," I was told. "Someday you will sit on that board. You just need a few more years of experience under your belt."

Time after time, my youth and inexperience were pointed out to me. And I was willing to pay my dues, learn my lessons, and wait my turn. As these more experienced people passed me, I would observe their lives to try to learn from them. I looked to see what kind of foundation they had built their lives on, which influential people they knew, how they conducted themselves. Sometimes I learned much by watching them. But many times I was disappointed. There were many people with years of experience under their belts but not much wisdom or skill to show for it.

That got me to wondering: *Why had experience helped some leaders and not others?* Slowly my confusion began to clear. What I had been taught all my life was not true: experience is not the best teacher! Some people learn and grow as a result of their experience; some people don't. Everybody has some kind of experience. It's what you do with that experience that matters.

How Will Experience Mark You?

We all begin our lives as empty notebooks. Every day we have an opportunity to record new experiences on our pages. With the turning of each page, we gain more knowledge and understanding. Ideally, as we progress our notebooks become filled with notations and observations. The problem is that not all people make the best use of their notebooks.

Some people seem to leave the notebook closed most of their lives. They rarely jot down anything at all. Others fill their pages, but they never take the time to reflect on them and gain greater wisdom and understanding. But a few not only make a record of what they experience; they linger over it and ponder its meaning. They reread what is written and reflect on it. Reflection turns experience into insight, so they not only live the experience but learn from it. They understand that time is on their side if they use their notebook as a learning tool, not just as a calendar. They have come to understand a secret. Experience teaches nothing, but evaluated experience teaches everything.

GAINING FROM EXPERIENCE

Do you know people who have lots of knowledge but little understanding? They may have means, but don't know the meaning of anything important? Even if they have a lot of know-how, they seem to possess little know-why? What is the problem with these individuals? Their life experience is void of reflection and evaluation. When twenty-five years go by, they don't gain twenty-five years of experience. They gain one year of experience twenty-five times!

If you want to gain from your experience—to become a wiser and more effective leader—there are some things about experience you need to know:

1. WE ALL EXPERIENCE MORE THAN WE UNDERSTAND

Baseball player Earl Wilson, the first black pitcher for the Boston Red Sox, quipped, "Experience enables you to recognize a mistake when you make it again." Let's face it: we're going to make mistakes. Too much happens to us in life for us to be able to understand all of it. Our experiences overwhelm our understanding. And no matter how smart we are, our understanding will never catch up with our experience.

So what is a person to do? Make the most of what we *can* understand. I do that in two ways. First, at the end of each day I try to remember to ask myself, "What did I learn today?" That prompts me to "review the page" of my notebook for the day. The second thing I do is take the last week of every year to spend time reviewing the previous twelve months. I reflect on my experiences—my successes and failures, my goals accomplished and dreams unmet, the relationships I built and the ones I lost. In this way, I try to help close some of the gap between what I experience and what I understand.

2. OUR ATTITUDE TOWARD UNPLANNED AND UNPLEASANT EXPERIENCES DETERMINES OUR GROWTH

Steve Penny, head of the S4 Leadership Network in Australia, observed, "Life is full of unforeseen detours. Circumstances happen which seem to completely cut across our plans. Learn to turn your detours into delights. Treat them as special excursions and learning tours. Don't fight them or you will never learn their purpose. Enjoy the moments and pretty soon you will be back on track again, probably wiser and stronger because of your little detour."

I must admit, having a positive attitude about life's detours is a constant battle for me. I prefer the expressway and a straight route to a winding scenic road. Anytime I find myself traveling on a detour, I'm looking for the quickest way out—not trying to enjoy the process. I know that's ironic for the guy who wrote *Failing Forward*, in which I wrote that the difference between average people and achieving people is their perception of and response to failure. Just because I know something is true and work to practice it doesn't mean it's easy.

In 2005, my close friend Rick Goad was diagnosed with pancreatic cancer. For one year I walked beside him through the uneven experiences created by this disease. In any given week, he would hope and be afraid, ask questions and find answers, have setbacks and possibilities. He endured a lot of ups and downs.

This experience was unexpected for Rick because he was still a young man—only in his forties. Throughout his ordeal I watched him live one day at a time, appreciate each moment, see the silver lining in the clouds, love his friends, and spend time with his God.

More than once he said to me, "John, I would not have chosen this for my life, but I also wouldn't trade this for anything."

Rick's detour ended in his death in 2006. It was heartbreaking. But Rick taught me and everyone else around him a lot during this difficult season. By watching him, we learned about how to live.

3. LACK OF EXPERIENCE IS COSTLY

At age sixty I now look back at my youth and I cringe at my naïveté. My toolbox of experience had only one tool in it: a hammer. If all you have is a hammer, everything looks like a nail. So I pounded and pounded. I fought many battles I shouldn't have. I enthusiastically led people down dead-end roads. I possessed the confidence that only the inexperienced can possess. I had no idea how little I knew.

Harry Golden remarked, "The arrogance of the young is a direct result of not having known enough consequences. The turkey that every day greedily approaches the farmer who tosses him grain is not wrong. It is just that no one ever told him about Thanksgiving."[1] I made plenty of mistakes as a young leader, but I was fortunate. None of them was disastrous. Most of the damage was self-inflicted, and the organizations I led didn't suffer terrible consequences for my inexperience.

4. EXPERIENCE IS ALSO COSTLY

Lack of experience may be costly—but so is experience. It's a fact that you cannot gain experience without paying a price. The great American novelist Mark Twain once remarked, "I know a man who grabbed a cat by the tail and he learned 40 percent more about cats than the man who didn't." You just have to hope that the price is not greater than the value of the experience you gain, and sometimes you cannot judge what the price will be until after you have gained the experience.

Ted W. Engstrom, former president of World Vision, used to tell a story about the governing board of a bank who chose a bright, charming, young man to succeed their retiring bank president. The young man came to the old man to ask for help.

The conversation began, "Sir, what is the main thing I must possess to successfully follow you as president of this bank?"

The crusty old man replied, "The ability to make decisions, decisions, decisions."

"How can I learn to do that?" the young man asked.

"Experience, experience, experience," replied the retiring president.

"But how do I get experience?"

The old man looked at him and said, "Bad decisions, bad decisions, bad decisions."

It is as the old saying goes: experience gives the test first and the lesson later. The acquisition of experience can be costly. But it's not as costly as not gaining experience.

5. NOT EVALUATING AND LEARNING FROM EXPERIENCE IS MORE COSTLY

It's a terrible thing to pay the price for experience and not receive the lesson. But that is often what happens with people. Why? Because when an experience is negative, people often run away from it. They're very quick to say, "I'll never do that again!"

Mark Twain had something to say on this subject too. He observed, "If a cat sits on a hot stove, that cat won't sit on that hot stove again. In fact, that cat won't sit on a cold stove either." A cat doesn't have the mental capacity to evaluate his experience and gain from it. The best he can hope to do is follow his instinct for survival. If we want to gain wisdom and improve as leaders, we need to do better than that. We need to heed the words of USA Today founder Allen Neuharth, who said, "Don't just learn something from every experience. Learn something positive."

6. EVALUATED EXPERIENCE LIFTS A PERSON ABOVE THE CROWD

People who make it a regular practice to reflect on their experiences, evaluate what went wrong and right, and learn from them are rare. But when you meet one, you know it. There is a parable of a fox, a wolf, and a bear. One day they went hunting together, and after each of them caught a deer, they discussed how to divide the spoils.

The bear asked the wolf how he thought it should be done. The wolf said everyone should get one deer. Suddenly the bear ate the wolf.

Then the bear asked the fox how he proposed to divvy things up. The fox offered the bear his deer and then said the bear ought to take the wolf's deer as well.

"Where did you get such wisdom?" asked the bear.

"From the wolf," replied the fox.

The school of life offers many difficult courses. Some we sign up for willingly. Others we find ourselves taking unexpectedly. All can teach us valuable lessons, but only if we desire to learn and are willing to reflect on their lessons. If you are, what will be the result? You may exemplify the sentiment expressed by Rudyard Kipling in his poem "If":

If you can keep your head when all about you
Are losing theirs and blaming it on you,
If you can trust yourself when all men doubt you
But make allowance for their doubting too,
If you can wait and not be tired by waiting,
Or being lied about, don't deal in lies,
Or being hated, don't give way to hating,
And yet don't look too good, nor talk too wise:

If you can dream—and not make dreams your master,
If you can think—and not make thoughts your aim;
If you can meet with Triumph and Disaster
And treat those two impostors just the same;
If you can bear to hear the truth you've spoken
Twisted by knaves to make a trap for fools,
Or watch the things you gave your life to, broken,
And stoop and build 'em up with worn-out tools:

If you can make one heap of all your winnings
And risk it all on one turn of pitch-and-toss,
And lose, and start again at your beginnings
And never breathe a word about your loss;

If you can force your heart and nerve and sinew
To serve your turn long after they are gone,
And so hold on when there is nothing in you
Except the Will which says to them: "Hold on!"

If you can talk with crowds and keep your virtue,
Or walk with kings—nor lose the common touch,
If neither foes nor loving friends can hurt you;
If all men count with you, but none too much,
If you can fill the unforgiving minute
With sixty seconds' worth of distance run,
Yours is the Earth and everything that's in it,
And—which is more—you'll be a Man, my son!

Not only will you be a man—or woman—of integrity and wisdom, you will also benefit your people because you will be a better leader.

7

WHAT AM I WILLING TO GIVE UP TO KEEP GROWING?

For everything you gain, you must give up something.

What is the key to going to the next level in your development? Put another way, what is the greatest obstacle you will face once you have begun achieving your goals and tasting success? I believe it is the ability to let go of what you have so that you can reach for something new. The greatest obstacle leaders face can be their own achievement. In other words, as Rick Warren says, "The greatest detriment to tomorrow's success is today's success."

In 1995, I faced one of the most difficult decisions of my life. I was twenty-six years into a highly successful career as a pastor. I was in as good a position as I could be. I was forty-eight years old and at the top of my game. The church I was leading, Skyline Wesleyan Church, was at that time the "flagship" church of the denomination. It had a national reputation and was highly influential. The church and I were highly respected. My reputation with the people was golden. I had spent more than a decade developing leaders, and the congregation was very solid. And it was in San Diego, California, one of the most beautiful cities in the country. It was ideal—both financially and professionally. I believe I could have settled in there and stayed until I retired. The only major obstacle that lay before me was the relocation of the church, which I believe we could have accomplished. (The leader who succeeded me has since accomplished it.)

I had only one problem. I wanted to go to the next level as a leader. I wanted to make a national and international impact. And I couldn't do it if I stayed there. I realized that the next stage of growth for me would require many difficult changes and much more time than I could give while leading the church. I understood that I needed to answer one critical question: am I willing to give up all that I have for a new level of growth?

WHAT IS THE NEXT LEVEL WORTH?

That's a question that every person must ask him- or herself more than once in a successful career. In *Leading Without Power*, Max DePree wrote, "By avoiding risk, we really risk what is most important in life—reaching toward growth, our potential and a true contribution to a common goal."

I started learning this lesson about trade-offs as a child. My father would often admonish me by saying, "Pay now—play later." In fact, he said it a lot because I was someone who loved to play and *never* wanted to pay! What he was trying to teach me was to do the difficult things first, and then enjoy myself. I learned from him that we all pay in life. Anything we get will exact a price from us. The question is, when will we pay? The longer we wait to pay, the greater the price. It is like interest that compounds. A successful life is a series of trade-offs. In my career, over and over I have traded security for opportunity. I've given up what many would consider an ideal position so that I could grow as a leader or make a bigger impact.

I've found that the higher we go, the harder it is to make trade-offs. Why? We have so much more that we risk giving up. People often talk about the sacrifices they had to make in the beginning of their careers. But in truth, most people have very little to give up in the beginning.

The only thing of value that they have is time. But as we climb higher, we have more, and we find it more difficult to let go of what we've worked for. That's why many climb partway up the mountain of their potential and then stop. They come to a place where they are unwilling to give up something in order to get the next thing. As a result, they stall—some forever.

As I debated the trade-offs of leaving the church to become a full-time writer, speaker, and developer of people, I sought advice from a few trusted mentors. One of them, author and consultant Fred Smith, passed on the following thoughts to me:

> Something in human nature tempts us to stay where we're comfortable. We try to find a plateau, a resting place, where we have comfortable stress and adequate finances. Where we have comfortable associations with people, without the intimidation of meeting new people and entering strange situations. Of course, all of us need to plateau for a time. We climb and then plateau for assimilation. But once we've assimilated what we've learned, we climb again. It's un-fortunate when we've done our last climb. When we have made our last climb, we are old, whether forty or eighty.

That pushed me over the edge. I resigned. I would strive to go to a new level or fail trying!

What Will You Trade?

Soon after I resigned, I did some reflecting on the price of growth, and I wrote a lesson called "Ten Trade-Offs Worth Making." I believe the lessons I learned that have served me well may also serve you.

1. Trade Affirmation for Accomplishment

I've already explained that when I began my career, I was a people pleaser. I wanted approval from my followers, admiration from my peers, and awards from my superiors. I was an affirmation junkie. But accolades are like smoke that quickly fades away. Awards turn to rust. And financial rewards are quickly spent. I decided that I would prefer to actually get something *done* than to just make myself look good. That decision paved the way for most of the other trades I would make in life.

2. TRADE SECURITY FOR SIGNIFICANCE

Success does not mean simply being busy. What you give your life to matters. The great leaders in history were great not because of what they owned or earned but because of what they gave their lives to accomplish. They made a difference!

I chose a career in which I expected to make a difference. But that did not exempt me from having to take risks to do things of greater significance. The same will be true for you, no matter what profession you have chosen.

3. TRADE FINANCIAL GAIN FOR FUTURE POTENTIAL

One of life's ironies for me is that I was never motivated by money, yet Margaret and I ended up doing well financially. Why? Because I was always willing to put future potential ahead of financial gain.

The temptation is almost always to go for the cash. But this goes back to the idea of pay now, play later. If you are willing to sacrifice financially on the front end for the possibility of greater potential, you are almost always given greater chances for higher rewards—including financially.

4. TRADE IMMEDIATE PLEASURE FOR PERSONAL GROWTH

If ever there was something our culture has a difficult time with, it is delayed gratification. If you look at the statistics on how much people are in debt and how little they put into savings, you can see that people are always seeking immediate pleasure.

When I was a kid, school bored me, and I couldn't wait to be done with it. I would have liked nothing better than to drop out, marry Margaret, my high school sweetheart, and play basketball. But because I wanted to have a career in leadership, I went to college, earned my degree, and waited until after graduation to marry Margaret. That was a *very long* four years.

Time after time, Margaret and I have put off or sacrificed pleasures, conveniences, or luxuries in order to pursue personal growth opportunities. We've never regretted it.

5. Trade Exploration for Focus

Some people like to dabble. The problem with dabbling is that you never really become great at anything. True, when you are young, you should try out new things—see where your strengths and interests lie. But the older you are, the more focused you should be. You can only go far if you specialize in something. If you study the lives of great men and women, you will find that they were very single-minded. Once you have found what you were created to do, stick with it.

6. Trade Quantity of Life for Quality of Life

I have to confess that I have a "more" mentality. If one is good, four is better. If somebody says he can hit a goal of twenty, I encourage him to reach for twenty-five. When I teach a one-hour leadership lesson on CD, I want to put so much content in it that the people who receive it will have to listen to it five times to get everything they can out of it.

Because of this natural inclination to do more, I've often had very little margin in my life. For years my calendar was booked solid, and I took very little time to relax. I remember asking my brother and his wife to come visit me, and Larry saying, "No, you're too busy. If we come, we won't ever see you."

I once read that the president of a large publishing company sought out a wise man to get his advice. After describing the chaos that was his life, he silently waited to hear something of value from the sage. The older man at first said nothing. He simply took a teapot and began pour-ing tea into a cup. And he kept pouring until the tea overflowed and began to cover the table.

"What are you doing?" the businessman exclaimed.

"Your life," responded the wise man, "is like a teacup, flowing over. There's no room for anything new. You need to pour out, not take more in."

It has been very difficult for me to change my mind-set from quan-tity to quality. Honestly, I'm still working on it. Having a heart attack in 1998 certainly made an impact on me in this area. So did having grand-children. I now carve out more time for the really important things in my life. I suggest you do the same.

7. TRADE ACCEPTABLE FOR EXCELLENT

This one is so obvious that it almost goes without saying. People do not pay for average. They are not impressed by anything that is merely acceptable. Leaders cannot rise up on the wings of mediocrity. If some-thing is worth doing, give it your best—or don't do it at all.

8. TRADE ADDITION FOR MULTIPLICATION

When people make the shift from doer to leader, they greatly increase the impact that their lives can make. It is a significant jump because, as I assert in *The 17 Indisputable Laws of Teamwork*, one is too small a number to achieve greatness. However, there is another jump that is more difficult and has even greater significance—changing from adder to multiplier.

Leaders who gather followers *add* to what they can accomplish. Leaders who develop leaders *multiply* their ability. How is that? For every leader they develop or attract, they gain not only that individual's horse-power but the horsepower of all the people that person leads. It has an incredible multiplying effect. Every great leader, regardless of where or when they led, was a leader of leaders. To go to the highest level of lead-ership, you must learn to be a multiplier.

9. Trade the First Half for the Second Half

In his book *Halftime*, Bob Buford says that most people who are successful in the first half of their life try to do the second half of their life in the same way. What he's really saying is that they reach a plateau and they are unwilling to trade what they have for a new way of doing things because it's much easier to stick with what's familiar.

If you are in the second half of life, you have probably spent much of your time paying the price for success. Don't waste it. Be willing to trade it for significance. Do things that will live on after you are gone. If you are in the first half, keep paying the price so that you have something to offer in your second half.

10. Trade Your Work for God for a Walk with God

As someone who has worked in ministry for many years, I understand the deep satisfaction of doing work that is for God. However, I also understand the trap of constantly doing *for* God without continually connecting *with* God.

If you are not a person of faith, then this may not make sense to you. However, if faith is a part of your life, remember that no matter how much value your work has, it cannot compare with a relationship with your Creator.

Are You Willing to Give Up to Go Up?

To achieve excellence, I think you have to learn to travel light. You must learn to off-load before trying to reload. You have to let go of one thing in order to grasp a new one. People naturally resist that. We want to stay in our comfort zone and hold on to what's familiar. Sometimes circumstances force us to give up something and we have the chance to gain something new. But more often than not, if we want to make positive trades, we have to maintain the right attitude and be willing to give up some things.

During the Civil War, President Abraham Lincoln was given a request for five hundred thousand additional recruits to fight in the army. Political advisors strongly recommended he turn it down since they thought honoring the request would prevent his reelection. But Lincoln's decision was firm.

"It is not necessary for me to be reelected," he said, "but it is necessary for the soldiers at the front to be reinforced by five hundred thousand men and I shall call for them. If I go down under the act, I will go down with my colors flying."

Lincoln is one of our greatest presidents because he was willing to give up everything—except final responsibility. That is the kind of attitude leaders need to have. Every new level of growth we hope to experience as leaders calls for a new level of change. You cannot have one without the other. If you want to be a better leader, get ready to make some trades.

As I've mentioned, I turned sixty in February of 2007. A few months before my birthday, I took the time to memorize the following prayer, because I wanted to pray it in the presence of my family and friends on my birthday. It says:

> Lord, as I grow older, I think I want to be known as . . .
> Thoughtful, rather than gifted,
> Loving, versus quick or bright,
> Gentle, over being powerful,
> A listener, more than a great communicator,
> Available, rather than a hard worker,
> Sacrificial, instead of successful,
> Reliable, not famous,
> Content, more than driven,
> Self-controlled, rather than exciting,
> Generous, instead of rich, and
> Compassionate, more than competent,
> I want to be a foot-washer.

I'm still striving to become that person. I'm still making trades.

Now more than ever, I am aware that significant birthdays can either mark the passage of time, or they can mark changes we've made in our lives to reach our potential and become the person we were created to be. With each passing year, I want to make good choices that make me a better person, help me become a better leader, and make a positive impact on others. That requires a willingness to keep making trades, because for everything you gain, you have to give up something.

LEADERSHIP

101

WHAT EVERY LEADER NEEDS TO KNOW

Published in Nashville, Tennessee, by Thomas Nelson. Thomas Nelson
is a registered trademark of Thomas Nelson, Inc.

Thomas Nelson, Inc., titles may be purchased in bulk for educational,
business, fund-raising, or sales promotional use. For information,
please e-mail SpecialMarkets@ThomasNelson.com.

Portions of this book were previously published in *Becoming a Person of Influence, The 21 Irrefutable Laws
of Leadership, The 21 Indispensable Qualities of a Leader,* and *Developing the Leader Within You.*

Library of Congress Cataloging-in-Publication

Maxwell, John C., 1947–
Leadership 101 / John C. Maxwell.
p. cm.
ISBN 13: 978-0-7852-6419-4
1. Leadership. I. Title: Leadership one hundred one. II. Title.
HM1261 .M3897 2002
303.3'4—dc21
2002009572

Contents

PART I

THE DEVELOPMENT OF A LEADER

I

WHY SHOULD I GROW
AS A LEADER?

The higher the leadership,
the greater the effectiveness.

I often open my leadership conferences by explaining what I call the Law of the Lid because it helps people understand the value of leadership. If you can get a handle on this principle, you will see the incredible impact of leadership on every aspect of life. So here it is: Leadership ability is the lid that determines a person's level of effectiveness. The lower an individual's ability to lead, the lower the lid on his potential. The higher the leadership, the greater the effectiveness. To give you an example, if your leadership rates an 8, then your effectiveness can never be greater than a 7. If your leadership is only a 4, then your effectiveness will be no higher than a 3. Your leadership ability—for better or for worse—always determines your effectiveness and the potential impact of your organization.

Let me tell you a story that illustrates the Law of the Lid. In 1930, two young brothers named Dick and Maurice moved from New Hampshire to California in search of the American Dream. They had just gotten out of high school, and they saw few opportunities back home. So they headed straight for Hollywood where they eventually found jobs on a movie studio set.

After a while, their entrepreneurial spirit and interest in the entertainment industry prompted them to open a theater in Glendale, a town about five miles northeast of Hollywood. But despite all their efforts, the brothers just couldn't make the business profitable, so they looked for a better business opportunity.

A NEW OPPORTUNITY

In 1937, the brothers opened a small drive-in restaurant in Pasadena, located just east of Glendale. As people in southern California became more dependent on their cars in the thirties, drive-in restaurants sprang up everywhere. Customers would drive into a parking lot around a small restaurant, place their orders with carhops, and receive their food on trays right in their cars. The food was served on china plates complete with glassware and metal utensils.

Dick and Maurice's tiny drive-in restaurant was a great success, and in 1940, they moved the operation to San Bernardino, a working-class boomtown fifty miles east of Los Angeles. They built a larger facility and expanded their menu from hot dogs, fries, and shakes to include barbecued beef and pork sandwiches, hamburgers, and other items. Their business exploded. Annual sales reached $200,000, and the brothers found themselves splitting $50,000 in profits every year—a sum that put them in the town's financial elite.

By 1948, their intuition told them that times were changing, so they made modifications to their restaurant business. They eliminated the carhops and started serving only walk-up customers. They reduced their menu and focused on selling hamburgers. They eliminated plates, glassware, and metal utensils, switching to paper products instead. They reduced their costs and the prices they charged customers. They also created what they called the Speedy Service System. Their kitchen became like an assembly line, where each person focused on service with speed. Their goal was to fill each customer's order in thirty seconds or less. And they succeeded. By the mid-1950s, annual revenue hit $350,000, and by then, Dick and Maurice split net profits of about $100,000 each year.

Who were these brothers? On the front of their small restaurant hung a neon sign that said simply MCDONALD'S HAMBURGERS. Dick and Maurice McDonald had hit the great American jackpot, and the rest, as they say, is history, right? Wrong. The McDonalds never went any further because their weak leadership put a lid on their ability to succeed.

THE STORY BEHIND THE STORY

It's true that the McDonald brothers were financially secure. Theirs was one of the most profitable restaurant enterprises in the country, and their genius was in customer service and kitchen organization, which led to a new system of food and beverage service. In fact, their talent was so widely known in food service circles that people from all over the country wanted to learn more about their methods. At one point, they received as many as three hundred calls and letters every month. That led them to the idea of marketing the McDonald's concept.

The idea of franchising restaurants had been around for several decades. To the McDonald brothers, it looked like a way to make money without having to open another restaurant themselves. In 1952, they tried it, but their effort was a dismal failure. The reason was simple: they lacked the leadership necessary to make it effective.

Dick and Maurice were good restaurant owners. They understood how to run a business, make their systems efficient, cut costs, and increase profits. They were efficient managers. But they were not leaders. Their thinking patterns clamped a lid down on what they could do and become. At the height of their success, Dick and Maurice found themselves smack-dab against the Law of the Lid.

THE BROTHERS PARTNER WITH A LEADER

In 1954, the brothers hooked up with a man named Ray Kroc, who *was* a leader. Kroc had been running a small company he founded, which sold machines for making milk shakes. McDonald's was one of his best customers, and as soon as he visited the store, he had a vision for its potential. In his mind he could see the restaurant going nationwide in hundreds of markets. He soon struck a deal with Dick and Maurice, and in 1955, he formed McDonald's System, Inc. (later called the McDonald's Corporation).

Kroc immediately bought the rights to a franchise so that he could use it as a model and prototype to sell other franchises. Then he began to assemble a team and build an organization to make McDonald's a nationwide entity.

In the early years, Kroc sacrificed a lot. Though he was in his mid-fifties, he worked long hours just as he had when he first got started in business thirty years earlier. He eliminated many frills at home, including his country club membership, which he later said added ten strokes to his golf game. During his first eight years with McDonald's, he took no salary. He also personally borrowed money from the bank and against his life insurance to help cover the salaries of a few key leaders he wanted on the team. His sacrifice and his leadership paid off. In 1961 for the sum of $2.7 million, Kroc bought the exclusive rights to McDonald's from the brothers, and he proceeded to turn it into an American institution and global entity. The "lid" in the life and leadership of Ray Kroc was obviously much higher than that of his predecessors.

In the years that Dick and Maurice McDonald had attempted to franchise their food service system, they managed to sell the concept to just fifteen buyers, only ten of whom actually opened restaurants. On the other hand, the leadership lid in Ray Kroc's life was sky high. Between 1955 and 1959, Kroc succeeded in opening 100 restaurants. Four years after that, there were 500 McDonald's. Today the company has opened more than 21,000 restaurants in no fewer than 100 countries.[1] Leadership ability—or more specifically the lack of leadership ability—was the lid on the McDonald brothers' effectiveness.

SUCCESS WITHOUT LEADERSHIP

I believe that success is within the reach of just about everyone. But I also believe that personal success without leadership ability brings only limited effectiveness. A person's impact is only a fraction of what it could be with good leadership. The higher you want to climb, the more you need leadership. The greater the impact you want to make, the greater your influence needs to be. Whatever you will accomplish is restricted by your ability to lead others.

Let me give you a picture of what I mean. Let's say that when it comes to success, you're an 8 (on a scale from 1 to 10). That's pretty good. I think it would be safe to say that the McDonald brothers were in that range. But let's also say that your leadership ability is only a 1. Your level of effectiveness would look like this:

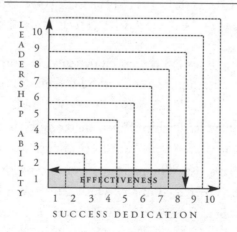

SUCCESS WITHOUT LEADERSHIP

To increase your level of effectiveness, you have a couple of choices. You could work very hard to increase your dedication to success and excellence—to work toward becoming a 10. It's possible that you could make it to that level, though the law of diminishing returns says that your success will increase only to a certain point, after which, it fails to increase in proportion to the amount of work you put into it. In other words, the effort it would take to increase those last two points might take more energy than it did to achieve the first eight. If you really killed yourself, you might increase your success by that 25 percent.

But you have another option. Let's say that instead you work hard to increase your level of *leadership*. Over the course of time, you develop yourself as a leader, and eventually, your leadership ability becomes, say, a 6.

By raising your leadership ability—without increasing your success dedication at all—you can increase your original effectiveness by 500 percent! If you were to raise your leadership to 8, where it matched your success dedication, you would increase your effectiveness by 700 percent! Leadership has a multiplying effect. I've seen its impact over and over again in all kinds of businesses and nonprofit organizations. And that's why I've taught leadership for more than twenty-five years.

TO CHANGE THE DIRECTION OF THE ORGANIZATION, CHANGE THE LEADER

Leadership ability is always the lid on personal and organizational effectiveness. If the leadership is strong, the lid is high. But if it's not, then the organization is limited. That's why in times of trouble, organizations naturally look for new leadership. When the country is experiencing hard times, it elects a new president. When a church is floundering, it searches for a new senior pastor. When a sports team keeps losing, it looks for a new head coach. When a company is losing money, it hires a new CEO.

A few years ago, I met Don Stephenson, the chairman of Global Hospitality Resources, Inc., of San Diego, California, an international hospitality advisory and consulting firm. Over lunch, I asked him about his organization. Today he primarily does consulting, but back then his company took over the management of hotels and resorts that weren't doing well financially. They oversaw many excellent facilities such as La Costa in southern California.

TO REACH THE HIGHEST LEVEL OF EFFECTIVENESS, YOU HAVE TO RAISE THE LID OF LEADERSHIP ABILITY.

Don said that whenever they came into an organization to take it over, they always started by doing two things: First, they trained all the staff to improve their level of service to the customers, and second, they fired the leader. When he told me that, I was at first surprised.

"You *always* fire him?" I asked. "Every time?"

"That's right. Every time," he said.

"Don't you talk to the person first—to check him out to see if he's a good leader?" I said.

"No," he answered. "If he'd been a good leader, the organization wouldn't be in the mess it's in."

And I thought to myself, *Of course. It's the Law of the Lid.* To reach the highest level of effectiveness, you have to raise the lid—one way or another.

The good news is that getting rid of the leader isn't the *only* way. Just as I teach in conferences that there is a lid, I also teach that you can raise it.

2

How Can I Grow As a Leader?

Leadership develops daily,
not in a day.

Becoming a leader is a lot like investing successfully in the stock market. If your hope is to make a fortune in a day, you're not going to be successful. What matters most is what you do day by day over the long haul. My friend Tag Short maintains, "The secret of our success is found in our daily agenda." If you continually invest in your leadership development, letting your "assets" compound, the inevitable result is growth over time.

When I teach leadership at conferences, people inevitably ask me whether leaders are born. I always answer, "Yes, of course they are . . . I've yet to meet one that came into the world any other way!" We all laugh, and then I answer the real question—whether leadership is something a person either possesses or doesn't.

Although it's true that some people are born with greater natural gifts than others, the ability to lead is really a collection of skills, nearly all of which can be learned and improved. But that process doesn't happen overnight. Leadership is complicated. It has many facets: respect, experience, emotional strength, people skills, discipline, vision, momentum, timing—the list goes on. As you can see, many factors that come into play in leadership are intangible. That's why leaders require so much seasoning to be effective. It was around the time I turned fifty that I truly began to understand the many aspects of leadership with clarity.

The Four Phases of Leadership Growth

Whether you do or don't have great natural ability for leadership, your development and progress will probably occur according to the following four phases:

Phase 1—I Don't Know What I Don't Know

Most people fail to recognize the value of leadership. They believe that leadership is only for a few—for the people at the top of the corporate ladder. They have no idea of the opportunities they're passing up when they don't learn to lead. This point was driven home for me when a college president shared with me that only a handful of students signed up for a leadership course offered by the school. Why? Only a few thought of themselves as leaders. If they had known that leadership is influence, and that in the course of each day most individuals usually try to influence at least four other people, their desire might have been sparked to learn more about the subject. It's unfortunate because as long as a person doesn't know what he doesn't know, he doesn't grow.

Phase 2—I Know What I Don't Know

Usually at some point in life, we are placed in a leadership position only to look around and discover that no one is following us. That's when we realize that we need to *learn* how to lead. And of course, that's when it's possible for the process to start. English Prime Minister Benjamin Disraeli wisely commented, "To be conscious that you are ignorant of the facts is a great step to knowledge."

SUCCESSFUL LEADERS ARE LEARNERS. AND THE
LEARNING PROCESS IS ONGOING, A RESULT OF
SELF-DISCIPLINE AND PERSEVERANCE.

That's what happened to me when I took my first leadership position in 1969. I had captained sports teams all my life and had been the student government president in college, so I already thought I was a leader. But when I tried to lead people in the real world, I found out the awful truth. That prompted me to start gathering resources and learning from them. I also had another idea: I wrote to the top ten leaders in my field and offered them one hundred dollars for a half hour of their time so that I could ask them questions. (That was quite a sum for me in 1969.) For the next several years, my wife, Margaret, and I planned every vacation around where those people lived. If a great leader in Cleveland said yes to my request, then that year we vacationed in Cleveland so that I could meet him. And my idea really paid off. Those men shared insights with me that I could have learned no other way.

PHASE 3—I GROW AND KNOW AND IT STARTS TO SHOW
When you recognize your lack of skill and begin the daily discipline of personal growth in leadership, exciting things start to happen.

Awhile back I was teaching a group of people in Denver, and in the crowd I noticed a really sharp nineteen-year-old named Brian. For a couple of days, I watched as he eagerly took notes. I talked to him a few times during breaks. When I got to the part of the seminar where I emphasize that leadership is a process, I asked Brian to stand up so that I could talk while everyone listened. I said, "Brian, I've been watching you here, and I'm very impressed with how hungry you are to learn and glean and grow. I want to tell you a secret that will change your life." Everyone in the whole auditorium seemed to lean forward.

"I believe that in about twenty years, you can be a *great* leader. I want to encourage you to make yourself a lifelong learner of leadership. Read books, listen to tapes regularly, and keep attending seminars. And whenever you come across a golden nugget of truth or a significant quote, file it away for the future.

"It's not going to be easy," I said. "But in five years, you'll see progress as your influence becomes greater. In ten years you'll develop a competence that makes your leadership highly effective. And in twenty years, when you're only thirty-nine years old, if you've continued to learn and grow, others will likely start asking you to teach them about leadership. And some will be amazed. They'll look at each other and say, 'How did he suddenly become so wise?'

"Brian, you can be a great leader, but it won't happen in a day. Start paying the price now."

What's true for Brian is also true for you. Start developing your leadership today, and someday you will experience the effects of this process.

PHASE 4—I SIMPLY GO BECAUSE OF WHAT I KNOW

When you're in phase 3, you can be pretty effective as a leader, but you have to think about every move you make. However, when you get to phase 4, your ability to lead becomes almost automatic. And that's when the payoff is larger than life. But the only way to get there is to recognize the process and pay the price.

TO LEAD TOMORROW, LEARN TODAY

Leadership is developed daily, not in a day—that is reality. The good news is that your leadership ability is not static. No matter where you're starting from, you can get better. That's true even for people who have stood on the world stage of leadership. While most presidents of the United States reach their peak while in office, others continue to grow and become better leaders afterward, such as former president Jimmy Carter. Some people questioned his ability to lead while in the White House. But in recent years, Carter's level of influence has continually increased. His high integrity and dedication in serving people through Habitat for Humanity and other organizations have made his influence grow. People are now truly impressed with his life.

FIGHTING YOUR WAY UP

There is an old saying: champions don't become champions in the ring— they are merely recognized there. That's true. If you want to see where someone develops into a champion, look at his daily routine. Former heavyweight champ Joe Frazier stated, "You can map out a fight plan or a life plan. But when the action starts, you're down to your reflexes. That's where your road work shows. If you cheated on that in the dark of the morning, you're getting found out now under the bright lights."[1] Boxing is a good analogy for leadership development because it is all about daily preparation. Even if a person has natural talent, he has to prepare and train to become successful.

One of this country's greatest leaders was a fan of boxing: President Theodore Roosevelt. In fact, one of his most famous quotes uses a boxing analogy:

> It is not the critic who counts, not the man who points out how the strong man stumbled, or where the doer of deeds could have done them better. The credit belongs to the man who is actually in the arena; whose face is marred by dust and sweat and blood; who strives valiantly; who errs and comes short again and again; who knows the great enthusiasms, the great devotions, and spends himself in a worthy cause; who, at best, knows in the end the triumph of high achievement; and who, at the worst, if he fails, at least fails while daring greatly, so that his place shall never be with those cold and timid souls who know neither victory nor defeat.

A boxer himself, Roosevelt was not only an effective leader, but he was the most flamboyant of all U.S. presidents.

A Man of Action

TR (which was Roosevelt's nickname) was known for regular boxing and judo sessions, challenging horseback rides, and long, strenuous hikes. A French ambassador who visited Roosevelt used to tell about the time that he accompanied the president on a walk through the woods. When the two men came to the banks of a stream that was too deep to cross by foot, TR stripped off his clothes and expected the dignitary to do the same so that they could swim to the other side. Nothing was an obstacle to Roosevelt.

His enthusiasm and stamina seemed boundless. As the vice presidential candidate in 1900, he gave 673 speeches and traveled 20,000 miles while campaigning for President McKinley. And years after his presidency, while preparing to deliver a speech in Milwaukee, Roosevelt was shot in the chest by a would-be assassin. With a broken rib and a bullet in his chest, Roosevelt insisted on delivering his one-hour speech before allowing himself to be taken to the hospital.

Roosevelt Started Slow

Of all the leaders this nation has ever had, Roosevelt was one of the toughest—both physically and mentally. But he didn't start that way. America's cowboy president was born in Manhattan to a prominent wealthy family. As a child, he was puny and very sickly. He had debilitating asthma, possessed very poor eyesight, and was painfully thin. His parents weren't sure he would survive.

When he was twelve, young Roosevelt's father told him, "You have the mind, but you have not the body, and without the help of the body the mind cannot go as far as it should. You must *make* the body." And make it he did. TR began spending time *every day* building his body as well as his mind, and he did that for the rest of his life. He worked out with weights, hiked, ice-skated, hunted, rowed, rode horseback, and boxed. By the time TR graduated from Harvard, he was ready to tackle the world of politics.

NO OVERNIGHT SUCCESS

Roosevelt didn't become a great leader overnight, either. His road to the presidency was one of slow, continual growth. As he served in various positions, ranging from New York City Police Commissioner to President of the United States, he kept learning and growing. He improved himself, and in time he became a strong leader.

Roosevelt's list of accomplishments is remarkable. Under his leadership, the United States emerged as a world power. He helped the country develop a first-class navy. He saw that the Panama Canal was built. He negotiated peace between Russia and Japan, winning a Nobel Peace Prize in the process. And when people questioned TR's leadership—since he had become president when McKinley was assassinated—he campaigned and was reelected by the largest majority of any president up to his time.

Ever the man of action, when Roosevelt completed his term as president in 1909, he immediately traveled to Africa where he led a scientific expedition sponsored by the Smithsonian Institution.

On January 6, 1919, at his home in New York, Theodore Roosevelt died in his sleep. Then Vice President Marshall said, "Death had to take him sleeping, for if Roosevelt had been awake, there would have been a fight." When they removed him from his bed, they found a book under his pillow. Up to the very last, TR was still striving to learn and improve himself.

If you want to be a leader, the good news is that you can do it. Everyone has the potential, but it isn't accomplished overnight. It requires perseverance. And you absolutely cannot ignore that becoming a leader is a process. Leadership doesn't develop in a day. It takes a lifetime.

PART II

THE TRAITS OF A LEADER

HOW CAN I BECOME DISCIPLINED?

The first person you lead is you.

I t's a tough road to the top. Not many people ever reach the place where they are considered one of the best at their work. And even fewer are believed to be *the* best—ever. Yet that's what Jerry Rice has achieved. He is called the best person ever to play wide receiver in football. And he has got the records to prove it.

People who know him well say he is a natural. Physically his God-given gifts are incredible, yet those alone have not made him great. The real key to his success has been his self-discipline. He works and prepares—day in and day out—unlike anyone else in professional football.

During practice in high school, Rice's coach, Charles Davis, made his players sprint twenty times up and down a forty-yard hill. On a particularly hot and muggy Mississippi day, Rice was ready to give up after eleven trips. As he sneaked toward the locker room, he realized what he was doing. "Don't quit," he told himself. "Because once you get into that mode of quitting, then you feel like it's okay." He went back and finished his sprints, and he has never been a quitter since.

As a professional player, he has become famous for his ability to sprint up another hill—a rugged 2.5-mile park trail in San Carlos, California—that Rice makes a regular part of his workout schedule. Other top players try to keep up with him on it, but they fall behind, astounded by his stamina. But that's only a part of Rice's regular routine. Even in the off-season, while other players are fishing or lying around enjoying downtime, Rice is working, his normal exercise routine lasting from 7:00 A.M. to noon. Someone once joked, "He is so well-conditioned that he makes Jamie Lee Curtis look like James Earl Jones."

"What a lot of guys don't understand about Jerry is that with him, football's a twelve-month thing," says NFL cornerback Kevin Smith. "He's a natural, but he still works. That's what separates the good from the great."

NO MATTER HOW GIFTED A LEADER IS, HIS GIFTS WILL
NEVER REACH THEIR MAXIMUM POTENTIAL WITHOUT
THE APPLICATION OF SELF-DISCIPLINE.

In 1997, Rice climbed another hill in his career: he made a comeback from a devastating injury. Prior to that, he had never missed a game in nineteen seasons of football, a testament to his disciplined work ethic and absolute tenacity. When he blew out his knee on August 31, 1997, people thought he was finished for the season. After all, only one player had ever had a similar injury and come back in the same season—Rod Woodson. He had rehabilitated his knee in four and a half months. Rice did it in three and a half—through sheer grit, determination, and incredible self-discipline. People had never seen anything like it before, and they might not again.

A DISCIPLINED DIRECTION

Jerry Rice is a perfect example of the power of self-discipline. No one achieves and sustains success without it. And no matter how gifted a leader is, his gifts will never reach their maximum potential without the application of self-discipline. It positions a leader to go to the highest level and is a key to leadership that lasts.

If you want to become a leader for whom self-discipline is an asset, follow these action points:

CHALLENGE YOUR EXCUSES

To develop a lifestyle of discipline, one of your first tasks must be to challenge and eliminate any tendency to make excuses. As French classical writer François La Rochefoucauld said, "Almost all our faults are more pardonable than the methods we think up to hide them." If you have several reasons why you can't be self-disciplined, realize that they are really just a bunch of excuses—all of which need to be challenged if you want to go to the next level as a leader.

REMOVE REWARDS UNTIL THE JOB IS DONE

Author Mike Delaney wisely remarked, "Any business or industry that pays equal rewards to its goof-offs and its eager-beavers sooner or later will find itself with more goof-offs than eager-beavers." If you lack self-discipline, you may be in the habit of having dessert before eating your vegetables.

A story illustrates the power of withholding rewards. An older couple had been at a campground for a couple of days when a family arrived at the site next to them. As soon as their sport-utility vehicle came to a stop, the couple and their three kids piled out. One child hurriedly unloaded ice chests, backpacks, and other items while the other two quickly put up tents. The site was ready in fifteen minutes.

The older couple was amazed. "You folks sure do work great together," the elderly gentleman told the dad admiringly.

"You just need a system," replied the dad. "Nobody goes to the bathroom until camp's set up."

STAY FOCUSED ON RESULTS

Anytime you concentrate on the difficulty of the work instead of its results or rewards, you're likely to become discouraged. Dwell on it too long, and you'll develop self-pity instead of self-discipline. The next time you're facing a must-do task and you're thinking of doing what's convenient instead of paying the price, change your focus. Count the benefits of doing what's right, and then dive in.

IF YOU KNOW YOU HAVE TALENT, AND YOU'VE SEEN A
LOT OF MOTION BUT LITTLE CONCRETE RESULTS—
YOU MAY LACK SELF-DISCIPLINE.

Author H. Jackson Brown Jr. quipped, "Talent without discipline is like an octopus on roller skates. There's plenty of movement, but you never know if it's going to be forward, backwards, or sideways." If you know you have talent, and you've seen a lot of motion—but little concrete results—you may lack self-discipline.

Look at last week's schedule. How much of your time did you devote to regular, disciplined activities? Did you do anything to grow and improve yourself professionally? Did you engage in activities promoting good health? Did you dedicate part of your income to savings or investments? If you've been putting off those things, telling yourself that you'll do them later, you may need to work on your self-discipline.

4

How Should I Prioritize My Life?

The discipline to prioritize and the ability
to work toward a stated goal are essential
to a leader's success.

Success can be defined as *the progressive realization of a predetermined goal.* This definition tells us that the discipline to prioritize and the ability to work toward a stated goal are essential to a leader's success. In fact, I believe they are the key to leadership.

Many years ago, while working toward a business degree, I learned about the Pareto Principle. It is commonly called the 20/80 principle. Although I received little information about this principle at the time, I began applying it to my life. Years later I find it is a most useful tool for determining priorities for any person's life or for any organization.

The Pareto Principle: The 20/80 Principle

Twenty percent of your priorities will give you 80 percent of your production, IF you spend your time, energy, money, and personnel on the top 20 percent of your priorities.

PRIORITIES   PRODUCTION

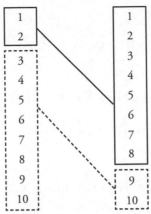

The solid lines on the illustration of the 20/80 Principle above represent a person or organization that spends time, energy, money, and personnel on the most important priorities. The result is a four-fold return in productivity. The dotted lines represent a person or organization that spends time, energy, money, and personnel on the lesser priorities. The result is a very small return.

EXAMPLES OF THE PARETO PRINCIPLE:

Time	20 percent of our time produces 80 percent of the results.
Counseling	20 percent of the people take up 80 percent of our time.
Products	20 percent of the products bring in 80 percent of the profit.
Reading	20 percent of the book contains 80 percent of the content.
Job	20 percent of our work gives us 80 percent of our satisfaction.
Speech	20 percent of the presentation produces 80 percent of the impact.

Donations 20 percent of the people will give 80 percent of the money.

Leadership 20 percent of the people will make 80 percent of the decisions.

Picnic 20 percent of the people will eat 80 percent of the food!

Every leader needs to understand the Pareto Principle in the area of people oversight and leadership. For example, 20 percent of the people in an organization will be responsible for 80 percent of the company's success. The following strategy will enable a leader to increase the productivity of an organization:

1. Determine which people are the top 20 percent producers.
2. Spend 80 percent of your "people time" with the top 20 percent.
3. Spend 80 percent of your personal development dollars on the top 20 percent.
4. Determine what 20 percent of the work gives 80 percent of the return and train an assistant to do the 80 percent less-effective work. This "frees up" the producer to do what he/she does best.
5. Ask the top 20 percent to do on-the-job training for the next 20 percent.

Remember, we teach what we know; we reproduce what we are. Like begets like. I teach this principle at leadership conferences, and I am often asked, "How do I identify the top 20 percent influencers/producers in my organization?" I suggest that you make a list of everyone in your company or department. Then ask yourself this question about each individual: "If this person takes a negative action against me or withdraws his or her support from me, what will the impact likely be?" If you won't be able to function, then put a check mark next to that name. If the person can help you or hurt you, but cannot make or break you in terms of your ability to get important things done, then don't put a check mark next to that name. When you get through making the check marks, you will have marked between 15 and 20 percent of the names. Those are the vital relationships that need to be developed and given the proper amount of resources needed to grow the organization.

ORGANIZE OR AGONIZE

Remember: it's not how hard you work; it's how smart you work. The ability to juggle three or four high priority projects successfully is a must for every leader.

A LIFE IN WHICH ANYTHING GOES WILL ULTIMATELY
BE A LIFE IN WHICH NOTHING GOES.

Prioritize Assignments

High Importance/High Urgency: Tackle these projects first.

High Importance/Low Urgency: Set deadlines for completion and get these projects worked into your daily routine.

Low Importance/High Urgency: Find quick, efficient ways to get this work done without much personal involvement. If possible, delegate it to a "can do" assistant.

Low Importance/Low Urgency: This is busy or repetitious work, such as filing. Stack it up and do it in one-half hour segments every week, get somebody else to do it, or don't do it at all. Before putting off until tomorrow something you can do today, study it clearly. Maybe you can postpone it indefinitely.

CHOOSE OR LOSE

Every person is an initiator or reactor when it comes to planning. An example is our calendar. The question is not, "Will my calendar be full?" but "Who will fill my calendar?" If we are leaders of others, the question is not, "Will I see people?" but "Whom will I see?" My observation is that leaders tend to initiate and followers tend to react. Note the difference:

Leaders	Followers
Initiate	React
Lead; pick up phone and make contact	Listen; wait for phone to ring
Spend time planning; anticipate problems	Spend time living day-to-day reacting to problems
Invest time with people	Spend time with people
Fill the calendar by priorities	Fill the calendar by requests

EVALUATE OR STALEMATE

Many times priorities are not black or white, but many tones of gray. I have found that the last thing one knows is what to put first. The following questions will assist your priority process:

What is required of me? A leader can give up anything except final responsibility. The question that must always be answered before accepting a new job is, "What is required of me?" In other words, what do I have to do that no one but me can do? Whatever those things are, they must be put high on the priority list. Failure to do them will cause you to be among the unemployed. There will be many responsibilities of the levels under your position, but only a few that require you to be the one and only one who can do them. Distinguish between what you have to do and what can be delegated to someone else.

What gives me the greatest return? The effort expended should approximate the results expected. A question I must continually ask myself is, "Am I doing what I do best and receiving a good return for the organization?" Three common problems in many organizations are:

- Abuse: Too few employees are doing too much.
- Disuse: Too many employees are doing too little.
- Misuse: Too many employees are doing the wrong things.

What is most rewarding? Life is too short not to be fun. Our best work takes place when we enjoy it. Some time ago I spoke at a leaders' conference where I attempted to teach this principle. The title of my lecture was "Take This Job and Love It." I encouraged the audience to find something they liked to do so much they would gladly do it for nothing. Then I suggested they learn to do it so well that people would be happy to pay them for it. You enjoy yourself because you are making your contribution to the world.

Success in your work will be greatly increased if the three Rs—Requirements, Return, Reward—are similar. In other words, if the requirements of my job are the same as my strengths that give me the highest return and doing those things brings me great pleasure, then I will be successful if I act on my priorities.

PRIORITY PRINCIPLES

PRIORITIES NEVER "STAY PUT"

Priorities continually shift and demand attention. H. Ross Perot said that anything that is excellent or praiseworthy stands moment-by-moment on the cutting edge and must be constantly fought for. Well-placed priorities always sit on "the edge."

To keep priorities in place:

- Evaluate: Every month review the three Rs (Requirements/Return/Reward).
- Eliminate: Ask yourself, "What am I doing that can be done by someone else?"
- Estimate: What are the top projects you are doing this month, and how long will they take?

YOU CANNOT OVERESTIMATE THE UNIMPORTANCE OF PRACTICALLY EVERYTHING

I love this principle. It's a little exaggerated but needs to be said. William James said that the art of being wise is "the art of knowing what to overlook." The petty and the mundane steal much of our time. Too many are living for the wrong things.

Dr. Anthony Campolo tells about a sociological study in which fifty people over the age of ninety-five were asked one question: "If you could live your life over again, what would you do differently?" It was an open-ended question, and a multiplicity of answers came from these eldest of senior citizens. However, three answers constantly reemerged and dominated the results of the study. Those answers were:

- If I had it to do over again, I would reflect more.
- If I had it to do over again, I would risk more.
- If I had it to do over again, I would do more things that would live on after I am dead.

A young concert violinist was asked the secret of her success. She replied, "Planned neglect." Then she explained, "When I was in school, there were many things that demanded my time. When I went to my room after breakfast, I made my bed, straightened the room, dusted the floor, and did whatever else came to my attention. Then I hurried to my violin practice. I found I wasn't progressing as I thought I should, so I reversed things. Until my practice period was completed, I deliberately neglected everything else. That program of planned neglect, I believe, accounts for my success."[1]

The Good Is the Enemy of the Best

Most people can prioritize when faced with right or wrong issues. The challenge arises when we are faced with two good choices. Now what should we do? What if both choices fall comfortably into the requirements, return, and reward of our work?

How to Break the Tie Between Two Good Options
- Ask your overseer or co-workers their preference.
- Can one of the options be handled by someone else? If so, pass it on and work on the one only you can do.
- Which option would be of more benefit to the customer?

Too many times we are like the merchant who was so intent on trying to keep the store clean that he would never unlock the front door. The real reason for running the store is to have customers come in, not to clean it up!

- Make your decision based on the purpose of the organization.

TOO MANY PRIORITIES PARALYZE US

Every one of us has looked at our desks filled with memos and papers, heard the phone ringing, and watched the door open all at the same time! Remember the "frozen feeling" that came over you?

William H. Hinson tells us why animal trainers carry a stool when they go into a cage of lions. They have their whips, of course, and their pistols are at their sides. But invariably they also carry a stool. Hinson says it is the most important tool of the trainer. He holds the stool by the back and thrusts the legs toward the face of the wild animal. Those who know maintain that the animal tries to focus on all four legs at once. In the attempt to focus on all four, a kind of paralysis overwhelms the animal, and it becomes tame, weak, and disabled because its attention is fragmented. (Now we will have more empathy for the lions.)

If you are overloaded with work, list the priorities on a separate sheet of paper *before* you take it to your boss and see what he will choose as the priorities.

The last of each month I plan and lay out my priorities for the next month. I sit down with my assistant and have her place those projects on the calendar. She handles hundreds of things for me on a monthly basis. However, when something is of High Importance/High Urgency, I communicate that to her so it will be placed above other things. All true leaders have learned to say no to the good in order to say yes to the best.

WHEN LITTLE PRIORITIES DEMAND TOO MUCH OF US, BIG PROBLEMS ARISE

Robert J. McKain said, "The reason most major goals are not achieved is that we spend our time doing second things first."

EFFICIENCY IS THE FOUNDATION FOR SURVIVAL.
EFFECTIVENESS IS THE FOUNDATION FOR SUCCESS.

Often the little things in life trip us up. A tragic example is an Eastern Airlines jumbo jet that crashed in the Everglades of Florida. The plane was the now-famous Flight 401, bound from New York to Miami with a heavy load of holiday passengers. As the plane approached the Miami airport for its landing, the light that indicates proper deployment of the landing gear failed to light. The plane flew in a large, looping circle over the swamps of the Everglades while the cockpit crew checked to see if the gear actually had not deployed, or if instead the bulb in the signal light was defective.

When the flight engineer tried to remove the light bulb, it wouldn't budge, and the other members of the crew tried to help him. As they struggled with the bulb, no one noticed the aircraft was losing altitude, and the plane simply flew right into the swamp. Dozens of people were killed in the crash. While an experienced crew of high-priced pilots fiddled with a seventy-five cent light bulb, the plane with its passengers flew right into the ground.

TIME DEADLINES AND EMERGENCIES FORCE US TO PRIORITIZE

We find this in Parkinson's Law: If you have only one letter to write, it will take all day to do it. If you have twenty letters to write, you'll get them done in one day. When is our most efficient time in our work? The week before vacation! Why can't we always run our lives the way we do the week before we leave the office, making decisions, cleaning off the desk, returning calls? Under normal conditions, we are efficient (doing things right). When time pressure mounts or emergencies arise, we become effective (doing the right things). Efficiency is the foundation for survival. Effectiveness is the foundation of success.

On the night of April 14, 1912, the great ocean liner, the *Titanic*, crashed into an iceberg in the Atlantic and sank, causing great loss of life.

One of the most curious stories to come from the disaster was of a woman who had a place in one of the lifeboats.

She asked if she could return to her stateroom for something and was given just three minutes. In her stateroom she ignored her own jewelry, and instead grabbed three oranges. Then she quickly returned to her place in the boat.

Just hours earlier it would have been ludicrous to think she would have accepted a crate of oranges in exchange for even one small diamond, but circumstances had suddenly transformed all the values aboard the ship. The emergency had clarified her priorities.

Too Often We Learn Too Late What Is Really Important

Gary Redding tells this story about Senator Paul Tsongas of Massachusetts. In January 1984 he announced that he would retire from the U.S. Senate and not seek reelection. Tsongas was a rising political star. He was a strong favorite to be reelected, and had even been mentioned as a potential future candidate for the Presidency or Vice Presidency of the United States.

A few weeks before his announcement, Tsongas had learned he had a form of lymphatic cancer that could not be cured but could be treated. In all likelihood, it would not greatly affect his physical abilities or life expectancy. The illness did not force Tsongas out of the Senate, but it did force him to face the reality of his own mortality. He would not be able to do everything he might want to do. So what were the things he really wanted to do in the time he had?

He decided that what he wanted most in life, what he would not give up if he could not have everything, was being with his family and watching his children grow up. He would rather do that than shape the nation's laws or get his name in the history books.

Shortly after his decision was announced, a friend wrote a note to congratulate Tsongas on having his priorities straight. The note read: "Nobody on his deathbed ever said, 'I wish I had spent more time on my business.'"

5

How Do I Develop Trust?

Trust is the foundation of leadership.

O ne of the most important lessons a leader can learn is how trust works. To me, it is a little like earning and spending pocket change. Each time you make a good leadership decision, it puts change into your pocket. Each time you make a poor one, you have to pay out some of your change to the people.

Every leader has a certain amount of change in his pocket when he starts in a new leadership position. From then on, he either builds up his change or pays it out. If he makes one bad decision after another, he keeps paying out change. Then one day, after making one last bad decision, he is going to reach into his pocket and realize he is out of change. It doesn't even matter if the blunder was big or small. When you're out of change, you're out as a leader.

A leader's history of successes and failures makes a big difference in his credibility. Your people know when you make mistakes. The real question is whether you're going to 'fess up. If you do, you can often quickly regain their trust. I've learned firsthand that when it comes to leadership, you just can't take shortcuts, no matter how long you've been leading your people.

TRUST IS THE FOUNDATION OF LEADERSHIP

There are three qualities a leader must exemplify to build trust: competence, connection, and character. People will forgive occasional mistakes based on ability, especially if they can see that you're still growing as a leader. But they won't trust someone who has slips in character. In that area, even occasional lapses are lethal. All effective leaders know this truth. PepsiCo chairman and CEO Craig Weatherup acknowledges, "People will tolerate honest mistakes, but if you violate their trust you will find it very difficult to ever regain their confidence. That is one reason that you need to treat trust as your most precious asset. You may fool your boss but you can never fool your colleagues or subordinates."

General H. Norman Schwarzkopf points to the significance of character: "Leadership is a potent combination of strategy and character. But if you must be without one, be without strategy." Character and leadership credibility always go hand in hand. Anthony Harrigan, president of the U.S. Business and Industrial Council, said,

> The role of character always has been the key factor in the rise and fall of nations. And one can be sure that America is no exception to this rule of history. We won't survive as a country because we are smarter or more sophisticated but because we are—we hope—stronger inwardly. In short, character is the only effective bulwark against internal and external forces that lead to a country's disintegration or collapse.

Character makes trust possible. And trust makes leadership possible.

CHARACTER COMMUNICATES

Character communicates many things to followers:

CHARACTER COMMUNICATES CONSISTENCY
Leaders without inner strength can't be counted on day after day

because their ability to perform changes constantly. NBA great Jerry West commented, "You can't get too much done in life if you only work on the days when you feel good." If your people don't know what to expect from you as a leader, at some point they won't look to you for leadership.

WHEN A LEADER'S CHARACTER IS STRONG, PEOPLE
TRUST HIM, AND THEY TRUST IN HIS ABILITY
TO RELEASE THEIR POTENTIAL.

Think about what happened in the late 1980s. Several high-profile Christian leaders stumbled and fell due to moral issues. That lack of consistency compromised their ability to lead their people. In fact, it gave a black eye to every pastor across the nation because it caused people to become suspicious of all church leaders, regardless of their personal track records. The flawed character of those fallen leaders destroyed the foundation for their leadership.

When I think of leaders who epitomize consistency of character, the first person who comes to mind is Billy Graham. Regardless of personal religious beliefs, everybody trusts him. Why? Because he has modeled high character for more than half a century. He lives out his values every day. He never makes a commitment unless he is going to keep it. And he goes out of his way to personify integrity.

CHARACTER COMMUNICATES POTENTIAL

John Morley observed, "No man can climb out beyond the limitations of his own character." That's especially true when it comes to leadership. Take, for instance, the case of NHL coach Mike Keenan. As of mid-1997, he had a noteworthy record of professional hockey victories: the fifth greatest number of regular-season wins, the third greatest number of play-off victories, six division titles, four NHL finals appearances, and one Stanley Cup.

Yet despite those commendable credentials, Keenan was unable to stay with a single team for any length of time. In eleven and a half seasons, he coached four different teams. And after his stint with the fourth team—the St. Louis Blues—he was unable to land a job for a long time. Why? Sportswriter E. M. Swift said of Keenan, "The reluctance to hire Keenan is *easily* explicable. Everywhere he has been, he has alienated players and management."[1] Evidently, his players didn't trust him. Neither did the owners, who were benefiting from seeing their teams win.

Craig Weatherup explains, "You don't build trust by talking about it. You build it by achieving results, always with integrity and in a manner that shows real personal regard for the people with whom you work."[2] When a leader's character is strong, people trust him, and they trust in his ability to release their potential. That not only gives followers hope for the future, but it also promotes a strong belief in themselves and their organization.

CHARACTER COMMUNICATES RESPECT

When you don't have strength within, you can't earn respect without. And respect is absolutely essential for lasting leadership. How do leaders earn respect? By making sound decisions, admitting their mistakes, and putting what's best for their followers and the organization ahead of their personal agendas.

A leader's good character builds trust among his followers. But when a leader breaks trust, he forfeits his ability to lead. I was again reminded of this while listening to a lesson taught by my friend Bill Hybels. Four times a year, he and I teach a seminar called "Leading and Communicating to Change Lives." Bill was conducting a session titled "Lessons from a Leadership Nightmare," and he shared observations and insights on some of the leadership mistakes made by Robert McNamara and the Johnson administration during the Vietnam War: the administration's inability to prioritize multiple challenges, its acceptance of faulty assumptions, and Johnson's failure to face serious staff conflicts. But in my opinion, the greatest insight Bill shared during that talk concerned the failure of American leaders, including McNamara, to face and publicly admit the terrible mistakes they had made concerning the war in Vietnam. Their actions broke trust with the American people, and the United States has been suffering from the repercussions ever since.

No leader can break trust with his people and expect to keep the same level of influence with them. Trust is the foundation of leadership. Violate your people's trust, and you're through as a leader.

HOW CAN I EFFECTIVELY
CAST VISION?

You can seize only what you can see.

O ne of the great dreamers of the twentieth century was Walt Disney. Any person who could create the first sound cartoon, first all-color cartoon, and first animated feature-length motion picture is definitely someone with vision. But Disney's greatest masterpieces of vision were Disneyland and Walt Disney World. And the spark for that vision came from an unexpected place.

Back when Walt's two daughters were young, he took them to an amusement park in the Los Angeles area on Saturday mornings. His girls loved it, and he did too. An amusement park is a kid's paradise, with wonderful atmosphere.

Walt was especially captivated by the carousel. As he approached it, he saw a blur of bright images racing around to the tune of energetic calliope music. But when he got closer and the carousel stopped, he could see that his eye had been fooled. He observed shabby horses with cracked and chipped paint. And he noticed that only the horses on the outside row moved up and down. The others stood lifeless, bolted to the floor.

The cartoonist's disappointment inspired him with a grand vision. In his mind's eye he could see an amusement park where the illusion didn't evaporate, where children and adults could enjoy a carnival atmosphere without the seedy side that accompanies some circuses or traveling carnivals. His dream became Disneyland. As Larry Taylor stated in *Be an Orange,* Walt's vision could be summarized as, "No chipped paint. All the horses jump."

Look Before You Lead

Vision is everything for a leader. It is utterly indispensable. Why? Because vision leads the leader. It paints the target. It sparks and fuels the fire within, and draws him forward. It is also the fire lighter for others who follow that leader. Show me a leader without vision, and I'll show you someone who isn't going anywhere. At best, he is traveling in circles.

To get a handle on vision and how it comes to be a part of a good leader's life, understand these things:

Vision Starts Within

When I'm teaching at conferences, someone will occasionally ask me to give him a vision for his organization. But I can't do it. You can't buy, beg, or borrow vision. It has to come from the inside. For Disney, vision was never a problem. Because of his creativity and desire for excellence, he always saw what *could* be.

If you lack vision, look inside yourself. Draw on your natural gifts and desires. Look to your calling, if you have one. And if you still don't sense a vision of your own, then consider hooking up with a leader whose vision resonates with you. Become his partner. That's what Walt Disney's brother, Roy, did. He was a good businessman and leader who could make things happen, but Walt provided the vision. Together, they made an incredible team.

Vision Draws on Your History

Vision isn't some mystical quality that comes out of a vacuum, as some people seem to believe. It grows from a leader's past and the history of the people around him. That was the case for Disney. But it's true for all leaders. Talk to any leader, and you're likely to discover key events in his past that were instrumental in the creation of his vision.

VISION MEETS OTHERS' NEEDS

True vision is far-reaching. It goes beyond what one individual can accomplish. And if it has real value, it does more than just *include* others; it *adds value* to them. If you have a vision that doesn't serve others, it's probably too small.

VISION HELPS YOU GATHER RESOURCES

One of the most valuable benefits of vision is that it acts like a magnet—attracting, challenging, and uniting people. It also rallies finances and other resources. The greater the vision, the more winners it has the potential to attract. The more challenging the vision, the harder the participants fight to achieve it. Edwin Land, the founder of Polaroid, advised, "The first thing you do is teach the person to feel that the vision is very important and nearly impossible. That draws out the drive in winners."

FOCUS ON LISTENING

Where does vision come from? To find the vision that is indispensable to leadership, you have to become a good listener. You must listen to several voices.

THE INNER VOICE

As I have already said, vision starts within. Do you know your life's mission? What stirs your heart? What do you dream about? If what you're pursuing doesn't come from a desire within—from the very depths of who you are and what you believe—you will not be able to accomplish it.

THE UNHAPPY VOICE

Where does inspiration for great ideas come from? From noticing what *doesn't* work. Discontent with the *status quo* is a great catalyst for vision. Are you on complacent cruise control? Or do you find yourself itching to change your world? No great leader in history has fought to prevent change.

THE SUCCESSFUL VOICE

Nobody can accomplish great things alone. To fulfill a big vision, you need a good team. But you also need good advice from someone who is ahead of you in the leadership journey. If you want to lead others to greatness, find a mentor. Do you have an adviser who can help you sharpen your vision?

THINK ABOUT WHAT YOU'D LIKE TO SEE CHANGE IN THE WORLD AROUND YOU.

THE HIGHER VOICE

Although it's true that your vision must come from within, you shouldn't let it be confined by your limited capabilities. A truly valuable vision must have God in it. Only He knows your full capabilities. Have you looked beyond yourself, even beyond your own lifetime, as you've sought your vision? If not, you may be missing your true potential and life's best for you.

To improve your vision, do the following:

Measure yourself. If you have previously thought about the vision for your life and articulated it, measure how well you are carrying it out. Talk to several key people, such as your spouse, a close friend, and key employees, asking them to state what they think your vision is. If *they* can articulate it, then *you* are probably living it.

Do a gut check. If you haven't done a lot of work on vision, spend the next several weeks or months thinking about it. Consider what really impacts you at a gut level. *What makes you cry? What makes you dream? What gives you energy?*

Also think about what you'd like to see change in the world around you. What do you see that isn't—but could be? Once your ideas start to become clearer, write them down and talk to a mentor about them.

From 1923 to 1955, Robert Woodruff served as president of Coca-Cola. During that time, he wanted Coca-Cola to be available to every American serviceman around the world for five cents, no matter what it cost the company. What a bold goal! But it was nothing compared to the bigger picture he could see in his mind's eye. In his lifetime, he wanted every person in the *world* to have tasted Coca-Cola. When you look deep into your heart and soul for a vision, what do *you* see?

PART III

THE IMPACT OF
A LEADER

7

WHY IS INFLUENCE IMPORTANT?

The true measure of leadership is influence—
nothing more, nothing less.

I f you don't have influence, you will *never* be able to lead others. So
how do you find and measure influence? Here's a story to answer that
question.

In late summer of 1997, people were jolted by two events that occurred
less than a week apart: the deaths of Princess Diana and Mother Teresa.
On the surface, the two women could not have been more different. One
was a tall, young, glamorous princess from England who circulated in the
highest society. The other, a Nobel Peace Prize recipient, was a small, elderly Catholic nun born in Albania, who served the poorest of the poor in
Calcutta, India.

What's incredible is that their impact was remarkably similar. In a
1996 poll published by the London *Daily Mail,* Princess Diana and
Mother Teresa were voted in first and second places as the world's two
most caring people. That's something that doesn't happen unless you
have a lot of influence. How did someone like Diana come to be
regarded in the same way as Mother Teresa? The answer is that she
demonstrated the power of influence.

DIANA CAPTURED THE WORLD'S IMAGINATION

In 1981, Diana became the most talked-about person on the globe when she married Prince Charles of England. Nearly one billion people watched Diana's wedding ceremony televised from St. Paul's Cathedral. And since that day, it seemed people never could get enough news about her. People were intrigued with Diana, a commoner who had once been a kindergarten teacher. At first she seemed painfully shy and totally overwhelmed by all the attention she and her new husband were receiving. Early in their marriage, some reports stated that Diana wasn't very happy performing the duties expected of her as a royal princess. However, in time she adjusted to her new role. As she started traveling and representing the royal family around the world at various functions, she quickly made it her goal to serve others and raise funds for numerous charitable causes. And during the process, she built many important relationships—with politicians, organizers of humanitarian causes, entertainers, and heads of state.

Diana started rallying people to causes such as medical research for AIDS, care for people with leprosy, and a ban on land mines. She was quite influential in bringing that last issue to the attention of the world's leaders. On a visit to the United States just months before her death, she met with members of the Clinton administration to convince them to support the Oslo conference banning the devices. And a few weeks later, they made changes in their position. Patrick Fuller of the British Red Cross said, "The attention she drew to the issue influenced Clinton. She put the issue on the world agenda, there's no doubt about that."[1]

THE EMERGENCE OF A LEADER

In the beginning, Diana's title had merely given her a platform to address others, but she soon became a person of influence in her own right. In 1996 when she was divorced from Prince Charles, she lost her title, but that loss didn't at all diminish her impact on others. Instead, her influence continued to increase while that of her former husband and in-laws declined—despite their royal titles and position.

Ironically, even in death Diana continued to influence others. When her funeral was broadcast on television and BBC Radio, it was translated into forty-four languages. NBC estimated that the total audience numbered as many as 2.5 billion people—more than twice the number of people who watched her wedding.

TRUE LEADERSHIP CANNOT BE AWARDED, APPOINTED, OR ASSIGNED. IT COMES ONLY FROM INFLUENCE.

Princess Diana has been characterized in many ways. But one word that I've never heard used to describe her is *leader*. Yet that's what she was. Ultimately, she made things happen because she was an influencer, and leadership is influence—nothing more, nothing less.

FIVE MYTHS ABOUT LEADERSHIP

There are plenty of misconceptions and myths that people embrace about leaders and leadership. Here are five common ones:

1. THE MANAGEMENT MYTH

A widespread misunderstanding is that leading and managing are one and the same. Up until a few years ago, books that claimed to be on leadership were often really about management. The main difference between the two is that leadership is about influencing people to follow, while management focuses on maintaining systems and processes. The best way to test whether a person can lead rather than just manage is to ask him to create positive change. Managers can maintain direction, but they can't change it. To move people in a new direction, you need influence.

2. THE ENTREPRENEUR MYTH

Frequently, people assume that all salespeople and entrepreneurs are leaders. But that's not always the case. You may remember the Ronco commercials that appeared on television years ago. They sold items such as the Veg-O-Matic, Pocket Fisherman, and Inside-the-Shell Egg Scrambler. Those products were the brainchildren of an entrepreneur named Ron Popeil. Called the salesman of the century, he has also appeared in numerous infomercials for products such as spray-on relief for baldness and food dehydrating devices.

Popeil is certainly enterprising, innovative, and successful, especially if you measure him by the $300 million in sales his products have earned. But that doesn't make him a leader. People may be buying what he has to sell, but they're not following him. At best, he is able to persuade people for a moment, but he holds no long-term influence with them.

3. THE KNOWLEDGE MYTH

Sir Francis Bacon said, "Knowledge is power." Most people, believing power is the essence of leadership, naturally assume that those who possess knowledge and intelligence are leaders. But that isn't automatically true. You can visit any major university and meet brilliant research scientists and philosophers whose ability to think is so high that it's off the charts, but whose ability to lead is so low that it doesn't even register on the charts. IQ doesn't necessarily equate to leadership.

4. THE PIONEER MYTH

Another misconception is that anyone who is out in front of the crowd is a leader. But being first isn't always the same as leading. For example, Sir Edmund Hillary was the first man to reach the summit of Mount Everest. Since his historic ascent in 1953, many people have "followed" him in achieving that feat. But that doesn't make Hillary a leader. He wasn't even the leader on that particular expedition. John Hunt was. And when Hillary traveled to the South Pole in 1958 as part of the Commonwealth Trans-Antarctic Expedition, he was accompanying another leader, Sir Vivian Fuchs. To be a leader, a person has to not only be out front, but also have people intentionally coming behind him, following his lead, and acting on his vision.

5. THE POSITION MYTH

The greatest misunderstanding about leadership is that people think it is based on position, but it's not. Stanley Huffty affirmed, "It's not the position that makes the leader; it's the leader that makes the position."

Look at what happened several years ago at Cordiant, the advertising agency formerly known as Saatchi & Saatchi. In 1994, institutional investors at Saatchi & Saatchi forced the board of directors to dismiss Maurice Saatchi, the company's CEO. What was the result? Several executives followed him out. So did many of the company's largest accounts, including British Airways and Mars, the candy maker. Saatchi's influence was so great that his departure caused the company's stock to fall immediately from $8⅝ to $4 per share.[2] Saatchi lost his title and position, but he continued to be the leader.

WHO'S THE REAL LEADER?

I personally learned the significance of influence when I accepted my first job out of college at a small church in rural Indiana. I went in with all the right credentials. I was hired as the senior pastor, which meant that I possessed the position and title of leader in that organization. I had the proper college degree. I had even been ordained. In addition, I had been trained by my father who was an excellent pastor and a very high-profile leader in the denomination. It made for a good-looking résumé—but it didn't make me a leader. At my first board meeting, I quickly found out who was the real leader of that church. By the time I took my next position three years later, I had learned the importance of influence. I recognized that hard work was required to gain influence in any organization and to earn the right to become the leader.

LEADERSHIP WITHOUT LEVERAGE

I admire and respect the leadership of my good friend Bill Hybels, the senior pastor of Willow Creek Community Church in South Barrington, Illinois, the largest church in North America. Bill says he believes that the church is the most leadership-intensive enterprise in society. A lot of businesspeople I know are surprised when they hear that statement, but I think Bill is right. What is the basis of his belief? Positional leadership doesn't work in volunteer organizations. If a leader doesn't have leverage—or influence—then he is ineffective. In other organizations, the person who has position has incredible leverage. In the military, leaders can use rank and, if all else fails, throw people into the brig. In business, bosses have tremendous leverage in the form of salary, benefits, and perks. Most followers are pretty cooperative when their livelihood is at stake.

FOLLOWERS IN VOLUNTARY ORGANIZATIONS
CANNOT BE FORCED TO GET ON BOARD.
IF THE LEADER HAS NO INFLUENCE WITH
THEM, THEN THEY WON'T FOLLOW.

But in voluntary organizations, such as churches, the only thing that works is leadership in its purest form. Leaders have only their influence to aid them. And as Harry A. Overstreet observed, "The very essence of all power to influence lies in getting the other person to participate." Followers in voluntary organizations cannot be forced to get on board. If the leader has no influence with them, then they won't follow. If you are a businessperson and you really want to find out whether your people are capable of leading, send them out to volunteer their time in the community. If they can get people to follow them while they're serving at the Red Cross, a United Way shelter, or their local church, then you know that they really do have influence—and leadership ability.

Here is my favorite leadership proverb: "He who thinks he leads, but has no followers, is only taking a walk." If you can't influence others, they won't follow you. And if they won't follow, you're not a leader. No matter what anybody else tells you, remember that leadership is influence—nothing more, nothing less.

8

How Does Influence Work?

Real leadership is being the person others
will gladly and confidently follow.

Sociologists tell us that even the most introverted individual influences ten thousand other people during his or her lifetime! This amazing statistic was shared with me by my associate Tim Elmore. Tim and I concluded that each one of us is both influencing and being influenced by others.

Influence Can Be Developed

The prominent leader of any group is quite easily discovered. Just observe the people as they gather. If an issue is to be decided, who is the person whose opinion seems most valuable? Who is the one with whom people quickly agree? Most importantly, who is the one the others follow?

Robert Dilenschneider, the CEO of Hill and Knowlton, a worldwide public relations agency, is one of the nation's major influence brokers. He skillfully weaves his persuasive magic in the global arena where governments and megacorporations meet. He wrote a book entitled *Power and Influence*, in which he shares the idea of the "power triangle" to help leaders get ahead. He says, "The three components of this triangle are communication, recognition, and influence. You start to communicate effectively. This leads to recognition and recognition in turn leads to influence."[1]

THE LEVELS OF LEADERSHIP

We can increase our influence and leadership potential if we understand the following levels of leadership:

LEVEL 1: POSITION—PEOPLE FOLLOW BECAUSE THEY HAVE TO

This is the basic entry level of leadership. The only influence you have is that which comes with a title. People who stay at this level get into territorial rights, protocol, tradition, and organizational charts. These things are not negative unless they become the basis for authority and influence, but they are poor substitutes for leadership skills.

A person may be "in control" because he has been appointed to a position. In that position he may have authority. But real leadership is more than having authority; it is more than having the technical training and following the proper procedures. Real leadership is being the person others will gladly and confidently follow. A real leader knows the difference between being the boss and being a leader.

- The boss drives his workers; the leader coaches them.
- The boss depends upon authority; the leader on goodwill.
- The boss inspires fear; the leader inspires enthusiasm.
- The boss says "I"; the leader, "we."
- The boss fixes the blame for the breakdown; the leader fixes the breakdown.

Characteristics of a "Positional Leader"

Security is based on title, not talent. The story is told of a private in World War I who shouted on the battlefield, "Put out that match!" only to find to his chagrin that the offender was General "Black Jack" Pershing. When the private, who feared severe punishment, tried to stammer out his apology, General Pershing patted him on the back and said, "That's all right, son. Just be glad I'm not a second lieutenant." The point should be clear. The higher the person's level of true ability and the resulting influence, the more secure and confident he becomes.

This level is often gained by appointment. All other levels are gained by ability. Leo Durocher was coaching at first base in an exhibition game the Giants were playing at West Point. One noisy cadet kept shouting at Leo and doing his best to upset him.

"Hey, Durocher," he hollered. "How did a little squirt like you get into the major leagues?"

Leo shouted back, "My congressman appointed me!"[2]

People will not follow a positional leader beyond his stated authority. They will only do what they have to do when they are required to do it. Low morale is always present. When the leader lacks confidence, the followers lack commitment. They are like the little boy who was asked by Billy Graham how to find the nearest post office. When the lad told him, Dr. Graham thanked him and said, "If you'll come to the convention center this evening you can hear me telling everyone how to get to heaven."

"I don't think I'll be there," the boy replied. "You don't even know your way to the post office."

Positional leaders have more difficulty working with volunteers, white collar workers, and younger people. Volunteers don't have to work in the organization, so there is no monetary leverage that a positional leader can use to make them respond. White collar workers are used to participating in decision-making and resent dictatorial leadership. Baby boomers in particular are unimpressed with symbols of authority.

The following characteristics must be exhibited with excellence on this level before you can advance to the next level.

Level 1: Position/Rights
- Know your job description thoroughly.

- Be aware of the history of the organization.
- Relate the organization's history to the people of the organization (in other words, be a team player).
- Accept responsibility.
- Do your job with consistent excellence.
- Do more than expected.
- Offer creative ideas for change and improvement.

LEVEL 2: PERMISSION—PEOPLE FOLLOW BECAUSE THEY WANT TO

Fred Smith says, "Leadership is getting people to work for you when they are not obligated."[3] That will only happen when you climb to the second level of influence. People don't care how much you know until they know how much you care. Leadership begins with the heart, not the head. It flourishes with a meaningful relationship, not more regulations.

A person on the "permission" level will lead by interrelationships. The agenda is not the pecking order but people development. On this level, the leader donates time, energy, and focus on the follower's needs and desires. A wonderful illustration of why it's so critical to put people and their needs first is found in the story of Henry Ford in Amitai Etzioni's book, *Modern Organizations*: "He made a perfect car, the Model T, that ended the need for any other car. He was totally product-oriented. He wanted to fill the world with Model T cars. But when people started coming to him and saying, 'Mr. Ford, we'd like a different color car,' he remarked, 'You can have any color you want as long as it's black.' And that's when the decline started."

People who are unable to build solid, lasting relationships will soon discover that they are unable to sustain long, effective leadership. Needless to say, you can love people without leading them, but you cannot lead people without loving them.

Caution! Don't try to skip a level. The most often skipped level is 2, *Permission*. For example, a husband goes from level 1, *Position*, a wedding day title, to level 3, *Production*. He becomes a great provider for the family, but in the process he neglects the essential relationships that hold a family together. The family disintegrates and so does the husband's business. Relationships involve a process that provides the glue and much of the staying power for long-term, consistent production.

The following characteristics must be mastered on this level before you can advance to the next one.

Level 2: Permission/Relationship
- Possess a genuine love for people.
- Make those who work with you more successful.
- See through other people's eyes.
- Love people more than procedures.
- Do "win-win" or don't do it.
- Include others in your journey.
- Deal wisely with difficult people.

LEVEL 3: PRODUCTION—PEOPLE FOLLOW BECAUSE OF WHAT YOU HAVE DONE FOR THE ORGANIZATION

On this level things begin to happen, good things. Profit increases. Morale is high. Turnover is low. Needs are being met. Goals are being realized. Accompanying the growth is the "big mo"—momentum. Leading and influencing others is fun. Problems are solved with minimum effort. Fresh statistics are shared on a regular basis with the people who undergird the growth of the organization. Everyone is results-oriented. In fact, results are the main reason for the activity.

This is a major difference between levels 2 and 3. On the "relationship" level, people get together just to get together. There is no other objective. On the "results" level, people come together to accomplish a purpose. They like to get together to get together, but they love to get together to accomplish something. In other words, they are results-oriented.

The following characteristics must be mastered with excellence before you can advance to the next level.

Level 3: Production/Results
- Initiate and accept responsibility for growth.
- Develop and follow a statement of purpose.
- Make your job description and energy an integral part of the statement of purpose.
- Develop accountability for results, beginning with yourself.
- Know and do the things that give a high return.
- Communicate the strategy and vision of the organization.
- Become a change-agent and understand timing.
- Make the difficult decisions that will make a difference.

LEVEL 4: PEOPLE DEVELOPMENT—PEOPLE FOLLOW BECAUSE OF WHAT YOU HAVE DONE FOR THEM

A leader is great, not because of his or her power, but because of his or her ability to empower others. Success without a successor is failure. A worker's main responsibility is doing the work himself. A leader's responsibility is developing others to do the work. The true leader can be recognized because somehow his people consistently demonstrate superior performances.

Loyalty to the leader reaches its highest peak when the follower has personally grown through the mentorship of the leader. Note the progression: At level 2, the follower loves the leader; at level 3, the follower admires the leader; at level 4, the follower is loyal to the leader. Why? You win people's hearts by helping them grow personally.

The core of leaders who surround you should all be people you have personally touched or helped to develop in some way. When that happens, love and loyalty will be exhibited by those closest to you and by those who are touched by your key leaders.

There is, however, a potential problem of moving up the levels of influence as a leader and becoming comfortable with the group of people you have developed around you. Many new people may view you as a "position" leader because you have had no contact with them. These two suggestions will help you become a people developer:

1. Walk slowly through the crowd. Have some way of keeping in touch with everyone.

2. Develop key leaders. I systematically meet with and teach those who are influencers within the organization. They in turn pass on to others what I have given them.

The characteristics that must be mastered at this level are listed below.

Level 4: People Development/Reproduction
- Realize that people are your most valuable asset.
- Place a priority on developing people.
- Be a model for others to follow.
- Pour your leadership efforts into the top 20 percent of your people.
- Expose key leaders to growth opportunities.
- Attract other winners/producers to the common goal.
- Surround yourself with an inner core that complements your leadership.

LEVEL 5: PERSONHOOD—PEOPLE FOLLOW BECAUSE OF WHO YOU ARE AND WHAT YOU REPRESENT

Most of us have not yet arrived at this level. Only a lifetime of proven leadership will allow us to sit at level 5 and reap the rewards that are eternally satisfying. I do know this—some day I want to sit atop this level. It's achievable.

The following characteristics define the Level 5 leader.

Level 5: Personhood/Respect
- Your followers are loyal and sacrificial.
- You have spent years mentoring and molding leaders.
- You have become a statesman/consultant, and are sought out by others.
- Your greatest joy comes from watching others grow and develop.
- You transcend the organization.

CLIMBING THE STEPS OF LEADERSHIP

Here are some additional insights on the leadership-levels process:

THE HIGHER YOU GO, THE LONGER IT TAKES.

Each time there is a change in your job or you join a new circle of friends, you start on the lowest level and begin to work yourself up the steps.

THE HIGHER YOU GO, THE HIGHER THE LEVEL OF COMMITMENT.

This increase in commitment is a two-way street. Greater commitment is demanded not only from you, but from the other individuals involved. When either the leader or the follower is unwilling to make the sacrifices a new level demands, influence will begin to decrease.

THE HIGHER YOU GO, THE EASIER IT IS TO LEAD.

Notice the progression from level two through level four. The focus goes from liking you, to liking what you do for the common interest of all concerned to liking what you do for them personally. Each level climbed by the leader and the followers adds another reason why people will want to follow.

THE HIGHER YOU GO, THE GREATER THE GROWTH.

Growth can only occur when effective change takes place. Change will become easier as you climb the levels of leadership. As you rise, other people will allow and even assist you in making the needed changes.

YOU NEVER LEAVE THE BASE LEVEL.

Each level stands upon the previous one and will crumble if the lower level is neglected. For example, if you move from a permission (relationships) level to a production (results) level and stop caring for the people who are following you and helping you produce, they might begin to develop a feeling of being used. As you move up in the levels, the deeper and more solid your leadership will be with a person or group of people.

IF YOU ARE LEADING A GROUP OF PEOPLE, YOU WILL
NOT BE ON THE SAME LEVEL WITH EVERYONE.

Not every person will respond the same way to your leadership.

FOR YOUR LEADERSHIP TO REMAIN EFFECTIVE, IT IS ESSENTIAL
THAT YOU TAKE THE OTHER INFLUENCERS WITHIN THE
GROUP WITH YOU TO THE HIGHER LEVELS.

The collective influence of you and the other leaders will bring the rest along. If this does not happen, divided interest and loyalty will occur within the group.

YOU MUST KNOW WHAT LEVEL YOU ARE ON
AT THIS MOMENT.

Since you will be on different levels with different people, you need to know which people are on which level. If the biggest influencers within the organization are on the highest levels and are supportive of you, then your success in leading others will be attainable. If the best influencers are on the highest levels and not supportive, then problems will soon arise.

Everyone is a leader because everyone influences someone. Not everyone will become a great leader, but everyone can become a better leader. Are you willing to unleash your leadership potential? Will you use your leadership skills to better mankind?

My Influence

> My life shall touch a dozen lives
> Before this day is done.
> Leave countless marks of good or ill,
> E'er sets the evening sun.

> This, the wish I always wish,
> The prayer I always pray:
> Lord, may my life help other lives
> It touches by the way.[4]

9

HOW CAN I EXTEND MY INFLUENCE?

The act of empowering others changes lives.

An English artist named William Wolcott went to New York in 1924 to record his impressions of that fascinating city. One morning he was visiting in the office of a former colleague when the urge to sketch came over him. Seeing some paper on his friend's desk, he asked, "May I have that?"

His friend answered, "That's not sketching paper. That's ordinary wrapping paper."

Not wanting to lose that spark of inspiration, Wolcott took the wrapping paper and said, "Nothing is ordinary if you know how to use it." On that ordinary paper Wolcott made two sketches. Later that same year, one of those same sketches sold for $500 and the other for $1,000, quite a sum for 1924.

People under the influence of an empowering person are like paper in the hands of a talented artist. No matter what they're made of, they can become treasures.

The ability to empower others is one of the keys to personal and professional success. John Craig remarked, "No matter how much work you can do, no matter how engaging your personality may be, you will not advance far in business if you cannot work through others." And business executive J. Paul Getty asserted, "It doesn't make much difference how much other knowledge or experience an executive possesses; if he is unable to achieve results through people, he is worthless as an executive."

PEOPLE UNDER THE INFLUENCE OF AN EMPOWERING PERSON ARE LIKE PAPER IN THE HANDS OF A TALENTED ARTIST.

When you become an empowerer, you work with and through people, but you do much more. You enable others to reach the highest levels in their personal and professional development. Simply defined, empowering is giving your influence to others for the purpose of personal and organizational growth. It's sharing yourself—your influence, position, power, and opportunities—with others for the purpose of investing in their lives so that they can function at their best. It's seeing people's potential, sharing your resources with them, and showing them that you believe in them completely.

You may already be empowering some people in your life without knowing it. When you entrust your spouse with an important decision and then cheerfully back him up, that's empowering. When you decide that your child is ready to cross the street by herself and give her your permission to do so, you have empowered her. When you delegate a challenging job to an employee and give her the authority she needs to get it done, you have empowered her.

The act of empowering others changes lives, and it's a win-win situation for you and the people you empower. Giving others your authority isn't like giving away an object, such as your car, for example. If you give away your car, you're stuck. You no longer have transportation. But empowering others by giving them your authority has the same effect as sharing information:

You haven't lost anything. You have increased the ability of others without decreasing yourself.

Qualifications of an Empowerer

Just about everyone has the potential to become an empowerer, but you cannot empower everyone. The process works only when certain conditions are met. You must have:

Position

You cannot empower people whom you don't lead. Leadership expert Fred Smith explained, "Who can give permission for another person to succeed? A person in authority. Others can encourage, but permission comes only from an authority figure: a parent, boss, or pastor."

Relationship

It has been said that relationships are forged, not formed. They require time and common experience. If you have made the effort to connect with people, then by the time you're ready to empower them, your relationship should be solid enough for you to be able to lead them. And as you do, remember what Ralph Waldo Emerson wrote: "Every man [or woman] is entitled to be valued by his [or her] best moments." When you value people and your relationships with them, you lay the foundation for empowering others.

Respect

Relationships cause people to want to be with you, but respect causes them to want to be empowered by you. Mutual respect is essential to the empowerment process. Psychiatrist Ari Kiev summed it up this way: "Everyone wants to feel that he counts for something and is important to someone. Invariably, people will give their love, respect, and attention to the person who fills that need." When you believe in people, care about them, and trust them, they know it. And that respect inspires them to want to follow where you lead.

Commitment

The last quality a leader needs to become an empowerer is commitment. US Air executive Ed McElroy stressed that "commitment gives us new power. No matter what comes to us—sickness, poverty, or disaster, we never turn our eye from the goal." The process of empowering others isn't always easy, especially when you start doing it for the first time. It's a road that has many bumps and sidetracks. But it is one that's worth traveling because the rewards are so great. Remember: when you empower people, you're not influencing just them; you're influencing all the people they influence. That's impact!

The Right Attitude

One more crucial element of empowering needs to be in place if you want to become a successful leader: you need to have the right attitude.

Many people neglect to empower others because they are insecure. They are afraid of losing their jobs to the people they mentor. They don't want to be replaced or displaced, even if it means that they would be able to move up to a higher position and leave their current one to be filled by the person they mentor. They're afraid of change. But change is part of empowerment—for the people you empower and for yourself. If you want to go up, there are things you have to be willing to give up.

WHEN IT COMES DOWN TO IT, EMPOWERING LEADERSHIP IS SOMETIMES THE ONLY REAL ADVANTAGE ONE ORGANIZATION HAS OVER ANOTHER IN OUR COMPETITIVE SOCIETY.

If you're not sure about where you stand in terms of your attitude toward the changes involved with empowering others, answer these questions:

QUESTIONS TO ASK BEFORE YOU GET STARTED

1. Do I believe in people and feel that they are my organization's most appreciable asset?
2. Do I believe that empowering others can accomplish more than individual achievement?
3. Do I actively search for potential leaders to empower?
4. Would I be willing to raise others to a level higher than my own level of leadership?
5. Would I be willing to invest time developing people who have leadership potential?
6. Would I be willing to let others get credit for what I taught them?
7. Do I allow others freedom of personality and process, or do I have to be in control?
8. Would I be willing to publicly give my authority and influence to potential leaders?
9. Would I be willing to let others work me out of a job?
10. Would I be willing to hand the leadership baton to the people I empower and truly root for them?

If you answer no to more than a couple of these questions, you may need an attitude adjustment. You need to believe in others enough to give them all you can and in yourself enough to know that it won't hurt you. Just remember that as long as you continue to grow and develop yourself, you'll always have something to give, and you won't need to worry about being displaced.

HOW TO EMPOWER OTHERS TO THEIR POTENTIAL

Once you have confidence in yourself and in the persons you wish to empower, you're ready to start the process. Your goal should be to hand over relatively small, simple tasks in the beginning and progressively increase their responsibilities and authority. The greener the people you're working with, the more time the process will take. But no matter whether they are raw recruits or seasoned veterans, it's still important to take them through the whole process. Use the following steps to guide you as you empower others:

1. EVALUATE THEM

The place to start when empowering people is to evaluate them. If you give inexperienced people too much authority too soon, you can set them up to fail. If you move too slowly with people who have lots of experience, you can frustrate and demoralize them.

Remember that all people have the potential to succeed. Your job is to see the potential, find out what they lack to develop it, and equip them with what they need. As you evaluate the people you intend to empower, look at these areas:

Knowledge. Think about what people need to know in order to do any task you intend to give them. Don't take for granted that they know all that you know. Ask them questions. Give them history or background information. Cast a vision by giving them the big picture of how their actions fit into the organization's mission and goals. Knowledge is not only power; it's empowering.

Skill. Examine the skill level of the people you desire to empower. Nothing is more frustrating than being asked to do things for which you have no ability. Your job as the empowerer is to find out what the job requires and make sure your people have what they need to succeed.

Desire. Greek philosopher Plutarch remarked, "The richest soil, if uncultivated, produces the rankest weeds." No amount of skill, knowledge, or potential can help people succeed if they don't have the desire to be successful. But when desire is present, empowerment is easy. As seventeenth-century French essayist Jean La Fontaine wrote, "Man is made so that whenever anything fires his soul, impossibilities vanish."

2. Model for Them

Even people with knowledge, skill, and desire need to know what's expected of them, and the best way to inform them is to show them. People do what people see.

The people you desire to empower need to see what it looks like to fly. As their mentor, you have the best opportunity to show them. Model the attitude and work ethic you would like them to embrace. And anytime you can include them in your work, take them along with you. There is no better way to help them learn and understand what you want them to do.

3. Give Them Permission to Succeed

As a leader and influencer, you may believe that everyone wants to be successful and automatically strives for success, probably as you have. But not everyone you influence will think the same way you do. You have to help others believe that they can succeed and show them that you want them to succeed. How do you do that?

Expect it. Author and professional speaker Danny Cox advised, "The important thing to remember is that if you don't have that inspired enthusiasm that is contagious—whatever you do have is also contagious." People can sense your underlying attitude no matter what you say or do. If you have an expectation for your people to be successful, they will know it.

Verbalize it. People need to hear you tell them that you believe in them and want them to succeed. Tell them often that you know they are going to make it. Send them encouraging notes. Become a positive prophet of their success. And reinforce your thoughts as often as you can.

Once people recognize and understand that you genuinely want to see them succeed and are committed to helping them, they will begin to believe they can accomplish what you give them to do.

4. Transfer Authority to Them

Many people are willing to give others responsibility. They gladly delegate tasks to them. But empowering others is more than sharing your workload. It's sharing your power and ability to get things done.

Management expert Peter Drucker asserted, "No executive has ever suffered because his subordinates were strong and effective." People become strong and effective only when they are given the opportunity to make decisions, initiate actions, solve problems, and meet challenges. When it comes down to it, empowering leadership is sometimes the only real advantage one organization has over another in our competitive society.

5. PUBLICLY SHOW YOUR CONFIDENCE IN THEM

When you first transfer authority to the people you empower, you need to tell them that you believe in them, and you need to do it publicly. Public recognition lets them know that you believe they will succeed. But it also lets the other people they're working with know that they have your support and that your authority backs them up. It's a tangible way of sharing (and spreading) your influence.

As you raise up leaders, show them and their followers that they have your confidence and authority. And you will find that they quickly become empowered to succeed.

6. SUPPLY THEM WITH FEEDBACK

Although you need to publicly praise your people, you can't let them go very long without giving them honest, positive feedback. Meet with them privately to coach them through their mistakes, miscues, and misjudgments. At first, some people may have a difficult time. During that early period, be a grace giver. Try to give them what they need, not what they deserve. And applaud any progress that they make. People do what gets praised.

7. RELEASE THEM TO CONTINUE ON THEIR OWN

No matter who you are working to empower—your employees, children, colleagues, or spouse—your ultimate aim should be to release them to make good decisions and succeed on their own. And that means giving them as much freedom as possible as soon as they are ready for it.

President Abraham Lincoln was a master at empowering his leaders. For example, when he appointed General Ulysses S. Grant as commander of the Union armies in 1864, he sent him this message: "I neither ask nor desire to know anything of your plans. Take the responsibility and act, and call on me for assistance."

That's the attitude you need as an empowerer. Give authority and responsibility, and offer assistance as needed. The person who has been the most empowering in my life is my father, Melvin Maxwell. He always encouraged me to be the best person I could be, and he gave me his permission and his power whenever he could. Years later when we talked about it, my father told me his philosophy: "I never consciously limited you as long as I knew what you were doing was morally right." Now that's an empowering attitude!

THE RESULTS OF EMPOWERMENT

If you head up any kind of organization—a business, club, church, or family—learning to empower others is one of the most important things you'll ever do as its leader. Empowerment has an incredibly high return. It not only helps the individuals you raise up by making them more confident, energetic, and productive, but it also has the ability to improve your life, give you additional freedom, and promote the growth and health of your organization.

As you empower others, you will find that most aspects of your life will change for the better. Empowering others can free you personally to have more time for the important things in your life, increase the effectiveness of your organization, increase your influence with others and, best of all, make an incredibly positive impact on the lives of the people you empower.

10

How Can I Make My
Leadership Last?

A leader's lasting value is measured by succession.

In 1997, one of the finest business leaders in the world died. His name was Roberto Goizueta, and he was the chairman and chief executive of the Coca-Cola Company. In a speech he gave to the Executives' Club of Chicago a few months before he died, Goizueta made this statement: "A billion hours ago, human life appeared on Earth. A billion minutes ago, Christianity emerged. A billion seconds ago, the Beatles performed on 'The Ed Sullivan Show.' A billion Coca-Colas ago . . . was yesterday morning. And the question we are asking ourselves now is, 'What must we do to make a billion Coca-Colas ago this morning?'"

Making Coca-Cola the best company in the world was Goizueta's lifelong quest, one he was still pursuing diligently when he suddenly, unexpectedly died. Companies that lose a CEO often go into turmoil, especially if his departure is unexpected, as Goizueta's was. Shortly before his death, Goizueta said in an interview with the *Atlanta Journal-Constitution* that retirement was "not on my radar screen. As long as I'm having the fun I'm having, as long as I have the energy necessary, as long as I'm not keeping people from their day in the sun, and as long as the board wants me to stay on, I will stay on." Just months after the interview, he was diagnosed with cancer. Six weeks later, he died.

Upon Goizueta's death, former president Jimmy Carter observed, "Perhaps no other corporate leader in modern times has so beautifully exemplified the American dream. He believed that in America, all things are possible. He lived that dream. And because of his extraordinary leadership skills, he helped thousands of others realize their dreams as well."

Goizueta's Legacy

The legacy left to the company by Goizueta is incredible. When he took over Coca-Cola in 1981, the company's value was $4 billion. Under Goizueta's leadership, it rose to $150 billion. That's an increase in value of more than 3,500 percent! Coca-Cola became the second most valuable corporation in America, ahead of the car makers, the oil companies, Microsoft, Wal-Mart, and all the rest. The only company more valuable was General Electric. Many of Coke's stockholders became millionaires many times over. Emory University in Atlanta, whose portfolio contains a large block of Coca-Cola stock, now has an endowment comparable to that of Harvard.

But high stock value wasn't the most significant thing Goizueta gave to the Coca-Cola company. Instead it was the way he left a legacy. When the CEO's death was announced, there was no panic among Coca-Cola stockholders. Paine Webber analyst Emanuel Goldman said that Goizueta "prepared the company for his not being there as well as any executive I've ever seen."

How did he do it? First, by making the company as strong as he possibly could. Second, by preparing a successor for the top position named Douglas Ivester. Mickey H. Gramig, writer for the *Atlanta Constitution*, reported, "Unlike some companies, which face a crisis when the top executive leaves or dies, Coca-Cola is expected to retain its status as one of the world's most admired corporations. Goizueta had groomed Ivester to follow his footsteps since the Georgia native's 1994 appointment to the company's No. 2 post. And as an indication of how strongly Wall Street felt about Coca-Cola's footings, the company's stock barely rippled six weeks ago when Goizueta was diagnosed with lung cancer."[1]

Doug Ivester, an accountant by training, started his career with Coca-Cola in 1979 as the assistant controller. Four years later, he was named chief financial officer. He was known for his exceptional financial creativity, and he was a major force in Goizueta's ability to revolutionize the company's approach to investment and the handling of debt. By 1989, Goizueta must have decided that Ivester had untapped potential, because he moved him out of his strictly financial role and sent him to Europe to obtain operating and international experience. A year later, Goizueta brought him back and named him president of Coca-Cola USA, where he oversaw expenditures and marketing. From there he continued to groom Ivester, and in 1994, there could be no doubt that Ivester would follow Goizueta into the top position. Goizueta made him president and chief operating officer.

What Roberto Goizueta did was very unusual. Few chief executives of companies today develop strong leaders and groom them to take over the organization. John S. Wood, a consultant at Egon Zehnder International Inc., has noted that "companies have not in the recent past been investing as heavily in bringing people up. If they're not able to grow them, they have to go get them." So why was Roberto Goizueta different? He knew the positive effect of mentoring firsthand.

Roberto Goizueta was born in Cuba and educated at Yale, where he earned a degree in chemical engineering. When he returned to Havana in 1954, he answered a newspaper ad for a bilingual chemist. The company hiring turned out to be Coca-Cola. By 1966, he had become vice president of technical research and development at the company's headquarters in Atlanta. He was the youngest man ever to hold such a position in the company. But in the early 1970s, something even more important happened. Robert W. Woodruff, the patriarch of Coca-Cola, took

Goizueta under his wing and began developing him. In 1975, Goizueta became the executive vice president of the company's technical division and took on other corporate responsibilities, such as overseeing legal affairs. And in 1980, with Woodruff's blessing, Goizueta became president and chief operating officer. One year later he was the chairman and chief executive. The reason Goizueta so confidently selected, developed, and groomed a successor in the 1990s is that he was building on the legacy that he had received in the 1970s.

LEADERS WHO LEAVE A LEGACY OF SUCCESSION . . .

Leaders who leave a legacy of succession for their organization do the following:

LEAD THE ORGANIZATION WITH A "LONG VIEW"

Just about anybody can make an organization look good for a moment—by launching a flashy new program or product, drawing crowds to a big event, or slashing the budget to boost the bottom line. But leaders who leave a legacy take a different approach. They lead with tomorrow as well as today in mind. That's what Goizueta did. He planned to keep leading as long as he was effective, yet he prepared his successor anyway. He always looked out for the best interests of the organization and its stockholders.

CREATE A LEADERSHIP CULTURE

The most stable companies have strong leaders at every level of the organization. The only way to develop such widespread leadership is to make developing leaders a part of your culture. That is a strong part of Coca-Cola's legacy. How many other successful companies do you know about that have had a succession of leaders come up within the ranks of their own organization?

PAY THE PRICE TODAY TO ASSURE SUCCESS TOMORROW

There is no success without sacrifice. Each organization is unique, and that dictates what the price will be. But any leader who wants to help his organization must be willing to pay that price to ensure lasting success.

VALUE TEAM LEADERSHIP ABOVE INDIVIDUAL LEADERSHIP

No matter how good he is, no leader can do it all alone. Just as in sports a coach needs a team of good players to win, an organization needs a team of good *leaders* to succeed. The larger the organization, the stronger, larger, and deeper the team of leaders needs to be.

WALK AWAY FROM THE ORGANIZATION WITH INTEGRITY

In the case of Coca-Cola, the leader didn't get the opportunity to walk away because he died an untimely death. But if he had lived, I believe Goizueta would have done just that. When it's a leader's time to leave the organization, he has got to be willing to walk away and let his successor do his own thing. Meddling only hurts him and the organization.

FEW LEADERS PASS IT ON

Max Dupree, author of *Leadership Is an Art,* declared, "Succession is one of the key responsibilities of leadership." Yet of all the characteristics of leadership, legacy is the one that the fewest leaders seem to learn. Achievement comes to someone when he is able to do great things for himself. Success comes when he empowers followers to do great things *with* him. Significance comes when he develops leaders to do great things *for* him. But a legacy is created only when a person puts his organization into the position to do great things *without* him.

I learned the importance of legacy the hard way. Because the church grew so much while I was in my first leadership position in Hillham, Indiana, I thought I was a success. When I began there, we had only three people in attendance. For three years, I built up that church, reached out to the community, and influenced many people's lives. When I left, our average attendance was in the high two hundreds, and our record was more than three hundred people. I had programs in place, and everything looked rosy to me. I thought I had really done something significant.

Eighteen months after I had moved to my second church, I had lunch with a friend I hadn't seen in a while, and he had just spent some time in Hillham. I asked him about how things were going back there, and I was surprised to hear his answer.

"Not too good," he answered.

"Really?" I said. "Why? Things were going great when I left. What's wrong?"

"Well," he said, "it's kind of fallen off. Some of the programs you got started kind of petered out. The church is running only about a hundred people. It might get even smaller before it's all over."

That really bothered me. A leader hates to see something that he put his sweat, blood, and tears into starting to fail. At first, I got ticked off at the leader who followed me. But then it hit me. If I had done a really good job there, it wouldn't matter what kind of leader followed me, good or bad. The fault was really mine. I hadn't set up the organization to succeed after I left. It was the first time I realized the significance of legacy.

PARADIGM SHIFT

After that, I started to look at leadership in a whole new way. Every leader eventually leaves his organization—one way or another. He may change jobs, get promoted, or retire. And even if a person refuses to retire, he is going to die. That made me realize that part of my job as a leader was to start preparing my people and organization for what inevitably lies ahead. That prompted me to change my focus from leading followers to developing leaders. My lasting value, like that of any leader, would be measured by my ability to give the organization a smooth succession.

My best personal succession story concerns my departure from Skyline Church. When I first arrived there in 1981, I made one of my primary goals the identification and development of leaders because I knew that our success depended on it. Over the fourteen years I was there, my staff and I developed literally hundreds of outstanding leaders, both volunteers and staff.

One of my greatest joys in life is knowing that Skyline is stronger now than when I left in 1995. Jim Garlow, who succeeded me as the senior pastor, is doing a wonderful job there. In the fall of 1997, Jim asked me to come back to Skyline and speak at a fund-raising banquet for the next phase of the building project, and I was delighted to honor his request.

About 4,100 people attended the event at the San Diego Convention Center, located on the city's beautiful bay. My wife, Margaret, and I really enjoyed the chance to see and talk with so many of our old friends. And of course, I felt privileged to be the evening's keynote speaker. It was quite a celebration—and quite a success. People pledged more than $7.8 million toward the building of the church's new facility.

As soon as I finished speaking, Margaret and I slipped out of the ballroom. We wanted the night to belong to Jim, since he was now the leader of Skyline. Because of that, we knew it would be best if we made a quick exit before the program was over. Descending the stairs, I grabbed her hand and gave it a squeeze. It was wonderful to know that what we started all those years ago was still going on. It's like my friend Chris Musgrove says, "Success is not measured by what you're leaving to, but by what you are leaving behind."

When all is said and done, your ability as a leader will not be judged by what you achieved personally or even by what your team accomplished during your tenure. You will be judged by how well your people and your organization did after you were gone. Your lasting value will be measured by succession.

RELATIONSHIPS

101

WHAT EVERY LEADER NEEDS TO KNOW

Published in Nashville, Tennessee, by Thomas Nelson.
Thomas Nelson is a registered trademark of Thomas Nelson, Inc.

Published in association with Yates & Yates, www.yates2.com

Scripture quotations noted NIV are from the HOLY BIBLE: NEW INTERNATIONAL VERSION®. © 1973, 1978, 1984 by International Bible Society. Used by permission of Zondervan Publishing House. All rights reserved.

Portions of this book were previously published in *Becoming a Person of Influence, The 17 Essential Qualities of a Team Player, The 21 Irrefutable Laws of Leadership, The 21 Indispensable Qualities of a Leader,* and *Your Road Map for Success.*

Library of Congress Cataloging-in-Publication Data
Maxwell, John C., 1947–
Relationships 101 : what every leader needs to know / John C. Maxwell.
p. cm.
"Portions of this book were previously published in *Becoming a person of influence, The 17 essential qualities of a team player, The 21 irrefutable laws of leadership, The 21 indispensable qualities of a leader,* and *Your road map for success.*"
ISBN: 978-0-7852-6351-7 (hardcover)
1. Leadership. 2. Interpersonal relations. 3. Success in business.
I. Title.
HD57.7 .M39427
658.4'092—dc22
2003021381

CONTENTS

PART I

THE NATURE
OF RELATIONSHIPS

I

WHY ARE RELATIONSHIPS IMPORTANT TO SUCCESS?

Relationships are the glue that holds team members together.

In the early 1960s, Michael Deaver was a young man with a political bent looking for a leader he could believe in and follow. The person he found was an actor-turned-politician named Ronald Reagan. In 1966, Reagan was elected governor of California, an office he would hold for two terms, from 1967 to 1975. During that tenure, Deaver became Reagan's deputy chief of staff, an office he also held when Reagan became the nation's fortieth president.

Deaver admired many things about the man he worked with for thirty years: his convictions and love of country, his understanding of himself, his skill as a communicator, and his honesty. Deaver said, "I would go so far as to say that he was actually incapable of dishonesty."[1] But perhaps what was most impressive about Ronald Reagan was his ability to relate to people.

Deaver commented, "Ronald Reagan was one of the shyest men I'd ever met."[2] Yet the president was able to connect with anyone, whether a head of state, a blue-collar worker, or a feisty member of the press. When asked about why Reagan had such rapport with the press corps, Deaver remarked, "Well, Reagan basically liked people, whether they were part of the press corps or whether they were just ordinary people. That comes through. While many of the press wouldn't agree with Reagan's policy, they genuinely liked him as a person."[3]

Part of Reagan's skill came from his natural charisma and glib verbal aptitude developed in Hollywood. But even greater was his ability to relate to people, something he honed while traveling the country for a decade as the spokesman for General Electric.

It's said that Reagan could make anyone feel like his best friend, even someone he'd never met before. But more important, he connected with the people closest to him. He truly cared about the people on his team. "The chief of staff, or the gardener, or a secretary would all be treated the same, as far as he was concerned," remembered Deaver. "They were all important."[4]

Deaver related a story that tells much about the connection the two men experienced. In 1975, Reagan gave a speech to a group of conservation-minded hunters in San Francisco, and the organization gave him a small bronze lion as a gift. At the time, Deaver admired it and told Governor Reagan how beautiful he thought it was.

Ten years later, Deaver prepared to bring his service to President Reagan to an end after having written his letter of resignation. Reagan asked Deaver to come to the Oval Office the next morning. As the deputy chief of staff entered the room, the president stood in front of his desk to greet him.

"Mike," he said, "all night I've been trying to think of something to give you that would be a reminder of all the great times we had together." Then Reagan turned around and picked up something from his desk. "You kinda liked this little thing, as I recall," the president said, his eyes moist. And he handed the bronze lion to Deaver, who was totally overcome. He couldn't believe that Reagan had remembered that about him all those years. That lion has held a place of honor in Deaver's home ever since.

Solid Relationships

Everyone liked being around Ronald Reagan because he loved people and connected with them. He understood that relationships were the glue that held his team members together—the more solid the relationships, the more cohesive his team.

Just about everything you do depends on teamwork. It doesn't matter whether you are a leader or follower, coach or player, teacher or student, parent or child, CEO or nonprofit worker; you will be involved with other people. The question is, will your involvement with others be successful? Your best chance for leadership also depends upon connecting with those on your team. Here is how you know whether you have built solid relationships with others. Look for the following five characteristics in your relationships:

1. Respect

When it comes to relationships, everything begins with respect, with the desire to place value on other people. Human relations author Les Giblin said, "You can't make the other fellow feel important in your presence if you secretly feel that he is a nobody."

The thing about respect is that you should show it to others, even before they have done anything to warrant it, simply because they are human beings. But at the same time, you should always expect to have to earn it from others. And the place you earn it the quickest is on difficult ground.

2. Shared Experiences

Respect can lay the foundation for a good relationship, but it alone is not enough. You can't be relational with someone you don't know. It requires shared experiences over time. And that's not always easy to achieve. For example, right after Brian Billick, coach of the Baltimore Ravens, won the 2001 Super Bowl, he was asked about the team's chances for repeating a championship season. He commented that it would be very difficult. Why? Because 25 to 30 percent of the team changes every year. Newer players don't have the shared experiences with the team that are needed to succeed.

3. TRUST

When you respect people and you spend enough time with them to develop shared experiences, you are in a position to develop trust. Trust is essential to all good relationships. Scottish poet George MacDonald observed, "To be trusted is a greater compliment than to be loved." Without trust, you cannot sustain any kind of relationship.

4. RECIPROCITY

One-sided personal relationships don't last. If one person is always the giver and the other is always the receiver, then the relationship will eventually disintegrate. The same is true of all relationships, including those on a team. For people to improve relationally, there has to be give-and-take so that everyone benefits as well as gives. Remember to ask your teammates, colleagues, and friends questions about their hopes, desires, and goals. Give people your full attention. Show others you care about them.

WHEN IT COMES TO RELATIONSHIPS, EVERYTHING
BEGINS WITH RESPECT, WITH THE DESIRE TO PLACE
VALUE ON OTHER PEOPLE.

---

5. MUTUAL ENJOYMENT

When relationships grow and start to get solid, the people involved begin to enjoy each other. Just being together can turn even unpleasant tasks into positive experiences.

How are you doing when it comes to being relational? Do you spend a lot of time and energy building solid relationships, or are you so focused on results that you tend to overlook (or overrun) others? If the latter is true of you, think about the wise words of George Kienzle and Edward Dare in *Climbing the Executive Ladder:* "Few things will pay you bigger dividends than the time and trouble you take to understand people. Almost nothing will add more to your stature as an executive and a person. Nothing will give you greater satisfaction or bring you more happiness." Becoming a highly relational person brings individual and team success.

WHAT DO I NEED TO
KNOW ABOUT OTHERS?

People don't care how much you know,
until they know how much you care.

I f your desire is to be successful and to make a positive impact on your world, you need the ability to understand others. Understanding others gives you the potential to influence every area of life, not just the business arena. For example, look at how understanding people helped this mother of a preschooler. She said:

> Leaving my four-year-old son in the house, I ran out to throw something in the trash. When I tried to open the door to get back inside, it was locked. I knew that insisting that my son open the door would have resulted in an hour-long battle of the wills. So in a sad voice, I said, "Oh, too bad. You just locked yourself in the house." The door opened at once.

Understanding people certainly impacts your ability to communicate with others. David Burns, a medical doctor and professor of psychiatry at the University of Pennsylvania, observed, "The biggest mistake you can make in trying to talk convincingly is to put your highest priority on expressing your ideas and feelings. What most people really want is to be listened to, respected, and understood. The moment people see that they are being understood, they become more motivated to understand your point of view." If you can learn to understand people—how they think, what they feel, what inspires them, how they're likely to act and react in a given situation—then you can motivate and influence them in a positive way.

WHY PEOPLE FAIL TO UNDERSTAND OTHERS

Lack of understanding concerning others is a recurrent source of tension in our society. I once heard an attorney say, "Half of all the controversies and conflicts that arise among people are caused not by differences of opinion or an inability to agree, but by the lack of understanding of one another." If we could reduce the number of misunderstandings, the courts wouldn't be as crowded, there would be fewer violent crimes, the divorce rate would go down, and the amount of everyday stress most people experience would drop dramatically.

If understanding is such an asset, why don't more people practice it? There are many reasons:

FEAR

Seventeenth-century American colonist William Penn advised, "Neither despise or oppose what thou dost not understand," yet many people seem to do exactly the opposite. When they don't understand others, they often react by becoming fearful. And once they start fearing others, they rarely try to overcome their fear in order to learn more about them. It becomes a vicious cycle.

Unfortunately, fear is evident in the workplace when it comes to employees' reactions toward their leaders. Yet in a healthy work environment, if you give others the benefit of the doubt and replace fear with understanding, everyone can work together positively. All people have to do is follow the advice of President Harry Truman, who said, "When we understand the other fellow's viewpoint—understand what he is trying to do—nine times out of ten he is trying to do right."

SELF-CENTEREDNESS

When fear isn't a stumbling block, self-centeredness often is. People are not self-centered on purpose; it's just in the nature of humans to think of their own interests first. If you want to see an example of that, play with a two-year-old child. He naturally chooses the best toys for himself and insists on his own way.

One way to overcome our natural self-centeredness is to try to see things from other people's perspectives. Talking to a group of salespeople, Art Mortell, author of *World Class Selling*, shared this experience: "Whenever I'm losing at chess, I consistently get up and stand behind my opponent and see the board from his side. Then I discover the stupid moves I've made because I can see it from his viewpoint. The salesperson's challenge is to see the world from the prospect's viewpoint."[1]

That's the challenge for every one of us, no matter what our profession. The following quote reminds us of what our priorities should be when dealing with other people:

A SHORT COURSE IN HUMAN RELATIONS

The least important word: I
The most important word: We
The two most important words: Thank you.
The three most important words: All is forgiven.
The four most important words: What is your opinion?
The five most important words: You did a good job.
The six most important words: I want to understand you better.

FAILURE TO APPRECIATE DIFFERENCES

The next logical step after leaving behind self-centeredness is learning to recognize and respect everyone else's unique qualities. Instead of trying to cast others in your image, learn to appreciate their differences. If someone has a talent that you don't have, great. The two of you can strengthen each other's weaknesses. If others come from a different culture, broaden your horizons and learn what you can from them. Your new knowledge will help you relate not only to them, but also to others.

Once you learn to appreciate other people's differences, you come to realize that there are many responses to leadership and motivation. Joseph Beck, onetime president of the Kenley Corporation, recognized that truth when he said that "different people are motivated in different ways. A good basketball coach, for example, knows when a player needs a 'kick in the pants.' The main difference is that all players need encouragement and only some need a 'kick in the pants.'"

FAILURE TO ACKNOWLEDGE SIMILARITIES

We all have emotional reactions to what's happening around us. To foster understanding, think of what your emotions would be if you were in the same position as the person you're interacting with. You know what you would want to happen in a given situation. Chances are that the person you're working with has many of the same feelings.

IF YOU TREAT EVERY PERSON YOU MEET AS IF HE
OR SHE WERE THE MOST IMPORTANT PERSON IN
THE WORLD, YOU'LL COMMUNICATE THAT HE
OR SHE IS SOMEBODY—TO YOU.

THINGS EVERYBODY NEEDS TO UNDERSTAND ABOUT PEOPLE

Knowing what people need and want is the key to understanding them. And if you can understand them, you can influence them and impact their lives in a positive way. What I know about understanding people can be summed up in the following list:

1. EVERYBODY WANTS TO BE SOMEBODY

There isn't a person in the world who doesn't have the desire to be someone, to have significance. Even the least ambitious and unassuming person wants to be regarded highly by others.

I remember the first time these feelings were stirred strongly within me. It was back when I was in the fourth grade and went to my first basketball game. I stood with my buddies in the balcony of the gym. The thing that I remember most wasn't the game; it was the announcement of the starting lineups. They turned all the lights out, and then some spotlights came on. The announcer called out the names of the starters, and they ran out to the middle of the floor one by one with everybody in the place cheering.

I hung over the balcony that day as a fourth-grade kid and said, "Wow, I'd like that to happen to me." In fact, by the time the introductions were over, I looked at my friend Bobby Wilson, and I said, "Bobby, when I get to high school, they're going to announce my name, and I'm going to run out in the spotlight to the middle of that basketball floor. And the people are going to cheer for me because I'm going to be somebody."

I went home that night and told my dad, "I want to be a basketball player." Soon afterward, he got me a Spalding basketball, and we put a goal on the garage. I used to shovel snow off that driveway to practice my foul shots and play basketball because I had a dream of becoming somebody.

It's funny how that kind of dream can impact your life. In the sixth grade, I played intramural basketball. Our team won a couple of games, so we got to go to the Old Mill Street Gym in Circleville, Ohio, where I'd seen that basketball game in the fourth grade. When we got there, instead of going out onto the floor with the rest of the players as they were warming up, I went to the bench where those high school players had been two years before. I sat right where they had, and I closed my eyes (the equivalent of turning the lights out in the gym). Then in my head I heard my name announced, and I ran out in the middle of the floor.

It felt so good to hear the imaginary applause that I thought, *I'll do it again!* So I did. In fact, I did it three times, and all of a sudden, I realized that my buddies weren't playing basketball; they were just watching me in disbelief. But I didn't care because I was one step closer to being the person I'd dreamed about becoming.

Everybody wants to be regarded and valued by others. In other words, everybody wants to be somebody. Once that piece of information becomes a part of your everyday thinking, you'll gain incredible insight into why people do the things they do. And if you treat every person you meet as if he or she were the most important person in the world, you'll communicate that he or she *is* somebody—to you.

2. NOBODY CARES HOW MUCH YOU KNOW UNTIL HE KNOWS HOW MUCH YOU CARE

The moment that people know that you care about them, the way they feel about you changes. Showing others that you care isn't always easy. Your greatest times and fondest memories will come because of people, but so will your most difficult, hurting, and tragic times. People are your greatest assets and your greatest liabilities. The challenge is to keep caring about them no matter what.

I came across an insightful quote called "Paradoxical Commandments of Leadership." Here's what it says:

> People are illogical, unreasonable, and self-centered—love them anyway.
>
> If you do good, people will accuse you of selfish ulterior motives—do good anyway.
>
> If you're successful, you'll win false friends and true enemies—succeed anyway.
>
> The good you do today will perhaps be forgotten tomorrow—do good anyway.
>
> Honesty and frankness make you vulnerable—be honest and frank anyway.
>
> The biggest man with the biggest ideas can be shot down by the smallest man with the smallest mind—think big anyway.

People favor underdogs but follow only hot dogs—fight for a few underdogs anyway.

What you spend years building may be destroyed overnight—build anyway.

People really need help but may attack you if you help them—help them anyway.

Give the world the best that you have and you will get kicked in the teeth—give the world the best that you have anyway.

If better is possible, then good is not enough.

That's the right way to treat people. Besides, you never know which people in your sphere of influence are going to rise up and make a difference in your life and the lives of others.

3. EVERYBODY NEEDS SOMEBODY

Contrary to popular belief, there are no such things as self-made men and women. Everybody needs friendship, encouragement, and help. What people can accomplish by themselves is almost nothing compared to their potential when working with others. And doing things with other people tends to bring contentment. Besides, Lone Rangers are rarely happy people. King Solomon of ancient Israel stated the value of working together this way:

Two are better than one,
     because they have a good return for their work:
If one falls down,
     his friend can help him up.
But pity the man who falls
     and has no one to help him up!
Also, if two lie down together, they will keep warm.
     But how can one keep warm alone?
Though one may be overpowered,
     two can defend themselves.
A cord of three strands is not quickly broken.[2]

Everybody needs somebody to come alongside and help. If you understand that, are willing to give to others and help them, and maintain the right motives, their lives and yours can change.

4. EVERYBODY CAN BE SOMEBODY WHEN SOMEBODY UNDERSTANDS AND BELIEVES HER

Once you understand people and believe in them, they really can become somebody. And it doesn't take much effort to help other people feel important. Little things, done deliberately at the right time, can make a big difference.

When was the last time you went out of your way to make people feel special, as if they were somebody? The investment required on your part is totally overshadowed by the impact it makes on them. Everyone you know and all the people you meet have the potential to be someone important in the lives of others. All they need is encouragement and motivation from you to help them reach their potential.

5. ANYBODY WHO HELPS SOMEBODY INFLUENCES A LOT OF BODIES

The final thing you need to understand about people is that when you help one person, you're really impacting a lot of other people. What you give to one person overflows into the lives of all the people that person impacts. The nature of influence is to multiply. It even impacts you because when you help others and your motives are good, you always receive more than you can ever give. Most people are so genuinely grateful when another person makes them feel special that they never tire of showing their gratitude.

CHOOSE TO UNDERSTAND OTHERS

In the end, the ability to understand people is a choice. It's true that some people are born with great instincts that enable them to understand how others think and feel. But even if you aren't instinctively a people person, you can improve your ability to work with others. Every person is capable of having the ability to understand, motivate, and ultimately influence others.

PART II

THE BUILDING BLOCKS OF RELATIONSHIPS

How Can I Encourage Others?

*Believing in people before they have proved themselves is the
key to motivating people to reach their potential.*

Everyone loves encouragement. It lifts them up when they're down
and motivates them when they're feeling discouraged. To be an
encourager, you need to believe the best in people, to have faith in them.
In fact, faith is essential for building and maintaining all positive relationships, yet it's a scarce commodity today. Take a look at the following
four facts about faith:

1. Most People Don't Have Faith in Themselves

Not long ago I saw a *Shoe* comic strip by Jeff MacNelly that showed
Shoe, the crusty newspaper editor, standing on the mound in a baseball
game. His catcher says to him, "You've got to have faith in your curve
ball." In the next frame Shoe remarks, "It's easy for him to say. When it
comes to believing in myself, I'm an agnostic."

That's the way too many people feel today. They have trouble believing
in themselves. They believe they will fail. Even when they see a light at the
end of the tunnel, they're convinced it's a train. They see a difficulty in

every responsibility. But the reality is that difficulties seldom defeat people; lack of faith in themselves usually does it. With a little faith in themselves, people can do miraculous things. But without it, they have a really tough time.

2. MOST PEOPLE DON'T HAVE SOMEONE WHO HAS FAITH IN THEM

In *Just for Today,* James Keller tells this story: "A sidewalk flower vendor was not doing any business. Suddenly a happy thought struck him and he put up this sign. 'This gardenia will make you feel important all day long for 10 cents.' All at once his sales began to increase."

In our society today, most people feel isolated. The strong sense of community that was once enjoyed by most Americans has become rare. And many people don't have the family support that was more common thirty or forty years ago. For example, evangelist Bill Glass noted, "Over 90 percent of prison inmates were told by parents while growing up, 'They're going to put you in jail.'" Instead of teaching their children to believe in themselves, some parents are tearing them down. For many people, even those who are closest to them don't believe in them. They have no one on their side. No wonder even a little thing like a flower can make a difference in how a person approaches the day.

3. MOST PEOPLE CAN TELL WHEN SOMEONE ELSE HAS FAITH IN THEM

People's instincts are pretty good at knowing when others have faith in them. They can sense if your belief is genuine or phony. And truly having faith in someone can change his or her life.

In his book *Move Ahead with Possibility Thinking,* my friend Robert Schuller, pastor of the Crystal Cathedral in Garden Grove, California, tells a wonderful story about an incident that changed his life as a boy. It occurred when his uncle had faith in him and showed it in his words and actions:

His car drove past the unpainted barn and stopped in a cloud of summer dust at our front gate. I ran barefooted across the splintery porch and saw my uncle Henry bound out of the car. He was tall, very handsome, and terribly alive with energy. After many years overseas in China, he was visiting our Iowa farm. He ran up to the old gate and put both of his big hands on my four-year-old shoulders. He smiled widely, ruffled my uncombed hair, and said, "Well! I guess you're Robert! I think you are going to be a preacher someday." That night I prayed secretly, "And dear God, make me a preacher when I grow up!" I believe that God made me a POSSIBILITY THINKER then and there.

Always remember that your goal is not to get people to think more highly of you. It's to get them to think more highly of themselves. Have faith in them, and they will begin to do exactly that.

4. Most People Will Do Anything to Live Up to Your Faith in Them

People rise or fall to meet your level of expectations for them. If you express skepticism and doubt in others, they will return your lack of confidence with mediocrity. But if you believe in them and expect them to do well, they will go the extra mile trying to do their best. And in the process, they and you benefit. John H. Spalding expressed the thought this way: "Those who believe in our ability do more than stimulate us. They create for us an atmosphere in which it becomes easier to succeed."

How to Become a Believer in People

I'm fortunate because I grew up in a positive, affirming environment. As a result, I have an easy time believing in people and expressing that belief. But I realize that not everyone had the benefit of a positive upbringing. Most people need to *learn* how to have faith in others. To build your belief in others, try using these suggestions, created using the initial letters of the word *BELIEVE*.

BELIEVE IN THEM BEFORE THEY SUCCEED

Everyone loves a winner. It's easy to have faith in people who have already proved themselves. It's much tougher to believe in people *before* they have proved themselves. But that is the key to motivating people to reach their potential. You have to believe in them first, before they become successful, and sometimes before you can persuade them to believe in themselves.

Some people in your life desperately want to believe in themselves but have little hope. As you interact with them, remember the motto of French World War I hero Marshal Ferdinand Foch: "There are no hopeless situations; there are only men and women who have grown hopeless about them." Every person has seeds of greatness within, even though they may currently be dormant. But when you believe in people, you water the seeds and give them the chance to grow.

EMPHASIZE THEIR STRENGTHS

Many people mistakenly think that to build relationships and be influential, they have to be an "authority" and point out others' deficiencies. People who try that approach become like Lucy from the comic strip *Peanuts* by Charles Schulz. In one strip Lucy told poor Charlie Brown, "You're in the shadow of your own goal posts! You are a miscue! You are three putts on the eighteenth green! You are a seven-ten split in the tenth frame . . . You are a missed free throw, a shanked nine iron and a called third strike! Do you understand? Have I made myself clear?" That's hardly a way to positively impact the life of another person!

The road to building positive relationships lies in exactly the opposite direction. The best way to show people your faith in them and motivate them is to focus your attention on their strengths. According to author and advertising executive Bruce Barton, "Nothing splendid has ever been achieved except by those who dared believe that something inside them was superior to circumstances." By emphasizing people's strengths, you're helping them believe that they possess what they need to succeed.

BELIEVING IN PEOPLE BEFORE THEY HAVE PROVED
THEMSELVES IS THE KEY TO MOTIVATING PEOPLE
TO REACH THEIR POTENTIAL.

Praise them for what they do well, both privately and publicly. Tell them how much you appreciate their positive qualities and their skills. And anytime you have the opportunity to compliment and praise them in the presence of their family and close friends, do it.

LIST THEIR PAST SUCCESSES

Even when you emphasize people's strengths, they may need further encouragement to show them you believe in them and to get them motivated. Entrepreneur Mary Kay Ash, founder of Mary Kay cosmetics, advised, "Everyone has an invisible sign hanging from his neck saying, 'Make me feel important!' Never forget this message when working with people." One of the best ways to do that is to help people remember their past successes.

The account of David and Goliath presents a classic example of how past successes can help a person have faith in himself. You may remember the story from the Bible. A nine-foot-tall Philistine champion named Goliath stood before the army of Israel and taunted them every day for forty days, daring them to send out a warrior to face him. On the fortieth day a young shepherd named David came to the front lines to deliver food to his brothers, who were in Israel's army. While he was there, he witnessed the giant's contemptuous display of taunts and challenges. David was so infuriated that he told King Saul he wanted to face the giant in battle. Here's what happened next:

Saul replied, "You are not able to go out against this Philistine and fight him; you are only a boy, and he has been a fighting man from his youth." But David said to Saul, "Your servant has been keeping his father's sheep. When a lion or a bear came and

carried off a sheep from the flock, I went after it, struck it and
rescued the sheep from its mouth. When it turned on me, I
seized it by its hair, struck it and killed it. Your servant has killed
both the lion and the bear . . . The LORD who delivered me from
the paw of the lion and the paw of the bear will deliver me from
the hand of this Philistine."[1]

David looked back on his past successes, and he had confidence in his
future actions. And of course, when he faced the giant, he felled him
like a tree, using nothing but a rock and sling. And when he cut off
Goliath's head, his success inspired his fellow countrymen; they routed
the Philistine army.

Not everyone has the natural ability to recognize past successes and draw
confidence from them. Some people need help. If you can show others
that they have done well in the past and help them see that their past victories have paved the way for future success, they'll be better able to move
into action. Listing past successes helps others believe in themselves.

INSTILL CONFIDENCE WHEN THEY FAIL

When you have encouraged people and put your faith in them, and
they begin to believe they can succeed in life, they soon reach a critical
crossroads. The first time or two that they fail—and they will fail because
it's a part of life—they have two choices. They can give in or go on.

Some people are resilient and willing to keep trying in order to succeed, even when they don't see immediate progress. But others aren't that
determined. Some will collapse at the first sign of trouble. To give them
a push and inspire them, you need to keep showing your confidence in
them, even when they're making mistakes or doing poorly.

One of the ways to do that is to tell about your past troubles and trau-
mas. Sometimes people think that if you're currently successful, you have
always been that way. They don't realize that you have had your share of
flops, failures, and fumbles. Show them that success is a journey—a
process, not a destination. When they realize that you have failed and yet

still managed to succeed, they'll realize that it's okay to fail. And their confidence will remain intact. They will learn to think the way baseball legend Babe Ruth did when he said, "Never let the fear of striking out get in the way."

Experience Some Wins Together

It's not enough just knowing failure is a part of moving forward in life. To really become motivated to succeed, people need to believe they can win.

Winning is motivation. Novelist David Ambrose acknowledged this truth: "If you have the will to win, you have achieved half your success; if you don't, you have achieved half your failure." Coming alongside others to help them experience some wins with you gives them reasons to believe they will succeed. And in the process, they sense victory. That's when incredible things begin to happen in their lives.

To help people believe they can achieve victory, put them in a position to experience small successes. Encourage them to perform tasks or take on responsibilities you know that they can handle and do well. And give them the assistance they need to succeed. In time as their confidence grows, they will take on more difficult challenges, but they will be able to face them with confidence and competence because of the positive track record they're developing.

Visualize Their Future Success

An experiment performed with laboratory rats measured their motivation to live under different circumstances. Scientists dropped a rat into a jar of water that had been placed in total darkness, and they timed how long the animal would continue swimming before it gave up and allowed itself to drown. They found that the rat lasted little more than three minutes.

Then they dropped another rat into the same kind of jar, but instead of placing it in total darkness, they allowed a ray of light to shine into it. Under those circumstances, the rat kept swimming for thirty-six hours. That's more than seven hundred times longer than the one in the dark! Because the rat could see, it continued to have hope.

If that is true of laboratory animals, think of how strong the effect of visualization can be on people, who are capable of higher reasoning. It's been said that a person can live forty days without food, four days without water, four minutes without air, but only four seconds without hope. Each time you cast a vision for others and paint a picture of their future success, you build them up, motivate them, and give them reasons to keep going.

EXPECT A NEW LEVEL OF LIVING

German statesman Konrad Adenaur observed: "We all live under the same sky, but we don't all have the same horizon." Make it your goal to help others see beyond today and their current circumstances and dream big dreams. When you put your faith in people, you help them expand their horizons and motivate them to move to a whole new level of living.

Putting your faith in others involves taking a chance. But the rewards outweigh the risks. Robert Louis Stevenson said, "To be what we are, and to become what we are capable of becoming, is the only end of life." When you put your faith in others, you help them reach their potential. You become an important relationship in their lives—and they in yours.

4

HOW CAN I CONNECT
WITH PEOPLE?

Always remember, the heart comes before the head.

I love communicating. It's one of my passions. Although I've spent more than thirty years speaking professionally, I'm always looking for ways to grow and keep improving in that area.

THE AUDIENCE'S BEST FRIEND

No doubt you've heard of Elizabeth Dole. She is a lawyer by trade, was a cabinet member in the Reagan and Bush administrations, and was the president of the American Red Cross. She is a marvelous communicator. Her particular gift, which I witnessed in San Jose one day, was making me and everyone else in her audience feel as though she was really our friend. She made me glad I was there. The bottom line is that she really knows how to connect with people.

In 1996, she demonstrated that ability to the whole country when she spoke at the Republican National Convention. If you watched it on television, you know what I'm talking about. When Elizabeth Dole walked out into the audience that night, they felt that she was their best friend. She was able to develop an amazing connection with them. I also felt that connection, even though I was sitting in my living room at home watching her on television. Once she finished her talk, I would have followed her anywhere.

BOB NEVER MADE THE CONNECTION

Also speaking at that convention was Bob Dole, Elizabeth's husband—not surprising since he was the Republican nominee for the presidential race. Anyone who watched would have observed a remarkable difference between the communication abilities of the two speakers. Where Elizabeth was warm and approachable, Bob appeared stern and distant. Throughout the campaign, he never seemed to be able to connect with the people.

Many factors come into play in the election of a president of the United States, but not least among them is the ability of a candidate to connect with his audience. A lot has been written about the Kennedy-Nixon debates of the 1960 election. One of the reasons John F. Kennedy succeeded was that he was able to make the television audience feel connected to him. The same kind of connection developed between Ronald Reagan and his audiences. And in the 1992 election, Bill Clinton worked extremely hard to develop a sense of connection with the American people—to do it he even appeared on the talk show *Arsenio* and played the saxophone.

> YOU CAN'T MOVE PEOPLE TO ACTION UNLESS YOU
> FIRST MOVE THEM WITH EMOTION. THE HEART
> COMES BEFORE THE HEAD.

I believe Bob Dole is a good man. But I also know he never connected with the people. Ironically, after the presidential race was over, he appeared on *Saturday Night Live,* a show that made fun of him during the entire campaign, implying that he was humorless and out of touch. On the show Dole came across as relaxed, approachable, and able to make fun of himself. And he was a hit with the audience. He had finally connected.

The Heart Comes First

You first have to touch people's hearts before you ask them for a hand. All great communicators recognize this truth and act on it almost instinctively. You can't move people to action unless you first move them with emotion. The heart comes before the head.

An outstanding orator and African-American leader of the nineteenth century was Frederick Douglass. It's said that he had a remarkable ability to connect with people and move their hearts when he spoke. Historian Lerone Bennett said of Douglass, "He could make people *laugh* at a slave owner preaching the duties of Christian obedience; could make them *see* the humiliation of a black maiden ravished by a brutal slave owner; could make them *hear* the sobs of a mother separated from her child. Through him, people could cry, curse, and *feel;* through him they could *live* slavery."

Connect in Public and Private

Connecting with people isn't something that needs to happen only when communicating to groups of people. It needs to happen with individuals. And the stronger the relationship between individuals, the more beneficial it will be and the more likely the follower will want to help the leader. That is one of the most important principles I've taught my staff over the years. My staff used to groan every time I would say, "People don't care how much you know until they know how much you care," but they also knew that it was true. You develop credibility with people when you connect with them and show that you genuinely want to help them.

Connect with People One at a Time

A key to connecting with others is recognizing that even in a group, you have to relate to people as individuals. General Norman Schwarzkopf remarked, "I have seen competent leaders who stood in front of a platoon and all they saw was a platoon. But great leaders stand in front of a platoon and see it as forty-four individuals, each of whom has aspirations, each of whom wants to live, each of whom wants to do good."[1] That's the only way to connect with people.

PUT A "10" ON EVERY PERSON'S HEAD

One of the best things you can do for people is to expect the best of them. I call it putting a "10" on everyone's head. It helps others think more highly of themselves, and at the same time, it also helps you. According to Jacques Wiesel, "A survey of one hundred self-made million-aires showed only one common denominator. These highly successful men and women could only see the good in people."

Benjamin Disraeli understood and practiced this concept, and it was one of the secrets of his charisma. He once said, "The greatest good you can do for another is not just to share your riches but to reveal to him his own." If you appreciate others, encourage them, and help them reach their potential, they will connect with you.

THE TOUGHER THE CHALLENGE, THE GREATER THE CONNECTION

Never underestimate the power of building relationships with people. If you've ever studied the lives of notable military commanders, you have probably noticed that the best ones understood how to connect with people. I once read that during World War I in France, General Douglas MacArthur told a battalion commander before a daring charge, "Major, when the signal comes to go over the top, I want you to go first, before your men. If you do, they'll follow." Then MacArthur removed the Distinguished Service Cross from his uniform and pinned it on the major. He had, in effect, awarded him for heroism before asking him to exhibit it. And of course, the major led his men, they followed him over the top, and they achieved their objective.

The Result of Connection in the Workplace

When a leader has done the work to connect with his people, you can see it in the way the organization functions. Among employees there are incredible loyalty and a strong work ethic. The vision of the leader becomes the aspiration of the people. The impact is incredible.

You can also see the results in other ways. On Boss's Day in 1994, a full-page ad appeared in *USA Today*. It was contracted and paid for by the employees of Southwest Airlines, and it was addressed to Herb Kelleher, the company's CEO:

> Thanks, Herb
> For remembering every one of our names.
> For supporting the Ronald McDonald House.
> For helping load baggage on Thanksgiving.
> For giving everyone a kiss (and we mean everyone).
> For listening.
> For running the only profitable major airline.
> For singing at our holiday party.
> For singing only once a year.
> For letting us wear shorts and sneakers to work.
> For golfing at The LUV Classic with only one club.
> For outtalking Sam Donaldson.
> For riding your Harley Davidson into Southwest Headquarters.
> For being a friend, not just a boss.
> Happy Boss's Day from Each One of Your 16,000 Employees.[2]

A display of affection like that occurs only when a leader has worked hard to connect with his people.

Don't ever underestimate the importance of building relational bridges between yourself and others around you. There's an old saying: To lead yourself, use your head; to lead others, use your heart. Always touch a person's heart before you ask him for a hand.

5

How Can I Become
a Better Listener?

Treat every person as if he or she were the
most important person in the world.

Edgar Watson Howe once joked, "No man would listen to you talk if he didn't know it was his turn next." Unfortunately, that accurately describes the way too many people approach communication—they're too busy waiting for their turn to really listen to others. But successful people understand the incredible value of becoming a good listener.

The ability to skillfully listen is the foundation to building positive relationships with others. When Lyndon B. Johnson was a junior senator from Texas, he kept a sign on his office wall that read, "You ain't learnin' nothin' when you're doin' all the talkin'." And Woodrow Wilson, the twenty-eighth American president, once said, "The ear of the leader must ring with the voices of the people."

THE VALUE OF LISTENING

Consider these benefits to listening:

Listening Shows Respect

A mistake that people often make in communicating is trying very hard to impress the other person. They try to make themselves appear smart, witty, or entertaining. But if you want to relate well to others, you have to be willing to focus on what they have to offer. Be *impressed* and *interested*, not *impressive* and *interesting*. Poet-philosopher Ralph Waldo Emerson acknowledged, "Every man I meet is in some way my superior, and I can learn of him." Remember that and listen, and the lines of communication will really open up.

Listening Builds Relationships

Dale Carnegie, author of *How to Win Friends and Influence People*, advised, "You can make more friends in two weeks by becoming a good listener than you can in two years trying to get people interested in you." Carnegie was incredibly gifted at understanding relationships. He recognized that people who are self-focused and who talk about themselves and their concerns all the time rarely develop strong relationships with others. David Schwartz noted in *The Magic of Thinking Big*, "Big people monopolize the listening. Small people monopolize the talking."

By becoming a good listener, you are able to connect with others on more levels and develop stronger, deeper relationships because you are meeting a need. Author C. Neil Strait pointed out that "everyone needs someone who he feels really listens to him." When you become that important listener, you help that person.

Listening Increases Knowledge

Wilson Mizner said, "A good listener is not only popular everywhere, but after a while he knows something." It's amazing how much you can learn about your friends and family, your job, the organization you work in, and yourself when you decide to really listen to others. But not everyone clues into this benefit. For example, I once heard a story about a tennis pro who was giving a lesson to a new student. After watching the novice take several swings at the tennis ball, the pro stopped him and suggested ways he could improve his stroke. But each time he did, the student interrupted him, gave a different opinion of the problem, and stated how it should be solved. After several interruptions, the pro began to nod his head in agreement.

When the lesson ended, a woman who had been watching said to the pro, "Why did you go along with that arrogant man's stupid suggestions?"

The pro smiled and replied, "I learned a long time ago that it is a waste of time to try to sell real *answers* to anyone who just wants to buy *echoes*."

Beware of putting yourself into a position where you think you know all the answers. Anytime you do, you'll be putting yourself in danger. It's almost impossible to think of yourself as "the expert" and continue growing and learning at the same time. All great learners are great listeners.

One common problem as people gain more authority is that they often listen to others less and less, especially the people who report to them. While it's true that the higher you go, the less you are required to listen to others, it's also true that your need for good listening skills increases. The farther you get from the front lines, the more you have to depend on others to get reliable information. Only if you develop good listening skills early, and then continue to use them, will you be able to gather the information you need to succeed.

As you proceed through life and become more successful, don't lose sight of your need to keep growing and improving yourself. And remember, a deaf ear is evidence of a closed mind.

LISTENING GENERATES IDEAS

Good companies have a reputation for listening to their people. Brinker International, owner of Chili's, On the Border, Romano's Macaroni Grill, and other restaurant chains, is one of the nation's best-run food service chains according to *Restaurants and Institutions* magazine. Almost 80 percent of its restaurants' menu items have come from suggestions made by unit managers.

What's good for effective companies is good for individuals. When you consistently listen to others, you never suffer for ideas. People love to contribute, especially when their leader shares the credit with them. If you give people opportunities to share their thoughts, and you listen with an open mind, there will always be a flow of new ideas. And even if you hear ideas that won't work, just listening to them can often spark other creative thoughts in you and others. You'll never know how close you are to a million-dollar idea unless you're willing to listen.

Listening Builds Loyalty

A funny thing happens when you don't make a practice of listening to people. They find others who will. Anytime employees, spouses, colleagues, children, or friends no longer believe they are being listened to, they seek out people who will give them what they want. Sometimes the consequences can be disastrous: the end of a friendship, lack of authority at work, lessened parental influence, or the breakdown of a marriage.

On the other hand, practicing good listening skills draws people to you. Everyone loves a good listener and is attracted to him or her. And if you consistently listen to others, valuing them and what they have to offer, they are likely to develop a strong loyalty to you, even when your authority with them is unofficial or informal.

Listening Is a Great Way to Help Others and Yourself

Roger G. Imhoff urged, "Let others confide in you. It may not help you, but it will surely help them." At first glance, listening to others may appear to benefit only them. But when you become a good listener, you put yourself in a position to help yourself too. You have the ability to develop strong relationships, gather valuable information, and increase your understanding of yourself and others.

How to Develop Listening Skills

To become a good listener, you have to want to hear. But you also need some skills to help you. Here are nine suggestions to help you become a better listener:

1. LOOK AT THE SPEAKER

The whole listening process begins with giving the other person your undivided attention. As you interact with someone, don't catch up on other work, shuffle papers, do the dishes, or watch television. Set aside the time to focus only on the other person. And if you don't have the time at that moment, then schedule it as soon as you can.

2. DON'T INTERRUPT

Most people react badly to being interrupted. It makes them feel disrespected. And according to Robert L. Montgomery, author of *Listening Made Easy*, "It's just as rude to step on other people's ideas as it is to step on their toes."

People who tend to interrupt others generally do so for one of these reasons:

- They don't place enough value on what the other person has to say.

- They want to impress others by showing how smart and intuitive they are.

- They're too excited by the conversation to let the other person finish talking.

If you are in the habit of interrupting other people, examine your motives and determine to make a change. Give people the time they need to express themselves. And don't feel that one of you has to speak all the time. Periods of silence can give you a chance to reflect on what's been said so that you can respond appropriately.

3. FOCUS ON UNDERSTANDING

Have you ever noticed how quickly most people forget the things they hear? Studies at institutions such as Michigan State, Ohio State, Florida State, and the University of Minnesota indicate that most people can recall only 50 percent of what they hear immediately after hearing it. And as the time passes, their ability to remember continues to drop. By the next day, their retention is usually down to 25 percent.

One way to combat that tendency is to aim for understanding rather than just remembering the facts. Lawyer, lecturer, and author Herb Cohen emphasized, "Effective listening requires more than hearing the words transmitted. It demands that you find meaning and understanding in what is being said. After all, meanings are not in words, but in people."

4. Determine the Need at the Moment

A lot of men and women find themselves in conflict because they occasionally communicate at cross-purposes. They neglect to determine the need of the other person at the moment of interaction. Men usually want to fix any problems they discuss; their need is resolution. Women, on the other hand, are more likely to tell about a problem simply to share it; they neither request nor desire solutions. Anytime you can determine the current need of the people you're communicating with, you can put whatever they say into the appropriate context. And you will be better able to understand them.

IF YOU SHOW PEOPLE HOW MUCH YOU CARE AND ASK QUESTIONS IN A NONTHREATENING WAY, YOU'LL BE AMAZED BY HOW MUCH THEY'LL TELL YOU.

---

5. Check Your Emotions

Most people carry around emotional baggage that causes them to react to certain people or situations. Sigmund Freud stated, "A man with a toothache cannot be in love," meaning that the toothache doesn't allow him to notice anything other than his pain. Similarly, anytime a person has an ax to grind, the words of others are drowned out by the sound of the grindstone.

Anytime that you become highly emotional when listening to another person, check your emotions—especially if your reaction seems to be stronger than the situation warrants. You don't want to make an unsuspecting person the recipient of your venting. Besides, even if your reactions are not due to an event from your past, you should always allow others to finish explaining their points of view, ideas, or convictions before offering your own.

6. SUSPEND YOUR JUDGMENT

Have you ever begun listening to another person tell a story and started to respond to it before he or she was finished? Just about everyone has. But the truth is that you can't jump to conclusions and be a good listener at the same time. As you talk to others, wait to hear the whole story before you respond. If you don't, you may miss the most important thing they intend to say.

7. SUM UP AT MAJOR INTERVALS

Experts agree that listening is most effective when it's active. John H. Melchinger suggests, "Comment on what you hear, and individualize your comments. For example, you can say, 'Cheryl, that's obviously very important to you.' It will help keep you on track as a listener. Get beyond, 'That's interesting.' If you train yourself to comment meaningfully, the speaker will know you are listening and may offer further information."

A technique for active listening is to sum up what the other person says at major intervals. As the speaker finishes one subject, paraphrase his or her main points or ideas before going on to the next one, and verify that you have gotten the right message. Doing that reassures the person and helps you stay focused on what he or she is trying to communicate.

8. ASK QUESTIONS FOR CLARITY

Have you ever noticed that top reporters are excellent listeners? Take someone like Barbara Walters, for example. She looks at the speaker, focuses on understanding, suspends judgment, and sums up what the person has to say. People trust her and seem to be willing to tell her just about anything. But she practices another skill that helps her to gather more information and increase her understanding of the person she is interviewing. She asks good questions.

If you want to become an effective listener, become a good reporter—not a stick-the-microphone-in-your-face-and-bark-questions-at-you reporter, but someone who gently asks follow-up questions and seeks clarification. If you show people how much you care and ask in a nonthreatening way, you'll be amazed by how much they'll tell you.

9. Always Make Listening Your Priority

The last thing to remember when developing your listening skills is to make listening a priority, no matter how busy you become or how far you rise in your organization. A remarkable example of a busy executive who made time for listening was the late Sam Walton, founder of Wal-Mart and one of the richest men in America. He believed in listening to what people had to say, especially his employees. He once flew his plane to Mt. Pleasant, Texas, landed, and gave instructions to his copilot to meet him about one hundred miles down the road. He then rode in a Wal-Mart truck just so that he could chat with the driver. We should all give listening that kind of priority.

Many people take for granted the ability to listen. Most people consider listening to be easy, and they view themselves as pretty good listeners. But while it's true that most people are able to hear, fewer are capable of really listening. However, it's never too late to become a good listener. It can change your life—and the lives of the people in your life.

PART III

THE GROWTH
OF RELATIONSHIPS

6

How Can I Build Trust with Others?

When your words and actions match,
people know they can trust you.

In his best-selling book *The Seven Habits of Highly Effective People,* Stephen Covey wrote about the importance of integrity to a person's success:

> If I try to use human influence strategies and tactics of how to get other people to do what I want, to work better, to be more motivated, to like me and each other—while my character is fundamentally flawed, marked by duplicity or insincerity—then, in the long run, I cannot be successful. My duplicity will breed distrust, and everything I do—even using so-called good human relations techniques—will be perceived as manipulative.
>
> It simply makes no difference how good the rhetoric is or even how good the intentions are; if there is little or no trust, there is no foundation or permanent success. Only basic goodness gives life to technique.[1]

Integrity is crucial for business and personal success. A joint study conducted by the UCLA Graduate School of Management and Korn/Ferry International of New York City surveyed 1,300 senior executives. Seventy-one percent of them said that integrity was the quality most needed to succeed in business. And a study by the Center for Creative Research discovered that though many errors and obstacles can be overcome by a person who wants to rise to the top of an organization, that person is almost never able to move up in the organization if he compromises his integrity by betraying a trust.

INTEGRITY IS ABOUT THE SMALL THINGS

Integrity is important to building relationships. And it is the foundation upon which many other qualities for success are built, such as respect, dignity, and trust. If the foundation of integrity is weak or fundamentally flawed, then success becomes impossible. As author and friend Cheryl Biehl points out, "One of the realities of life is that if you can't trust a person at all points, you can't truly trust him or her at any point." Even people who are able to hide their lack of integrity for a period of time will eventually experience failure, and their relationships will suffer.

It's crucial to maintain integrity by taking care of the little things. Many people misunderstand that. They think they can do whatever they want when it comes to the small things because they believe that as long as they don't have any major lapses, they're doing well. But ethical principles are not flexible. A little white lie is still a lie. Theft is theft—whether it's $1, $1,000, or $1 million. Integrity commits itself to character over personal gain, to people over things, to service over power, to principle over convenience, to the long view over the immediate.

Nineteenth-century clergyman Philips Brooks maintained, "Character is made in the small moments of our lives." Anytime you break a moral principle, you create a small crack in the foundation of your integrity. And when times get tough, it becomes harder to act with integrity, not easier. Character isn't created in a crisis; it only comes to light. Everything you have done in the past—and the things you have neglected to do—come to a head when you're under pressure.

Developing and maintaining integrity require constant attention. Josh Weston, former chairman and CEO of Automatic Data Processing, Inc., says, "I've always tried to live with the following simple rule: 'Don't do what you wouldn't feel comfortable reading about in the newspapers the next day.'" That's a good standard all of us should keep.

INTEGRITY IS AN INSIDE JOB

One of the reasons many people struggle with integrity issues is that they tend to look outside themselves to explain any deficiencies in character. But the development of integrity is an inside job. Take a look at the following three truths about integrity that go against common thinking:

1. INTEGRITY IS NOT DETERMINED BY CIRCUMSTANCES

It's true that our upbringing and circumstances affect who we are, especially when we are young. But the older we get, the greater the number of choices we make—for good or bad. Two people can grow up in the same environment, even in the same household, and one will have integrity and the other won't. Your circumstances are as responsible for your character as a mirror is for your looks. Who you see only reflects who you are.

2. INTEGRITY IS NOT BASED ON CREDENTIALS

In ancient times, brick makers, engravers, and other artisans used a symbol to mark the things they created. The symbol that each one used was his "character." The value of the work was in proportion to the skill with which the object was made. And only if the quality of the work was high was the character esteemed. In other words, the quality of the person and his work gave value to his credentials. If the work was good, so was the character. If it was bad, then the character was viewed as poor.

The same is true for us today. Character comes from who we are. But some people would like to be judged not by who they are, but by the titles they have earned or the position they hold, regardless of the nature of their character. Their desire is to influence others by the weight of their credentials rather than the strength of their character. But credentials can never accomplish what character can. Look at some differences between the two:

CREDENTIALS	CHARACTER
Are transient	Is permanent
Turn the focus to rights	Keeps the focus on responsibilities
Add value to only one person	Adds value to many people
Look to past accomplishments	Builds a legacy for the future
Often evoke jealousy in others	Generates respect and integrity
Can only get you in the door	Keeps you there

No number of titles, degrees, offices, designations, awards, licenses, or other credentials can substitute for basic, honest integrity when it comes to the power of influencing others

3. INTEGRITY IS NOT TO BE CONFUSED WITH REPUTATION

Certainly a good reputation is valuable. King Solomon of ancient Israel stated, "A good name is more desirable than great riches."[2] But a good reputation exists because it is a reflection of a person's character. If a good reputation is like gold, then having integrity is like owning the mine. Worry less about what others think, and give your attention to your inner character. D. L. Moody wrote, "If I take care of my character, my reputation will take care of itself."

If you struggle with maintaining your integrity, and you're doing all the right things on the *outside*—but you're still getting the wrong results—something is wrong and still needs to be changed on the *inside*. Look at the questions on the following page. They may help you nail down areas that need attention.

Questions to Help You Measure Your Integrity

1. How well do I treat people if I gain nothing?

2. Am I transparent with others?

3. Do I role-play based on the person(s) I'm with?

4. Am I the same person in the spotlight as I am when I'm alone?

5. Do I quickly admit wrongdoing without being pressed to do so?

6. Do I put people ahead of my personal agenda?

7. Do I have an unchanging standard for moral decisions, or do circumstances determine my choices?

8. Do I make difficult decisions, even when they have a personal cost attached to them?

9. When I have something to say about people, do I talk *to* them or *about* them?

10. Am I accountable to at least one other person for what I think, say, and do?

Don't be too quick to respond to the questions. If character development is a serious area of need in your life, your tendency may be to skim through the questions, giving answers that describe how you wish you were rather than who you actually are. Take some time to reflect on each question, honestly considering it before answering. Then work on the areas where you're having the most trouble.

Integrity Is Your Best Friend

Integrity is your best friend. It will never betray you or put you in a compromising position. It keeps your priorities right. When you're tempted to take shortcuts, it helps you to stay the right course. When others criticize you unfairly, it helps you keep going and take the high road of not striking back. And when others' criticism is valid, integrity helps you to accept what they say, learn from it, and keep growing.

IF A GOOD REPUTATION IS LIKE GOLD, THEN HAVING INTEGRITY IS LIKE OWNING THE MINE.

Abraham Lincoln once stated, "When I lay down the reins of this administration, I want to have one friend left. And that friend is inside myself." You could almost say that Lincoln's integrity was his best friend while he was in office because he was criticized so viciously. Here is a description of what he faced as explained by Donald T. Phillips:

> Abraham Lincoln was slandered, libeled and hated perhaps more intensely than any man ever to run for the nation's highest office. . . . He was publicly called just about every name imaginable by the press of his day, including a grotesque baboon, a third-rate country lawyer who once split rails and now splits the Union, a coarse vulgar joker, a dictator, an ape, a buffoon, and others. The *Illinois State Register* labeled him "the craftiest and most dishonest politician that ever disgraced an office in America." Severe and unjust criticism did not subside after Lincoln took the oath of office, nor did it come only from Southern sympathizers. It came from within the Union itself, from Congress, from some factions within the Republican party, and initially, from within his own cabinet. As president, Lincoln learned that, no matter what he did, there were going to be people who would not be pleased.[3]

Through it all, Lincoln was a man of principle. And as Thomas Jefferson wisely said, "God grant that men of principle shall be our principal men."

INTEGRITY IS YOUR FRIENDS' BEST FRIEND

Integrity is your best friend. And it's also one of the best friends that your friends will ever have. When the people around you know that you're a person of integrity, they know that you want to influence them because of the opportunity to add value to their lives. They don't have to worry about your motives.

If you're a basketball fan, you probably remember Red Auerbach. He was the president and general manager of the Boston Celtics from 1967 to 1987. He truly understood how integrity adds value to others, especially when people are working together on a team. And he had a method of recruiting that was different from that of most NBA team leaders. When he reviewed a prospective player for the Celtics, his primary concern was the young man's character. While others focused almost entirely on statistics and individual performance, Auerbach wanted to know about a player's attitude. He figured that the way to win was to find players who would give their best work for the benefit of the team. A player who had outstanding ability but whose character was weak or whose desire was to promote only himself was not really an asset.

It has been said that you don't really know people until you have observed them when they interact with a child, when the car has a flat tire, when the boss is away, and when they think no one will ever know. But people with integrity never have to worry about that. No matter where they are, who they are with, or what kind of situation they find themselves in, they are consistent and live by their principles.

BECOME A PERSON OF INTEGRITY

In the end, you can bend your actions to conform to your principles, or you can bend your principles to conform to your actions. It's a choice you have to make. If you want to be successful, then you better choose the path of integrity because all other roads ultimately lead to ruin.

To become a person of integrity, you need to go back to the fundamentals. You may have to make some tough choices, but they'll be worth it.

COMMIT YOURSELF TO HONESTY, RELIABILITY, AND CONFIDENTIALITY

Integrity begins with a specific, conscious decision. If you wait until a moment of crisis before settling your integrity issues, you set yourself up to fail. Choose today to live by a strict moral code, and determine to stick with it no matter what happens.

DECIDE AHEAD OF TIME THAT YOU DON'T HAVE A PRICE

President George Washington perceived that "few men have the virtue to withstand the highest bidder." Some people can be bought because they haven't settled the money issue before the moment of temptation. The best way to guard yourself against a breach in integrity is to make a decision today that you won't sell your integrity: not for power, revenge, pride, or money—any amount of money.

EACH DAY, DO WHAT YOU SHOULD DO BEFORE WHAT YOU WANT TO DO

A big part of integrity is following through consistently on your responsibilities. Our friend Zig Ziglar says, "When you do the things you have to do when you have to do them, the day will come when you can do the things you want to do when you want to do them." Psychologist-philosopher William James stated the idea more strongly: "Everybody ought to do at least two things each day that he hates to do, just for the practice."

With integrity, you can experience freedom. Not only are you less likely to be enslaved by the stress that comes from bad choices, debt, deceptiveness, and other negative character issues, but you are free to influence others and add value to them in an incredible way. And your integrity opens the door for you to experience continued success.

If you know what you stand for and act accordingly, people can trust you. You are a model of the character and consistency that other people admire and want to emulate. And you've laid a good foundation, one that makes it possible for you to build positive relationships.

7

WHAT IS MY MOST
IMPORTANT RELATIONSHIP?

Succeed at home, and all other relationships become easier.

Did you know that according to the Bureau of Labor Statistics, families dissolve at a greater rate in the United States than in any other major industrialized country? And we also lead in the number of fathers absent from the home. U.S. divorce laws are the most permissible in the world, and people are using them at an alarming rate.[1] To some people, marriages and families have become acceptable casualties in the pursuit of success.

But many people are now realizing that the hope of happiness at the expense of breaking up a family is an illusion. You can't give up your marriage or neglect your children and gain true success. Building and maintaining strong families benefit us in every way, including in helping us become successful. Family life expert Nick Stinnet asserted more than a decade ago, "When you have a strong family life, you receive the message that you are loved, cared for, and important. *The positive intake of love, affection, and respect . . . gives you inner resources to deal with life more successfully*" (emphasis added).

WORKING TO STAY TOGETHER

Fairly early in our marriage, Margaret and I realized that in my career, I would often have the opportunity to travel. And we decided that any time I got the chance to go someplace interesting or to attend an event that we knew would be exciting, she would come along with me, even when it was difficult financially. We've done a pretty good job of following through on that commitment over the years.

Margaret and I, with our kids Elizabeth and Joel Porter, have been to the capitals of Europe, the jungles of South America, the teeming cities of Korea, the rugged outback of Australia, and on safari in South Africa. We've met wonderful people of every race and a multitude of nationalities. We've had the chance to see and do things that will remain in our memories for the rest of our lives. I decided early on, what would it profit me to gain the whole world and lose my family?

I know that I wouldn't have experienced any measure of success in life without Margaret. But my gratitude to her and the children doesn't come from what they've brought me. It comes from who they are to me. When I reach the end of my days, I don't want Margaret, Elizabeth, or Joel Porter to say that I was a good author, speaker, pastor, or leader. My desire is that the kids think I'm a good father and that Margaret thinks I'm a good husband. That's what matters most. It's the measure of true success.

STEPS TO BUILDING A STRONG FAMILY

Good marriages and strong families are joys, but they don't just happen on their own. Dr. R. C. Adams, who studied thousands of marriages over a ten-year period, found that only 17 percent of the unions he studied could be considered truly happy. And Jarle Brors, former director of the Institute of Marriage and Family Relations in Washington, D.C., said, "We are finally realizing that we have to go back to the basics in order to reestablish the type of families that give us the type of security that children can grow up in." If we want to have solid families and healthy marriages, we have to work hard to create them.

If you have a family—or you intend to have one in the future—take a look at the following guidelines. They have helped to develop the Maxwell family, and I believe they can help you to strengthen yours.

EXPRESS APPRECIATION FOR EACH OTHER

I once heard someone joke that home is the place where family members go when they are tired of being nice to other people. Unfortunately, some homes seem to work that way. A salesman spends his day treating his clients with the utmost kindness, often in the face of rejection, in order to build his business, but he is rude to his wife when he comes home. Or a doctor spends the day being caring and compassionate with her patients, but she comes home exhausted and blows up with her children.

To build a strong family, you have to make your home a supportive environment. Psychologist William James observed, "In every person from the cradle to the grave, there is a deep craving to be appreciated." Feeling appreciated brings out the best in people. And when that appreciation comes in the home and is coupled with acceptance, love, and encouragement, the bonds between family members grow, and the home becomes a safe haven for everyone.

WHAT WOULD IT PROFIT ME TO GAIN THE WHOLE WORLD AND LOSE MY FAMILY?

I've heard that for every negative remark to a family member, it takes four positive statements to counteract the damage. That's why it's so important to focus on the positive aspects of each other's personality and express unconditional love for each other, both verbally and nonverbally. Then the home becomes a positive environment for everyone.

STRUCTURE YOUR LIVES TO SPEND TIME TOGETHER

It's been said that the American home has become a domestic cloverleaf upon which family members pass each other while en route to a multitude of places and activities. That seems to be true. When I was a kid, I spent a lot of time with my parents, brother, and sister. We went on family vacations, usually in the car. As a parent, it's been harder for me to keep that tradition alive. We've been good about planning and taking vacations together, but sometimes we've had to be creative to have time together. For example, when the children were younger, I always tried to drive them to school in the morning to spend some time with them. But with all the things going on in our busy lives, we found that the only way to get time together was to plan it carefully.

Every month, I spend several hours examining my travel schedule, figuring out what lessons I need to write, thinking about the projects I have to complete, and so on. And at that time, I'll plan my work for the whole month. But before I mark any dates for work, I write in all the important dates for family activities. I'll block out time for birthdays, anniversaries, ball games, theater performances, graduation ceremonies, concerts, and romantic dinners. And I'll also schedule special one-on-one time with Margaret and each of the kids so that we can continue to build our relationships. Then once those are set, I'll plan my work schedule around them. I've done this for years, and it's been the only thing that's prevented my work from squeezing my family out of the schedule. I've found that if I don't strategically structure my life to spend time with my family, it won't happen.

DEAL WITH CRISIS IN A POSITIVE WAY

Every family experiences problems, but not all families respond to them in the same way. And that often separates a family that's close from one that's barely holding together. I've noticed that some people pursuing success seem to avoid the home environment. I suspect that one reason is that they are not able to handle family crisis situations well. They find it easier to try to avoid the problems altogether. But that's not a solution.

M. Scott Peck, author of *The Road Less Traveled,* has offered some remarkable insights on the subject of problems and how we handle them:

It is in this whole process of meeting and solving problems that life has meaning. Problems are the cutting edge that distinguishes between success and failure. Problems call forth our courage and wisdom; indeed they create our courage and our wisdom. It is only because of problems that we grow mentally and spiritually. . . . It is through the pain of confronting and resolving problems that we learn. As Benjamin Franklin said, "Those things that hurt, instruct."

If we are to grow as families and be successful at home as well as in the other areas of our lives, we must learn to cope with the difficulties we find there. Here are some strategies to help you with the problem-solving process:

- *Attack the problem, never the person.* Always try to be supportive of each other. Remember, you're all on the same side. So don't take your frustrations out on people. Instead, attack the problem.

- *Get all the facts.* Nothing can cause more damage than jumping to false conclusions during a crisis. Don't waste your emotional or physical energy chasing down a wrong problem. Before you try to find solutions, be sure you know what's really going on.

- *List all the options.* This may sound a bit analytical, but it really helps because you can look at emotional subjects with some objectivity. Besides, if you had a problem at work, you would probably be willing to go through this process. Give any family problem at least as much time and energy as you would a professional one.

- *Choose the best solution.* As you decide on a solution, always remember that people are your priority. Make your choices accordingly.

- *Look for the positives in the problem.* As Dr. Peck said, the tough things give us a chance to grow. No matter how bad things look at the moment, just about everything has something positive that comes from it.

- *Never withhold love.* No matter how bad things get or how angry you are, never withhold your love from your spouse or children. Sure, tell them how you feel. Acknowledge the problems. But continue loving family members unconditionally through it all.

This last point is the most important of all. When you feel loved and supported by your family, you can weather nearly any crisis. And you can truly enjoy success.

COMMUNICATE CONTINUALLY

An article in the *Dallas Morning News* reported that the average couple married ten years or more spends only thirty-seven minutes a week in meaningful communication. I could hardly believe it. Compare that to the fact that the average American spends almost five times longer than that watching television every day! No wonder so many marriages are in trouble. Just like anything else, good communication doesn't develop by itself. It must be developed, and that process takes time and effort. Here are some suggestions for helping you do exactly that:

- *Develop platforms for communication.* Be creative about finding reasons to talk to each other. Take walks together as a family where you can talk. Call your spouse a couple of times during the day. Meet for lunch one day a week. Offer to drive the kids to soccer practice so you can talk. Communication can happen almost anywhere.

- *Control communication killers.* The television and the telephone probably steal the most family communication time. Restrict the amount of time you give them, and you'd be amazed by how much time you have to talk.

- *Encourage honesty and transparency in conversations.* Differences of opinion are healthy and normal in a family. Encourage all family members to speak their minds, and then when they do, never criticize or ridicule them.

- *Adopt a positive communication style.* Be conscious of the way you interact with your family members. You may have adopted a style that stifles open communication. If you're in the habit of using any communication style other than a cooperative one, begin working immediately to change. You'll have to do that if you want to build your relationship with your family.

SHARE THE SAME VALUES

Today, families don't give values the same priority or attention as they once did. Boston College education professor William Kilpatrick said, "There is a myth that parents don't have the right to instill their values in their children. Once again, the standard dogma here is that children must create their own values. But of course, children have precious little chance to do that. . . . Does it make sense for parents to remain neutral bystanders when everyone else from script writers, to entertainers, to advertisers, to sex educators insist on selling their values to children?"[2]

Common values strengthen a family and are especially beneficial to children as they grow up. A study conducted by the Search Institute showed that in single-parent homes, children whose parent expresses and enforces standards thrive at twice the rate of children who don't have values promoted in a similar way.[3] And that doesn't even take into account whether the values are what we would consider positive.

The best way to get started in working toward sharing common values in your family is to identify the values you want to instill. If you're like most families, you've never done that before. But to be able to live them out, you first have to find them out. They are the three to seven things you're willing to go to the mat for.

Let me list for you the five we've identified in the Maxwell family so that you have an idea of what I'm talking about:

1. Commitment to God
2. Commitment to personal and family growth
3. Commonly shared experiences

    4. Confidence in ourselves and others

    5. The desire to make a contribution in life

The values you choose will undoubtedly be different from ours, but you need to identify them. If you've never done it before, set aside some time to talk about your values with your spouse and children. If your kids are older, include them in the process of identifying the values. Make it a discussion time. And never be reluctant to take on the role of model and teacher of your family's values. If you don't do it, someone else will.

BUILD YOUR MARRIAGE

Finally, if you are married, the best thing you can do to strengthen your family is to build your marriage relationship. It's certainly the best thing you can do for your spouse, but it also has an incredibly positive impact on your children. My friend Josh McDowell wisely stated, "The greatest thing a father can do for his children is to love their mother." And the greatest thing a mother can do for her children is to love their father.

A common missing ingredient in many marriages is dedication to make things work. Marriages may start because of love, but they finish because of commitment. Sexuality researcher Dr. Alfred Kinsey, who studied six thousand marriages and three thousand divorces, revealed that "there may be nothing more important in a marriage than a determination that it shall persist. With such a determination, individuals force themselves to adjust and to accept situations which would seem sufficient grounds for a breakup, if continuation of the marriage were not the prime objective." If you want to help your spouse, your children, and yourself, then become committed to building and sustaining a strong marriage.

NBA coach Pat Riley said, "Sustain a family life for a long period of time and you can sustain success for a long period of time. First things first. If your life is in order you can do whatever you want." There is definitely a correlation between family success and personal success. Not only does building strong family relationships lay the groundwork for future success, but it also gives life deeper meaning.

I believe that few people have ever been truly successful without a positive, supportive family. No matter how great people's accomplishments are, I think they're still missing something when they're working without the benefit of those close relationships. True, some people are called to be single, but they are rare. For most people, a good family helps you know your purpose and develop your potential, and it helps you enjoy the journey along the way with an intensity that isn't possible otherwise. And when it comes to sowing seeds that benefit others, who could possibly derive greater benefit from you than your own family members?

8

How Can I Serve and Lead
People at the Same Time?

You've got to love your people more than your position.

U.S. Army General H. Norman Schwarzkopf displayed highly successful leadership abilities in commanding the allied troops in the Persian Gulf War, just as he had done throughout his career, beginning in his days at West Point.

In Vietnam he turned around a battalion that was in shambles. The First Battalion of the Sixth Infantry—known as the "worst of the sixth"—went from laughingstock to effective fighting force and were selected to perform a more difficult mission. That turned out to be an assignment to what Schwarzkopf described as "a horrible, malignant place" called the Batangan Peninsula. The area had been fought over for thirty years, was covered with mines and booby traps, and was the site of numerous weekly casualties from those devices.

Schwarzkopf made the best of a bad situation. He introduced procedures to greatly reduce casualties, and whenever a soldier *was* injured by a mine, he flew out to check on the man, had him evacuated using his chopper, and talked to the other soldiers to boost their morale.

On May 28, 1970, a man was injured by a mine, and Schwarzkopf, then a colonel, flew to the man's location. While the helicopter was evacuating the injured soldier, another soldier stepped on a mine, severely injuring his leg. The man thrashed around on the ground, screaming and wailing. That's when everyone realized the first mine hadn't been a lone booby trap. They were all standing in the middle of a minefield.

Schwarzkopf believed the injured man could survive and even keep his leg—but only if he stopped flailing around. There was only one thing he could do. He had to go after the man and immobilize him. Schwarzkopf wrote,

> I started through the minefield, one slow step at a time, staring at the ground, looking for telltale bumps or little prongs sticking up from the dirt. My knees were shaking so hard that each time I took a step, I had to grab my leg and steady it with both hands before I could take another . . . It seemed like a thousand years before I reached the kid.

The 240-pound Schwarzkopf, who had been a wrestler at West Point, then pinned the wounded man and calmed him down. It saved his life. And with the help of an engineer team, Schwarzkopf got him and the others out of the minefield.

The quality that Schwarzkopf displayed that day could be described as heroism, courage, or even foolhardiness. But I think the word that best describes it is *servanthood*. On that day in May, the only way he could be effective as a leader was to serve the soldier who was in trouble.

HAVING A SERVANT'S HEART

When you think of servanthood, do you envision it as an activity performed by relatively low-skilled people at the bottom of the positional totem pole? If you do, you have a wrong impression. Servanthood is not about position or skill. It's about attitude. You have undoubtedly met people in service positions who have poor attitudes toward servanthood: the rude worker at the government agency, the waiter who can't be bothered with taking your order, the store clerk who talks on the phone with a friend instead of helping you.

Just as you can sense when a worker doesn't want to help people, you can just as easily detect whether someone has a servant's heart. And the truth is that the best leaders desire to serve others, not themselves.

What does it mean to embody the quality of servanthood? A true servant leader:

1. PUTS OTHERS AHEAD OF HIS OWN AGENDA

The first mark of servanthood is the ability to put others ahead of yourself and your personal desires. It is more than being willing to put your agenda on hold. It means intentionally being aware of other people's needs, available to help them, and able to accept their desires as important.

2. POSSESSES THE CONFIDENCE TO SERVE

The real heart of servanthood is security. Show me someone who thinks he is too important to serve, and I'll show you someone who is basically insecure. How we treat others is really a reflection of how we think about ourselves. Philosopher-poet Eric Hoffer captured that thought:

> The remarkable thing is that we really love our neighbor as ourselves; we do unto others as we do unto ourselves. We hate others when we hate ourselves. We are tolerant toward others when we tolerate ourselves. We forgive others when we forgive ourselves. It is not love of self but hatred of self which is at the root of the troubles that afflict our world.

Only secure leaders give power to others. It's also true that only secure people exhibit servanthood.

3. Initiates Service to Others

Just about anyone will serve if compelled to do so. And some will serve in a crisis. But you can really see the heart of someone who initiates service to others. Great leaders see the need, seize the opportunity, and serve without expecting anything in return.

4. Is Not Position-Conscious

Servant leaders don't focus on rank or position. When Colonel Norman Schwarzkopf stepped into that minefield, rank was the last thing on his mind. He was one person trying to help another. If anything, being the leader gave him a greater sense of obligation to serve.

5. Serves Out of Love

Servanthood is not motivated by manipulation or self-promotion. It is fueled by love. In the end, the extent of your influence and the quality of your relationships depend on the depth of your concern for others. That's why it's so important for leaders to be willing to serve.

How to Become a Servant

To improve your servanthood, do the following:

- *Perform small acts.* When was the last time you performed small acts of kindness for others? Start with those closest to you: your spouse, children, parents. Find ways today to do small things that show others you care.

- *Learn to walk slowly through the crowd.* I learned this great lesson from my father. I call it walking slowly through the crowd. The next time you attend a function with a number of clients, colleagues, or employees, make it your goal to connect with others by circulating among them and talking to people. Focus on each person you meet. Learn his name if you don't know it already.

  Make your agenda getting to know each person's needs, wants, and desires. Then later when you go home, make a note to yourself to do something beneficial for half a dozen of those people.

IT IS TRUE THAT THOSE WHO WOULD BE GREAT
MUST BE LIKE THE LEAST AND THE SERVANT OF ALL.

- *Move into action.* If an attitude of servanthood is conspicuously absent from your life, the best way to change it is to start serving. Begin serving with your body, and your heart will eventually catch up. Sign up to serve others for six months at your church, a community agency, or a volunteer organization. If your attitude still isn't good at the end of your term, do it again. Keep at it until your heart changes.

Where is your heart when it comes to serving others? Do you desire to become a leader for the perks and benefits? Or are you motivated by a desire to help others?

If you really want to become the kind of leader that people want to follow, you will have to settle the issue of servanthood. If your attitude is to be served rather than to serve, you may be headed for trouble. It is true that those who would be great must be like the least and the servant of all.

Albert Schweitzer wisely stated, "I don't know what your destiny will be, but one thing I know: The ones among you who will be really happy are those who have sought and found how to serve." If you want to be successful on the highest level, be willing to serve on the lowest. That's the best way to build relationships.

SUCCESS

101

WHAT EVERY LEADER NEEDS TO KNOW

Published in Nashville, Tennessee, by Thomas Nelson.
Thomas Nelson is a registered trademark of Thomas Nelson, Inc.

Published in association with Yates & Yates, www.yates2.com

Thomas Nelson, Inc., titles may be purchased in bulk for educational, business, fund-raising, or sales promotional use. For information, please e-mail SpecialMarkets@ThomasNelson.com.

Portions of this book have been previously published in *Your Road Map for Success, Failing Forward, The 360° Leader, Winning with People, The 21 Indispensable Qualities of a Leader,* and *The 17 Essential Qualities of a Team Player* by John C. Maxwell.

Library of Congress Cataloging-in-Publication Data

Maxwell, John C., 1947–
Success 101 : what every leader needs to know / John C. Maxwell.
p. cm.
ISBN 978-1-4002-8023-0
1. Success in business--Handbooks, manuals, etc. I. Title.
HF5386.M4449 2008
658.4'09--dc22
2008026082

CONTENTS

PART I

THE RIGHT PICTURE OF SUCCESS

WHAT IS SUCCESS?

You cannot achieve what you have not defined.

The problem for most people who want to be successful is not that they can't achieve success. The main obstacle for them is that they misunderstand success. Maltbie D. Babcock said, "One of the most common mistakes and one of the costliest is thinking that success is due to some genius, some magic, something or other which we do not possess."

THE TRADITIONAL PICTURE OF SUCCESS

What is success? What does it look like? Most people have a vague picture of what it means to be a successful person that looks something like this:

The wealth of Bill Gates,
the physique of Arnold Schwarzenegger
   (or Marilyn Monroe),
the intelligence of Albert Einstein,
the athletic ability of Michael Jordan,
the business prowess of Donald Trump,

the social grace and poise of Jackie Kennedy,
the imagination of Walt Disney, and
the heart of Mother Teresa.

That sounds absurd, but it's closer to the truth than we would like to admit. Many of us picture success as looking like one other than who we are—and we especially can't be eight other people! And more important than that, you shouldn't want to be. If you tried to become just like even one of these other people, you wouldn't be successful. You would be a bad imitation of them, and you would eliminate the possibility of becoming the person you were meant to be.

THE RIGHT PICTURE OF SUCCESS

So how do you get started on the journey toward success? What does it take to be a success? Two things are required: the right picture of success and the right principles for getting there.

The picture of success isn't the same for any two people because we're all created differently as unique individuals. But the process is the same for everyone. It's based on principles that do not change. After more than thirty-five years of knowing successful people and studying the subject, I have developed the following definition of success:

Success is . . .
Knowing your purpose in life,
Growing to reach your maximum potential, and
Sowing seeds that benefit others.

You can see by this definition that success is a journey rather than a destination. No matter how long you live or what you decide to do in life, you will never exhaust your capacity to grow toward your potential or run out of opportunities to help others. When you see success as a journey, you'll never have the problem of trying to "arrive" at an elusive final destination. And you'll never find yourself in a position where you have accomplished some final goal, only to discover that you're still unfulfilled and searching for something else to do.

Another benefit of focusing on the journey of success instead of on arriving at a destination or achieving a goal is that you have the potential to become a success *today*. The very moment that you make the shift to finding your purpose, growing to your potential, and helping others, successful is something you *are right now*, not something you vaguely hope one day to be.

To get a better handle on these aspects of success, let's take a look at each one of them:

KNOWING YOUR PURPOSE

Nothing can take the place of knowing your purpose. Millionaire industrialist Henry J. Kaiser, the founder of Kaiser Aluminum as well as the Kaiser-Permanente health care system, said, "The evidence is overwhelming that you cannot begin to achieve your best unless you set some aim in life." Or put another way, if you don't try actively to discover your purpose, you're likely to spend your life doing the wrong things.

I believe that God created every person for a purpose. According to psychologist Viktor Frankl, "Everyone has his own specific vocation or mission in life. Everyone must carry out a concrete assignment that demands fulfillment. Therein he cannot be replaced, nor can his life be repeated. Thus everyone's task is as unique as his specific opportunity to implement it." Each of us has a purpose for which we were created. Our responsibility—and our greatest joy—is to identify it.

Here are some questions to ask yourself to help you identify your purpose:

For what am I searching? All of us have a strong desire buried in our hearts, something that speaks to our deepest thoughts and feelings, something that sets our souls on fire. Some people have a strong sense of what that is when they're just children. Others take half a lifetime to discover it. But no matter what, it's there. You only need to find it.

Why was I created? Each of us is different. No one else in the world has exactly the same gifts, talents, background, or future. That's one of the reasons it would be a serious mistake for you to try to be someone other than yourself.

Think about your unique mix of abilities, the resources available to you, your personal history, and the opportunities around you. If you objectively identify these factors and discover the desire of your heart, you will have done a lot toward discovering your purpose in life.

Do I believe in my potential? You cannot consistently act in a manner inconsistent with the way you see yourself. If you don't believe that you have potential, you will never try to reach it. And if you aren't willing to work toward reaching your potential, you will never be successful.

You should take the advice of President Theodore Roosevelt, who said, "Do what you can, with what you have, where you are." If you do that with your eyes fixed on your life purpose, what else can be expected of you?

When do I start? Some people live their lives from day to day, allowing others to dictate what they do and how they do it. They never try to discover their true purpose for living. Others know their purpose, yet never act on it. They are waiting for inspiration or permission or an invitation to get started. But if they wait much longer, they'll never get going. So the answer to the question "When do I start?" is NOW.

GROWING TO YOUR POTENTIAL

Novelist H. G. Wells held that wealth, notoriety, place, and power are no measures of success whatsoever. The only true measure of success is the ratio between what we might have been and what we have become. In other words, success comes as the result of growing to our potential.

It's been said that our potential is God's gift to us, and what we do with it is our gift to him. But at the same time, our potential is probably our greatest untapped resource. Henry Ford observed, "There is no man living who isn't capable of doing more than he thinks he can do."

We have nearly limitless potential, yet too few ever try to reach it.

Why? The answer lies in this: We can do *anything*, but we can't do *everything*. Many people let everyone around them decide their agenda in life. As a result, they never really dedicate themselves to *their* purpose in life. They become a jack-of-all-trades, master of none—rather than a jack-of-few-trades, focused on one.

If that describes you more than you'd like, you're probably ready to take steps to make a change. Here are four principles to put you on the road to growing toward your potential:

1. Concentrate on One Main Goal. Nobody ever reached her potential by scattering herself in twenty directions. Reaching your potential requires focus. That's why it's so important for you to discover your purpose. Once you've decided where to focus your attention, you must decide what you are willing to give up to do it. And that's crucial. There can be no success without sacrifice. The two go hand in hand. If you desire to accomplish little, sacrifice little. But if you want to accomplish great things, be willing to sacrifice much.

2. Concentrate on Continual Improvement. David D. Glass, chief executive officer of Wal-Mart stores, was once asked whom he admired most. His answer was Wal-Mart founder Sam Walton. He remarked, "There's never been a day in his life, since I've known him, that he didn't improve in some way." Commitment to continual improvement is the key to reaching your potential and to being successful. Each day you can become a little bit better than you were yesterday. It puts you one step closer to your potential. And you'll also find that what you *get* as the result of your growth is not nearly as important as what you *become* along the way.

3. Forget the Past. My friend Jack Hayford, founding pastor of Church on the Way in Van Nuys, California, commented, "The past is a dead issue, and we can't gain any momentum moving toward tomorrow if we are dragging the past behind us." Unfortunately, that's what too many people do; they drag the past with them wherever they go. And as a result, they never make any progress.

I like the attitude of Cyrus Curtis, who once owned the *Saturday Evening Post.* He had a sign hanging in his office that announced, "Yesterday ended last night." It was his way of reminding himself and his employees that the past is done, and we should be looking forward, not back.

Maybe you've made a lot of mistakes in your life, or you've had an especially difficult past with many obstacles. Work your way through it and move on. Don't let it prevent you from reaching your potential.

If you need inspiration, think of other people who overcame seemingly insurmountable obstacles, such as Booker T. Washington. He was born into slavery and was denied access to the resources available to white society, but he never let that prevent him from pursuing his potential. He founded the Tuskegee Institute and the National Black Business League. He said, "I have learned that success is to be measured not so much by the position that one has reached in life as by the obstacles which one has overcome while trying to succeed."

Think of Helen Keller, who lost her sight and hearing at nineteen months old. Helen overcame her severe disabilities, went on to graduate from Radcliffe College, and became an author, noted lecturer, and champion for people who are blind.

Think of Franklin Delano Roosevelt. In 1921, at the age of thirty-nine, he had a severe case of polio, which left him disabled and in terrible pain. He never walked again without assistance. But he didn't let that stop him from pursuing his potential. Eight years later, he became the governor of New York, and in 1932, he was elected president of the United States.

No doubt, you can think of others who have overcome tragedies or past mistakes to pursue their potential. You may even know personally some people who fought back from adversity to become successful. Let them inspire you. No matter what you've faced in the past, you have the *potential* to overcome it.

4. *Focus on the Future.* Baseball Hall of Famer Yogi Berra declared, "The future isn't what it used to be." Although that may be true, it's still the only place we have to go. Your potential lies ahead of you—whether you're eight, eighteen, forty-eight, or eighty. You still have room to improve yourself. You can become better tomorrow than you are today. As the Spanish proverb says, "He who does not look ahead remains behind."

SOWING SEEDS THAT BENEFIT OTHERS

When you know your purpose in life and are growing to reach your maximum potential, you're well on your way to being a success. But there is one more essential part of the journey: helping others. Without that aspect, the journey can be a lonely and shallow experience.

It's been said that we make a living by what we get, but we make a life by what we give. Physician, theologian, and philosopher Albert Schweitzer stated it even more strongly: "The purpose of human life is to serve, and to show compassion and the will to help others." For him, the journey of fulfilling his purpose led to Africa, where he served people for many years.

For you, sowing seeds that benefit others probably won't mean traveling to another country to serve the poor—unless that is the purpose you were born to fulfill. (And if it is, you won't be satisfied until that's what you're doing.) However, if you're like most people, helping others is something you can do right here at home, whether it's spending more time with your family, developing an employee who shows potential, helping people in the community, or putting your desires on hold for the sake of your team at work. The key is to find your purpose and help others while you're pursuing it. Entertainer Danny Thomas insisted that "all of us are born for a reason, but all of us don't discover why. Success in life has nothing to do with what you gain in life or accomplish for yourself. It's what you do for others."

The journey toward success and fulfillment will not look the same for everyone because the picture of success is different for every person. But the principles used to take the journey don't change. They can be applied at home, in school, at the office, on the ball field, and in church. That's what the remainder of this book is about—the principles that can help you work toward knowing your purpose, growing to your potential, and sowing seeds that benefit others. It doesn't matter where you are now. You can learn and apply these ideas. You can be successful today.

What Direction Should I Go?

You will never go farther than your dreams take you.

If you live in a town near the ocean, you may have seen advertisements for "cruises to nowhere." Maybe you've even been on one. People get on board a cruise ship, and when they leave the pier, instead of setting out for a lush island or other exotic location, they go out to sea and travel in circles for a couple of days. Meanwhile they dine on sumptuous meals, lounge around the pool, enjoy the shows, and participate in onboard activities. It's similar to checking into a fine hotel or resort.

The problem for a lot of people is that their lives are too much like those cruises. They're on a trip with no set destination, no charted course. They're in a holding pattern, and they occupy their time pursuing pleasures or engaging in activities that don't have any lasting benefit. Meanwhile, they travel in circles. In the end, they finish no better than they started. A cruise to nowhere may be a fun way to occupy a few days of vacation time, but it's no way to spend your life.

As I mentioned before, success is a journey. You don't suddenly become successful when you arrive at a particular place or achieve a certain goal. But that doesn't mean you should travel without identifying a destination. You can't fulfill your purpose and grow toward your potential if you don't know what direction you should be going. You need to identify and sail toward your destination. In other words, you need to discover your dream.

THE POWER OF A DREAM

I believe that each of us has a dream placed in the heart. I'm not talking about wanting to win the lottery. That kind of idea comes from a desire to escape our present circumstances, not to pursue a heartfelt dream. I'm talking about a vision deep inside that speaks to the very soul. It's the thing we were born to do. It draws on our talents and gifts. It appeals to our highest ideals. It sparks our feelings of destiny. It is inseparably linked to our purpose in life. The dream starts us on the success journey.

When I look for the name of a person who identified and lived out his dream, I think of auto industry pioneer and visionary Henry Ford. He asserted, "The whole secret of a successful life is to find out what it is one's destiny to do, and then do it."

Ford's dream grew out of his interest in anything mechanical. From boyhood, he had a passion for studying and tinkering with machinery. He taught himself about steam engines, clocks, and combustion engines. He traveled around the countryside doing repair work for free, just so he could get his hands on machines. He became a mechanic and watchmaker. He even worked as a night engineer for the Detroit Edison Company.

Ford became increasingly intrigued by the idea of the automobile, and he devoted more and more of his attention to it. In 1896, he built his first car in a shed behind his house. After that, he continued to think about how to improve his early efforts, and he studied the work of other car builders, including that of Ransom E. Olds, who manufactured the first Oldsmobile in 1900.

Out of his love for machinery and intrigue over the automobile grew Ford's dream: the creation of an inexpensive mass-produced automobile.

Until then, the new horseless carriage had been an expensive luxury item, available to only the rich. But Ford was determined to put the automobile within the reach of the common person. In 1899, he helped form the Detroit Motor Company. But when his fellow organizers balked at the idea of manufacturing their product inexpensively in order to sell it to the masses, he left the company. However, he held on to his dream, and his efforts finally paid off. In 1903, he organized the Ford Motor Company and began to produce the Model T. The first year his new company produced just under 6,000 cars. But only eight years later, they produced more than 500,000. And they managed to reduce the initial retail price from $850 to only $360. Ford's dream became a reality.

Ford has been called a genius and has been credited with the birth of the assembly line and mass production. But no matter what he had going for him, his greatest asset was his dream and his willingness to devote himself to it.

A dream does many things for us:

A Dream Gives Us Direction

Have you ever known a person who didn't have a clue concerning what she wanted in life, yet was highly successful? I haven't either. We all need something worthwhile to aim for. A dream provides us with that. It acts as a compass, telling us the direction we should travel. And until we've identified that right direction, we'll never know for sure that our movement is actually progress. Our actions are just as likely to take us backward instead of forward. If you move in *any* direction other than toward your dream, you'll miss out on the opportunities necessary to be successful.

A Dream Increases Our Potential

Without a dream, we may struggle to see potential in ourselves because we don't look beyond our current circumstances. But with a dream, we begin to see ourselves in a new light, as having greater potential and being capable of stretching and growing to reach it. Every opportunity we meet, every resource we discover, every talent we develop, becomes a part of our potential to grow toward that dream. The greater the dream, the greater the potential. E. Paul Hovey said, "A blind man's world is bounded by the limits of his touch; an ignorant man's world by the limits of his knowledge; a great man's world by the limits of his vision." If your vision—your dream—is great, then so is your potential for success.

A DREAM HELPS US PRIORITIZE

A dream gives us hope for the future, and it also brings us power in the present. It makes it possible for us to prioritize everything we do. A person who has a dream knows what he is willing to give up in order to go up. He is able to measure everything he does according to whether or not it contributes to the dream, concentrating his attention on the things that bring him closer to it and giving less attention to everything that doesn't.

Ironically, many people do exactly the opposite. Rather than focus on their one dream and let go of the less important things, they want to keep every option open. But when they do, they actually face more problems because decision making becomes overly complicated for them. They are like a performer who spins plates. You might have seen one of those acts on an old television variety program such as *The Ed Sullivan Show*. The performer puts a plate on top of a long, thin rod and spins it. As long as the plate is spinning, it balances on the end of the rod. He then places the rod in a device so that it stands on end. Then he does the same thing with another rod and plate, and then another. He keeps adding plates until he has a whole bunch of them spinning. As he goes, he must occasionally stop, run back, and put more spin on the previous plates so that they don't fall.

A performer who is really good at this can get quite a few plates spinning very quickly in the beginning. But as time goes by, even the good ones find it harder to make any progress adding new plates because they're spending all their time going back to keep the previous ones spinning. Getting that last plate up and spinning usually takes an incredibly long time.

Keeping all your options open is a lot like that. At first, it's fun to have so many possibilities open before you. It seems to be an excellent idea. But as time goes by, you can't make any progress because you spend all your time preserving the options rather than moving forward.

When you have a dream, you don't have that problem. You can expend your time and energy only on the "plates" that bring you closer to your dream. You can allow all the others to stop spinning and crash to the floor. They are unimportant. That knowledge frees up your time to concentrate on the few things that make a difference, and it keeps you on the right track.

A DREAM ADDS VALUE TO OUR WORK

A dream puts everything we do into perspective. Even the tasks that aren't exciting or immediately rewarding take on added value when we know they ultimately contribute to the fulfillment of a dream. Each activity becomes an important piece in that bigger picture. It reminds me of the story of a reporter who talked to three construction workers pouring concrete at a building site. "What are you doing?" he asked the first worker. "I'm earning a paycheck," he grumbled.

The reporter asked the same question of a second laborer, who looked over his shoulder and said, "What's it look like I'm doing? I'm pouring concrete."

Then he noticed a third man, who was smiling and whistling as he worked. "What are you doing?" he asked the third worker.

He stopped what he was doing and said excitedly, "I'm building a shelter for the homeless." He wiped his hands clean on a rag and then pointed, "Look, over there is where the kitchen will be. And that over there is the women's dormitory. This here . . ."

Each man was doing the same job. But only the third was motivated by a larger vision. The work he did was fulfilling a dream, and it added value to all his efforts.

Vince Lombardi stated, "I firmly believe that any man's finest hour—his greatest fulfillment to all he holds dear—is that moment when he has worked his heart out in a good cause and lies exhausted on the field of battle—victorious." A dream provides the perspective that makes that kind of effort possible.

A DREAM PREDICTS OUR FUTURE

Katherine Logan said, "A vision foretells what may be ours. It is an invitation to do something. With a great mental picture in mind we go from one accomplishment to another, using the materials about us only as stepping-stones to that which is higher and better and more satisfying. We thus become possessors of the unseen values which are eternal."

When we have a dream, we're not just spectators sitting back, hoping that everything turns out all right. We're taking an active part in shaping the purpose and meaning of our lives. And the winds of change don't simply blow us here and there. Our dream, when pursued, is the most likely predictor of our future. That doesn't mean we have any guarantees, but it does increase our chances for success tremendously.

WHERE WILL YOUR DREAM TAKE YOU?

Dare to dream and act on that dream. Do it in spite of problems, circumstances, and obstacles. History is filled with men and women who faced adversity and achieved success in spite of it. For example, the Greek orator Demosthenes stuttered! The first time he tried to make a public speech, he was laughed off the rostrum. But he had a dream of being a notable speaker. He pursued that dream and grew toward his potential. It is said that he used to put pebbles in his mouth and practice speaking over the sound of the crashing surf at the seashore. His persistence paid off. He lived his dream: he became the greatest orator of the ancient world.

Others dared to dream and became successes. Napoleon, despite humble parentage, became an emperor. Beethoven brought to life his inner vision for music when he composed symphonies, even after he lost his hearing. Charles Dickens dreamed of becoming a writer and became the most-read novelist in Victorian England—despite being born into poverty.

Oliver Wendell Holmes noted, "The great thing in this world is not so much where we are but in what direction we are moving." This is also one of the great things about having a dream. You can pursue your dream no matter where you are today. And what happened in the past isn't as important as what lies ahead in the future. As the saying goes, "No matter what a person's past may have been, his future is spotless." You can begin pursuing your dream today!

3

WHAT ROLE DOES FAILURE PLAY IN SUCCESS?

You will not succeed unless you are willing to fail.

Too many people believe the process of achieving success is supposed to be easy. The great American inventor Thomas Edison observed that attitude among people. And this is how he responded to it:

> Failure is really a matter of conceit. People don't work hard because, in their conceit, they imagine they'll succeed without ever making an effort. Most people believe that they'll wake up some day and find themselves rich. Actually, they've got it half right, because eventually they do wake up.

Each of us has to make a choice. Are we going to sleep life away, avoiding failure at all costs? Or are we going to wake up and realize this: failure is simply a price we pay to achieve success.

FAILURE IS NOT . . .

If you can change your perspective on failure, it will help you to persevere—and ultimately achieve your desires. So how should you judge failure? By taking a look at seven things failure is *not*:

1. PEOPLE THINK FAILURE IS AVOIDABLE . . . IT'S NOT

Everybody fails, errs, and makes mistakes. You've heard the saying "To err is human, to forgive divine." Alexander Pope wrote that more than 250 years ago. And he was only paraphrasing a saying that was common 2,000 years ago, during the time of the Romans. Things today are the same as they were then: if you're a human being, you're going to make mistakes.

You're probably familiar with Murphy's Law and the Peter Principle. Recently I came across something called "Rules for Being Human." I think it describes well the state we're in as people:

Rule #1: You will learn lessons.
Rule #2: There are no mistakes—only lessons.
Rule #3: A lesson is repeated until it is learned.
Rule #4: If you don't learn the easy lessons, they get *harder.* (Pain is one way the universe gets your attention.)
Rule #5: You'll know you've learned a lesson when your actions change.

You see, writer Norman Cousins was right when he said, "The essence of man is imperfection." So know that you're going to make mistakes.

2. PEOPLE THINK FAILURE IS AN EVENT . . . IT'S NOT

Growing up, I thought that success and failure came in a moment. The best example I can think of is taking a test. If you got an F, it meant you failed. But I've come to realize that failure is a process. If you flunk a test, it doesn't mean you just failed a one-time event. The F shows that you neglected the process leading up to the test.

Failure is like success. It's not someplace you arrive. Just as success is not a single event, neither is failure. Success or failure comes from how you deal with life along the way. Truly, no one can conclude that he's failed until he breathes his last breath. Until then, he's still in process and the jury is still out.

3. PEOPLE THINK FAILURE IS OBJECTIVE ... IT'S NOT

When you err—whether you miscalculate crucial figures, miss a deadline, blow a deal, make a poor choice concerning your children, or otherwise fumble a ball—what determines whether that action was a failure? Do you look at the size of the problem it causes or the amount of money it costs you or your organization? Is it determined by how much heat you have to take from your boss or by the criticism of your peers? No. Failure isn't determined that way. The real answer is that *you* are the only person who can really label what you do a failure. It's subjective. Your perception of and response to your mistakes determine whether your actions are failure.

Did you know that entrepreneurs almost never get their first business off the ground? Or their second? Or their third? According to Tulane University business professor Lisa Amos, the average for entrepreneurs is 3.8 failures before they finally make it in business. They are not deterred by problems, mistakes, or errors. Why? Because they don't see setbacks as failure. They recognize that three steps forward and two steps back *still* equals one step forward. And as a result, they overcome average and become achievers.

4. PEOPLE THINK FAILURE IS THE ENEMY ... IT'S NOT

Most people try to avoid failure like the plague. They're afraid of it. But it takes adversity to create success. Basketball coach Rick Pitino states it even more strongly: "Failure is good," he says. "It's fertilizer. Everything I've learned about coaching I've learned from making mistakes." People who see failure as the enemy are captive to those who conquer it. Herbert V. Brocknow believes "the fellow who never makes a mistake takes his orders from one who does." Observe any highly successful person, and you'll discover a person who doesn't see a mistake as the enemy. That is true in any endeavor. As musicologist Eloise Ristad said, "When we give ourselves permission to fail, we at the same time give ourselves permission to excel."

5. PEOPLE THINK FAILURE IS IRREVERSIBLE . . . IT'S NOT

There's an old saying in Texas: "It doesn't matter how much milk you spill as long as you don't lose your cow." In other words, mistakes are not irreversible. Keep everything in perspective. The problems come when you see only the spilled milk and not the bigger picture. People who see failure correctly take it in stride.

> Mistakes don't make them want to give up.
> Success doesn't make them think that they are set up.

Every event—whether good or bad—is just one small step in the process of living. Or as Tom Peters says, "If silly things were not done, intelligent things would never happen."

6. PEOPLE THINK FAILURE IS A STIGMA . . . IT'S NOT

Mistakes are not permanent markers. I love the perspective of Senator Sam Ervin Jr. He remarked, "Defeat may serve as well as victory to shake the soul and let the glory out." That's the way we need to look at failure.

When you make mistakes, don't let them get you down. And don't let yourself think of them as a stigma. Make each failure a step to success.

7. PEOPLE THINK FAILURE IS FINAL . . . IT'S NOT

Even what may appear to be a huge failure doesn't need to keep you from achieving. Take a look at the story of Sergio Zyman. He was the mastermind behind New Coke, something that marketing consultant Robert McMath sees as one of the greatest product failures of all time.[1]

Zyman, who successfully introduced Diet Coke, believed that Coca-Cola needed to act boldly to reverse its twenty-year market decline against its rival Pepsi. His solution was to stop offering the drink that had been popular for nearly a hundred years, change the formula, and offer it as New Coke. The move was an abysmal failure that lasted seventy-nine days and cost the company about $100 million. People hated New Coke. And it caused Zyman to leave the company.

But Zyman's problems with New Coke didn't keep him down. In fact, he doesn't even see them as failure. Years later when asked if it was a mistake, Zyman answers, "No, categorically."

A failure? "No."

A blunder, a misstep, a bust? "Another word between bust and, uh, something else," he replies. "Now if you say to me, 'The strategy that you guys embarked on didn't work,' I'll say, 'Yeah, absolutely it didn't work. But the totality of the action ended up being positive.'" Ultimately, the return of Coca-Cola Classic made the company stronger.

Zyman's assessment was confirmed by Roberto Goizueta, the late chairman and chief executive of the Coca-Cola Company. He hired Zyman back at Coca-Cola in 1993.

"Judge the results," said Goizueta. "We get paid to produce results. We don't get paid to be right."[2]

EMBRACE FAILURE

How can you help yourself learn a new definition of failure and develop a different perspective concerning failure and success? By making mistakes. Chuck Braun of Idea Connection Systems encourages trainees to think differently through the use of a mistake quota. He gives each student a quota of thirty mistakes to make for each training session. And if a student uses up all thirty? He or she receives another thirty. As a result, the students relax, think of mistakes in a whole new light, and begin learning.

As you approach your next big project or assignment, give yourself a reasonable mistake quotient. How many mistakes should you expect to achieve? Twenty? Fifty? Ninety? Give yourself a quota and try to hit it before bringing the task to completion. Remember, mistakes don't define failure. They are merely the price of achievement on the journey toward success.

4

How Do I Get Started?

The first step toward success is leading yourself
exceptionally well.

Have you ever worked with people who didn't lead themselves very well? We often think that self-leadership is about making good decisions every day, when the reality is that we need to make a few critical decisions in major areas of life and then manage those decisions day to day.

Here's a classic example of what I mean. Have you ever made a New Year's resolution to exercise? You probably already believe that exercise is important. Making a decision to do it isn't that hard, but managing that decision—and following through—is much more difficult. Let's say, for example, that you sign up for a health club membership the first week of January. When you sign on, you're excited. But the first time you show up at the gym, there's a mob of people. There are so many cars that police are directing traffic. You drive around for fifteen minutes, and finally find a parking place—four blocks away. But that's okay; you're there for exercise anyway, so you walk to the gym.

Then when you get inside the building, you have to wait to even get into the locker room to change. But you think, *That's okay. I want to get into shape. This is going to be great.* You think that until you finally get dressed and discover all the machines are being used. Once again you have to wait. Finally, you get on a machine—it's not the one you really wanted, but hey, you'll take it—and you exercise for twenty minutes. When you see the line for the shower, you decide to skip it, take your clothes, and just change at home.

On your way out, you see the manager of the club, and you decide to complain about the crowds. She says, "Don't worry about it. Come back in three weeks, and you can have the closest parking place and your choice of machines. Because by then, 98 percent of the people who signed up will have dropped out!"

It's one thing to decide to exercise. It's another to actually follow through with it. As everyone else drops out, you will have to decide whether you will quit like everyone else or if you will stick with it. And that takes self-management.

WHAT SUCCESSFUL PEOPLE MUST SELF-MANAGE

If you want to be successful and gain credibility with your boss and others, focus on taking care of business in these seven areas:

1. MANAGE YOUR EMOTIONS

It's important for everybody to manage emotions. Nobody likes to spend time around an emotional time bomb who may "go off" at any moment. Leaders and other successful people know when to display emotions and when to delay them. Sometimes they show them so that their teammates can feel what they're feeling. It stirs them up. Is that manipulative? I don't think so, as long as people are doing it for the good of the team and not for their own gain. Because leaders see more than others and ahead of others, they often experience the emotions first. By letting the team know what you're feeling, you're helping them to see what you're seeing.

Other times leaders have to hold their feelings in check. In his book *American Soldier*, Gen. Tommy Franks wrote about a devastating incident that occurred in Vietnam when he was a junior officer and the example that was set for him in this area by Lt. Col. Eric Antilla, who put the men he commanded ahead of his own emotional needs:

> I studied Eric Antilla's eyes. I knew he was gripped by anguish, but he never let it show. We were at war; he was commanding troops in combat. And his quiet resolve in meeting this catastrophe gave us all strength. In an hour he would grieve, but now he stood rock solid. In war, it is necessary that commanders be able to delay their emotions until they can afford them.[1]

When I say that successful people should delay their emotions, I'm not suggesting that they deny them or bury them. The bottom line in managing your emotions is that you should put others—not yourself—first in how you handle and process them. Whether you delay or display your emotions should not be for your own gratification. You should ask yourself, *What does the team need?* not, *What will make me feel better?*

2. Manage Your Time

Time management issues are tough, but they are especially difficult for people who are neither at the top or bottom of an organization. Leaders at the top can delegate. Workers at the bottom usually punch a time clock. They get paid an hourly wage, and they do what they can while they're on the clock. People in the middle who are trying to be successful are often expected to put in long hours to get work done. Because of that, they need to manage their time well.

Time is valuable. Psychiatrist and author M. Scott Peck said, "Until you value yourself, you won't value your time. Until you value your time, you will not do anything with it." In *What to Do Between Birth and Death* (Wm. Morrow & Co., 1992), Charles Spezzano says that people don't pay for things with money; they pay for them with time. If you say to yourself, *In five years, I'll have put enough away to buy that vacation house*, then what you are really saying is that the house will cost you five years—one-twelfth of your adult life. "The phrase *spending your time* is not a metaphor," said Spezzano. "It's how life works."

Instead of thinking about what you do and what you buy in terms of money, instead think about them in terms of time. Think about it. What is worth spending your life on? Seeing your work in that light just may change the way you manage your time.

3. MANAGE YOUR PRIORITIES

Most people are generalists. They know a lot about a lot of things. However, most successful individuals are highly focused. The old proverb is true: If you chase two rabbits, both will escape. So what should you do? You should still try to get yourself to the point where you can manage your priorities and focus your time in this way:

80 percent of the time—work where you are strongest
15 percent of the time—work where you are learning
5 percent of the time—work in other necessary areas

This may not be easy to achieve, but it is what you should strive for. If you have people working for you, try to give them the things you aren't good at but they are. Or if possible, trade some duties with your colleagues so that each of you is playing to your strength. Remember, the only way to move up from the middle is to gradually shift from generalist to specialist, from someone who does many things well to someone who focuses on a few things she does exceptionally well.

The secret to making the shift is often discipline. In *Good to Great*, Jim Collins wrote:

Most of us lead busy, but undisciplined lives. We have ever-expanding "to do" lists, trying to build momentum by doing, doing, doing—and doing more. And it rarely works. Those who build the good-to-great companies, however, made as much use of "stop doing" lists as the "to do" lists. They displayed a remarkable amount of discipline to unplug all sorts of extraneous junk.[2]

You must be ruthless in your judgment of what you should not do. Just because you like doing something doesn't mean it should stay on your to-do list. If it is a strength, do it. If it helps you grow, do it. If your leader says you must handle it personally, do it. Anything else is a candidate for your "stop doing" list.

4. Manage Your Energy

Some people have to ration their energy so that they don't run out. Up until a few years ago, that wasn't me. When people asked me how I got so much done, my answer was always, "High energy, low IQ." From the time I was a kid, I was always on the go. I was six years old before I realized my name wasn't "Settle Down."

Now that I'm past sixty, I do have to pay attention to my energy level. In *Thinking for a Change*, I shared one of my strategies for managing my energy. When I look at my calendar every morning, I ask myself, *What is the main event?* That is the one thing to which I cannot afford to give anything less than my best. That one thing can be for my family, my employees, a friend, my publisher, the sponsor of a speaking engagement, or my writing time. I always make sure I have the energy to do it with focus and excellence.

Even people with high energy can have that energy sucked right out of them under difficult circumstances. I've observed that leaders in the middle of an organization often have to deal with what I call "the ABCs energy-drain."

> *Activity Without Direction*—doing things that don't seem to matter
> *Burden Without Action*—not being able to do things that really matter

Conflict Without Resolution—not being able to deal with what's
the matter

If you find that you are in an organization where you often must deal
with these ABCs, then you will have to work extra hard to manage your
energy well. Either that or you need to look for a new place to work.

5. MANAGE YOUR THINKING

Poet and novelist James Joyce said, "Your mind will give back to you
exactly what you put into it." The greatest enemy of good thinking is busyness. If you find that the pace of life is too demanding for you to stop and
think during your workday, then get into the habit of jotting down the
three or four things that need good mental processing or planning that you
can't stop to think about. Then carve out some time later when you can
give those items some good think-time. That may be thirty minutes at
home the same day, or you may want to keep a running list for a whole
week and then take a couple of hours on Saturday. Just don't let the list get
so long that it disheartens or intimidates you.

I encouraged readers in *Thinking for a Change* to have a place to think,
and I wrote about the "thinking chair" I have in my office. I don't use that
chair for anything else other than my think-time. I've discovered since the
book's publication that I didn't explain clearly enough how to correctly use
the thinking chair. People at conferences told me that they sat in their own
thinking chairs and nothing happened. I explain to them that I don't sit in
that thinking chair without an agenda, just hoping that a good idea hits me.
What I usually do is think about the things I've jotted down because I
couldn't think about them during a busy day. I take the list to my chair, put
it in front of me, and give each item as much think-time as it needs.
Sometimes I'm evaluating a decision I've already made. Sometimes I'm
thinking through a decision I will have to make. Sometimes I'm developing
a strategy. Other times I'm trying to be creative in fleshing out an idea.

I want to encourage you to try managing your thinking in this way.
If you've never done it before, you will be amazed by the payoff. A

minute of thinking is often more valuable than an hour of talk or unplanned work.

6. MANAGE YOUR WORDS

Legendary basketball coach John Wooden said, "Show me what you can do; don't just tell me what you can do." Successful people value action. And if they are going to stop what they're doing long enough to listen, the words they hear need to have value. Make them count.

In *The Forbes Scrapbook of Thoughts on the Business Life* (Triumph Books, 1995), Emile de Girardin is quoted as saying, "The power of words is immense. A well-chosen word has often sufficed to stop a flying army, to change defeat into victory, and to save an empire." If you wish to make sure that your words carry weight, then weigh them well. The good news is that if you manage your thinking and take advantage of focused think-time, you will probably see improvement in the area of managing your words too.

David McKinley, a successful leader in a large organization in Plano, Texas, told me a story about something that happened in his first job after graduate school. He was preparing to make an important call on someone, and he decided that he should ask the top leader to go with him. When they got there, David, in his enthusiasm, just wouldn't stop talking. He didn't give his leader a chance to do anything but watch until the very end of their visit.

As they returned to the car, David's boss told him, "I might as well have stayed at the office." He went on to explain how his presence was superfluous. David told me, "I learned a huge lesson that day about staying 'in bounds' when I was with the senior leader. His honest counsel and correction strengthened our relationship and has served me well throughout my life." If you have something worthwhile to say, say it briefly and well. If you don't, sometimes the best thing to do is remain silent.

7. MANAGE YOUR PERSONAL LIFE

You can do everything right at work and manage yourself well there, but if your personal life is a mess, it will eventually turn everything else sour. What would it profit a person to climb to the top of the organizational chart but to lose a marriage or alienate the children? As someone who spent many years counseling people, I can tell you, no career success is worth it.

For years one of my definitions of *success* has been this: having those closest to me love and respect me the most. That is what is most important. I want the love and respect of my wife, my children, and my grandchildren before I want the respect of anyone I work with. Don't get me wrong. I want the people who work with me to respect me, too, but not at the expense of my family. If I blow managing myself at home, then the negative impact will spill over into every area of my life, including work.

LEAD YOURSELF FIRST

If you want to influence others, you must always lead yourself first. If you can't, you have no credibility. That applies whether the influence you desire to exert is on the people above you, beside you, or below you. The better you are at making sure you're doing what you should be doing, the better chance you have for making an impact on others and being successful.

PART II

THE CORE QUALITIES FOR SUCCESS

5

HOW WELL DO I
WORK WITH PEOPLE?

It is no exaggeration to say that the ability to work with people
is the most important ingredient for success.

What kind of price would you put on good people skills? Ask the successful CEOs of major corporations what characteristic is most needed for success in leadership positions, and they'll tell you it's the ability to work with people. Interview entrepreneurs to find out what separates the successes from the failures, and they'll tell you it is skill with people. Talk to top salespeople and they'll tell you that people knowledge is much more important than mere product knowledge. Sit down with teachers and tradesmen, shop foremen and small business owners, pastors and parents, and they'll tell you that people skills make the difference between those who excel and those who don't. People skills are invaluable. It doesn't matter what you want to do. If you can win with people, you can win!

WHAT KIND OF PERSON ARE YOU?

For years psychologists have attempted to divide people into various categories. Sometimes an observant poet can do a better job. Ella Wheeler Wilcox did so in the poem "Which Are You?":

There are two kinds of people on earth today;
Just two kinds of people, no more, I say.

Not the sinner and saint, for it's well understood,
That the good are half-bad and the bad half-good.

Not the rich and the poor, for to rate a man's wealth,
You must first know the state of his conscience and health.

Not the humble and proud, for in life's little span,
Who puts on vain airs, is not counted a man.

Not the happy and sad, for the swift flying years
Bring each man his laughter and each man his tears.

No; the two kinds of people on earth I mean,
Are the people who lift, and the people who lean.
Wherever you go, you will find the earth's masses,
Are always divided in just these two classes.

And oddly enough, you will find too, I ween,
There's only one lifter to twenty who lean.

In which class are you? Are you easing the load,
Of overtaxed lifters, who toil down the road?
Or are you a leaner, who lets others share
Your portion of labor, and worry and care?[1]

These are good questions we must ask ourselves, because our answers will have a huge impact on our relationships. I think Wilcox was on the right track. People do tend to add value to others, lessening their load and lifting them up, or they take away value from others, thinking only of themselves and taking people down in the process. But I would take that one step farther. I believe the intensity with which we lift or lower others can determine that there are really *four* kinds of people when it comes to relationships:

1. Some People Add Something to Life— We Enjoy Them

Many people in this world desire to help others. These people are adders. They make the lives of others more pleasant and enjoyable. They're the lifters Wilcox wrote about. Evangelist D. L. Moody advised people to . . .

> do all the good you can,
> to all the people you can,
> in all the ways you can,
> as long as ever you can.

Moody was an adder.

People who add value to others almost always do so *intentionally*. I say that because adding value to others requires a person to give of himself, and that rarely occurs by accident. I have endeavored to become an adder. I like people, and I want to help them. I make it my goal to be a friend.

Recently the CEO of a large corporation invited me to speak on leadership for his organization. After teaching his executives and conducting sessions for his managers, I had gained enough credibility with him that he wanted to do something nice for me.

"John, I like what you've done for us," he said as we sat one day in his office. "Now, what can I do for you?"

"Nothing," I replied. "You don't need to do anything for me." The corporation had, of course, paid me for the times I had spoken, and I had really enjoyed the experience. His people were sharp and eager to learn.

"Oh, come on," he said. "Everybody wants *something*. What do you want?"

"Look, doesn't everybody need an easy friend? Somebody who doesn't want anything?" I answered, looking him in the eye. "I just want to be an easy friend."

He chuckled and said, "Okay, you'll be my easy friend." And that's who I have endeavored to be. Author Frank Tyger says, "Friendship consists of a willing ear, an understanding heart and a helping hand." That's what I'm trying to give my friend.

2. SOME PEOPLE SUBTRACT SOMETHING FROM LIFE— WE TOLERATE THEM

In *Julius Caesar*, playwright William Shakespeare's Cassius asserts, "A friend should bear his friend's infirmities, but Brutus makes mine greater than they are." That's what subtracters do. They do not bear our burdens, and they make heavier the ones we already have. The sad thing about subtracters is that what they do is usually unintentional. If you don't know how to add to others, then you probably subtract by default.

In relationships, receiving is easy. Giving is much more difficult. It's similar to the difference between building something and tearing it down. It takes a skilled craftsman much time and energy to build a beautiful chair. It takes no skill whatsoever to smash that chair in a matter of moments.

3. SOME PEOPLE MULTIPLY SOMETHING IN LIFE— WE VALUE THEM

Anyone who wants to can become an adder. It takes only a desire to lift people up and the intentionality to follow through. But to go to another level in relationships—to become a multiplier—one must be intentional, strategic, and skilled. The greater the talent and resources a person possesses, the greater his potential to become a multiplier.

I am fortunate. I have a lot of multipliers in my life, highly gifted people who want to see me succeed, people such as Todd Duncan, Rick Goad, and Tom Mullins. Each of these men has a servant's heart. They are tops in their fields. They value partnership. They're always generating great ideas. And they're passionate about making a difference. They help me to sharpen my vision and maximize my strengths.

You probably have people like that in your life, people who live to help you succeed and have the skills to help you along the way. If you can think of people who have played the role of multiplier in your life, stop and take some time to call or write them and let them know what they've meant in your life.

4. Some People Divide Something in Life—We Avoid Them

R. G. LeTourneau, inventor of numerous kinds of heavy earth-moving equipment, says that his company used to make a scraper that was known as Model G. One day a customer asked a salesman what the *G* stood for. The salesman, like many people in his profession, was quick on his feet, and he replied, "The *G* stands for *gossip*, because like a tale-bearer, this machine moves a lot of dirt and moves it fast!"

Dividers are people who will really "take you to the basement," meaning they'll take you down as low as they can, as often as they can. They're like the company president who sent his personnel director a memo saying, "Search the organization for an alert, aggressive young man who could step into my shoes—and when you find him, fire him."

Dividers are so damaging because, unlike subtracters, their negative actions are usually intentional. They are hurtful people who make themselves look or feel better by trying to make someone else do worse than they do. As a result, they damage relationships and create havoc in people's lives.

TAKE OTHERS TO A HIGHER LEVEL

I believe that deep down everyone—even the most negative person—wants to be a lifter. We all want to be a positive influence in the lives of others. And we can be. If you want to lift people up and add value to their lives, keep the following in mind:

LIFTERS COMMIT THEMSELVES TO DAILY ENCOURAGEMENT

Roman philosopher Lucius Annaeus Seneca observed, "Wherever there is a human being, there is an opportunity for kindness." Encourage others, and do it daily.

LIFTERS KNOW THE LITTLE DIFFERENCE THAT SEPARATES HURTING AND HELPING

The little things you do every day have a greater impact on others than you might think. A smile, rather than a frown, can make someone's day. A kind word instead of criticism lifts an individual's spirits rather than dragging him down.

You hold the power to make another person's life better or worse by the things you do today. Those closest to you—your spouse, children, or parents—are most affected by what you say and do. Use that power wisely.

LIFTERS INITIATE THE POSITIVE IN A NEGATIVE ENVIRONMENT

It's one thing to be positive in a positive or neutral environment. It's another to be an instrument of change in a negative environment. Yet that's what lifters try to do. Sometimes that requires a kind word, other times it takes a servant's action, and occasionally it calls for creativity.

American revolutionary Ben Franklin told in his autobiography about asking a favor to create a positive connection in a negative environment. In 1736, Franklin was being considered for a position as clerk of the general assembly. Only one person stood in the way of his nomination, a powerful man who did not like Franklin.

Franklin wrote, "Having heard that he had in his library a certain very scarce book, I wrote a note to him, expressing my desire of perusing that book and requesting he would do me the favor of lending it to me." The man was flattered and delighted by the request. He loaned Franklin the book, and the two became lifelong friends.

Lifters Understand Life Is Not a Dress Rehearsal

Here's a quote I've always loved: "I expect to pass through this world but once. Any good therefore that I can do, or any kindness that I can show to any fellow creature, let me do it now. Let me not defer or neglect it, for I shall not pass this way again."[2] People who lift others don't wait until tomorrow or some other "better" day to help people. They act now!

Everyone is capable of becoming a person who lifts up others. You don't have to be rich. You don't have to be a genius. You don't have to have it all together. You do have to care about people and initiate lifting activities. Don't let another day go by without lifting up the people in your life. Doing that will positively change the relationships you already have and open you up to many more.

6

DO OTHERS
FIND ME TRUSTWORTHY?

Trust is the foundation of all relationships.

I f you've traveled through smaller airports or have much experience flying in corporate aircraft, you've probably seen or flown in a Learjet. I've had the opportunity to fly in one a couple of times, and it's quite an experience. They're small—capable of carrying only five or six passengers—and very fast. It's like climbing into a narrow tube with jet engines strapped to it.

I have to admit, the whole experience of riding in a Learjet is pretty exhilarating. But by far the most amazing thing to me about it is the time it saves. I've traveled literally millions of miles on airlines, and I'm accustomed to long drives to airports, car rental returns, shuttles, terminal congestion, and seemingly endless delays. It can be a nightmare. Flying on a Learjet can easily cut travel time in half.

The father of this amazing airplane was a man named Bill Lear. An inventor, aviator, and business leader, Lear held more than 150 patents, including those of the automatic pilot, car radio, and eight-track tapes (you can't win them all). Lear was a pioneer in his thinking, and in the

1950s, he could see the potential for the manufacture of small corporate jets. It took him several years to make his dream a reality, but in 1963, the first Learjet made its maiden voyage, and in 1964 he delivered his first production jet to a client.

Lear's success was immediate, and he quickly sold many aircraft. But not long after he got his start, Lear learned that two aircraft he'd built had crashed under mysterious circumstances. He was devastated. At that time, fifty-five Learjets were privately owned, and Lear immediately sent word to all of the owners to ground their planes until he and his team could determine what had caused the crashes. The thought that more lives might be lost was far more important to him than any adverse publicity that action might generate in the media.

As he researched the ill-fated flights, Lear discovered a potential cause, but he couldn't verify the technical problem on the ground. There was only one sure way to find out whether he had diagnosed the problem correctly. He would have to try to re-create it personally—in the air.

It was a dangerous process, but that's what he did. As he flew the jet, he nearly lost control and almost met the same fate as the other two pilots. But he did manage to make it through the tests, and he was able to verify the defect. Lear developed a new part to correct the problem and fitted all fifty-five planes with it, eliminating the danger.

Grounding the planes cost Lear a lot of money. And it planted seeds of doubt in the minds of potential customers. As a result, he needed two years to rebuild the business. But Lear never regretted his decision. He was willing to risk his success, his fortune, and even his life to solve the mystery of those crashes—but not his integrity. And that takes character.

The Importance of Character

How a person deals with the circumstances of life tells you many things about his character. Crisis doesn't necessarily make character, but it certainly does reveal it. Adversity is a crossroads that makes a person choose one of two paths: character or compromise. Every time he chooses character, he becomes stronger, even if that choice brings negative consequences. As Nobel prize–winning author Alexander Solzhenitsyn noted, "The meaning of earthly existing lies, not as we have grown used to thinking, in prospering, but in the development of the soul." The development of character is at the heart of our development not just as leaders, but as human beings.

What must every person know about character?

1. CHARACTER IS MORE THAN TALK

Anyone can *say* that he has integrity, but action is the real indicator of character. Your character determines who you are. Who you are determines what you see. What you see determines what you do. That's why you can never separate a person's character from his actions. If a person's actions and intentions are continually working against each other, then look to his character to find out why.

2. TALENT IS A GIFT, BUT CHARACTER IS A CHOICE

We have no control over a lot of things in life. We don't get to choose our parents. We don't select the location or circumstances of our birth and upbringing. We don't get to pick our talents or IQ. But we do choose our character. In fact, we create it every time we make choices— to cop out or dig out of a hard situation, to bend the truth or stand under the weight of it, to take the easy money or pay the price. As you live your life and make choices today, you are continuing to create your character.

3. CHARACTER BRINGS LASTING SUCCESS WITH PEOPLE

True leadership always involves other people. (As the leadership proverb says, if you think you're leading and no one is following you, then you're only taking a walk.) Followers do not trust leaders whose character they know to be flawed, and they will not continue following them.

4. People Cannot Rise Above the Limitations of Their Character

Have you ever seen highly talented people suddenly fall apart when they achieved a certain level of success? The key to that phenomenon is character. Steven Berglas, a psychologist at Harvard Medical School and author of *The Success Syndrome,* says that people who achieve great heights but lack the bedrock character to sustain them through the stress are headed for disaster. He believes they are destined for one or more of the four As: *arrogance,* painful feelings of *aloneness,* destructive *adventure-seeking,* or *adultery.* Each is a terrible price to pay for weak character.

Examine Yourself

If you've found yourself being sucked in by one of the four As that Berglas identifies, call a time-out. Do what you must to step away from some of the stress of your success, and seek professional help. Don't think that the valley you're in will pass with time, more money, or increased prestige. Unaddressed cracks in character only get deeper and more destructive with time.

If you're not struggling in any of these four areas, you should still examine the condition of your character. Ask yourself whether your words and actions match—all the time. When you say you'll finish an assignment, do you always follow through? If you tell your children that you'll make it to their recital or ball game, are you there for it? Can people trust your handshake as they would a legal contract?

As you lead others at home, at work, and in the community, recognize that your character is your most important asset. G. Alan Bernard, president of Mid Park, Inc., stated, "The respect that leadership must have requires that one's ethics be without question. A leader not only stays above the line between right and wrong, he stays well clear of the 'gray areas.'"

BUILDING CHARACTER

To improve your character, do the following:

SEARCH FOR THE CRACKS

Spend some time looking at the major areas of your life (work, marriage, family, service, etc.), and identify anywhere you might have cut corners, compromised, or let people down. Write down every instance you can recall from the past two months.

LOOK FOR PATTERNS

Examine the responses that you just wrote down. Is there a particular area where you have a weakness, or do you have a type of problem that keeps surfacing? Detectable patterns will help you diagnose character issues.

FACE THE MUSIC

The beginning of character repair comes when you face your flaws, apologize, and deal with the consequences of your actions. Create a list of people to whom you need to apologize for your actions; then follow through with sincere apologies.

REBUILD

It's one thing to face up to your past actions. It's another to build a new future. Now that you've identified any areas of weakness, create a plan that will prevent you from making the same mistakes again.

A man took his young daughter to a carnival, and she immediately ran over to a booth and asked for cotton candy. As the attendant handed her a huge ball of it, the father asked, "Sweetheart, are you sure you can eat all that?" "Don't worry, Dad," she answered, "I'm a lot bigger on the inside than on the outside."

That's what real character is—being bigger on the inside.

7

HOW SKILLED AM I
IN MY WORK?

To hit the mark, aim above it.

Benjamin Franklin always thought of himself as an ordinary citizen. One of seventeen children, Franklin was the son of a tradesman, a candlemaker, who was far from wealthy. He experienced a typical childhood. He attended school for only two years, and at age twelve, he was apprenticed to his brother in the printing trade.

Franklin worked hard and lived a simple life, governing his actions according to a set of thirteen virtues, upon which he graded himself daily. At age twenty he started his own printing business. Had Franklin been content to work at his trade, his name would be little more than a footnote in Philadelphia's history. Yet he lived an extraordinary life. He was one of the fathers of American independence and a great leader of the emerging nation. He coauthored the Declaration of Independence, and he later helped write the Treaty of Paris and the Constitution of the United States. (He was the only man who signed all three.) And he was selected to perform a difficult and dangerous secret diplomatic mission to Paris during the war to secure military and financial support for the Revolution.

What gave a Northern tradesman the opportunity to exert so much influence among the wealthy, predominately Southern landholders who headed the war for independence? I believe it was Franklin's incredible competence.

Benjamin Franklin excelled at everything he touched for seven decades. When he started his own printing business in 1726, people believed Philadelphia could not support a third printer, but Franklin quickly established a reputation as the most skilled and industrious printer in town. But the Philadelphia tradesman wasn't content with only that accomplishment.

Franklin's mind was curious, and he continually sought ways to improve himself and others. He expanded into publishing, his work including the noted *Poor Richard's Almanack*. He did extensive experiments with electricity and coined many of the terms still associated with its use. He invented numerous items such as the potbellied stove, the catheter, and bifocals. And when he traveled frequently across the Atlantic Ocean, he took it upon himself to chart the Gulf Stream. His attitude toward life could be seen in an aphorism he wrote for his almanac: "Hide not your talents. They for use were made. What's a sundial in the shade?"

The evidences of Franklin's talents were many. He helped establish Philadelphia's first library. He started the nation's first fire department. He developed the concept of daylight saving time. And he held many posts serving the government.

For the most part, Franklin was recognized for his ability. But sometimes he had to let his competence speak for itself. During a time when he was working on improvements in agriculture, he discovered that plaster made grains and grasses grow better, but he had a difficult time convincing his neighbors about the discovery. His solution? When spring arrived, he went to a field close to a path, dug out some letters into the dirt with his hands, put plaster into the ruts, and then sowed seed over the whole area. As people passed that way in following weeks, they could see green letters growing brighter than the rest of the field. They said simply, "This has been plastered." People got the message.

RAISE YOUR LEVEL OF COMPETENCE

We all admire people who display high competence, whether they are precision craftsmen, world-class athletes, or successful business leaders. But the truth is that you don't have to be Fabergé, Michael Jordan, or Bill Gates to excel in the area of competence. If you want to cultivate that quality, here's what you need to do.

1. SHOW UP EVERY DAY

There's a saying, "All things come to him who waits." Unfortunately sometimes, it's just the leftovers from the people who got there first. Responsible people show up when they're expected. But highly competent people take it a step farther. They don't show up in body only. They come ready to play every day—no matter how they feel, what kind of circumstances they face, or how difficult they expect the game to be.

2. KEEP IMPROVING

Like Benjamin Franklin, all highly competent people continually search for ways to keep learning, growing, and improving. They do that by asking *why*. After all, the person who knows *how* will always have a job, but the person who knows *why* will always be the boss.

3. FOLLOW THROUGH WITH EXCELLENCE

I've never met a person I considered competent who didn't follow through. I bet it's the same for you. Willa A. Foster remarked, "Quality is never an accident; it is always the result of high intention, sincere effort, intelligent direction and skillful execution; it represents the wise choice of many alternatives." Performing at a high level of excellence is always a choice, an act of the will.

4. ACCOMPLISH MORE THAN EXPECTED

Highly competent people always go the extra mile. For them, good enough is never good enough. In *Men in Mid-Life Crisis,* Jim Conway writes that some people feel "a weakening of the need to be a great man and an increasing feeling of 'let's just get through this the best way we can.' Never mind hitting home runs. Let's just get through the ball game without getting beaned." Successful people cannot afford to have that kind of attitude. They need to do the job, and then some, day in and day out.

5. INSPIRE OTHERS

Highly competent people do more than perform at a high level. They inspire and motivate other people to do the same. While some rely on relational skills alone to survive, effective people combine these skills with high competence to take their organizations to new levels of excellence and influence.

HOW COMPETENT ARE YOU?

Where do you stand when it comes to getting the job done? Do you attack everything you do with fervor and perform at the highest level possible? Or is good enough sometimes good enough for you?

When you think about people who are competent, you're really considering only three types of people:

1. Those who can see what needs to happen.

2. Those who can make it happen.

3. Those who can make things happen when it really counts.

When it comes to your profession, where do you consistently perform? Are you a thinker, a doer, or a clutch player? The better you are, the greater potential for influence you will have with your people.

GETTING IN THE GAME

To improve your competence, do the following:

GET YOUR HEAD IN THE GAME

If you've been mentally or emotionally detached from your work, it's time to reengage. First, rededicate yourself to your job. Determine to give it an appropriate amount of your undivided attention. Second, figure out why you have been detached. Do you need new challenges? Are you in conflict with your boss or co-workers? Are you in a dead-end job? Identify the source of the problem, and create a plan to resolve it.

REDEFINE THE STANDARD

If you're not performing at a consistently high level, reexamine your standards. Are you shooting too low? Do you cut corners? If so, hit your mental reset button, and outline more demanding expectations for yourself.

FIND THREE WAYS TO IMPROVE

Nobody keeps improving without being intentional about it. Do a little research to find three things you can do to improve your professional skills. Then dedicate the time and money to follow through on them.

I read an editorial in *Texas Business* not long ago that said, "We are truly the lost generation, huffing and puffing down the fast track to nowhere, always looking to the dollar sign for direction. That's the only standard we recognize. We have no built-in beliefs, no ethical boundaries."

You're only as good as your private standards. When was the last time you gave a task your absolute best even though nobody but you would know about it?

8

DO I KEEP GOING
WHEN OTHERS DON'T?

Quitters never win and winners never quit.

In the summer of 2001, my wife, Margaret, and I went to England for ten days with our friends Dan and Patti Reiland, Tim and Pam Elmore, and Andy Steimer. We've been close to the Reilands and Elmores about twenty years, and we've done a lot of traveling together, so we were really looking forward to the trip. And though we haven't known Andy nearly as long, he's become a good friend—and he's been to England so many times that he was acting almost like our unofficial tour guide.

As we prepared for the trip, several of us had specific interests and historic sites we wanted to include. For instance, I wanted to visit all the places related to John Wesley, the renowned evangelist of the eighteenth century. For more than thirty years, I've studied Wesley, read all his writings, and collected his books. So we went to Epworth, where he grew up, to Wesley's Chapel in London, and to many of the places where he preached. For Tim, we visited Cambridge and other sites related to apologist, professor, and author C. S. Lewis. Andy had only one must-see place on his list, since he had been to England so many times: Winston Churchill's war rooms.

Three of us wanted to walk in the places where our heroes had walked, to get a glimpse of history and maybe understand the sense of destiny one of these great leaders or thinkers must have experienced. Then there was Dan. Sure, Dan enjoyed sharing our interests. He loves the subject of leadership, he's read C. S. Lewis's works, and he is ordained as a Wesleyan pastor. And he had a great time visiting our preferred sites. But the one place he absolutely *had* to see was the crosswalk where the Beatles had been photographed for the *Abbey Road* album. Dan wanted us to get our picture taken walking across the street, just as John, Ringo, Paul, and George had.

Now, I like the Beatles, and I thought it might be fun to visit the site. But to Dan, it was more than a big deal. It was essential. If we didn't make it to Abbey Road, then his trip just wouldn't have been complete. Because of that, every day as we set out from our London hotel on our itinerary, Dan would press us intently: "Now, guys, we're going to make it to Abbey Road, right?"

On the last day, we were scheduled to finally make our Abbey Road trek. Everyone except Margaret got up at six o'clock and piled into two cabs to make the trip across town to the street outside the recording studio where the Beatles recorded their last album. Dan was so excited that I thought he was going to bounce off the walls of the cab.

When we got there, we couldn't believe it. The street was closed! Big construction trucks were everywhere, and orange cones filled the crosswalk. It looked as if we had made the trip for nothing. Because we would be leaving London later that afternoon, we wouldn't get another opportunity for the picture. Dan would have to go home empty-handed.

We decided to get out of the cabs anyway, just to check out the situation. We figured there might be heavy construction occurring on the tiny street. However, we discovered that a huge crane, which was located about a half mile away, was scheduled to come down the street sometime in the afternoon, and that's why the road was closed. That gave me hope that we might succeed after all. None of us wanted Dan to be disappointed, and I always love a challenge. So we went to work.

We struck up a conversation with the workmen who had closed the road. At first, they had no idea what we wanted. Then when they understood why we were there, they folded their arms, stood as solid as the Rock of Gibraltar, and told us it couldn't be done. It was their turf, it was their job, and they were not going to move. However, I did have to laugh when we talked to one worker who was about twenty-five years old. When we said that Dan wanted a photo like the one on the Beatles' album, and that the original had been taken on that very spot, the young man said, "Really? It was here?"

We talked to the guys some more. We joked. We offered to take them all out to lunch. And we told them how far we had come and how much the whole thing meant to Dan. "You can be Dan's heroes," I explained. After a while, I could see they were beginning to soften. Finally a big, burly guy with a thick accent said, "Oh, let's help the Yanks out. What could it hurt?"

The next thing we knew, it was like they were working for us. They began clearing cones and moving trucks. They even let Patti, Dan's wife, climb up onto one of the trucks to take the picture so that it would be from the same angle as the Beatles' original shot. Quickly we lined up: first Tim, then Andy, then me (with my shoes off like Paul McCartney), and finally Dan. It was a moment we won't soon forget, and the photo sits on my desk today to remind me of it.

Working with Persistence

On that summer day in London, did we succeed because of extraordinary talent? No. Was it because of our timing? Certainly not, since our timing got us into trouble in the first place. Was it power or sheer numbers? No, there were only six of us. We succeeded because we were tenacious. Our desire to get that picture was so strong that success for our little team was almost inevitable.

It's appropriate to finish the discussion of the essential qualities of a team player by talking about tenacity because tenacity is crucial to success. Even people who lack talent and fail to cultivate some of the other vital qualities of a team player have a chance to contribute to the team and help it succeed if they possess a tenacious spirit.

Being tenacious means . . .

1. GIVING ALL THAT YOU HAVE, NOT MORE THAN YOU HAVE

Some people who lack tenacity do so because they mistakenly believe that being tenacious demands from them more than they have to offer. As a result, they don't push themselves. However, being tenacious requires that you give 100 percent—not more, but certainly not less. If you give your all, you afford yourself every opportunity possible for success.

Look at the case of General George Washington. During the entire course of the Revolutionary War, he won only three battles. But he gave all he had, and when he did win, it counted. British general Cornwallis, who surrendered to Washington at Yorktown to end the war, said to the American commander, "Sir, I salute you not only as a great leader of men, but as an indomitable Christian gentleman who wouldn't give up."

2. WORKING WITH DETERMINATION, NOT WAITING ON DESTINY

Tenacious people don't rely on luck, fate, or destiny for their success. And when conditions become difficult, they keep working. They know that trying times are no time to quit trying. And that's what makes the difference. For the thousands of people who give up, there is always someone like Thomas Edison, who remarked, "I start where the last man left off."

3. QUITTING WHEN THE JOB IS DONE, NOT WHEN YOU'RE TIRED

Robert Strauss stated that "success is a little like wrestling a gorilla. You don't quit when you're tired—you quit when the gorilla is tired." If you want your team to succeed, you have to keep pushing beyond what you *think* you can do and find out what you're really capable of. It's not the first but the last step in the relay race, the last shot in the basketball game, the last yard with the football into the end zone that makes the difference, for that is where the game is won. Motivational author Napoleon Hill summed it up: "Every successful person finds that great success lies just beyond the point when they're convinced their idea is not going to work." Tenacity hangs on until the job is finished.

How tenacious are you? When others have given up, do you keep hanging on? If it's the bottom of the ninth inning and there are two outs, have you already lost the game mentally, or are you ready to rally the team to victory? If the team hasn't found a solution to a problem, are you willing to keep plugging away to the very end in order to succeed? If you sometimes give up before the rest of the team does, you may need a strong dose of tenacity.

HOW TO BECOME MORE TENACIOUS

A. L. Williams says, "You beat 50 percent of the people in America by working hard. You beat another 40 percent by being a person of honesty and integrity and standing for something. The last 10 percent is a dog-fight in the free enterprise system." To improve your tenacity . . .

WORK HARDER AND/OR SMARTER

If you tend to be a clock-watcher who never works beyond quitting time no matter what, then you need to change your habits. Put in an additional sixty to ninety minutes of work every day by arriving at work thirty to forty-five minutes early and staying an equal amount of time after your normal hours. If you are someone who already puts in an inordinate number of hours, then spend more time planning to make your working hours more efficient.

STAND FOR SOMETHING

To succeed, you must act with absolute integrity. However, if you can add to that the power of purpose, you will possess an additional edge. Write on an index card how your day-to-day work relates to your overall purpose. Then review that card daily to keep your emotional fires burning.

MAKE YOUR WORK A GAME

Nothing feeds tenacity like our natural competitive nature. Try to harness that by making your work a game. Find others in your organization who have similar goals and create a friendly competition with them to motivate you and them.

ACCOMPLISHING THE IMPOSSIBLE

People said it couldn't be done—building a railroad from sea level on the coast of the Pacific Ocean into the Andes Mountains, the second-highest mountain range on earth after the Himalayans. Yet that is what Ernest Malinowski, a Polish-born engineer, wanted to do. In 1859, he proposed building a rail line from Callao on the coast of Peru into the country's interior—to an elevation of more than fifteen thousand feet. If he was successful, it would be the highest railway in the world.

The Andes are treacherous mountains. The altitude makes work difficult, but add to that frigid conditions, glaciers, and the potential for volcanic activity. And the mountains climb from sea level to tens of thousands of feet in a very short distance. Climbing to high altitude in the jagged mountains would require switchbacks, zigzags, and numerous bridges and tunnels.

But Malinowski and his work crews succeeded. Jans S. Plachta states, "There are approximately hundred tunnels and bridges, some of which are major engineering feats. It is difficult to visualize how this task could have been accomplished with relatively primitive construction equipment, high altitudes, and mountainous terrain as obstacles." The railroad still stands today as a testament to the tenacity of the men who built it. No matter what happened to them during the process, Malinowski and his team never, never, never quit.

9

AM I STRIVING
TO KEEP LEARNING?

The day you stop growing is the beginning
of the end of your success.

I f you see the image of a little man sporting a tiny moustache, carrying a cane, and wearing baggy pants, big, clumsy shoes, and a derby hat, you know immediately that it's Charlie Chaplin. Just about everyone recognizes him. In the 1910s and 1920s, he was *the* most famous and recognizable person on the planet. If we looked at today's celebrities, the only person even in the same category as Chaplin in popularity would be Michael Jordan. And to measure who is the bigger star, we would have to wait another seventy-five years to find out how well everyone remembers Michael.

When Chaplin was born, nobody would have predicted great fame for him. Born into poverty as the son of English music hall performers, he found himself on the street as a small child when his mother was institutionalized. After years in workhouses and orphanages, he began working on the stage to support himself. By age seventeen, he was a veteran performer. In 1914, while just in his mid-twenties, he worked for Mack

Sennett at Keystone Studios in Hollywood making $150 a week. During that first year in the movie business, he made thirty-five films working as an actor, writer, and director. Everyone recognized his talent immediately, and his popularity grew. A year later, he earned $1,250 a week. Then in 1918, he did something unheard-of. He signed the entertainment industry's first $1 million contract. He was rich; he was famous; and he was the most powerful filmmaker in the world—at the ripe old age of twenty-nine.

Chaplin was successful because he had great talent and incredible drive. But those traits were fueled by teachability. He continually strived to grow, learn, and perfect his craft. Even when he was the most popular and highest-paid performer *in the world,* he wasn't content with the status quo.

Chaplin explained his desire to improve to an interviewer:

When I am watching one of my pictures presented to an audience, I always pay close attention to what they don't laugh at. If, for example, several audiences do not laugh at a stunt I mean to be funny, I at once begin to tear that trick to pieces and try to discover what was wrong in the idea or in the execution of it. If I hear a slight ripple at something I had not expected to be funny, I ask myself why that particular thing got a laugh.

That desire to grow made him successful economically, and it brought a high level of excellence to everything he did. In those early days, Chaplin's work was hailed as marvelous entertainment. As time went by, he was recognized as a comic genius. Today many of his movies are considered masterpieces, and he is appreciated as one of the greatest filmmakers of all time. Screenwriter and film critic James Agee wrote, "The finest pantomime, the deepest emotion, the richest and most poignant poetry were in Chaplin's work."

If Chaplin had replaced his teachability with arrogant self-satisfaction when he became successful, his name would be right up there along with

Ford Sterling or Ben Turpin, stars of silent films who are all but forgotten today. But Chaplin kept growing and learning as an actor, director, and eventually film executive. When he learned from experience that filmmakers were at the mercy of studios and distributors, he started his own organization, United Artists, along with Douglas Fairbanks, Mary Pickford, and D. W. Griffith. The film company is still in business today.

Keep Moving!

Successful people face the danger of contentment with the *status quo.* After all, if a successful person already possesses influence and has achieved a level of respect, why should he keep growing? The answer is simple:

> Your growth determines who you are.
> Who you are determines who you attract.
> Who you attract determines the success of your organization.

If you want to grow your organization, *you* have to remain teachable.

Allow me to give you five guidelines to help you cultivate and maintain a teachable attitude:

1. Cure Your Destination Disease

Ironically, lack of teachability is often rooted in achievement. Some people mistakenly believe that if they can accomplish a particular goal, they no longer have to grow. It can happen with almost anything: earning a degree, reaching a desired position, receiving a particular award, or achieving a financial goal.

But effective people cannot afford to think that way. The day they stop growing is the day they forfeit their potential—and the potential of the organization. Remember the words of Ray Kroc: "As long as you're green, you're growing. As soon as you're ripe, you start to rot."

2. Overcome Your Success

Another irony of teachability is that success often hinders it. Effective people know that what got them there doesn't keep them there. If you have been successful in the past, beware. And consider this: if what you did yesterday still looks big to you, you haven't done much today.

3. Swear Off Shortcuts

My friend Nancy Dornan says, "The longest distance between two points is a shortcut." That's really true. For everything of value in life, you pay a price. As you desire to grow in a particular area, figure out what it will really take, including the price, and then determine to pay it.

4. Trade In Your Pride

Teachability requires us to admit we don't know everything, and that can make us look bad. In addition, if we keep learning, we must also keep making mistakes. But as writer and expert craftsman Elbert Hubbard said, "The greatest mistake one can make in life is to be continually fearing you will make one." You cannot be prideful and teachable at the same time. Emerson wrote, "For everything you gain, you lose something." To gain growth, give up your pride.

5. Never Pay Twice for the Same Mistake

Teddy Roosevelt asserted, "He who makes no mistakes, makes no progress." That's true. But the person who keeps making *the same* mistakes also makes no progress. As a teachable person, you will make mistakes. Forget them, but always remember what they taught you. If you don't, you will pay for them more than once.

When I was a kid growing up in rural Ohio, I saw this sign in a feed store: "If you don't like the crop you are reaping, check the seed you are sowing." Though the sign was an ad for seeds, it contained a wonderful principle.

What kind of crop are you reaping? Do your life and leadership seem to be getting better day after day, month after month, year after year? Or are you constantly fighting just to hold your ground? If you're not where you hoped you would be by this time in your life, your problem may be lack of teachability. When was the last time you did something for the first time? When was the last time you made yourself vulnerable by diving into something for which you weren't the expert? Observe your attitude toward growing and learning during the next several days or weeks to see where you stand.

NEVER STOP GROWING

To improve your teachability, do the following:

OBSERVE HOW YOU REACT TO MISTAKES

Do you admit your mistakes? Do you apologize when appropriate? Or are you defensive? Observe yourself. And ask a trusted friend's opinion. If you react badly—or you make no mistakes at all—you need to work on your teachability.

TRY SOMETHING NEW

Go out of your way today to do something different that will stretch you mentally, emotionally, or physically. Challenges change us for the better. If you really want to start growing, make new challenges part of your daily activities.

LEARN IN YOUR AREA OF STRENGTH

Read six to twelve books a year on leadership or your field of specialization. Continuing to learn in an area where you are already an expert prevents you from becoming jaded and unteachable.

After winning his third world championship, bull rider Tuff Hedeman didn't have a big celebration. He moved on to Denver to start the new season—and the whole process over again. His comment: "The bull won't care what I did last week." Whether you're an untested rookie or a successful veteran, if you want to be a champion tomorrow, be teachable today.

PART III

SUCCESS AT THE NEXT LEVEL

10

AM I WILLING TO DO
THE TOUGH JOBS?

*Successful people do the things that unsuccessful
people are unwilling to do.*

I t's said that an aid group in South Africa once wrote to missionary
and explorer David Livingstone, asking, "Have you found a good
road to where you are? If so, we want to know how to send other men to
join you."

Livingstone replied, "If you have men who will come only if they
know there is a good road, I don't want them. I want men who will come
even if there is no road at all." That's what top leaders want from the
people working for them: they want individuals who are willing to do
what others won't.

Few things gain the appreciation of a top leader more quickly than
an employee with a whatever-it-takes attitude. That is what successful
people must have. They must be willing and able to think outside of
their job description, to be willing to tackle the kinds of jobs that others
are too proud or too frightened to take on. These things are what often
elevate successful people above their peers.

WHAT IT MEANS TO DO
WHAT OTHERS WON'T

Perhaps you already possess a whatever-it-takes mind-set, and if a task is honest, ethical, and beneficial, you're willing to take it on. If so, good for you! Now all you need is to know how to direct that attitude into action so that you're doing the things that will make the greatest impact and create influence with others. Here are the top ten things I recommend you do to become a successful person and a good leader:

1. SUCCESSFUL PEOPLE TAKE THE TOUGH JOBS

The ability to accomplish difficult tasks earns others' respect very quickly. In *Developing the Leader Within You,* I point out that one of the quickest ways to gain leadership is problem solving.

> Problems continually occur at work, at home, and in life in general. My observation is that people don't like problems, weary of them quickly, and will do almost anything to get away from them. This climate makes others place the reins of leadership into your hands—if you are willing and able to either tackle their problems or train them to solve them. Your problem-solving skills will always be needed because people always have problems.[1]

Not only does taking on tough jobs earn you respect, but it also helps you become a better leader. You learn resiliency and tenacity during tough assignments, not easy ones. When tough choices have to be made and results are difficult to achieve, leaders are forged.

2. SUCCESSFUL PEOPLE PAY THEIR DUES

Former U.S. senator Sam Nunn said, "You have to pay the price. You will find that everything in life exacts a price, and you will have to decide whether the price is worth the prize." To become a successful person, you will have to pay a price. You will have to give up other opportunities in order to lead. You will have to sacrifice some personal goals for the sake of others. You will have to get out of your comfort zone and do things you've never done before. You will have to keep learning and growing when you don't feel like it. You will have to repeatedly put others ahead of yourself. And if you desire to be a really good leader, you will have to do these things without fanfare or complaint. But remember, as NFL legend George Halas said, "Nobody who ever gave their best ever regretted it."

3. Successful People Work in Obscurity

I think very highly of the importance of leadership. I guess that's obvious for a guy whose motto is "Everything rises and falls on leadership." Occasionally someone will ask me about how ego fits into the leadership equation. They'll want to know what keeps a leader from having a huge ego. I think the answer lies in each leader's pathway to leadership. If people paid their dues and gave their best in obscurity, ego is usually not a problem.

One of my favorite examples of this occurred in the life of Moses in the Old Testament. Though born a Hebrew, he lived a life of privilege in the palace of Egypt until he was forty years old. But after killing an Egyptian, he was exiled to the desert for forty years. There God used him as a shepherd and father, and after four decades of faithful service in obscurity, Moses was called to leadership. Scripture says by that time he was the most humble man in the world. Bill Purvis, the senior pastor of a large church in Columbus, Georgia, said, "If you do what you can, with what you have, where you are, then God won't leave you where you are, and He will increase what you have."

English novelist and poet Emily Bronte said, "If I could I would always work in silence and obscurity, and let my efforts be known by their results." Not everyone wants to be out of the spotlight as she did. But it's important for a leader to learn to work in obscurity because it is a test of personal integrity. The key is being willing to do something because it matters, not because it will get you noticed.

4. SUCCESSFUL PEOPLE SUCCEED WITH DIFFICULT PEOPLE

People working at the bottom of an organization usually have no choice concerning whom they work with. As a result, they often have to work with difficult people. In contrast, people at the top almost never have to work with difficult people because they get to choose who they work with. If someone they work with becomes difficult, they often let that person go or move him or her out.

For leaders in the middle, the road is different. They have some choice in the matter, but not complete control. They may not be able to get rid of difficult people, but they can often avoid working with them. But good leaders—ones who learn to lead up, across, and down—find a way to succeed with people who are hard to work with. Why do they do it? Because it benefits the organization. How do they do it? They work at finding common ground and connect with them. And instead of putting these difficult people in their place, they try to put themselves in their place.

5. SUCCESSFUL PEOPLE PUT THEMSELVES ON THE LINE

If you want to be successful, you must distinguish yourself from your colleagues. How do you do that, especially while paying your dues or working in obscurity? One way is to take a risk. You cannot play it safe and stand out at the same time.

Here's the tricky thing about taking risks when you work in an organization. You should never be casual about risking what's not yours. I call that "betting with other people's money." You don't have the right to put the organization on the line. Nor would it be right for you to create high risk for others in the organization. If you are going to take a risk, you need to put *yourself* on the line. Play it smart, but don't play it safe.

6. SUCCESSFUL PEOPLE ADMIT FAULTS BUT NEVER MAKE EXCUSES

It's easier to move from failure to success than from excuses to success.

And you will have greater credibility with your leader if you admit your shortcomings and refrain from making excuses. I guarantee that. Of course, that doesn't mean you don't need to produce results. Baseball coach and tutor McDonald Valentine said, "The higher the level you play, the less they accept excuses."

A good time to make mistakes and learn is before you are recognized by others as successful. That's when you want to discover your identity and work things out. You can discover your leadership strengths before you have a leadership position. If you fall short in an area, you can work to overcome your mistakes. If you keep falling short in the same way, you may learn how to overcome an obstacle, or you may discover an area of weakness where you will need to collaborate with others. But no matter what, don't make excuses. Steven Brown, president of the Fortune Group, summed up this issue: "Essentially there are two actions in life: performance and excuses. Make a decision as to which you will accept from yourself."

7. Successful People Do More Than Expected

Expectations are high for people at the top. And, unfortunately, in many organizations the expectations for people at the bottom are low. But expectations are mixed in the middle of an organization. So if you work in an organization and you do more than is expected of you, you stand out, and often there can be wonderful, serendipitous results.

When Chris Hodges, a senior pastor who is a donor and volunteer trainer with EQUIP, was working as a staff member at a large church in Baton Rouge, his boss, Larry Stockstill, had the opportunity to become the host of a live television show. Chris had no responsibilities related to the show, and was, in fact, rather low in the organization's hierarchy. But he knew that the show was important to Larry, so Chris took it upon himself to go down to the studio to see the first taping. As it turned out, he was the only staff member to do so.

There was great excitement in the studio as the hour of the first broadcast approached. That excitement quickly turned to panic when the guest who was scheduled to appear on the show called in to say he was having a problem getting there. The guest wasn't worried, because he thought they could just start the taping later. What he didn't realize was that the show was scheduled to go on the air live!

In that moment, Larry looked around, saw Chris, and said, "You're going to be my guest today." The crew scrambled, put a microphone on Chris, slapped some makeup on his face, and sat him down in the chair next to Larry. Then to Chris's great shock, when the lights turned on and the cameras started rolling, Larry introduced Chris as his cohost.

Chris ended up being on that show with Larry every week for two and a half years. The experience changed him forever. Not only did it build his relationship with his leader, but it also made him well-known in the community. More important, he learned to think on his feet and become a better communicator, skills that serve him well every day of his life. And it all happened because he decided to do more than was expected of him.

8. Successful People Are the First to Step Up and Help

In *25 Ways to Win with People*, I point out that being the first to help others is a great way to make them feel like a million bucks. It lets them know you care. The kind of influence you gain from helping a peer is also gained with your leader when you step up and help others. Haven't you found the following to be true?

- The first person to volunteer is a hero and is given the "10" treatment.
- The second person is considered a helper and viewed as only slightly above average.
- The third person, along with everyone after, is seen as a follower and is ignored.

It doesn't matter whom you're helping, whether it's your boss, a peer, or someone working for you. When you help someone on the team, you help the whole team. And when you help the team, you're helping your leaders. And that gives them reasons to notice and appreciate you.

9. SUCCESSFUL PEOPLE PERFORM TASKS THAT ARE "NOT THEIR JOB"

Few things are more frustrating for a leader than having someone refuse to do a task because it is "not his job." (In moments like those, most of the top leaders I know are tempted to invite such people to be without a job altogether!) Successful people don't think in those terms. They understand the Law of the Big Picture from *The 21 Irrefutable Laws of Leadership*: "The goal is more important than the role."

A successful person's goal is to get the job done, to fulfill the vision of the organization and its leader. That often means doing whatever it takes. As a leader "moves up," that more often takes the form of hiring someone to get it done, but leaders in the middle often don't have that option. So instead, they jump in and get it done themselves.

10. SUCCESSFUL PEOPLE TAKE RESPONSIBILITY FOR THEIR RESPONSIBILITIES

I recently saw a cartoon where a dad is reading a book to his little boy at bedtime. The title on the cover of the book says, *The Story of Job*, and the boy has only one question for his father: "Why didn't he sue someone?"

Isn't that the way a lot of people think these days? Their knee-jerk reaction to adversity is to blame someone else. That's not the case with successful people. They take hold of their responsibilities and follow through with them 100 percent.

Lack of responsibility can be a deal breaker when it comes to the people who work for me. When my employees don't get the job done, certainly I become disappointed. But I'm willing to work with them to help them improve—if they are taking responsibility for themselves. I know they will work at getting better if they take ownership and have teachable spirits. We have no starting point for improvement, however, if they don't get the job done and they fail to take responsibility. In such cases, it's time to move on and find someone else to take their place.

WHAT ARE YOU WILLING TO DO?

J. C. Penney said, "Unless you are willing to drench yourself in your work beyond the capacity of the average man, you are just not cut out for positions at the top." I'd say that you're not cut out for leadership in the middle either! People who want to be effective are willing to do what others won't. And because of that, their leaders are willing to resource them, promote them, and be influenced by them.

AM I READY TO
STEP UP MY GAME?

Successful people become go-to players.

The Law of the Catalyst in *The 17 Indisputable Laws of Teamwork* states that winning teams have players who make things happen. That's always true—whether in sports, business, government, or some other arena. Those team members who can make things happen are their go-to players. They demonstrate consistent competence, responsibility, and dependability.

SUCCESSFUL TEAMS HAVE GO-TO PLAYERS

Everyone admires go-to players and looks to them when the heat is on—not only their leaders, but also their followers and peers. When I think of go-to players, I mean people who always produce.

1. GO-TO PLAYERS PRODUCE WHEN THE PRESSURE'S ON

There are many different kinds of people in the workplace, and you can measure them according to what they do for the organization:

Go-to players are the people who find a way to make things happen no matter what. They don't have to be in familiar surroundings. They don't have to be in their comfort zones. The circumstances don't have to be fair or favorable. The pressure doesn't hinder them either. In fact, if anything, the more pressure there is, the better they like it. They always produce when the heat is on.

2. Go-To Players Produce When the Resources Are Few

In 2004 when *Today Matters* came out and I was frequently being asked to speak on the subject, I was once booked to do back-to-back sessions in Little Rock, Arkansas. After the first session, the site ran out of books. When the leader of the organization I was speaking for found out, he mobilized some of his people and sent them out to all the bookstores in town to buy more copies of the book so that his people could have access to them right after my second speaking session. I think he ended up buying every copy in town.

The thing I loved about it was that he wanted his people to benefit from the book, and he knew that if he didn't have it there after I spoke, they probably wouldn't get a copy. So he made it happen—even though he had to buy the books at full retail and resell them for that same amount. It took a lot of effort and provided no financial return. What a leader!

3. Go-To Players Produce When the Momentum Is Low

Organizations have only three kinds of people when it comes to momentum. There are momentum breakers—people who sabotage the leader or organization and actually sap momentum as a result. These people have terrible attitudes and represent the bottom 10 percent of the organization. (At General Electric, Jack Welch made it his goal every year to identify and fire these people.) The second group is comprised of the momentum takers—people who merely take things as they come. They neither create nor diminish momentum; they simply flow with it. These people represent the middle 80 percent.

The final group is the momentum makers—the people who move

things forward and create momentum. These are the leaders in the organization and comprise the top 10 percent. These momentum makers make progress. They overcome obstacles. They help move others along. They actually create energy in the organization when the rest of the team is feeling tired or discouraged.

4. GO-TO PLAYERS PRODUCE WHEN THE LOAD IS HEAVY

Good employees always have the desire to be helpful to their leaders. I've worked with many of them over the years. I always appreciate it when someone who works with me says, "I've finished my work. Can I do something for you?" But there is another level of play that some go-to players reach, and you can see it in their ability to carry a heavy load anytime their leader needs it. They don't help the leader with a heavy load only when theirs is light. They do it anytime their leader's load is heavy.

Linda Eggers, Tim Elmore, and Dan Reiland are examples of heavy load lifters for me. For years, when I've been pressed, they've taken tasks from me and completed them with excellence. Dan Reiland is so incredible at this that he continues to do it even now—and he doesn't even work for me anymore. He does it as a friend.

The keys to becoming this kind of player are availability and responsibility. Being a heavy load lifter is really an attitude issue, not a position issue. If you have the willingness and capacity to lift the load of your leaders when they need it, you will have influence with them.

5. GO-TO PLAYERS PRODUCE WHEN THE LEADER IS ABSENT

The greatest opportunity for a leader in the middle of an organization to distinguish himself is when the leader is absent. It is at those times that a leadership vacuum exists, and leaders can rise up to fill it. True, when leaders know they will be absent, they usually designate a leader to stand in for them. But even then, there are still opportunities for people to step up, take responsibility, and shine.

If you step forward to lead when there is a leadership vacuum, you may have a very good chance of distinguishing yourself. You should also know, however, that when people step up to fill that vacuum, it almost always exposes their true colors. If their motives are good, and they desire to lead for the good of the organization, it will show through. If they are attempting a power grab for personal gain and their own advancement, that will show through too.

6. GO-TO PLAYERS PRODUCE WHEN THE TIME IS LIMITED

I love a sign I saw at a small business called "The 57 Rules to Deliver the Goods." Beneath the title it read:

Rule 1: Deliver the Goods
Rule 2: The Other 56 Don't Matter

That's the philosophy of go-to players. They deliver no matter how tough the situation is.

LOOK FOR YOUR OPPORTUNITY TO STEP UP

As I was working on this chapter, Rod Loy told me a story about when he was a leader in the middle of an organization. At a large meeting, his leader announced a new program that he said was in place. Rod listened with interest, because he had not been aware of it. It sounded great, but then his leader announced that Rod would be leading the program, and anyone who was interested in it could talk to him about it after the meeting.

Rod had not been informed of his role in this program, but that did not matter. During the rest of the meeting while his leader spoke, Rod quickly sketched out the design and action plan for the program. When the meeting was over and people approached him, he communicated his plan and launched it. Rod said it may not have been his best work, but it was good work under the circumstances. It created a win for the organization, preserved his leader's credibility, and served the people well.

You may never find yourself in the kind of situation Rod did. But if you adopt the positive attitude and tenacity of a go-to player, and take every opportunity to make things happen, you will probably perform as he did under similar circumstances. If you do, your leader will come to rely on you, and the people we rely on increase their influence and credibility every day we work with them.

AM I READY TO LEAD AT THE NEXT LEVEL?

To reach the next level, lead others to success.

Growing organizations are always looking for good people to step up to the next level and lead. How do they find out if a person is qualified to make that jump? By looking at that person's track record in his or her current position. The key to moving up as an emerging leader is to focus on being successful where you are and leading well on that level, not on moving up the ladder. If you are successful where you are, I believe you will be given an opportunity to succeed at a higher level.

TO MOVE UP, LEARN TO LEAD

As you strive to become the most successful person you can be, keep the following things in mind:

1. LEADERSHIP IS A JOURNEY THAT STARTS WHERE YOU ARE, NOT WHERE YOU WANT TO BE

Recently, while I was driving in my car, a vehicle to the left of me attempted to turn right from the middle lane and caused an accident. Fortunately, I was able to slow down quickly and lessen the impact; but still, my air bags deployed, and both cars were greatly damaged.

The first thing I noticed after I stopped and took stock of the situation was that the little computer screen in my car was showing my exact location according to the GPS system. I stared at it a moment, wondering why the car was telling me my exact latitude and longitude. And then I thought, *Of course!* If you're in real trouble and you call for help, the first thing emergency workers will want to know is your location. You can't get anywhere until you first know where you are.

Leadership is similar. To know how to get where you want to go, you need to know where you are. To get where you want to go, you need to focus on what you're doing now. Award-winning sportswriter Ken Rosenthals said, "Each time you decide to grow again, you realize you are starting at the bottom of another ladder." You need to have your eyes fixed on your current responsibilities, not the ones you wish to have someday. I've never known a person focused on yesterday to have a better tomorrow.

2. LEADERSHIP SKILLS ARE THE SAME, BUT THE "LEAGUE OF PLAY" CHANGES

If you get promoted, don't think that because your new office is just a few feet down the hall from your old place that the difference is just a few steps. When you get "called up" to another level of leadership, the quality of your game must rise quickly.

No matter what level you're working on, leadership skills are needed at that level. Each new level requires a higher degree of skill. The easiest place to see this is in sports. Some players can make the jump from recreational league to high school. Fewer can make it from high school to college. And only a handful can make it to the professional level.

Your best chance of making it into the next "league of play" is to grow on the current level so that you will be able to go to the next level.

3. GREAT RESPONSIBILITIES COME ONLY AFTER HANDLING SMALL ONES WELL

When I teach at a conference or go to a book signing, people sometimes confide in me that they desire to write books too. "How do I get started?" they ask.

"How much writing do you do now?" I ask in return.

Some tell me about articles and other pieces they are writing, and I simply encourage them; but most of the time they sheepishly respond, "Well, I haven't really written anything yet."

"Then you need to start writing," I explain. "You've got to start small and work up to it."

Leadership is the same. You've got to start small and work up to it. A person who has never led before needs to try to influence one other person. Someone who has some influence should try to build a team. Just start with what's necessary.

St. Francis of Assisi said, "Start doing what is necessary; then do what is possible; and suddenly you are doing the impossible." All good leadership begins where you are. It was Napoleon who said, "The only conquests which are permanent and leave no regrets are our conquests over ourselves." The small responsibilities you have before you now comprise the first great leadership conquest you must make. Don't try to conquer the world until you've taken care of things in your own backyard.

4. LEADING AT YOUR CURRENT LEVEL CREATES YOUR RÉSUMÉ FOR GOING TO THE NEXT LEVEL

When you go to see a doctor for the first time, you are usually asked a lot of questions about your family history. In fact, there are usually more questions about that than there are about your lifestyle. Why? Because family history, more than anything else, seems to be what determines your health.

When it comes to leadership success, history is also similarly dispro-portionate. Your track record where you work now is what leaders will look at when trying to decide if you can do a job. I know that when I interview someone for a job, I put 90 percent of the emphasis on the track record.

If you want to get the chance to lead on another level, then your best chance for success is to lead well where you are now. Every day that you lead and succeed, you are building a résumé for your next job.

5. WHEN YOU CAN LEAD VOLUNTEERS WELL, YOU CAN LEAD ALMOST ANYONE

At a recent President's Day conference where we were discussing leadership development, a CEO asked me, "How can I pick the best leader out of a small group of leaders? What do I look for?"

There are many things that indicate someone has leadership poten-tial—the ability to make things happen, strong people skills, vision, desire, problem-solving skills, self-discipline, a strong work ethic. But there is one really great test of leadership that is almost foolproof, and that is what I suggested: "Ask them to lead a volunteer group."

If you want to test your own leadership, then try leading volunteers. Why is that so difficult? Because with volunteers, you have no leverage. It takes every bit of leadership skill you have to get people who don't have to do anything to do what you ask. If you're not challenging enough, they lose interest. If you push too hard, they drop out. If your people skills are weak, they won't spend any time with you. If you can-not communicate the vision, they won't know where to go or why.

If you lead others and your organization has any kind of community service focus, encourage the people on your team to volunteer. Then watch to see how they do. If they thrive in that environment, then you know that they possess many of the qualifications to go to another level in your organization.

LIVING ON THE NEXT LEVEL

Donald McGannon, former CEO of Westinghouse Broadcasting Corporation, stated, "Leadership is action, not position." Taking action—and helping others to do the same in a coordinated effort—is the essence of leadership. Do those things where you are, and you won't remain long there.

TEAMWORK

101

WHAT EVERY LEADER NEEDS TO KNOW

© 2008 by John C. Maxwell

All rights reserved. No portion of this book may be reproduced, stored in a retrieval system, or transmitted in any form or by any means—electronic, mechanical, photocopy, recording, scanning, or other—except for brief quotations in critical reviews or articles, without the prior written permission of the publisher.

Published in Nashville, Tennessee, by Thomas Nelson. Thomas Nelson is a registered trademark of Thomas Nelson, Inc.

Published in association with Yates & Yates, www.yates2.com

Thomas Nelson, Inc., titles may be purchased in bulk for educational, business, fund-raising, or sales promotional use. For information, please e-mail SpecialMarkets@ThomasNelson.com.

Portions of this book have been previously published in *The 17 Indisputable Laws of Teamwork*, *Talent Is Never Enough*, *Developing Leaders Around You*, *The 360° Leader*, *Winning with People*, *The 21 Irrefutable Laws of Leadership*, and *The 17 Essential Qualities of a Team Player* by John C. Maxwell.

ISBN: 978-1-4002-0395-6

Library of Congress Cataloging-in-Publication Data

Maxwell, John C., 1947–
Teamwork 101 : what every leader needs to know / John C. Maxwell.
p. cm.
Includes bibliographical references.
ISBN 978-1-4002-8025-4
1. Teams in the workplace. 2. Teams in the workplace—Psychological aspects. I. Title.
II. Title: Teamwork one hundred one. III. Title: Teamwork one hundred and one.
HD66.M379 2009
658.4'022—dc22
2009028195

Printed in the United States of America
12 13 14 15 QG 5 4 3 2 1

CONTENTS

PART I

THE POWER OF TEAMWORK

I

Why Is Teamwork
So Important?

One is too small a number to achieve greatness.

Who are your personal heroes? Okay, maybe you don't have heroes exactly. Then let me ask you this: Which people do you admire most? Who do you wish you were more like? Which people fire you up and get your juices flowing? Do you admire . . .

- Business innovators, such as Jeff Bezos, Fred Smith, or Bill Gates?
- Great athletes, such as Michael Jordan, Marion Jones, or Mark McGwire?
- Creative geniuses, such as Pablo Picasso, Buckminster Fuller, or Wolfgang Amadeus Mozart?
- Pop-culture icons, such as Madonna, Andy Warhol, or Elvis Presley?
- Spiritual leaders, such as John Wesley, Billy Graham, or Mother Teresa?
- Political leaders, such as Charlemagne, Alexander the Great, or Winston Churchill?

- Revolutionary thinkers, such as Marie Curie, Thomas Edison, or Albert Einstein?

Or maybe your list includes people in a field I did not mention.

It's safe to say that we all admire achievers. And we Americans especially love pioneers and bold individualists, people who fight alone, despite the odds or opposition: the settler who carves a place for himself in the wilds of the frontier, the Old West sheriff who resolutely faces an enemy in a gunfight, the pilot who bravely flies solo across the Atlantic Ocean, and the scientist who changes the world through the power of his mind.

THE MYTH OF THE LONE RANGER

Nothing of significance was ever achieved by an individual acting alone. Look below the surface and you will find that all seemingly solo acts are really team efforts. Frontiersman Daniel Boone had companions from the Transylvania Company as he blazed the Wilderness Road. Sheriff Wyatt Earp had his two brothers and Doc Holliday looking out for him. Aviator Charles Lindbergh had the backing of nine businessmen from St. Louis and the services of the Ryan Aeronautical Company, which built his plane. Even Albert Einstein, the scientist who revolutionized the world with his theory of relativity, didn't work in a vacuum. Of the debt he owed to others for his work, Einstein once remarked, "Many times a day I realize how much my own outer and inner life is built upon the labors of my fellow men, both living and dead, and how earnestly I must exert myself in order to give in return as much as I have received." It's true that the history of our country is marked by the accomplishments of many strong leaders and innovative individuals who took considerable risks. But those people always were part of teams.

Economist Lester C. Thurow commented:

There is nothing antithetical in American history, culture, or traditions to teamwork. Teams were important in America's history—wagon trains conquered the West, men working together on the assembly line in American industry conquered the world, a successful national strategy and a lot of teamwork put an American on the moon first (and thus far, last). But American mythology extols only the individual . . . In America, halls of fame exist for almost every conceivable activity, but nowhere do Americans raise monuments in praise of teamwork.

I must say that I don't agree with all of Thurow's conclusions. After all, I've seen the U.S. Marine Corps war memorial in Washington, D.C., commemorating the raising of the flag on Iwo Jima. But he is right about something. Teamwork is and always has been essential to building this country. And that statement can be made about every country around the world.

THE VALUE OF TEAMWORK

A Chinese proverb states, "Behind an able man there are always other able men." The truth is that teamwork is at the heart of great achievement. The question isn't whether teams have value. The question is whether we acknowledge that fact and become better team players. That's why I assert that *one is too small a number to achieve greatness.* You cannot do anything of *real* value alone.

I challenge you to think of *one* act of genuine significance in the history of humankind that was performed by a lone human being. No matter what you name, you will find that a team of people was involved. That is why President Lyndon Johnson said, "There are no problems we cannot solve together, and very few that we can solve by ourselves."

C. Gene Wilkes, in his book *Jesus on Leadership*, observed that the power of teams not only is evident in today's modern business world, but it also has a deep history that is evident even in biblical times. Wilkes asserts:

- Teams involve more people, thus affording more resources, ideas, and energy than would an individual.

- Teams maximize a leader's potential and minimize her weaknesses. Strengths and weaknesses are more exposed in individuals.
- Teams provide multiple perspectives on how to meet a need or reach a goal, thus devising several alternatives for each situation. Individual insight is seldom as broad and deep as a group's when it takes on a problem.
- Teams share the credit for victories and the blame for losses. This fosters genuine humility and authentic community. Individuals take credit and blame alone. This fosters pride and sometimes a sense of failure.
- Teams keep leaders accountable for the goal. Individuals connected to no one can change the goal without accountability.
- Teams can simply do more than an individual.

If you want to reach your potential or strive for the seemingly impossible—such as communicating your message two thousand years after you are gone—you need to become a team player. It may be a cliché, but it is nonetheless true: Individuals play the game, but teams win championships.

WHY DO WE STAND ALONE?

Knowing all that we do about the potential of teams, why do some people still want to do things by themselves? I believe there are a number of reasons.

1. EGO

Few people are fond of admitting that they can't do everything, yet that is a reality of life. There are no supermen or superwomen. As Kerry Walls, one of the people on my INJOY Group team, says, "Spinning more plates doesn't increase your talent—it increases your likelihood of dropping a plate." So the question is not whether you can do everything by yourself; it's how soon you're going to realize that you can't.

Philanthropist Andrew Carnegie declared, "It marks a big step in your development when you come to realize that other people can help you do a better job than you could do alone." To do something really big, let go of your ego, and get ready to be part of a team.

2. Insecurity

In my work with leaders, I've found that some individuals fail to promote teamwork because they feel threatened by other people. Sixteenth-century Florentine statesman Niccolo Machiavelli probably made similar observations, prompting him to write, "The first method for estimating the intelligence of a ruler is to look at the men he has around him."

I believe that insecurity, rather than poor judgment or lack of intelligence, most often causes leaders to surround themselves with weak people. As I stated in *The 21 Irrefutable Laws of Leadership*, only secure leaders give power to others. That is the Law of Empowerment. On the other hand, insecure leaders usually fail to build teams because of one of two reasons: either they want to maintain control over everything for which they are responsible, or they fear being replaced by someone more capable. In either case, leaders who fail to promote teamwork undermine their own potential and erode the best efforts of the people with whom they work. They would benefit from the advice of President Woodrow Wilson: "We should not only use all the brains we have, but all that we can borrow."

3. Naïveté

Consultant John Ghegan keeps a sign on his desk that says, "If I had it to do all over again, I'd get help." That remark accurately represents the feelings of the third type of people who fail to become team builders. They naively underestimate the difficulty of achieving big things. As a result, they try to go it alone.

Some people who start out in this group turn out okay in the end. They discover that their dreams are bigger than their capabilities, they realize they won't accomplish their goals solo, and they adjust. They make team building their approach to achievement. But some others learn the truth too late, and as a result, they never accomplish their goals. And that's a shame.

4. Temperament

Some people aren't very outgoing and simply don't think in terms of team building and team participation. As they face challenges, it never occurs to them to enlist others to achieve something.

As a people person, I find that hard to relate to. Whenever I face any kind of challenge, the very first thing I do is think about the people I want on the team to help with it. I've been that way since I was a kid. I've always thought, *Why take the journey alone when you can invite others along with you?*

I understand that not everyone operates that way. But whether or not you are naturally inclined to be part of a team is really irrelevant. If you do everything alone and never partner with other people, you create huge barriers to your own potential. Dr. Allan Fromme quipped, "People have been known to achieve more as a result of working with others than against them." What an understatement! It takes a team to do anything of lasting value. Besides, even the most introverted person in the world can learn to enjoy the benefits of being on a team. (That's true even if someone isn't trying to accomplish something great.)

My friend Chuck Swindoll wrote a piece in *The Finishing Touch* that sums up the importance of teamwork:

> Nobody is a whole team . . . We need each other. You need someone and someone needs you. Isolated islands we're not. To make this thing called life work, we gotta lean and support. And relate and respond. And give and take. And confess and forgive. And reach out and embrace and rely . . . Since none of us is a whole, independent, self-sufficient, super-capable, all-powerful hotshot, let's quit acting like we are. Life's lonely enough without our playing that silly role. The game is over. Let's link up.

For the person trying to do everything alone, the game really is over. If you want to do something big, you must link up with others.

WHAT IS THE IMPACT OF
GOOD TEAMWORK?

There are some things only a team can accomplish.

R ecently had the opportunity to tour the aircraft carrier USS
Enterprise while it was at sea. The entire experience was fantastic,
but the highlight for me was sitting with Rear Admiral Raymond Spicer,
commander of the *Enterprise's* carrier strike group, and watching F/A-18
Hornet jets taking off and landing at night. What an incredible sight!

There was beauty in the way the jets shot off the deck and others
landed, coming to a halt in a mere two seconds. But what struck me even
more was the number of people who seemed to be involved in the
process and the teamwork that was required. When I asked Admiral
Spicer about it, he put me in contact with Lt. Commander Ryan Smith,
the V2 Division officer, who explained the process to me. He said:

The pilot is seated at the controls of an F/A-18 Hornet as the jet
is accelerated from 0 to nearly 160 mph in the span of less than
three seconds. As the aircraft climbs away from the carrier, she
raises the landing gear and is suddenly alone in the black of
night. There are few examples of solitary combat in today's era
of modern, networked warfare, but an aviator seated in the

cockpit of one of today's Navy fighters still seems like an example in which the accomplishment of a particular objective is entirely dependent on the talent, skill, and effort of one particular, highly trained individual. However, the singular act of catapulting a jet off of the end of one of these carriers is the result of the complex orchestration of scores of individuals, each with a mastery of his or her own specific task. It is the efforts and coordination of these individuals, most of whom are just barely high school graduates, which serve as a truly inspiring example of teamwork.[1]

He then went on to explain the process. Hours before that jet taxis to the catapult for launching, it is being inspected by a team of mechanics and technicians. While the pilot is receiving a briefing on the mission, including weather, target information, radio procedures, and navigational information (all of which are produced by teams of sailors), the aircraft is going through an equally rigorous period of prepa-ration. The preflight routine ends only when the pilot has reviewed the aircraft's maintenance records and inspected the aircraft for flight.

Thirty minutes prior to the aircraft's launch time, a specific sequence of steps begins that is always followed with precision. The aircraft carrier's air boss calls for engine starts, a test to make certain that the jets are in proper working order, while the pilot runs through his pre-taxi checks. The aircraft's plane captain is listening to the engines and watching the movement of each control surface as the pilot does his checks. Once it is determined that everything is okay, the aircraft is then topped off with fuel.

Meanwhile, the aircraft handling officer, seated in flight deck control and using a tabletop model of the carrier's flight deck and aircraft, reviews the launch sequence plan with the deck caller. The aircraft handling officer radios the deck caller, telling him which aircraft are reported to be "up" and ready to taxi.

The deck caller leads three separate teams of plane directors and other sailors from the carrier's Flight Deck Division, and each team is responsible for a different area of the flight deck. These teams ensure that each aircraft to be launched is safely unchained, directed around other parked aircraft (often with only inches of clearance), and put in line to be launched—sometimes as the deck of the carrier is pitching and rolling. When the deck caller gets the okay, the aircraft goes to one of the four catapults.

On deck, final maintenance checkers walk alongside the aircraft and inspect each panel and component as crew members from the Catapult and Arresting Gear Division hook the aircraft up to the catapult mechanism and ready it for launch. Below deck, other teams are using hydraulics and other equipment to control steam from the nuclear reactor that will be used to power the catapult.

At this time, ordnance personnel arm the aircraft's weapons. The catapult officer then confirms the weight of the aircraft with the pilot. He also makes note of the wind over the deck and ambient conditions. He performs calculations to determine the precise amount of energy needed to achieve flight.

Even with all of this preparation, no jet would be able to take off if the ship weren't in the proper position. The ship's navigational team, which makes calculations to determine the required speed and heading, has relayed information to the bridge, and by now the ship has completed its turn and has accelerated to proper speed on its directed course. The aircraft is finally almost ready for launch.

The aircraft is hydraulically tensioned into the catapult. At this point, the pilot applies full power to the aircraft's engines and checks to be sure the aircraft is functioning. If the pilot determines that the aircraft is ready for flight, he signals the catapult officer by saluting him. If the catapult officer also receives a thumbs-up from the squadron final checker, he will then give the fire signal to a catapult operator who depresses the fire button and sends the aircraft on its way.

What's amazing is that three more aircraft can be launched right behind it in less than a minute, each having gone through that same procedure. And in just a matter of minutes, that same flight deck can be prepared to receive landing aircraft, one coming on final approach just as the previous one is taxied out of the landing area.

Teamwork Truths

I can think of few things that require such a high degree of precision teamwork with so many different groups of people as the launching of a jet from an aircraft carrier. It's easy to see that teamwork is essential for the task. However, a task doesn't *have* to be complex to need teamwork. In 2001, when I wrote *The 17 Indisputable Laws of Teamwork*, the first law I included was the Law of Significance, which says, "One is too small a number to achieve greatness." If you want to do anything of value, teamwork is required.

Teamwork not only allows a person to do what he couldn't otherwise do; it also has a compounding effect on all he possesses—including talent. If you believe one person is a work of God (which I do), then a group of talented people committed to working together is a work of art. Whatever your vision or desire, teamwork makes the dream work.

Working together with other people toward a common goal is one of the most rewarding experiences of life. I've led or been part of many different kinds of teams—sports teams, work teams, business teams, ministry teams, communication teams, choirs, bands, committees, boards, you name it. I've observed teams of nearly every type in my travels around the world. And talking to leaders, developing teams, counseling with coaches, and teaching and writing on teamwork have influenced my thinking when it comes to teams. What I've learned, I want to share with you:

1. Teamwork Divides the Effort and Multiplies the Effect

Would you like to get better results from less work? I think everyone would. That's what teamwork provides.

It's common sense that people working together can do more than an individual working alone. So why are some people reluctant to engage in teamwork? It can be difficult in the beginning. Teams don't usually come together and develop on their own. They require leadership and cooperation. While that may be more work on the front end, the dividends it pays on the back end are tremendous and well worth the effort.

2. TALENT WINS GAMES, BUT TEAMWORK WINS CHAMPIONSHIPS

A sign in the New England Patriots' locker room states, "Individuals play the game, but teams win championships." Obviously the Patriot players understand this. Over a four-year period, they won the Super Bowl three times.

Teams that repeatedly win championships are models of teamwork. For more than two decades, the Boston Celtics dominated the NBA. Their team has won more championships than any other in NBA history, and at one point during the fifties and sixties, the Celtics won eight championships in a row. During their run, the Celtics never had a player lead the league in scoring. Red Auerbach, who coached the Celtics and then later moved to their front office, always emphasized teamwork. He asserted, "One person seeking glory doesn't accomplish much; everything we've done has been the result of people working together to meet our common goals."

It's easy to see the fruit of teamwork in sports. But it is at least as important in business. Harold S. Geneen, who was director, president, and CEO of ITT for twenty years, observed, "The essence of leadership is the ability to inspire others to work together as a team—to stretch for a common objective." If you want to perform at the highest possible level, you need to be part of a team.

3. TEAMWORK IS NOT ABOUT YOU

The Harvard Business School recognizes a team as a small number of people with complementary skills who are committed to a common purpose, performance goals, and approach for which they hold themselves mutually accountable. Getting those people to work together is sometimes a challenge. It requires good leadership. And the more talented the team members, the better the leadership that is needed. The true measure of team leadership is not getting people to work. Neither is it getting people to work hard. The true measure of a leader is getting people to work hard together!

I've studied exceptional team leaders and coaches. Here are what just a few say about getting people to work together:

PAUL "BEAR" BRYANT, legendary Alabama football coach: "In order to have a winner, the team must have a feeling of unity. Every player must put the team first ahead of personal glory."

BUD WILKINSON, author of *The Book of Football Wisdom*: "If a team is to reach its potential, each player must be willing to subordinate his personal goals to the good of the team."

LOU HOLTZ, coach of college football national championship teams: "The freedom to do your own thing ends when you have obligations and responsibilities. If you want to fail yourself—you can—but you cannot do your own thing if you have responsibilities to team members."

MICHAEL JORDAN, most talented basketball player of all time and six-time world champion: "There are plenty of teams in every sport that have great players and never win titles. Most of the time, those players aren't willing to sacrifice for the greater good of the team. The funny thing is, in the end, their unwillingness to sacrifice only makes individual goals more difficult to achieve. One thing I believe to the fullest is that if you think and achieve as a team, the individual accolades will take care of themselves. Talent wins games, but teamwork and intelligence win championships."[2]

All great teams are the result of their players making decisions based on what's best for the rest. That's true in sports, business, the military, and volunteer organizations. And it's true at every level, from the part-time support person to the coach or CEO. The best leaders also put their team first. C. Gene Wilkes observed:

> Team leaders genuinely believe that they do not have all the answers—so they do not insist on providing them. They believe they do *not* need to make all key decisions—so they do not do so. They believe they *cannot* succeed without the combined contributions of all the other members of the team to a common end—so they avoid any action that might constrain inputs or intimidate anyone on the team. Ego is their predominant concern.

Highly talented teams possess players with strong egos. One secret of successful teamwork is converting individual ego into team confidence, individual sacrifice, and synergy. Pat Riley, NBA champion coach, says, "Teamwork requires that everyone's efforts flow in a single direction. Feelings of significance happen when a team's energy takes on a life of its own."

4. GREAT TEAMS CREATE COMMUNITY

All effective teams create an environment where relationships grow and teammates become connected to one another. To use a term that is currently popular, they create a *sense of community*. That environment of community is based on trust. Little can be accomplished without it.

On good teams, trust is a nonnegotiable. On winning teams, players extend trust to one another. Initially that is a risk because their trust can be violated and they can be hurt. At the same time that they are giving trust freely, they conduct themselves in such a way to earn trust from others. They hold themselves to a high standard. When everyone gives freely and bonds of trust develop and are tested over time, players begin to have faith in one another. They believe that the person next to them will act with consistency, keep commitments, maintain confidences, and support others. The stronger the sense of community becomes, the greater their potential to work together.

Developing a sense of community in a team does not mean there is never conflict. All teams experience disagreements. All relationships have tension. But you can work them out. My friend Bill Hybels, who leads a congregation of more than twenty thousand people, acknowledges this:

> The popular concept of unity is a fantasy land where disagreements never surface and contrary opinions are never stated with force. Instead of unity, we use the word *community*. We say, "Let's not pretend we never disagree. We're dealing with the lives of 16,000 people [at the time]. The stakes are high. Let's not have people hiding their concerns to protect a false notion of unity. Let's face the disagreement and deal with it in a good way."
>
> The mark of community . . . is not the absence of conflict. It's the presence of a reconciling spirit. I can have a rough-and-tumble leadership meeting with someone, but because we're committed to the community, we can still leave, slapping each other on the back, saying, "I'm glad we're still on the same team." We know no one's bailing out just because of a conflicting position.

When a team shares a strong sense of community, team members can resolve conflicts without dissolving relationships.

5. ADDING VALUE TO OTHERS ADDS VALUE TO YOU

"My husband and I have a very happy marriage," a woman bragged. "There's nothing I wouldn't do for him, and there's nothing he wouldn't do for me. And that's the way we go through life—doing nothing for each other!" That kind of attitude is a certain road to disaster for any team—including a married couple.

Too often people join a team for their personal benefit. They want a supporting cast so that they can be the star. But that attitude hurts the team. When even the most talented person has a mind to serve, special things can happen. Former NBA great Magic Johnson paraphrased John F. Kennedy when he stated, "Ask not what your teammates can do for you. Ask what you can do for your teammates." That wasn't just talk for Johnson. Over the course of his career with the Los Angeles Lakers, he started in every position during championship games to help his team.

U.S. president Woodrow Wilson asserted, "You are not here merely to make a living. You are here in order to enable the world to live more amply, with greater vision, with a finer spirit of hope and achicvement. You are here to enrich the world, and to impoverish yourself if you forget the errand." People who take advantage of others inevitably fail in business and relationships. If you desire to succeed, then live by these four simple words: *add value to others*. That philosophy will take you far.

3

CAN MY TEAM
ACCOMPLISH THE DREAM?

As the challenge escalates, the need for teamwork elevates.

In 1935, twenty-one-year-old Tenzing Norgay made his first trip to Mount Everest. He worked as a porter for a British team of mountaineers. A Sherpa born in the high altitudes of Nepal, Tenzing had been drawn to the mountain from the time that Westerners began visiting the area with the idea of climbing to the mountain's peak. The first group had come in 1920. Fifteen years later, climbers were still trying to figure out how to conquer the mountain.

The farthest this expedition would go was up to the North Col, which was at an altitude of 22,000 feet. (A is a flat area along a mountain's ridge between peaks.) And it was just below that col that the climbing party made a gruesome discovery. They came across a wind-shredded tent. And in that tent was a skeleton with a little frozen skin stretched over the bones. It was sitting in an odd position, with one boot off and the laces of the other boot between its bony fingers.

HARSHEST PLACE ON THE PLANET

Mountain climbing is not for the faint of heart, because the world's highest peaks are some of the most inhospitable places on earth. Of course, that hasn't stopped people from attempting to conquer mountains. Everest, the world's highest peak at 29,035 feet, is remote. The altitude incapacitates all but the hardiest and most experienced climbers, and the weather is ruthlessly unforgiving. Experts believe that the bodies of 120 failed climbers remain on the mountain today.[1]

The body Tenzing and the others found in 1935 was that of Maurice Wilson, an Englishman who had sneaked into Tibet and tried to climb the mountain secretly, without the permission of the Tibetan government. Because he was trying to make the ascent quietly, he had hired only three porters to climb the mountain with him. As they approached the North Col, those men had refused to go any farther with him. Wilson decided to try to make the climb on his own. That decision killed him.

MEASURE THE COST

Only someone who has climbed a formidable mountain knows what it takes to make it to the top. For thirty-two years, between 1920 and 1952, seven major expeditions tried—and failed—to make it to the top of Everest. An experienced climber, Tenzing Norgay was on six of those expeditions. His fellow climbers joked that he had a third lung because of his ability to climb tirelessly while carrying heavy loads.

NOT A CASUAL STROLL

In 1953, Tenzing embarked on his seventh expedition to Everest with a British group led by Colonel John Hunt. By then, he was respected not only as a porter who could carry heavy loads at high altitudes, but also as a mountaineer and full-fledged expedition member, an honor unusual at that time for a Sherpa. The year before he had climbed to a height of 28,250 feet with a Swiss team. Up to then, that was the closest any human being had come to the top of the mountain.

Tenzing was also engaged to be the British group's for the trip, the Sherpa leader who would hire, organize, and lead the porters for the journey. That was no small task. To hope to get just two people from base camp up to the summit, the team brought ten high-altitude climbers, including a New Zealander named Edmund Hillary. Altogether, the men would require two and a half *tons* of equipment and food. Those supplies couldn't be trucked or airlifted to the base of the mountain. They had to be delivered to Kathmandu and *carried* on the backs of men and women 180 miles up and down Himalayan ridges and over rivers crossed by narrow rope-and-plank bridges to the base camp. Tenzing would have to hire between two and three hundred people just to get the supplies in the vicinity of the mountain. Supplies needed by the party above the base camp would have to be carried up the mountain by another forty porters, each a Sherpa with extensive mountain experience.

IT TAKES A TEAM

For each level that the climbers reached, a higher degree of teamwork was required. One set of men would exhaust themselves just to get equipment up the mountain for the next group. Two-man teams would work their way up the mountain, finding a path, cutting steps, securing ropes. And then they would be finished, having spent themselves to make the next leg of the climb possible for another team. Of the teamwork involved, Tenzing remarked:

> You do not climb a mountain like Everest by trying to race ahead on your own, or by competing with your comrades. You do it slowly and carefully, by unselfish teamwork. Certainly I wanted to reach the top myself; it was the thing I had dreamed of all my life. But if the lot fell to someone else I would take it like a man, and not a cry-baby. For that is the mountain way.[2]

The team of climbers, using the "mountain way," ultimately made it possible for two pairs to make an attempt at reaching the summit. The first consisted of Tom Bourdillon and Charles Evans. When they tried and failed, the other team got its chance. That team consisted of Tenzing and Edmund Hillary. Tenzing wrote of the first team:

They were worn-out, sick with exhaustion, and, of course, terribly disappointed that they had not reached the summit themselves. But still . . . they did everything they could to advise and
help us. And I thought, Yes, that is how it is on a mountain. That
is how a mountain makes men great. For where would Hillary
and I have been without the others? Without the climbers who
had made the route and the Sherpas who had carried the loads?
It was only because of the work and sacrifice of all of them that
we were now to have our chance at the top.[3]

They made the most of their chance. On May 29, 1953, Tenzing
Norgay and Edmund Hillary accomplished what no other human being ever
had: they stood on the summit of Mount Everest, the world's highest peak!

Could Tenzing and Hillary have made it alone? The answer is no.
Could they have made it without a great team? Again, the answer is no.
Why? Because *as the challenge escalates, the need for teamwork elevates.*
That's the Law of Mount Everest.

What Is Your Everest?

You may not be a mountain climber, and you may not have any desire to
reach the summit of Everest. But I bet you have a dream. I say that with
confidence because deep down everybody has one—even the people who
haven't figured out what theirs is yet. If you have a dream, you need a
team to accomplish it.

How do you approach the task of putting together a team to accomplish
your dream? I think the best way to start is to ask yourself three questions:

1. "What Is My Dream?"

It all starts with this question because your answer reveals *what could
be.* Robert Greenleaf remarked, "Nothing much happens without a dream.
For something really great to happen, it takes a really great dream."

What lies in your heart? What do you see as a possibility for your life?

What would you like to accomplish during your time on this earth? Only a dream will tell you such things. As Harlem Renaissance poet Langston Hughes wrote:

> *Hold fast to dreams for if dreams die,*
> *Life is a broken-winged bird that cannot fly.*
> *Hold fast to dreams for when dreams go,*
> *Life is a barren field frozen with snow.*

If you want to do something great, you must have a dream. But a dream is not enough. You can fulfill a dream only if you are part of a team.

2. "WHO IS ON MY TEAM?"

This second question tells you *what is*. It measures your current situation. Your potential is only as good as your current team. That's why you must examine who is joining you on your journey. A mountain climber like Maurice Wilson, who had only three halfhearted companions, was never able to accomplish his dream of climbing the mountain. However, someone like Tenzing Norgay, who always climbed Everest with the best mountaineers in the world, was able to make it to the top. A great dream with a bad team is nothing more than a nightmare.

3. "WHAT SHOULD MY DREAM TEAM LOOK LIKE?"

The truth is that your team must be the size of your dream. If it's not, then you won't achieve it. You simply cannot achieve an ultimate number ten dream with a number four team. It just doesn't happen. If you want to climb Mount Everest, you need a Mount Everest–sized team. There's no other way to do it. It's better to have a great team with a weak dream than a great dream with a weak team.

FOCUS ON THE TEAM, NOT THE DREAM

One mistake I've seen people repeatedly make is focusing too much attention on their dream and too little on their team. But the truth is that if you build the right team, the dream will almost take care of itself.

Every dream brings challenges of its own. The kind of challenge determines the kind of team you need to build. Consider a few examples:

TYPE OF CHALLENGE	TYPE OF TEAM REQUIRED
New challenge	Creative team
Controversial challenge	United team
Changing challenge	Fast and flexible team
Unpleasant challenge	Motivated team
Diversified challenge	Complementary team
Long-term challenge	Determined team
Everest-sized challenge	Experienced team

If you want to achieve your dream—I mean, really do it, not just imagine what it would be like—then grow your team. But as you do so, make sure your motives are right. Some people gather a team just to benefit themselves. Others do it because they enjoy the team experience and want to create a sense of community. Still others do it because they want to build an organization. The funny thing about these reasons is that if you're motivated by *all* of them, then your desire to build a team probably comes from wanting to add value to everyone on the team. But if your desire to build the team comes as the result of only one of these reasons, you probably need to examine your motives.

HOW TO GROW A TEAM

When the team you have doesn't match up to the team of your dreams, then you have only two choices: Give up your dream, or grow up your team. Here is my recommendation concerning how to do the latter.

1. DEVELOP TEAM MEMBERS

The first step to take with a team that's not realizing its potential is to help individual team members grow. If you're leading the team, then one of your most important responsibilities is to see the potential that people don't see in themselves, and draw it out. When you accomplish this, you're doing your job as a leader.

Think about the people on your team, and determine what they need based on the following categories:

- Enthusiastic beginner—needs direction
- Disillusioned learner—needs coaching
- Cautious completer—needs support
- Self-reliant achiever—needs responsibility

Always give the people who are already on your team a chance to grow and bloom. That's what early British explorer Eric Shipton did with a young, inexperienced kid named Tenzing in 1935, and his country was rewarded eighteen years later with a successful climb of the world's highest peak.

2. ADD KEY TEAM MEMBERS

Even if you give every person on your team a chance to learn and grow, and all of them make the most of the opportunities, you may find that you still lack the talent needed to accomplish your dream. That's when it's time to recruit that talent. Sometimes all the team needs is one key person with talent in an area to make the difference between success and failure.

3. CHANGE THE LEADERSHIP

Various team challenges require different kinds of leadership. If a team has the right talent but still isn't growing, sometimes the best thing you can do is ask someone from the team who has previously been a follower to step into a leadership role. That transition may occur only for a short season, or it may be more permanent.

The challenge of the moment often determines the leader for that challenge. Why? Because every person on the team has strengths and weaknesses that come into play. That was the case for the Everest team as they faced every stage of the journey. Colonel Hunt chose the climbers and led the expedition, casting vision, modeling unselfish service, and making critical decisions about who would take which part. Tenzing chose the porters, leading, organizing, and motivating them to build the camps at each stage of the mountain. And the climbing teams took turns leading, cutting the trail up the mountain so that Hillary and Tenzing could make the final climb to the summit. When a particular challenge emerged, so did a leader to meet it. And everyone worked together, doing his part.

If your team is facing a big challenge, and it doesn't seem to be making any progress "up the mountain," then it might be time to change leaders. There may be someone on the team more capable for leading during this season.

4. REMOVE INEFFECTIVE MEMBERS

Sometimes a team member can turn a winning team into a losing one, either through lack of skill or a poor attitude. In those cases you must put the team first and make changes for the greater good.

Tenzing faced that situation during the 1953 Everest expedition. During early days of travel, there were continual flare-ups between the porters and the British team of climbers, and as sirdar, Tenzing was constantly stuck in the middle trying to work things out. After repeatedly negotiating the peace between the two parties, Tenzing discovered that the source of the problem was two Sherpas who were stirring up dissension. He promptly fired them and sent them home. Peace was quickly restored. If your team keeps breaking down or falling short, you may need to make changes in your team.

Growing a team is demanding and time-consuming. But if you want to achieve your dream, you have no other choice. The greater the dream, the greater the team. *As the challenge escalates, the need for teamwork elevates.* That is the Law of Mount Everest.

4

How Do I Develop
a Team That Lasts?

Create an environment that unleashes new leaders.

If you are the leader in your organization, then I want to spend a few moments with you in this special section. Many leaders in the middle of organizations are highly frustrated. They have great desire to lead and succeed; yet their leaders are often a greater hindrance than help to them. More than two-thirds of the people who leave their jobs do so because of an ineffective or incompetent leader. People don't leave their company—they leave their leader.

As a leader, you have the power the way nobody else does to create a positive leadership culture where potential leaders flourish. If you create that environment, then people with leadership potential will learn, gain experience, and come into their own. They will become the kind of team leaders who make an organization great.

If you're willing to work at making your organization a place where leaders lead and do it well, you'll need to shift your focus from

leading the people and the organization, to . . .
leading the people, finding leaders, and leading the
    organization, to . . .

leading the people, developing the leaders, and
    leading the organization, to . . .
leading and empowering the leaders while they lead
    the organization, to . . .
serving the leaders as they lead the organization.

Depending on where you're starting from, that process may take several years, and it may be a tough climb. But think of the alternative. Where will your organization be in five years if you don't raise up leaders in an environment that unleashes team leaders?

The Leader's Daily Dozen

If you're ready to revolutionize your organization, then I want to encourage you to start the process by adopting what I call the "Leader's Daily Dozen." Every morning when you get up and get ready to lead your organization, make a commitment to these twelve power-unleashing activities.

1. Place a High Value on People

The first shift for turning your organization into a leader-friendly environment must occur inside of you. You only commit yourself to things you value. And fundamentally, if you don't value people, you will never create a culture that develops leaders.

Most leaders focus on two things: the vision and the bottom line. The vision is what usually excites us most, and taking care of the bottom line keeps us in business. But between the vision and the bottom line are all the people in your organization. What's ironic is that if you ignore the people and only pay attention to these other two things, you will lose the people and the vision (and probably the bottom line). But if you focus on the people, you have the potential to win the people, the vision, and the bottom line.

When Jim Collins studied great companies and came to discover and define what he called level five leaders, he noticed that these excellent leaders didn't take the credit for their organization's accomplishments. In fact, they were incredibly humble and gave the credit to their people. Without a doubt, level five leaders place a high value on people.

Many companies say they value their people and their customers. Those are trendy things to say, but talk is cheap. If you want to know whether this is a value in your organization, then talk to people who know your organization well but don't work for it. What would they say? Their answers would probably give you the most accurate picture.

But you know your own heart better than anyone else. It all starts with you. You need to ask yourself: *Do I place a high value on people?*

2. COMMIT RESOURCES TO DEVELOP PEOPLE

Once when I was flying to Dallas with Zig Ziglar, he asked if I ever received letters from people thanking me. When I acknowledged that I did, he asked, "When you get those letters, what do people thank you for?" I had never really thought about that before, but the answer was clear. People almost always said thanks for a book I had written or some other resource I had produced.

"It's the same for me," Zig said. "Isn't that interesting? You and I are known for our speaking, but that's not what prompts people to write."

I've done a lot of speaking over the past thirty-five years. I love doing it, and I do think it has value. Events are great for creating lots of energy and enthusiasm, but if you want to facilitate growth, you need resources. They are better for development because they are process oriented. You can take them with you. You can refer back to them. You can dig into the meat and skip the fluff—and you can go at your own pace.

Once when I was teaching leaders at a large corporation, one of the event's organizers stated from the platform that people were their organization's most appreciable asset. I applauded his sentiment, but I also expanded on it for the leaders in the room. His statement is true only if you develop those people.

It takes a lot of effort to develop leaders. The first question a leader usually asks is, "What is it going to cost?" My answer is, "Whatever amount it costs, it won't be as high as the cost of not developing your people."

Once again, I have a question for you. Ask yourself, Am I committed to providing resources for leadership development?

3. Place a High Value on Leadership

People who run a one-person business may not have to worry about leadership. But for people who lead organizations, leadership is always an issue. Anytime you have two or more people working together, leadership comes into play. In some organizations, all the emphasis is placed on effort, and leadership isn't even on people's radar. What a mistake.

All good leaders recognize the importance of leadership and place a high value on it. I love what General Tommy Franks said about the ultimate leaders in the middle of the military—the sergeants:

> The months in the desert had reinforced my longstanding conviction that sergeants really were the backbone of the Army. The average trooper depends on NCOs for leadership by personal example. I thought of Sam Long and Scag, of Staff Sergeant Kittle—they had been examples of what a sergeant should be. If a noncommissioned officer is dedicated to his troops, the squad or section will have hard, realistic training, hot food when it's available, and the chance to take an occasional shower. If a sergeant is indifferent to the needs of his soldiers, their performance will suffer, and their lives might be wasted. A smart officer works hard to develop good NCOs.[1]

The American military understands the value of leadership and always places a high value on it. If you value leadership, leaders will emerge to add value to the organization.

This time the question to ask yourself is very simple: Do I place a high value on leadership in my organization?

4. Look for Potential Leaders

If leadership is on your radar and you value it, you will continually be on the lookout for potential leaders. Several years ago I did a lesson for one of my leadership development tape clubs that taught leaders what to look for in potential leaders. It was called "Searching for Eagles," and for many years it was our most requested lesson. These are the top ten characteristics of "eagles":

- They make things happen.
- They see opportunities.
- They influence the opinions and actions of others.
- They add value to you.
- They draw winners to them.
- They equip other eagles to lead.
- They provide ideas that help the organization.
- They possess an uncommonly great attitude.
- They live up to their commitments.
- They show fierce loyalty to the organization and the leader.

As you begin to search for potential leaders, look for people who possess these qualities. Meanwhile, ask yourself: *Am I continually looking for potential leaders?*

5. Know and Respect Your People

As you find leaders and develop them, you will get to know them better as individuals. But there are also other characteristics that are common to all leaders that you should keep in mind as you take them through the development process.

- People want to see results.
- People want to be effective—they want to do what they do well.
- People want to be in the picture.
- People want to be appreciated.
- People want to be a part of the celebration.

As you select people to develop, work to strike a balance between these universal desires and the individual needs of your people. Try to tailor the development process for each individual as much as you can. To do that, continually ask yourself, *Do I know and respect my people?*

6. Provide Your People with Leadership Experiences

It is impossible to learn leadership without actually leading. After all, leadership is action. One of the places where many leaders miss developmental opportunities comes in what we delegate. Our natural tendency is to give others tasks to perform rather than leadership functions to fulfill. We need to make a shift. If we don't delegate leadership—with authority as well as accountability—our people will never gain the experience they need to lead well.

The question you must ask yourself is, Am I providing my people with leadership experiences?

7. Reward Leadership Initiative

Taking initiative is such an important part of leadership. The best leaders are proactive. They make things happen. Most leaders are initiators, but that doesn't mean that every leader feels comfortable when others use their initiative. Just because they trust their own instincts doesn't mean they trust the instincts of their people.

It's true that emerging leaders often want to take the lead before they are really ready to. But potential leaders can only become full-fledged leaders if they are allowed to develop and use their initiative. So what's the solution? Good timing! If you rush the timing, you short-circuit the growth process. If you hold leaders back when they're ready to move, you stunt their growth.

One of the things that can help you navigate the timing issue is recognizing whether your mind-set is one of scarcity or abundance. If you believe that the world has only a limited amount of resources, a finite number of opportunities, and so forth, then you may be reluctant to let your leaders take risks—because you may think that the organization will not be able to recover from mistakes. On the other hand, if you believe opportunities are unlimited, that resources are renewable and unlimited, you will be more willing to take risks. You will not doubt your ability to recover.

How are you doing in this area? Ask yourself, *Do I reward leadership initiative?*

8. PROVIDE A SAFE ENVIRONMENT WHERE PEOPLE ASK QUESTIONS, SHARE IDEAS, AND TAKE RISKS

Pulitzer Prize–winning historian Garry Wills said, "Leaders have a say in what they are being led to. A leader who neglects that soon finds himself without followers." It takes secure leaders at the top to let the leaders working for them be full participants in the organization's leadership process. If leaders in the middle question them, they don't take it personally. When they share ideas, the leaders cannot afford to feel threatened. When people lower than they are in the organization want to take risks, they need to be willing to give them room to succeed or fail.

Leadership by its very nature challenges. It challenges out-of-date ideas. It challenges old ways of doing things. It challenges the status quo. Never forget that what gets rewarded gets done. If you reward complacency, you will get complacency from your leaders in the middle. But if you can remain secure and let them find new ways of doing things— ways that are better than yours—the organization will move forward more quickly.

Instead of trying to be Mr. Answerman or Ms. Fix-it, when your leaders start coming into their own, move more into the background. Try taking on the role of wise counselor and chief encourager. Welcome the desire of your best leaders to innovate and improve the organization. After all, I think you'll agree that a win for the organization is a win for you.

So what role are you playing in your organization? Are you "the expert," or are you more of an advisor and advocate? Ask yourself, *Am I providing an environment where people can ask questions, share ideas, and take risks?*

9. Grow with Your People

I've talked to a lot of leaders during my career, and I've detected a number of different attitudes toward growth. Here's how I would summarize them:

- I have already grown.
- I want my people to grow.
- I'm dedicated to helping my people grow.
- I want to grow along with my people.

Guess which attitude fosters an organization where people are growing?

When people in an organization see the leader growing, it changes the culture of the organization. It immediately removes many barriers between the leader and the rest of the people, putting you on the same level with them, which makes the leader much more human and accessible. It also sends a clear message to everyone: make growth a priority.

So the question I want you to ask yourself is very simple: *Am I growing with my people?*

10. Draw People with High Potential into Your Inner Circle

When Mark Sanborn, author of *The Fred Factor*, spoke at one of our leadership events, he made a remark that really stuck with me: "It's better to have a group of deer led by a lion than a group of lions led by a deer." Why? Because even if you have a group of deer, if they are led by a lion, they will act like a pride of lions. Isn't that a great analogy? It's really true. When people spend time with someone and are directed by them, they learn to think the way that person thinks and do what that person does. Their performance starts to rise according to the capability of their leader.

When I was working on *Developing the Leaders Around You*, I often took an informal poll at conferences to find out how people came to be leaders. I asked if they became leaders because (a) they were given a position; (b) there was a crisis in the organization; or (c) they had been mentored. More than 80 percent indicated that they were leaders because someone had mentored them in leadership—had taken them through the process.

The best way to develop high-caliber leaders is to have them mentored by a high-caliber leader. If you lead your organization, you are probably the best (or at least one of the best) leader in the organization. If you are not already doing so, you need to handpick the people with the greatest potential, invite them into your inner circle, and mentor them. It doesn't matter if you do it with one or with a dozen, whether you work one-on-one or in a group setting. The main thing is that you need to be giving your best to your best people.

Are you doing that? What is your answer to the question, Am I drawing people with potential into my inner circle?

11. COMMIT YOURSELF TO DEVELOPING A LEADERSHIP TEAM

When I started out as a leader, I tried to do everything myself. Until I was about age forty, I thought I could do it all. After my fortieth birthday, I finally realized that if I didn't develop other leaders, my potential was only a fraction of what it could be. So for the next decade, developing people into good leaders was my focus. But even that has its limitations. I realize now that to reach the highest level of leadership, I must continually develop leadership teams.

Let's face it. No one does everything well. I can't do it all—can you? I wrote the *The 21 Irrefutable Laws of Leadership*, which contains every leadership principle I know based on a lifetime of learning and leading. I can't do all of the twenty-one laws well. So I need help.

You do too. If you want your organization to reach its potential, if you want it to go from good to great (or even average to good), you need to develop a team of leaders, people who can fill in each other's gaps, people who challenge and sharpen one another. If we try to do it all ourselves, we will never get beyond the glass ceiling of our own leadership limitations.

How are you in this area? Ask yourself, Am I committed to developing a leadership team?

12. Unleash Your Leaders to Lead

As leaders, if we feel any uncertainty or insecurity about the leadership development process, it is usually not related to the training we give. The uncertainty we feel comes when we contemplate releasing our leaders to lead. It is not dissimilar to what parents feel with their kids. My children are grown and have families of their own, but when they were teenagers, the hardest thing for my wife and me was releasing them to go their own way and make their own decisions. It is scary, but if you don't let them try out their wings, they will never learn to fly.

As I have grown older, I have come to think of myself as a lid lifter. That is my main function as a team leader. If I can lift the leadership lids for the members of my team, then I am doing my job. The more barriers I remove for my people, the more likely they are to rise up to their potential. And what's really great is that when the leaders are lid lifters for the leaders in the middle of an organization, then those leaders become load lifters for the ones at the top. If you become dedicated to developing and releasing team leaders, your organization will change—and so will your life.

PART II

THE DYNAMICS OF TEAMWORK

5

WHAT ARE THE CHARACTERISTICS OF A GOOD TEAM?

Great teams have everyone on the same page.

In all my years of people development and team building, I have found that all successful teams share some common characteristics. If you, as a player, team leader, or coach, can cultivate these qualities in your group of leaders, they will become a cohesive team capable of leaping tall buildings or performing any other required task. Here are those characteristics:

THE TEAM MEMBERS CARE FOR ONE ANOTHER

All great teams begin with this quality. It is the foundation upon which everything is built. Teams that don't bond can't build. Why? Because they never become a cohesive unit.

One of the best descriptions of this quality that I've ever come across was given by college football coach Lou Holtz. He said that he had once watched a television program that examined why men died for their country. In the program, which looked at United States Marines, the French Foreign Legion, and the British Commandos, it was noted that men died for their country because of the love they had for their fellow man. In the show, they interviewed a soldier who had been wounded in combat and was recovering in a hospital when he heard his unit was going back out on a dangerous mission. The soldier escaped from the hospital and went with them, only to be wounded again. When asked why he did it, he said that after you work and live with people, you soon realize your survival depends on one another. For a team to be successful, the teammates have to know they will look out for one another.

I have found that one of the best ways to get members of a team to care about one another is to get them together outside of a work context in order to build relationships. Every year in our organization we plan retreats and other events that put our people together in social settings. And during those times, we also make sure they spend part of their time with staff members they don't know very well. That way they're not only building relationships, they're being prevented from developing cliques.

THE TEAM MEMBERS KNOW WHAT IS IMPORTANT

One of the things I enjoy most about a team experience is how the team functions as a single unit. All of its parts have a common goal and purpose. This quality is developed by making sure each team member knows what is important to the team. This quality, like the previous one, is foundational to team building. Without it team members cannot truly work together.

In a sport such as basketball, the players on a team recognize that scoring is what is important. When a team is more effective at scoring than the opponent, it wins. Because the team members know that, they spend their time improving and perfecting their ability to score. That is their focus. In contrast, in many organizational settings, the team members don't know what it means to "score." They may have a list of duties, but they don't know how those duties go together to make a score. It would be the equivalent of a basketball player who knew how to set a pick, dribble, and pass, but who never knew all these skills were used together to score baskets.

If just one player on a basketball team doesn't know what is important to the team, it makes him ineffective. And when he is in the game, it is impossible for the team to succeed. The same is true in any organization. Anyone who doesn't know what's important to the team not only fails to contribute to the team, but actually *prevents the team from achieving success*. That is why it is so important for the leader of the team to identify what is important to the team and to communicate that information to her team members.

THE TEAM MEMBERS COMMUNICATE WITH ONE ANOTHER

The third foundational quality of an effective team is communication. Just as it is important for the team leader to communicate what is important to the team, the individual members of the team must communicate with one another. Without it, the players are likely to work against each other. Important tasks can be left undone, and team members can find themselves duplicating work.

Anyone who has played basketball is familiar with the situation in which two players go up for a rebound and fight each other for the ball, only to find that they are on the same team. On teams where players communicate with one another, a third player will shout, "Same team!" to make sure they don't lose the ball while trying to take it away from one another. That is what communication on the team is all about: letting each other know what's going on so the team's best interest is protected.

The same is true in nonsporting organizations. Clear and formal lines of communication must be established. But even more important, an atmosphere of positive communication must be established and encouraged on a daily basis. People on the team must be made to feel that they are in an environment where it is safe to offer suggestions or criticism without feeling threatened, freely trade information in the spirit of cooperation, and discuss ideas without being negatively criticized. Open communication among teammates increases productivity.

THE TEAM MEMBERS GROW TOGETHER

Once the members of the team care for one another, have a common goal, and communicate with one another, they are ready to start growing. In an organization, it is the team leader's responsibility to orchestrate the team's growth. He must make sure his people grow both personally and professionally. And he must ensure that their growth happens together—as a team.

When I work on growing my team members, I take several different approaches. First, we all learn together on a regular basis, at least once a month. In this way, I there are some things everyone in the organization knows, and they share the common experience of learning these things together, regardless of their position or responsibilities.

Second, I regularly build small teams of learners. I periodically have groups of three or four work together on a project that requires them to learn. It builds strong relational bonds between those people. It's a good idea, by the way, to vary the members of these teams so that different people are learning to work together. It also gives you an idea about the particular chemistry of different groups as they work together.

Finally, I frequently send different people to conferences, workshops, and seminars. When they return, I ask them to teach others in the organization what they've learned. It gets everyone used to teaching and learning from each other. Shared experiences and the give-and-take of communication are the greatest ways to promote team growth.

THERE IS A TEAM FIT

As people who care about one another grow together and work toward a common goal, they get to know each other better. They start to appreciate each other's strengths and become aware of each other's weaknesses. They begin to recognize and appreciate each player's unique qualities. And that leads to the development of a team "fit."

The type of fit a team has depends on many things. It is more than just the way a group of people with particular talents come together. We have probably all seen teams made up of talented players at each position who should have been able to play well together but couldn't. Despite their talents, they didn't have the right chemistry.

A good team fit requires an attitude of partnership. Every team member must respect the other players. They must desire to contribute to the team, and they must come to expect a contribution from every other person. Above all, they must learn to trust each other. It is trust that makes it possible for them to rely on one another. It allows them to make up for each other's weaknesses instead of trying to exploit them. It enables one team member to say to the other, "You go ahead and do this task because you are better at it than I am," without shame or manipulation. Trust allows team members to begin working as a single unit, to begin accomplishing the things that together they recognize as important. Once the players know and trust one another, and develop a fit, the team's personality will begin to emerge.

THE TEAM MEMBERS PLACE THEIR INDIVIDUAL RIGHTS BENEATH THE BEST INTEREST OF THE TEAM

Once team members believe in the goals of their team and begin to develop genuine trust in one another, they will be in a position to demonstrate true teamwork. Their mutual trust will make it possible for them to place their own rights and privileges beneath the best interest of the team.

Notice that I mention the team members will be in a *position* to demonstrate true teamwork. That does not necessarily mean that they will. For there to be teamwork, several things must happen. First, they must genuinely believe that the value of the team's success is greater than the value of their own individual interests. They will be able to believe it only if they care about one another and if their leader has effectively cast the vision of what is important. Then they will recognize that their success will come with the team's success.

Second, for team members to place their individual rights beneath the team's best interest, personal sacrifice must be encouraged and then rewarded—by the team leader and the other members of the team. As this happens, the people will come to identify themselves more and more with the team. At that point they will recognize that individualism wins trophies, but teamwork wins pennants.

EACH TEAM MEMBER PLAYS A SPECIAL ROLE

As the team fit becomes stronger and each person is willing to put the team first, people begin to recognize their different roles on the team. They can do this because they know what must be accomplished to win, and they know their teammates' capabilities. With that knowledge and some encouragement from the team leader, people will gladly assume appropriate roles. Philip Van Auken, in *The Well-Managed Ministry*, recognizes this as the *Niche Principle*. He says, "People who occupy a special place on the team feel special and perform in a special way. Team niches humanize teamwork."

In an ideal situation, each person's role is built on his or her greatest strengths. That way each person's talents can be maximized. But it doesn't always work exactly that way. Because the team's success is what is most important, sometimes the team members must be flexible. For example, anyone who follows professional basketball has heard of Magic Johnson. He played for the Los Angeles Lakers during the 1980s, when they were one of the best teams. His greatest talent was his ability to make plays happen, especially assists using incredible look-away passes. But Johnson was a player who was always willing to fill whatever role the team needed. Over several seasons, he started in NBA championship games as a guard, forward, and center. He may be the only professional basketball player who has ever done that.

The important thing is that all the team members take a role that fits the goals and needs of the organization as well as their own personal talents and abilities. When any role is not filled, the whole team suffers.

If you are a team leader, you must recognize what roles need to be filled by your team members for the team to accomplish its goal. And when you see a role not being filled, you must make adjustments to the team to make sure the job gets done.

AN EFFECTIVE TEAM HAS A GOOD BENCH

In sports, the bench may be the most misunderstood resource of the team. Many "starting" players believe that they are important, while the people on the bench are not. They believe they could do without them. Others who spend much of their time on the bench don't recognize their own contribution. Some mistakenly believe they don't have to bother preparing the way the starters do, that they don't have to be ready to play. But the truth is that a good bench is indispensable. Without a good bench, a team will never succeed.

The first thing a good bench gives is depth. In sports, many teams can produce a winning season. But when the level of competition goes up, such as in a play-off or a national tournament, a team without depth just can't make it. If the team does not have good reserve players, it will not be able to go the distance. I have yet to see a championship team that did not have a good bench. In fact, developing a good bench is what much of this book is about: selecting, equipping, and developing people to do their best and get the job done when they are needed.

Another property of a team's bench is that it sets the tone for the whole team's level of play. This is true because the team's preparation depends on the bench. In sports, teams practice against their own players. If the starters practice only against weak players, their performance will not improve. But a good bench causes them to do their best all the time, to constantly improve. The same is true in any organization. If the level of play in the organization is high every day, then the team's performance will be top-notch when it really counts.

Finally, a good bench is a requirement for a successful team because it provides a place for a weary player to rest. On successful teams, when one of the players cannot make it any farther due to fatigue or injury, his teammates carry the load and give him a rest. This is possibly the finest quality of teamwork—the willingness of one player to step up his level of play and go the extra mile for his teammate in a time of need. It is the ultimate indication of a player's desire to put the team and its goals first.

The Team Members Know Exactly Where the Team Stands

In sports, the ability to know where their team stands at every moment during a game separates the great players from the adequate players. That quality, as much as talent, enables a player to move from one level of play up to the next, such as from college to the pros. Coaches have different terms for this quality. A football coach, for instance, might call it *football sense*. A basketball coach might call it *court sense* or *vision*. It is the ability to know how many seconds are left on the clock, how many points they are down, and which players are hot or hurt on each team. It is a quality that makes players, and therefore teams, great.

Outside of sports, the quality could be called *organizational sense*. It is the ability to know what is happening within the organization, how the organization stands in reference to its goals, how it stacks up against the competition, how the different players are doing, and how much more they can give in order to get the team where it needs to go. Not all team members are equally gifted with this sense. It is the job of the team leader to keep all of the players informed. He must get them to check on the team's progress and listen to the other players to know where the team stands. If all the team members are informed of where the team stands, they are in a better position to know what it is going to take for the team to succeed.

The Team Members Are Willing to Pay the Price

Time after time, success comes down to sacrifice—willingness to pay the price. The same is true of a winning team. Each member of the team must be willing to sacrifice time and energy to practice and prepare. He must be willing to be held accountable. He must be willing to sacrifice his own desires. He must be willing to give up part of himself for the team's success.

It all comes down to the desire and dedication of the individuals on the team. It's as true in business as it is in sports. It's even true in war. In an interview with David Frost, General Norman Schwarzkopf, commander of the Allied forces in the Gulf War, was asked, "What's the greatest lesson you've learned out of all this?" He replied:

I think that there is one really fundamental military truth. And that's that you can add up the correlation of forces, you can look at the number of tanks, you can look at the number of airplanes, you can look at all these factors of military might and put them together. But unless the soldier on the ground, or the airman in the air, has the will to win, has the strength of character to go into battle, believes that his cause is just, and has the support of his country . . . all the rest of that stuff is irrelevant.

Without each person's conviction that the cause is worth the price, the battle will never be won, and the team will not succeed. There must be commitment.

When you build a team within your organization, you will be capable of a level of success you never thought possible. Teamwork for a worthwhile vision makes it possible for common people to attain uncommon results. And when the team members are not common people, but leaders, their accomplishments can multiply.

6

WHAT DOES IT MEAN
TO BE A TEAM PLAYER?

The best players put the team first.

When the situation is life or death, most people worry more about taking care of themselves than anyone else. Not Philip Toosey. As an officer in the British army during World War II, he had plenty of opportunities to preserve himself, but instead, he always looked out for his team.

In 1927, when the twenty-three-year-old Toosey joined the Territorial Army, a kind of army reserve, he did so because he wanted to do more than merely develop in his career in banking and commodities trading. He had other interests. He was a good athlete and enjoyed playing rugby, but many of his friends were applying for service, so he decided to join as well. He was commissioned as a second lieutenant in an artillery unit, where he excelled as a leader and battery commander. In time, he moved up in rank to major.

In 1939, he and his unit were called up to active service as war broke out in Europe. He briefly served in France, was evacuated at Dunkirk, and was subsequently shipped overseas to serve in the Pacific. There he was part of the failed attempt to defend the Malay Peninsula and then finally Singapore from Japanese aggression. By that time, Toosey had been promoted to lieutenant colonel and was in command of the 135th regiment of the army's Eighteenth Division. And although he and his men fought well during the campaign, British forces were repeatedly required to retreat until they fell all the way back to Singapore.

It was there that Toosey displayed the first of many characteristically unselfish acts. When the British realized that surrender was inevitable, Toosey was ordered to leave his men and ship out so that his expertise as an artillery officer might be preserved and used elsewhere. He refused. He later recalled:

> I could not really believe my ears but being a Territorial [rather than a regular army officer] I refused. I got a tremendous rocket and was told to do as I was told. However I was able to say that as a Territorial all orders were a subject of discussion. I pointed out that as a Gunner I had read the Manual of Artillery Training, Volume II, which says quite clearly that in any withdrawal the Commanding Officer leaves last.[1]

He knew the negative effect that abandoning his men would have on their morale, so he stayed with them. Accordingly, when the Allied forces in Singapore surrendered to the Japanese in February 1942, Toosey became a prisoner of war along with his men.

Toosey soon found himself in a POW camp at Tamarkan near a major river called the Kwae Yai. As senior officer, he was in command of the Allied prisoners. His assignment from the Japanese was to build bridges across the river. (*The Bridge on the River Kwai* was based on the events that occurred at this camp, but Toosey was nothing like the character Colonel Nicholson in the movie.)

When first confronted by the orders of his Japanese captors, Toosey wanted to refuse. After all, the Hague Convention of 1907, which the Japanese had ratified, prohibited prisoners of war from being forced to do work that would help their enemies in the war effort. But Toosey also knew that refusal would bring reprisals, which he described as "immediate, physical, and severe."[2] Biographer Peter N. Davies observed, "Toosey, in fact, quickly realized that he had no real option in this matter and accepted that the vital question was not whether the troops were to perform the tasks laid down, but how many were to die in the process."[3]

Toosey chose to ask the prisoners to cooperate with their captors, but he risked his life daily by standing up for his men and arguing for increased rations, regular working hours, and a day off each week. He later said, "If you took responsibility as I did, it increased your suffering very considerably."[4] He suffered regular beatings and was made to stand at attention in the sun for twelve hours, yet his badgering caused improved conditions for the prisoners. And remarkably, during the ten months that work was being done on the bridges, only nine prisoners died.

Later, as the commander of a POW camp hospital, Toosey was known to do everything possible to aid the welfare of his men, including hiking to meet in person every single group of prisoners who arrived at the camp, even in the dead of night. He worked with the black market in order to obtain medicine, food, and other supplies, even though detection would have meant certain death. He insisted on taking responsibility for an illegal radio if it were to be found by Japanese guards. And when the war ended, Toosey's first concern was to find the men of his regiment. He traveled three hundred miles to be reunited with them and determine that they were safe.

After he returned to England, Toosey took three weeks of vacation and then went back to his prewar work with the merchant bank Barings. He never sought glory for his endeavors during the war, nor did he complain about the movie *The Bridge on the River Kwai*, though he evidently hated it. The only thing in his later life related to the war was his work for the Far East Prisoners of War Federation to help other former POWs. It was another act characteristic of a man who always put his team ahead of himself.

CULTIVATING SELFLESSNESS

Poet W. H. Auden quipped, "We're here on earth to do good for others. What the others are here for, I don't know." No team succeeds unless its players put others on the team ahead of themselves. Being selfless isn't easy, but it is necessary.

As a team member, how do you cultivate an attitude of selflessness? Begin by doing the following:

1. BE GENEROUS

St. Francis of Assisi stated, "All getting separates you from others; all giving unites to others." The heart of selflessness is generosity. It not only helps to unite the team, but it also helps to advance the team. If team members are willing to give of themselves generously to the team, then it is being set up to succeed.

2. AVOID INTERNAL POLITICS

One of the worst forms of selfishness can be seen in people who are playing politics on the team by posturing or positioning themselves for their own benefit, regardless of how it might damage relationships on the team. But good team players worry about the benefit of their teammates more than themselves. That kind of unselfishness helps teammates and benefits the giver. The remarkable scientist Albert Einstein observed, "A person first starts to live when he can live outside of himself."

3. DISPLAY LOYALTY

If you show loyalty to the people on your team, they will return loyalty in kind. That was certainly the case for Colonel Toosey. Time and time again, he put himself on the line for his men, and as a result they worked hard, served him well, and completed whatever mission they had been given—even in the most difficult of circumstances. Loyalty fosters unity, and unity breeds team success.

4. VALUE INTERDEPENDENCE OVER INDEPENDENCE

In America, we value independence highly because it is often accompanied by innovation, hard work, and a willingness to stand for what's right. But independence taken too far is a characteristic of selfishness, especially if it begins to harm or hinder others. Seneca asserted, "No man can live happily who regards himself alone, who turns everything to his own advantage. You must live for others if you wish to live for yourself."

TO BECOME MORE SELFLESS . . .

PROMOTE SOMEONE OTHER THAN YOURSELF

If you are in the habit of talking up your achievements and promoting yourself to others, determine to keep silent about yourself and praise others for two weeks. Find positive things to say about people's actions and qualities, especially to their superiors, family, and close friends.

TAKE A SUBORDINATE ROLE

Most people's natural tendency is to take the best place and to let others fend for themselves. All day today, practice the discipline of serving, letting others go first, or taking a subordinate role. Do it for a week and see how it affects your attitude.

GIVE SECRETLY

Writer John Bunyan maintained, "You have not lived today successfully unless you've done something for someone who can never repay you." If you give to others on your team without their knowing, they cannot repay you. Try it. Get in the habit of doing it, and you may not be able to stop.

7

HOW DO I GO ABOUT BUILDING A WINNING TEAM?

A leader's investment in the team pays dividends.

Everyone knows that teamwork is a good thing; in fact, it's essential! But how does it really work? What makes a winning team? Why do some teams go straight to the top, seeing their vision become reality, while others seem to go nowhere?

Teams come in all shapes and sizes. If you're married, you and your spouse are a team. If you are employed by an organization, you and your colleagues are a team. If you volunteer your time, you and your fellow workers are a team. As Dan Devine joked, "A team is a team is a team. Shakespeare said that many times." Although the gifted playwright might not have said exactly that, the concept is nonetheless true. That's why teamwork is so important.

HOW TO INVEST IN TEAM BUILDING

I believe that most people recognize that investing in team building brings benefits to everyone on the team. The question for most people isn't *why*, but *how*. Allow me to share with you ten steps you can take to invest in building your team. You can implement these practices whether you are a player or coach, employee or employer, follower or leader. There is always someone on the team who can benefit from what you have to offer. And when everyone on the team is investing, then the benefits are like those of compound interest. They multiply. Here is how to get started:

1. MAKE THE DECISION TO BUILD A TEAM . . . THIS STARTS THE INVESTMENT IN THE TEAM

It's said that every journey begins with the first step. Deciding that people on the team are worth developing is the first step in building a better team. That requires *commitment*.

2. GATHER THE BEST TEAM POSSIBLE . . . THIS ELEVATES THE POTENTIAL OF THE TEAM

As I've previously mentioned, the better the people on the team, the greater the potential. There's only one kind of team that you may be a part of where you *shouldn't* go out and find the best players available, and that's family. You need to stick with those teammates through thick and thin. But every other kind of team can benefit from the recruitment of the very best people available.

3. PAY THE PRICE TO DEVELOP THE TEAM . . . THIS ENSURES THE GROWTH OF THE TEAM

When Morgan Wootten extended himself to benefit the kid who had two and a half strikes against him, he and his family had to pay a price to help that boy. It wasn't convenient or comfortable. It cost them in energy, money, and time.

It will cost you to develop your team. You will have to dedicate time that could be used for personal productivity. You will have to spend money that could be used for personal bene-fit. And sometimes you will have to set aside your personal agenda. But the benefit to the individuals—and the team—is worth the price. Everything you give is an investment.

4. Do Things Together as a Team . . . This Provides Community for the Team

I once read the statement, "Even when you've played the game of your life, it's the feeling of teamwork that you'll remember. You'll forget the plays, the shots, and the scores, but you'll never forget your teammates." That describes the community that develops among teammates who spend time doing things together.

The only way to develop community and cohesiveness among your teammates is to get them together, not just in a professional setting but in personal ones as well. There are lots of ways to get yourself connected with your teammates, and to connect them with one another. Many families who want to bond find that camping does the trick. Business colleagues can socialize outside of work (in an appropriate way). The *where* and *when* are not as important as the fact that team members share common experiences.

5. Empower Team Members with Responsibility and Authority . . . This Raises Up Leaders for the Team

The greatest growth for people often occurs as a result of the trial and error of personal experience. Any team that wants people to step up to a higher level of performance—and to higher levels of leadership—must give team members authority as well as responsibility. If you are a leader on your team, don't protect your position or hoard your power. Give it away. That's the only way to empower your team.

6. Give Credit for Success to the Team . . . This Lifts the Morale of the Team

Mark Twain said, "I can live for two months on one good compliment." That's the way most people feel. They are willing to work hard if they receive recognition for their efforts. That's why Napoleon Bonaparte observed, "A soldier will fight long and hard for a bit of colored ribbon." Compliment your teammates. Talk up their accomplishments. And if you're the leader, take the blame but never the credit. Do that and your team will always fight for you.

7. WATCH TO SEE THAT THE INVESTMENT IN THE TEAM IS PAYING OFF . . . THIS BRINGS ACCOUNTABILITY TO THE TEAM

If you put money into an investment, you expect a return—maybe not right away, but certainly over time. How will you know whether you are gaining or losing ground on that investment? You have to pay attention to it and measure its progress.

The same is true of an investment in people. You need to observe whether you are getting a return for the time, energy, and resources you are putting into them. Some people develop quickly. Others are slower to respond, and that's okay. The main outcome you want to see is progress.

8. STOP YOUR INVESTMENT IN PLAYERS WHO DO NOT GROW . . . THIS ELIMINATES GREATER LOSSES FOR THE TEAM

One of the most difficult experiences for any team member is leaving a teammate behind. Yet that is what you must do if someone on your team refuses to grow or change for the benefit of teammates. That doesn't mean that you love the person less. It just means you stop spending your time trying to invest in someone who won't or can't make the team better.

9. CREATE NEW OPPORTUNITIES FOR THE TEAM . . . THIS ALLOWS THE TEAM TO STRETCH

There is no greater investment you can make in building a team than giving it new opportunities. When a team has the possibility of taking new ground or facing new challenges, it has to stretch to meet them. That process not only gives the team a chance to grow, but it also benefits every individual. Everyone has the opportunity to grow toward his or her potential.

10. GIVE THE TEAM THE BEST POSSIBLE CHANCE TO SUCCEED . . . THIS GUARANTEES THE TEAM A HIGH RETURN

James E. Hunton says, "Coming together is a beginning. Keeping together is progress. Working together is success." One of the most essential tasks you can undertake is to clear obstacles so that the team has the best possible chance to work toward success. If you are a team member, that may mean making a personal sacrifice or helping others work together better. If you are a leader, that means creating an energized environment for the team and giving each person what he needs at any given time to ensure success.

Investing in building a team almost guarantees a high return for the effort because a team can do so much more than individuals. Or as Rex Murphy, one of my conference attendees, told me, "Where there's a will there's a way; where there's a team, there's more than one way."

8

HOW DOES A WEAK PLAYER
IMPACT THE TEAM?

A weak link harms the leader's credibility
and the team's chances for success.

As much as any team likes to measure itself by its best people, the truth is that *the strength of the team is impacted by its weakest link.* No matter how much people try to rationalize it, compensate for it, or hide it, a weak link will eventually come to light.

YOUR TEAM IS NOT FOR EVERYONE

One of the mistakes I often made early in my career as a team leader was that I thought everyone who was on my team should remain on the team. That was true for several reasons. First, I naturally see the best in people. When I look at individuals with potential, I see all that they can become—even if they don't see it. And I try to encourage and equip them to become better. Second, I truly like people. I figure the more who take the trip, the bigger the party. Third, because I have vision and believe my goals are worthwhile and beneficial, I sometimes naively assume that everyone will want to go along with me.

But just because I wanted to take everyone with me didn't mean that it would always work out that way. My first memorable experience with this occurred in 1980 when I was offered an executive position at Wesleyan World Headquarters in Marion, Indiana. When I accepted the position, I invited my assistant to come with me to be a part of the new team I was building. So she and her husband considered my offer and went to Marion to look around. I'll never forget when they came back. As I excitedly talked about the coming challenges and how we could begin to tackle them, I began to realize from the expressions on their faces that something was wrong. And that's when they told me. They weren't going.

That statement took me completely by surprise. In fact, I was sure that they were making a mistake and told them so, doing my best to convince them to change their minds. But my wife, Margaret, gave me some very good advice. She said, "John, your problem is that you want to take everybody with you. But not everyone is going to go on the journey. Let it go." It was a hard lesson for me to learn—and sometimes it still is.

From that experience and others I've had since then, I've discovered that when it comes to teamwork . . .

1. Not Everyone Will Take the Journey

Some people don't want to go. My assistant and her husband wanted to stay in Lancaster, Ohio, where they had built relationships for many years. For other people the issue is their attitude. They don't want to change, grow, or conquer new territory. They hold fast to the status quo. All you can do with people in this group is kindly thank them for their past contributions and move on.

2. Not Everyone Should Take the Journey

Other people shouldn't join a team because it's a matter of their agenda. They have other plans, and where you're going isn't the right place for them. The best thing you can do for people in this category is wish them well, and as far as you are able, help them on their way so that they achieve success in their venture.

3. NOT EVERYONE CAN TAKE THE JOURNEY

For the third group of people, the issue is ability. They may not be capable of keeping pace with their teammates or helping the group get where it wants to go. How do you recognize people who fall into this category? They're not very hard to identify.

- They can't keep pace with other team members.
- They don't grow in their area of responsibility.
- They don't see the big picture.
- They won't work on personal weaknesses.
- They won't work with the rest of the team.
- They can't fulfill expectations for their area.

If you have people who display one or more of those characteristics, then you need to acknowledge that they are weak links.

That's not to say that they are necessarily bad people. In fact, some teams exist to serve weak links or help them become stronger. It depends on the team's goals. For example, when I was a senior pastor, we reached out to people in the community with food and assistance. We helped people with addictions, divorce recovery, and many other difficulties. Our goal was to serve them. It's good and appropriate to help people who find themselves in those circumstances. But putting them on the team while they are still broken and weak doesn't help them, and it hurts the team—even to the extent of making the team incapable of accomplishing its goal of service.

What can you do with people on your team who are weak links? You really have only two choices: you need to train them or trade them. Of course, your first priority should always be to try to train people who are having a hard time keeping up. Help can come in many forms: giving people books to read, sending them to conferences, presenting them with new challenges, pairing them with mentors. I believe that people often rise to your level of expectations. Give them hope and training, and they usually improve.

But what should you do if a team member continually fails to meet expectations, even after receiving training, encouragement, and opportunities to grow? My father used to have a saying: "Water seeks its own level." Somebody who is a weak link on your team might be capable of becoming a star on another team. You need to give that person an opportunity to find his level somewhere else.

THE IMPACT OF A WEAK LINK

If you are a team leader, you cannot avoid dealing with weak links. Team members who don't carry their own weight slow down the team, and they have a negative effect on your leadership. Several things may happen when a weak link remains on the team:

1. THE STRONGER MEMBERS IDENTIFY THE WEAK ONE

A weak link cannot hide (except in a group of weak people). If you have strong people on your team, they always know who isn't performing up to the level of everyone else.

2. THE STRONGER MEMBERS HAVE TO HELP THE WEAK ONE

If your people must work together as a team to do their work, then they have only two choices when it comes to a weak teammate. They can ignore the person and allow the team to suffer, or they can help him and make the team more successful. If they are team players, they will help.

3. THE STRONGER MEMBERS COME TO RESENT THE WEAK ONE

Whether strong team members help or not, the result will always be the same: resentment. No one likes to lose or fall behind consistently because of the same person.

4. THE STRONGER MEMBERS BECOME LESS EFFECTIVE

Carrying someone else's load in addition to your own compromises your performance. Do that for a long time, and the whole team suffers.

5. The Stronger Members Question the Leader's Ability

Anytime the leader allows a weak link to remain a part of the team, the team members forced to compensate for the weak person begin to doubt the leader's courage and discernment. You lose the respect of the best when you don't deal properly with the worst.

Many team members may be able to avoid the hard decision of dealing with subpar members, but leaders can't. In fact, one of the differences between leaders and followers is action. Followers often know what to do, but they are unwilling or unable to follow through. But know this: if other people on the team make decisions for you because you are unwilling or unable to make them, then your leadership is being compromised, and you're not serving the team well.

Strengthening the Chain

Weak team members always take more of the team's time than strong ones. One reason is that the more competent people have to give their time to compensate for those who don't carry their share of the load. The greater the difference in competence between the more accomplished performers and the less accomplished ones, the greater the detriment to the team. For example, if you rate people on a scale from 1 to 10 (with 10 being the best), a 5 among 10s really hurts the team, where an 8 among 10s often does not.

Let me show you how this works. When you first put together a group of people, their talents come together in a way that is analogous to addition. So visually a 5 among 10s looks like this:

$$10 + 10 + 10 + 10 + 5 = 45$$

The difference between this team and great ones with five 10s is like the difference between 50 and 45. That's a difference of 10 percent. But once a team comes together and starts to develop chemistry, synergy, and momentum, it's analogous to multiplication. That's when a weak link really starts to hurt the team. It's the difference between this:

$$10 \times 10 \times 10 \times 10 \times 10 = 100{,}000$$

and this:

$$10 \times 10 \times 10 \times 10 \times 5 = 50{,}000$$

That's a difference of 50 percent! The power and momentum of the team may be able to compensate for a weak link for a while, but not forever. A weak link eventually robs the team of momentum—and potential.

Ironically, weak links are less aware than stronger members of their weaknesses and shortcomings. They also spend more time guarding their turf, saving their positions, and holding on to what they have. And know this: when it comes to interaction between people, the weaker person usually controls the relationship. For example, someone with a good self-image is more flexible than a person with a poor self-image. An individual with a clear vision acts more readily than someone without one. A person with superb ability and high energy accomplishes more and works longer than an individual with lesser gifts. If the two people journey together, the stronger member must constantly work with and wait on the weaker one. That controls what happens on the journey.

If your team has a weak link who can't or won't rise to the level of the team—and you've done everything you can to help the person improve—then you've got to take action. When you do, heed the advice of authors Danny Cox and John Hoover. If you need to remove somebody from the team, be discreet, be clear, be honest, and be brief. Then, once the person is gone, be open about it with the rest of the team while maintaining respect for the person you let go.[1] And if you start to have second thoughts before or afterward, remember this: as long as a weak link is part of the team, everyone else on the team will suffer.

9

How Do I Create Positive Energy on the Team?

*Put completing teammates ahead of
competing with them.*

Chris Hodges, a good leader who is a native of Baton Rouge, is well-known for telling Boudreaux jokes, a type of humor popular in Louisiana. Recently on a trip for EQUIP, he told me this one (I'll try to capture the accent in writing as best I can—just think Justin Wilson):

> A group of Cajuns was sitting around bragging about how successful they were. Thibideaux says, "I just bought me another shrimp boat, yeah, and I got me a crew of ten people workin' for me."
>
> "Dat ain't nottin'," says Landry. "I been promoted at the refinery, and now I got fifty men workin' for me."
>
> Boudreaux hears this, and he doesn't want to look bad in front of his friends, so he says, "Oh yeah, well I got three hundred people under me."
>
> Thibideaux says, "What you talkin' 'bout, Boudreaux? You mow lawns all day."
>
> "Dat's true," says Boudreaux, "but now I'm cuttin' da grass at the cemetery, and I got three hundred people under me."

There's nothing wrong with competition. The problem for many leaders is that they end up competing against their peers in their own organization in a way that hurts the team and them. It all depends on how you handle competition and how you channel it. In healthy working environments, there is both competition and teamwork. The issue is to know when each is appropriate. When it comes to your teammates, you want to compete in such a way that instead of *competing* with them, you are *completing* them. Those are two totally different mind-sets.

COMPETING	VS.	COMPLETING
Competing		Completing
Scarcity mind-set		Abundance mind-set
Me first		Organization first
Destroys trust		Develops trust
Thinks win-lose		Thinks win-win
Single thinking		Shared thinking
(my good ideas)		(our great ideas)
Excluding others		Including others

Winning at all costs will cost you when it comes to your peers. If your goal is to beat your peers, then you will never be able to influence them.

HOW TO BALANCE COMPETING AND COMPLETING

The bottom line is that the success of the whole team is more important than any individual wins. Organizations need both competition and teamwork to win. When those two elements exist in the right balance, great team chemistry is the result.

So how do you balance competing and completing? How do you learn to easily shift from one to the other? Here's what I recommend.

1. ACKNOWLEDGE YOUR NATURAL DESIRE TO COMPETE

About four or five years after I graduated from college, I went back to play in an alumni basketball game against the college's then-current team. Back when I played for the team, I had been a shooting guard, but this time they assigned me to cover the team's point guard. As I watched him in warm-ups, I knew I was in trouble. He was a lot faster than I was. So I quickly developed a strategy.

The first time he tried to take the ball inside to the hoop, I fouled him. I don't mean I tapped his hand as he shot the ball. I mean I really fouled him—hard. He got up, limped to the line for his free throws, and clanged both of them off the back of the rim. So far, so good.

The next time his team came down the floor and he tried to set up a shot from outside, I fouled him hard again. As he got up, he started grumbling under his breath.

Soon after that when there was a loose ball, I dove after it, but I also made sure I landed right on top of him. I wasn't as big then as I am now, but I was heavier than he was.

He popped up and barked at me, "You're playing too hard. It's only a game."

"Okay," I said with a grin, "then let me win."

It doesn't matter who you are or what you do, competitiveness is a natural leadership instinct. I haven't met a leader yet who didn't like to win. I look back now and recognize that I wasn't very mature. The good news is that the alumni team won the game. The bad news is that I didn't make a friend that day.

The key to being competitive is channeling it in a positive way. If you squash it, you lose an edge that motivates you to do some of your best work. If you let it run wild, you run over your teammates and alienate them. But if you control it and direct it, competitiveness can help you succeed.

2. EMBRACE HEALTHY COMPETITION

Every winning team I've ever seen or been a part of experienced healthy competition among team members. Healthy competition does so many positive things for a team, many of which cannot be achieved through anything else.

Healthy competition helps bring out your best. How many world records do you suppose are set when a runner runs alone? I don't know of one! People function at peak capacity when they have someone else pushing them. That's true whether you're learning, practicing, or playing in the game.

Healthy competition promotes honest assessment. What is the quickest way for you to measure your effectiveness in your profession? Maybe you have long-term measurements in place, such as monthly or yearly goals. But what if you want to know how you're doing today? How would you go about measuring it? You could look at your to-do list. But what if you set the bar too low for yourself? You could ask your boss. But maybe the best way would be to see what others in your line of work are doing. If you are significantly behind or ahead of them, wouldn't that tell you something? And if you were behind, wouldn't you try to figure out what you're doing wrong? It may not be the only way to assess yourself, but it certainly can provide a good reality check.

Healthy competition creates camaraderie. When people compete together, it often creates a connection between them, whether they are on the same team or opposing teams. When competition is ongoing and friendly on the same team, it creates an even stronger bond that can lead to great camaraderie.

Healthy competition doesn't become personal. Competition between teammates is ultimately about having fun. When competition is healthy, teammates remain friends when the game is done. They play against each other for the thrill of it, and when they're done, they can walk away together without hard feelings.

I love the joke about the rooster who dragged an ostrich egg into the henhouse. He laid it down for all the hens to see and said, "I don't want to intimidate you girls, but I just want to show you what they're doing up the road." Competition can definitely help motivate a team to get going.

3. PUT COMPETITION IN ITS PROPER PLACE

The whole goal of healthy competition is to leverage it for the corporate win. Competition in practice helps teammates improve one another for game day. If it is channeled correctly, it is used to beat the other team.

Of course, some leaders can take this to the extreme. Tommy Lasorda, former manager of the Los Angeles Dodgers, has told the story about the day his team was scheduled to play on the road against the Cincinnati Reds. In the morning, Lasorda went to mass. As he settled into his pew, the manager of the Reds, Johnny McNamara, happened to come into the same church and sit down in the same pew.

The men eyed one another, but neither spoke.

When mass was over, they had begun to walk out when Lasorda discovered that the other manager had paused to light a candle. He figured that gave the Reds an edge. "When he left, I went down and blew that candle out," Lasorda said. "All throughout the game, I kept hollering to him, 'Hey, Mac, it ain't gonna work. I blew it out.' We clobbered them that day, 13–2."

4. KNOW WHERE TO DRAW THE LINE

No matter how much you desire to win, if you want to cultivate the ability to compete in a healthy way, you must make sure you never cross the line by "going for the throat" with your peers, because if you do, you will alienate them. And that line is not difficult to define. I'd say that when competitiveness raises the bar and makes others better, that's healthy. Anytime it lowers morale and hurts the team, it's unhealthy and out of line.

When I was leading Skyline Church in the San Diego area, my staff was very competent and very competitive. The core group who always led the charge consisted of Dan Reiland, Sheryl Fleisher, and Tim Elmore. They all had their own departments and areas of expertise, but they were always competing, always trying to one-up each other. Their friendly competition kept them on their toes, and it inspired the rest of the staff to join in and do their best. But as hard-driving and competitive as they were, if any one of them had a problem, the others were right there, ready to jump in and lend a hand. They always put the team's win ahead of their own.

Today those three leaders are out doing different things in different organizations across the country, but they remain friends. They keep in touch, share stories, and still help one another whenever they can. The kind of bond that develops when you compete together doesn't die easily. They have a deep respect for each other that continues to give them credibility—and influence—with one another.

How Can I Harness the
Team's Creativity?

Make sure the best idea always wins.

Imagine that you're getting ready to go into an important project meeting that will be attended by your boss and several people who are on the same level as you in the organization. Let's say that you were picked from among your peers by your boss to lead the meeting, and you see this time as your chance to shine. You've done your homework and then some. You've spent countless hours thinking through the project, brainstorming, planning, and endeavoring to foresee any obstacles that could be ahead. Based on your preliminary discussions with your staff and your peers, you feel that your ideas are better than anything you've heard from anyone else.

So you begin the meeting with great confidence. But before long, the agenda is not proceeding the way you expected or planned. Your boss makes a comment and sends the flow of the discussion in an entirely new direction. At first you think, .

And then one of your peers launches in with an idea. You don't think much of it, but everyone else seems to think it's wonderful. A couple of other people in the room springboard off of that initial idea and begin to build on it. You can feel the energy in the room starting to build. Ideas are sparking. And everyone is clearly moving away from everything you've spent weeks planning—the idea that was your "baby."

What do you do?

For most people in those circumstances, their natural instinct would be to fight for their ideas. After all, by then they would have made quite an investment in them:

- *The Intellectual Investment*—it takes hours of thinking, planning, and problem solving spent to gather, create, and refine an idea.
- *The Physical Investment*—getting ready for an important meeting or presentation usually takes a lot of time, effort, and resources.
- *The Emotional Investment*—when people come up with something they see as a good idea, it's hard to keep themselves from thinking about not only what the idea could do for the company but also what it could do for them and their careers.

By this time, they become pretty attached to their ideas, and it becomes difficult to let those ideas die, especially when someone else who didn't do any work may come in and get all the credit.

IDEAS: THE LIFEBLOOD OF AN ORGANIZATION

If you desire to harness the creativity of your team, then you need to resist the temptation to fight for your idea when it's not the best idea. Why? Because good ideas are too important to the organization. Harvey Firestone, founder of the Firestone Tire and Rubber Company, said, "Capital isn't so important in business. Experience isn't so important. You can get both of these. What is important is ideas. If you have ideas, you have the main asset you need, and there isn't any limit to what you can do with your business and your life. They are any man's greatest asset—ideas."

Great organizations possess people throughout the organization who produce great ideas. That is how they become great. The progress they make and the innovations they create don't come down from on high. Their creative sessions are not dominated by top-down leaders. Nor does every meeting become a kind of wrestling match to see who can dominate everyone else. People come together as teams, peers work together, and they make progress because they want the best idea to win.

Leaders in the organization who help to surface good ideas are creating what an organization needs most. They do that by producing synergy among their peers. And they will develop influence with their peers because when they are present, they make the whole team better.

WHAT LEADS TO THE BEST IDEAS?

To let the best idea win, you must first generate good ideas. And then you must work to make them even better. How do team leaders do that? How do they help the team find the best ideas? I believe they follow this pattern:

1. TEAM LEADERS LISTEN TO ALL IDEAS

Finding good ideas begins with an open-minded willingness to listen to all ideas. Mathematician and philosopher Alfred North Whitehead said, "Almost all really new ideas have a certain aspect of foolishness when they are first produced." During the brainstorming process, shutting down any ideas might prevent you from discovering the good ones.

In *Thinking for a Change*, one of the eleven thinking skills I recommend people learn is shared thinking. It is faster than solo thinking, is more innovative, and has greater value. Most important, I believe, is the fact that great thinking comes when good thoughts are shared in a collaborative environment where people contribute to them, shape them, and take them to the next level. A good team leader helps to create such an environment.

2. TEAM LEADERS NEVER SETTLE FOR JUST ONE IDEA

I think many times leaders are too quick to settle on one idea and run with it. That is because leaders are so action oriented. They want to go. They want to make something happen. They want to take the hill! The problem is that they sometimes fight their way to the top of the hill only to find that it's not the right one.

One idea is never enough. Many ideas make us stronger. I once heard an analyst say he thought that was the reason the communist bloc fell at the end of the twentieth century. Communism created a system based primarily on only one idea. If anyone tried to do things a different way, they were knocked down or shipped out.

In contrast, democracy is a system based on a multitude of ideas. If people want to try something different, they have the chance to float their idea and see what happens. If it catches on, it moves forward. If not, it is replaced by another idea. Because of that freedom, in democratic countries creativity is high, opportunities are unlimited, and the potential for growth is astounding. The democratic system can be messy, but that is also true of any endeavor that's creative and collaborative.

The same kind of free-market mentality that drives the largest economy in the world can also drive organizations. If people are open to ideas and options, they can keep growing, innovating, and improving.

3. Team Leaders Look in Unusual Places for Ideas

Good leaders are attentive to ideas; they are always searching for them. And they cultivate that attentiveness and practice it as a regular discipline. As they read the newspaper, watch a movie, listen to their colleagues, or enjoy a leisure activity, they are always on the lookout for ideas or practices they can use to improve their work and their leadership.

If you desire to find good ideas, you have to search for them. Rarely does a good idea come looking for you.

4. Team Leaders Don't Let Personality Overshadow Purpose

When someone you don't like or respect suggests something, what is your first reaction? I bet it's to dismiss it. You've heard the phrase "Consider the source." That's not a bad thing to do, but if you're not careful, you may very likely throw out the good with the bad.

Don't let the personality of someone you work with cause you to lose sight of the greater purpose, which is to add value to the team and advance the organization. If that means listening to the ideas of people with whom you have no chemistry, or worse, a difficult history, so be it. Set aside your pride and listen. And in cases where you must reject the ideas of others, make sure you reject only the idea and not the person.

5. TEAM LEADERS PROTECT CREATIVE PEOPLE AND THEIR IDEAS

Ideas are such fragile things, especially when they first come to light. Advertising executive Charlie Brower said, "A new idea is delicate. It can be killed by a sneer or a yawn; it can be stabbed to death by a quip and worried to death by a frown on the right man's brow."

If you desire the best idea to win, then become a champion of creative people and their contributions to your organization. When you discover peers who are creative, promote them, encourage them, and protect them. Pragmatic people often shoot down the ideas of creative people. Leaders who value creativity can help the creative people around them thrive and keep generating ideas that benefit the organization.

6. TEAM LEADERS DON'T TAKE REJECTION PERSONALLY

When your ideas are not received well by others, do your best not to take it personally. When someone in a meeting does that, it can kill the creative process, because at that point the discussion is no longer about the ideas or helping the organization; it becomes about the person whose feelings are hurt. In those moments, if you can stop competing and focus your energy on creating, you will open the way for the people around you to take their creativity to the next level.

Mel Newhoff is executive vice president of Bozell Worldwide, a top advertising agency. In his industry, ideas are everything. Newhoff has some good advice about the big picture concerning ideas and how to approach your inter-action with others in relation to them:

Be passionate about your work, and have the integrity to stand up for your ideas. But also know when to compromise.

Without passion you will not be taken seriously. If you don't defend your ideas, no one else will either. When principle is involved, don't budge.

But there is another side to this also. There are very few real "absolutes" in life. Most matters involve taste or opinion, not principle. In these areas recognize that you can compromise. If you become someone who can never compromise, you will forfeit opportunities to those who can.

Being an encouraging leader and leading across is not about getting your own way. It's not about winning at all costs. It's about winning respect and influence with your peers so that you can help the whole team win. Should you be passionate and determined, believing in yourself and your ability to contribute? Definitely. Should you hold on to your deeply held values and stand on principle when those are in jeopardy? Absolutely. But never forget that having a collaborative spirit helps the organization. When you think in terms of *our* idea instead of *my* idea or *her* idea, you're probably on track to helping the team win. That should be your motivation, not just trying to win friends and influence people. But I think you'll find that if you let the best idea win, you will win friends and influence people.

EQUIPPING

101

WHAT EVERY LEADER NEEDS TO KNOW

Published in Nashville, Tennessee, by Thomas Nelson. Thomas Nelson is a registered trademark of Thomas Nelson, Inc.

Thomas Nelson, Inc., titles may be purchased in bulk for educational, business, fund-raising, or sales promotional use. For information, please e-mail SpecialMarkets@ThomasNelson.com.

Portions of this book have been taken from *Developing the Leaders Around You,* *The 17 Essential Qualities of a Team Player,* and *The 17 Indisputable Laws of Teamwork.*

Library of Congress Cataloging-in-Publication Data

Maxwell, John C., 1947–
Equipping 101 / John C. Maxwell.
p. cm.
Includes bibliographical references.
ISBN: 978-0-7852-6352-4 (hardcover)
1. Teams in the workplace. 2. Leadership. 3. Career development.
4. Mentoring. I. Title.
HD66.M377 2004
658.3'14—dc22
2003021379

Contents

PART I

EQUIPPING
FOR SUCCESS

I

WHY DO I NEED TO
EQUIP OTHERS?

One is too small a number to achieve greatness.

Who are your personal heroes? Okay, maybe you don't have heroes exactly. Then let me ask you this: Which people do you admire most? Who do you wish you were more like? What people fire you up and get your juices flowing? Do you admire . . .

- Business innovators, such as Sam Walton, Fred Smith, or Bill Gates?

- Great athletes, such as Michael Jordan, Tiger Woods, or Mark McGwire?

- Creative geniuses, such as Pablo Picasso, Buckminster Fuller, or Wolfgang Amadeus Mozart?

- Pop-culture icons, such as Marilyn Monroe, Andy Warhol, or Elvis Presley?

- Spiritual leaders, such as John Wesley, Billy Graham, or Mother Teresa?

- Political leaders, such as Alexander the Great, Charlemagne, or Winston Churchill?

- Film industry giants, such as D. W. Griffith, Charlie Chaplin, or Steven Spielberg?

- Architects and engineers, such as Frank Lloyd Wright, the Starrett brothers, or Joseph Strauss?

- Revolutionary thinkers, such as Marie Curie, Thomas Edison, or Albert Einstein?

Or maybe your list includes people in a field I didn't mention.

It's safe to say that we all admire achievers. And we Americans especially love pioneers and bold individualists, people who fight alone, despite the odds or opposition: the settler who carves a place for himself in the wilds of the frontier, the Old West sheriff who resolutely faces an enemy in a gunfight, the pilot who bravely flies solo across the Atlantic Ocean, and the scientist who changes the world through the power of his mind.

THE MYTH OF THE LONE RANGER

As much as we admire solo achievement, the truth is that no lone individual has done anything of value. The belief that one person can do something great is a myth. There are no real Rambos who can take on a hostile army by themselves. Even the Lone Ranger wasn't really a loner. Everywhere he went he rode with Tonto!

Nothing of significance was ever achieved by an individual acting alone. Look below the surface and you will find that all seemingly solo acts are really team efforts. Frontiersman Daniel Boone had companions from the Transylvania Company as he blazed the Wilderness Road. Sheriff Wyatt Earp had his two brothers and Doc Holliday looking out for him. Aviator Charles Lindbergh had the backing of nine businessmen from St. Louis and the services of the Ryan Aeronautical Company, which built his plane.

Even Albert Einstein, the scientist who revolutionized the world with his theory of relativity, didn't work in a vacuum. Of the debt he owed to others for his work, Einstein once remarked, "Many times a day I realize how much my own outer and inner life is built upon the labors of my fellow men, both living and dead, and how earnestly I must exert myself in order to give in return as much as I have received." It's true that the history of our country is marked by the accomplishments of many strong leaders and innovative individuals who took considerable risks. But those people always were part of teams.

Economist Lester C. Thurow commented on the subject:

> There is nothing antithetical in American history, culture, or traditions to teamwork. Teams were important in America's history—wagon trains conquered the West, men working together on the assembly line in American industry conquered the world, a successful national strategy and a lot of teamwork put an American on the moon first (and thus far, last). But American mythology extols only the individual . . . In America, halls of fame exist for almost every conceivable activity, but nowhere do Americans raise monuments in praise of teamwork.

I must say that I don't agree with all of Thurow's conclusions. After all, I've seen the U.S. Marine Corps war memorial in Washington, D.C., commemorating the raising of the flag on Iwo Jima. But he is right about something. Teamwork is and always has been essential to building this country. And that statement can be made about every country around the world.

A Chinese proverb states, "Behind an able man there are always other able men." And the truth is that teamwork is at the heart of great achievement. The question isn't whether teams have value. The question is whether we acknowledge that fact and become better team players. That's why I assert that one is too small a number to achieve greatness. You cannot do anything of real value alone. If you truly take this to heart, you will begin to see the value of developing and equipping your team players.

> "BEHIND AN ABLE MAN THERE ARE ALWAYS
> OTHER ABLE MEN."—CHINESE PROVERB

I challenge you to think of one act of genuine significance in the history of humankind that was performed by a lone human being. No matter what you name, you will find that a team of people was involved. That is why President Lyndon Johnson said, "There are no problems we cannot solve together, and very few that we can solve by ourselves."

C. Gene Wilkes, in his book, *Jesus on Leadership,* observed that the power of teams not only is evident in today's modern business world, but it also has a deep history that is evident even in biblical times. Wilkes asserts:

- Teams involve more people, thus affording more resources, ideas, and energy than would an individual.

- Teams maximize a leader's potential and minimize her weaknesses. Strengths and weaknesses are more exposed in individuals.

- Teams provide multiple perspectives on how to meet a need or reach a goal, thus devising several alternatives for each situation.

- Teams share the credit for victories and the blame for losses. This fosters genuine humility and authentic community.

- Teams keep leaders accountable for the goal.

- Teams can simply do more than an individual.

If you want to reach your potential or strive for the seemingly impossible—such as communicating your message two thousand years after you are gone—you need to become a team player. It may be a cliché, but it is nonetheless true: individuals play the game, but teams win championships.

WHY DO WE STAND ALONE?

Knowing all that we do about the potential of teams, why do some people still want to do things by themselves? I believe there are a number of reasons.

1. EGO

Few people are fond of admitting that they can't do everything, yet that is a reality of life. There are no supermen or superwomen. So the question is not whether you can do everything by yourself; it's how soon you're going to realize that you can't.

Philanthropist Andrew Carnegie declared, "It marks a big step in your development when you come to realize that other people can help you do a better job than you could do alone." To do something really big, let go of your ego, and get ready to be part of a team.

2. INSECURITY

In my work with leaders, I've found that some individuals fail to promote teamwork and fail to equip their team members for leadership because they feel threatened by other people. Sixteenth-century Florentine statesman Niccolò Machiavelli probably made similar observations, prompting him to write, "The first method for estimating the intelligence of a ruler is to look at the men he has around him."

I believe that insecurity, rather than poor judgment or lack of intelligence, most often causes leaders to surround themselves with weak people. Only secure leaders give power to others. On the other hand, insecure leaders usually fail to build teams because of one of two reasons: Either they want to maintain control over everything for which they are responsible, or they fear being replaced by someone more capable. In either case, leaders who fail to promote teamwork undermine their own potential and erode the best efforts of the people with whom they work. They would benefit from the advice of President Woodrow Wilson: "We should not only use all the brains we have, but all that we can borrow."

> "THE FIRST METHOD FOR ESTIMATING THE INTELLIGENCE
> OF A RULER IS TO LOOK AT THE MEN HE HAS
> AROUND HIM."—NICCOLÒ MACHIAVELLI

3. NAIVETÉ

Consultant John Ghegan keeps a sign on his desk that says, "If I had it to do all over again, I'd get help." That remark accurately represents the feelings of the third type of people who fail to become team builders. They naively underestimate the difficulty of achieving big things. As a result, they try to go it alone.

Some people who start out in this group turn out okay in the end. They discover that their dreams are bigger than their capabilities, they realize they won't accomplish their goals solo, and they adjust. They make team building their approach to achievement. But some others learn the truth too late, and as a result, they never accomplish their goals. And that's a shame.

4. TEMPERAMENT

Some people aren't very outgoing and simply don't think in terms of team building and equipping. As they face challenges, it never occurs to them to enlist others to achieve something.

As a people person, I find that hard to relate to. Whenever I face any kind of challenge, the very first thing I do is to think about the people I want on the team to help with it. I've been that way since I was a kid. I've always thought, *Why take the journey alone when you can invite others along with you?*

I understand that not everyone operates that way. But whether or not you are naturally inclined to be part of a team is really irrelevant. If you do everything alone and never partner with other people, you create huge barriers to your own potential. Dr. Allan Fromme quipped, "People have been known to achieve more as a result of working with others than against them." What an understatement! It takes a team to do anything of lasting value. Besides, even the most introverted person in the world can learn to enjoy the benefits of being on a team. (That's true even if someone isn't trying to accomplish something great.)

A few years ago my friend Chuck Swindoll wrote a piece in *The Finishing Touch* that sums up the importance of teamwork. He said,

> Nobody is a whole team . . . We need each other. You need someone and someone needs you. Isolated islands we're not. To make this thing called life work, we gotta lean and support. And relate and respond. And give and take. And confess and forgive. And reach out and embrace and rely . . . Since none of us is a whole, independent, self-sufficient, super-capable, all-powerful hotshot, let's quit acting like we are. Life's lonely enough without our playing that silly role. The game is over. Let's link up.

For the person trying to do everything alone, the game really is over. If you want to do something big, you must link up with others. One is too small a number to achieve greatness.

HOW CAN I ADOPT
A TEAM MIND-SET?

Investing in a team almost guarantees a high return for the effort,
because a team can do so much more than individuals.

He's one of the greatest team builders in all of sports, yet you've probably never heard of him. Here is a list of his impressive accomplishments:

- Forty consecutive basketball seasons with at least twenty wins
- Five national championships
- Number one ranking in his region in twenty of the last thirty-three years
- Lifetime winning percentage of .870

His name is Morgan Wootten. And why have most people never heard of him? Because he is a high school basketball coach!

When asked to name the greatest basketball coach of all time, most people would respond with one of two names: Red Auerbach or John Wooden. But do you know what John Wooden, the UCLA coach called the Wizard of Westwood, had to say about Morgan Wootten? He was emphatic in his appraisal: "People say Morgan Wootten is the best high school coach in the country. I disagree. I know of no finer coach at any level—high school, college, or pro. I've said it elsewhere and I'll say it here: I stand in awe of him."[1]

That's a pretty strong recommendation from the man who won ten NCAA national championships and coached some of the most talented players in the game, including Kareem Abdul-Jabbar. (By the way, when Kareem was in high school at Power Memorial Academy, his team lost only one game—to Morgan Wootten's team!)

No Plan to Be a Team Builder

Morgan Wootten never planned to coach a team. He was a decent athlete in high school, but nothing special. However, he was an excellent talker. When he was growing up, his ambition was to be an attorney. But when he was a nineteen-year-old college student, a friend tricked him into accepting a job coaching baseball, a game he knew little about, to kids from an orphanage. The team had no uniforms and no equipment. And despite working hard, the boys lost all sixteen of their games.

During that first season, Wootten fell in love with those kids. When they asked him to come back and coach football, he couldn't refuse them. Besides, he had played football in high school, so he knew something about it. The orphanage team went undefeated and won the Washington, D.C., Catholic Youth Organization (CYO) championship. But more important, Wootten began to realize that he wanted to invest his time in children, not in court cases.

Even that first year he made a difference in the lives of kids. He remembers one boy in particular who had started stealing and kept being brought back to the orphanage by the police. He described the boy as having "two and a half strikes against him already." Wootten let the boy know he was headed for trouble. But he also took the boy under his wing. Wootten recalled:

We started spending some time together. I took him to my house and he'd enjoy Mom's meals. He spent weekends with us. He became friends with my brother and sisters. He's still in Washington today and doing quite well and known to a lot of people. Anyone would be proud to call him their son. He was bound for a life of crime and jail, however, and maybe a lot worse, until someone gave him the greatest gift a parent can give a child—his time.

Giving of himself to the people on his teams is something Wootten has done every year since then. NCAA basketball coach Marty Fletcher, a former player and assistant under Wootten, summarized his talent this way: "His secret is that he makes whomever he is with feel like the most important person in the world."[2]

CREATING A DYNASTY

It wasn't long before Wootten was invited to become an assistant coach at a local powerhouse high school. Then with a couple of years' experience under his belt, he became head coach at DeMatha High School.

When he started at the school in 1956, Wootten was taking over a bunch of losing teams. He called together all of the students who wanted to play sports at DeMatha, and he told them:

Fellas, things are going to change. I know how bad DeMatha's teams have been during these last few years, but that's over with. We're going to win at DeMatha and we're going to build a tradition of winning. Starting right now . . . But let me tell you how we're going to do it. We're going to outwork every team we ever play . . . With a lot of hard work and discipline and dedication, people are going to hear about us and respect us, because DeMatha will be a winner.[3]

That year, the football team won half of its games, which was quite an accomplishment. In basketball and baseball, they were division champions. His teams have been winning ever since. DeMatha has long been considered a dynasty.

On October 13, 2000, Wootten was inducted into the Naismith Basketball Hall of Fame in Springfield, Massachusetts. At that time, his teams had amassed a record of 1,210-183. Over the years, more than 250 of his players have won college scholarships. Twelve players from his high school teams went on to play in the NBA.[4]

It's Not About Basketball

But winning games and honors isn't what excites Wootten most. It's investing in the kids. Wootten says:

> Coaches at every level have a tendency to lose sight of their purpose at times, especially after success arrives. They start to put the cart before the horse by working harder and harder to develop their teams, using their boys or girls to do it, gradually forgetting that their real purpose should be to develop the kids, using their teams to do it.[5]

Wootten's attitude reaps rewards not only for the team, but also for the individuals on the team. For example, for a twenty-six-year stretch, every single one of Wootten's seniors earned college scholarships—not just starters but bench players too.

Equipping your team compounds over time. Morgan Wootten equips his players because it is the right thing to do, because he cares about them. That practice has made his players good, his teams successful, and his career remarkable. He is the first basketball coach to have won 1,200 games at any level. Developing people pays off in every way.

How to Invest in Your Team

I believe that most people recognize that investing in a team brings benefits to everyone on the team. The question for most people isn't why, but how. Allow me to share with you ten steps you can take to invest in your team.

Here is how to get started:

1. Make the Decision to Build a Team—This Starts the Investment in the Team

It's said that every journey begins with the first step. Deciding that people on the team are worth equipping and developing is the first step in building a better team. That requires commitment.

2. Gather the Best Team Possible—This Elevates the Potential of the Team

The better the people on the team, the greater the potential. There's only one kind of team that you may be a part of where you shouldn't go out and find the best players available, and that's family. You need to stick with those teammates through thick and thin. But every other kind of team can benefit from the recruitment of the very best people available.

3. Pay the Price to Develop the Team—This Ensures the Growth of the Team

When Morgan Wootten extended himself to benefit the kid who had two-and-a-half strikes against him, he and his family had to pay a price to help that boy. It wasn't convenient or comfortable. It cost them in energy, money, and time.

It will cost you to develop your team. You will have to dedicate time that could be used for personal productivity. You will have to spend money that could be used for personal benefit. And sometimes you will have to set aside your personal agenda.

4. Do Things Together As a Team—This Provides Community for the Team

I once read the statement, "Even when you've played the game of your life, it's the feeling of teamwork that you'll remember. You'll forget the plays, the shots, and the scores, but you'll never forget your teammates." That is describing the community that develops among teammates who spend time doing things together.

DECIDING THAT PEOPLE ON THE TEAM ARE WORTH EQUIPPING AND DEVELOPING IS THE FIRST STEP IN BUILDING A BETTER TEAM.

The only way to develop community and cohesiveness among your teammates is to get them together, not just in a professional setting but in personal ones as well. There are lots of ways to get yourself connected with your teammates and to connect them with one another. Many families who want to bond find that camping does the trick. Business colleagues can socialize outside work (in an appropriate way). The where and when are not as important as the fact that team members share common experiences.

5. Empower Team Members with Responsibility and Authority—This Raises Up Leaders for the Team

The greatest growth for people often occurs as a result of the trial and error of personal experience. Any team that wants people to step up to a higher level of performance—and to higher levels of leadership—must give team members authority as well as responsibility. If you are a leader on your team, don't protect your position or hoard your power. Give it away. That's the only way to empower your team.

6. Give Credit for Success to the Team—This Lifts the Morale of the Team

Mark Twain said, "I can live for two months on one good compliment."

That's the way most people feel. They are willing to work hard if they receive recognition for their efforts. Compliment your teammates. Talk up their accomplishments. And if you're the leader, take the blame but never the credit. Do that and your team will always fight for you.

"I CAN LIVE FOR TWO MONTHS ON ONE GOOD
COMPLIMENT."—MARK TWAIN

---

7. WATCH TO SEE THAT THE INVESTMENT IN THE TEAM IS PAYING OFF—THIS BRINGS ACCOUNTABILITY TO THE TEAM

If you put money into an investment, you expect a return—maybe not right away, but certainly over time. How will you know whether you are gaining or losing ground on that investment? You have to pay attention to it and measure its progress.

The same is true of an investment in people. You need to observe whether you are getting a return for the time, energy, and resources you are putting into them. Some people develop quickly. Others are slower to respond, and that's okay. The main outcome you want to see is progress.

8. STOP YOUR INVESTMENT IN PLAYERS WHO DO NOT GROW—THIS ELIMINATES GREATER LOSSES FOR THE TEAM

One of the most difficult experiences for any team member is leaving a teammate behind. Yet that is what you must do if someone on your team refuses to grow or change for the benefit of teammates. That does not mean that you love the person less. It just means you stop spending your time trying to invest in someone who won't or can't make the team better.

9. CREATE NEW OPPORTUNITIES FOR THE TEAM—THIS ALLOWS THE TEAM TO STRETCH

There is no greater investment you can make in a team than giving it new opportunities. When a team has the possibility of taking new ground or facing new challenges, it has to stretch to meet them. That process not only gives the team a chance to grow, but it also benefits every individual. Everyone has the opportunity to grow toward his or her potential.

10. Give the Team the Best Possible Chance to Succeed—This Guarantees the Team a High Return

James E. Hunton says, "Coming together is a beginning. Keeping together is progress. Working together is success." One of the most essential tasks you can undertake is to clear obstacles so that the team has the best possible chance to work toward success. If you are a team member, that may mean making a personal sacrifice or helping others to work together better. If you are a leader, that means creating an energized environment for the team and equipping each person with what he needs at any given time to ensure success.

Investing in a team almost guarantees a high return for the effort, because a team can do so much more than individuals. Or as Rex Murphy, one of my conference attendees, told me: "Where there's a will there's a way; where there's a team, there's more than one way."

My Personal Investment—and Return

Once you have experienced what it means to invest in your team, you will never be able to stop. Thinking about my team—about how the teammates add value to me as I add value to them—brings me abundant joy. And just like my investment and their return, my joy continues to compound.

At this stage of my life, everything I do is a team effort. When I first started teaching seminars, I did everything. Certainly there were other people pitching in, but I was just as likely to pack and ship a box as I was to speak. Now, I show up and teach. My wonderful team takes care of everything else. Even the book you're reading was a team effort. I would do anything for the people on my team because they do everything for me:

My team makes me better than I am.

My team multiplies my value to others.

My team enables me to do what I do best.

My team gives me more time.

My team represents me where I cannot go.

My team provides community for our enjoyment.

My team fulfills the desires of my heart.

If your current team experiences are not as positive as you would like, then it's time to increase your level of investment. Building and equipping a team for the future is just like developing a financial nest egg. It may start slowly, but what you put in brings a high return—similar to the way that compound interest works with finances. Try it and you will find that investing in the team compounds over time.

PART II

EQUIPPING THE RIGHT PEOPLE

3

WHOM SHOULD
I EQUIP?

Those closest to the leader will determine the
success level of that leader.

One night, after working quite late, I grabbed a copy of *Sports Illustrated*, hoping its pages would lull me to sleep. It had the opposite effect. On the back cover was an advertisement that caught my eye and got my emotional juices flowing. It featured a picture of John Wooden, the coach who led the UCLA Bruins for many years. The caption beneath his picture read, "The guy who puts the ball through the hoop has ten hands."

John Wooden was a great basketball coach. Called the Wizard of Westwood, he brought ten national basketball championships to UCLA in a span of twelve years. Two back-to-back championships are almost unheard of in the world of competitive sports, but he led the Bruins to *seven titles in a row*. It took a consistent level of superior play, good coaching, and hard practice. But the key to the Bruins's success was Coach Wooden's unyielding dedication to his concept of teamwork.

He knew that if you oversee people and you wish to develop leaders, you are responsible to: (1) appreciate them for who they are; (2) believe that they will do their very best; (3) praise their accomplishments; and (4) accept your personal responsibility to them as their leader.

Coach Bear Bryant expressed this same sentiment when he said: "I'm just a plowhand from Arkansas, but I have learned how to hold a team together—how to lift some men up, how to calm others down, until finally they've got one heartbeat together as a team. There's always just three things I say: 'If anything goes bad, I did it. If anything goes semi-good, then we did it. If anything goes real good, they did it.' That's all it takes to get people to win." Bear Bryant won people and games. Until a few years ago, he held the title of the winningest coach in the history of college football, with 323 victories.

Great leaders—the truly successful ones who are in the top 1 percent—all have one thing in common. They know that acquiring and keeping good people is a leader's most important task. An organization cannot increase its productivity—but people can! The asset that truly appreciates within any organization is people. Systems become dated. Buildings deteriorate. Machinery wears. But people can grow, develop, and become more effective if they have a leader who understands their potential value.

If you really want to be a successful leader, you must develop and equip other leaders around you. You must find a way to get your vision seen, implemented, and contributed to by your team. The leader sees the big picture, but he needs other leaders to help make his mental picture a reality.

Most leaders have followers around them. They believe the key to leadership is gaining more *followers.* Few leaders surround themselves with other *leaders,* but the ones who do bring great value to their organizations. And not only is their burden lightened, but their vision is carried on and enlarged.

WHOM YOU EQUIP REALLY MATTERS

The key to surrounding yourself with other leaders is to find the best people you can, then equip them to become the best leaders they can be. Great leaders produce other leaders. Let me tell you why:

Those Closest to the Leader Will Determine the Success Level of That Leader

The greatest leadership principle that I have learned in over thirty years of leadership is that those closest to the leader will determine the success level of that leader. A negative reading of this statement is also true: those closest to the leader will determine the level of failure for that leader. In other words, the people close to me "make me or break me." The determination of a positive or negative outcome in my leadership depends upon my ability as a leader to develop and equip those closest to me. It also depends upon my ability to recognize the value that others bring to my organization. My goal is not to draw a following that results in a crowd. My goal is to develop leaders who become a movement.

Stop for a moment and think of the five or six people closest to you in your organization. Are you developing them? Do you have a game plan for their growth? Are they being properly equipped for leadership? Have they been able to lift your load?

Within my organization leadership development is continually emphasized. In their first training session, I give new leaders this principle: *As a potential leader you are either an asset or a liability to the organization.* I illustrate this truth by saying, "When there's a problem, a 'fire' in the organization, you as a leader are often the first to arrive at the scene. You have in your hands two buckets. One contains water and the other contains gasoline. The 'spark' before you will either become a greater problem because you pour the gasoline on it, or it will be extinguished because you use the bucket of water."

Every person within your organization also carries two buckets. The question a leader needs to ask is, "Am I training them to use the gasoline or the water?"

An Organization's Growth Potential Is Directly Related to Its Personnel Potential

When conducting leadership conferences, I often make the statement, "Grow a leader—grow the organization." A company cannot grow without until its leaders grow within.

I am often amazed at the amount of money, energy, and marketing focus organizations spend on areas that will not produce growth. Why advertise that the customer is number one when the personnel have not been trained in customer service? When customers arrive, they will know the difference between an employee who has been trained to give service and one who hasn't. Slick brochures and catchy slogans will never overcome incompetent leadership.

In 1981 I became Senior Pastor of Skyline Wesleyan Church in San Diego, California. This congregation had averaged 1,000 in attendance from 1969 to 1981, and it was obviously on a plateau. When I assumed leadership responsibilities, the first question I asked was, "Why has the growth stopped?" I needed to find an answer, so I called my first staff meeting and gave a lecture titled *The Leadership Line*. My thesis was, "Leaders determine the level of an organization." I drew a line across a marker board and wrote the number 1,000. I shared with the staff that for thirteen years the average attendance at Skyline was 1,000. I knew the staff could lead 1,000 people effectively. What I did not know was whether they could lead 2,000 people. So I drew a dotted line and wrote the number 2,000, and I placed a question mark between the two lines. I then drew an arrow from the bottom 1,000 to the top 2,000 line and wrote the word "change."

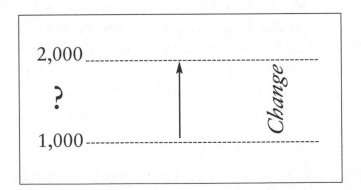

It would be my responsibility to equip them and help them make the necessary changes to reach our new goal. When the leaders changed positively, I knew the growth would come automatically. Now, I had to help them change themselves, or I knew I would literally have to change them by hiring others to take their places.

From 1981 to 1995 I gave this lecture at Skyline on three occasions. The last time, the number 4,000 was placed on the top line. As I discovered, the numbers changed, but the lecture didn't. The strength of any organization is a direct result of the strength of its leaders. Weak leaders equal weak organizations. Strong leaders equal strong organizations. Everything rises and falls on leadership.

POTENTIAL LEADERS HELP CARRY THE LOAD

Businessman Rolland Young said, "I am a self-made man, but I think if I had it to do over again, I would call in someone else!" Usually leaders fail to develop other leaders either because they lack training or because they possess wrong attitudes about allowing and encouraging others to come alongside them. Often, leaders wrongly believe that they must compete with the people close to them instead of working with them. Great leaders have a different mind-set. In *Profiles in Courage*, President John F. Kennedy wrote, "The best way to go along is to get along with others." This kind of positive interaction can happen only if the leader has an attitude of interdependency with others and is committed to win-win relationships.

EVERYTHING RISES AND FALLS ON LEADERSHIP.

Take a look at differences between the two views leaders possess about people:

WINNING BY COMPETITIVENESS	WINNING BY COOPERATION
Look at others as enemies	Look at others as friends
Concentrate on yourself	Concentrate on others
Become suspicious of others	Become supportive of others
Win only if you are good	Win if you or others are good

WINNING BY COMPETITIVENESS	WINNING BY COOPERATION
Winning determined by your skills	Winning determined by the skills of many
Small victory	Large victory
Some joy	Much joy
There are winners and losers	There are only winners

Peter Drucker was correct when he said, "No executive has ever suffered because his people were strong and effective." The leaders around me lift my load in many ways. Here are two of the most important ones:

1. *They become a sounding board for me.* As a leader, I sometimes hear counsel that I don't want to hear but need to hear. That's the advantage of having leaders around you—having people who know how to make decisions. Followers tell you what you *want* to hear. Leaders tell you what you *need* to hear.

I have always encouraged those closest to me to give me advice on the front end. In other words, an opinion before a decision has potential value. An opinion after the decision has been made is worthless. Alex Agase, a college football coach, once said, "If you really want to give me advice, do it on Saturday afternoon between one and four o'clock, when you've got twenty-five seconds to do it, between plays. Don't give me advice on Monday. I know the right thing to do on Monday."

"NO EXECUTIVE HAS EVER SUFFERED BECAUSE HIS PEOPLE WERE STRONG AND EFFECTIVE."—PETER DRUCKER

---

2. *They possess a leadership mind-set.* Fellow leaders do more than work with the leader, they think like the leader. It gives them the power to lighten the load. This becomes invaluable in areas such as decision making, brainstorming, and providing security and direction to others.

A majority of my time is spent away from the office speaking at conferences and events. Therefore, it is essential that I have leaders in my organizations who can carry on effectively while I am gone. And they do. It happens because I have spent my life finding and developing potential leaders. The results are very gratifying.

LEADERS ATTRACT POTENTIAL LEADERS

Birds of a feather really do flock together. I really believe that it takes a leader to know a leader, grow a leader, and show a leader. I have also found that it takes a leader to attract a leader.

Attraction is the obvious first step to equipping others, yet I find many people in leadership positions who are unable to accomplish this task. Good leaders are able to attract potential leaders because:

- Leaders think like them.
- Leaders express feelings that other leaders sense.
- Leaders create an environment that attracts potential leaders.
- Leaders are not threatened by people with great potential.

For example, a person in a leadership position who is a "5" on a scale of 1 to 10 will not attract a leader who is a "9." Why? Because leaders naturally size up any crowd and migrate to other leaders who are at the same or higher level.

Any leader who has only followers around him will be called upon to continually draw on his own resources to get things done. Without other leaders to carry the load, he will become fatigued and burnt out. Have you asked yourself lately, "Am I tired?" If the answer is yes, you may have a good reason for it, as this humorous story illustrates:

Somewhere in the world there is a country with a population of 220 million. Eighty-four million are over sixty years of age, which leaves 136 million to do the work. People under twenty years of age total 95 million, which leaves 41 million to do the work.

There are 22 million employed by the government, which leaves 19 million to do the work. Four million are in the Armed Forces, which leaves 15 million to do the work. Deduct 14,800,000, the number in state and city offices, and that leaves 200,000 to do the work. There are 188,000 in hospitals or insane asylums, so that leaves 12,000 to do the work.

It is of interest to note that in this country 11,998 people are in jail, so that leaves just two people to carry the load. That's you and me—and brother, I'm getting tired of doing everything myself!

Unless you want to carry the whole load yourself, you need to be developing and equipping leaders.

EQUIPPED LEADERS EXPAND AND ENHANCE THE FUTURE OF THE ORGANIZATION

One of the things my father taught me was the importance of people above all other elements in an organization. He was the president of a college for sixteen years. One day, as we sat on a campus bench, he explained that the most expensive workers on campus were not the highest paid. The most expensive ones were the people who were nonproductive. He explained that developing leaders took time and cost money. You usually had to pay leaders more. But such people were an invaluable asset. They attracted a higher quality of person, they were more productive, and they continued to add value to the organization. He closed the conversation by saying, "Most people produce only when they feel like it. Leaders produce even when they don't feel like it."

"MOST PEOPLE PRODUCE ONLY WHEN THEY FEEL
LIKE IT. LEADERS PRODUCE EVEN WHEN
THEY DON'T FEEL LIKE IT."
—MELVIN MAXWELL

The More People You Lead, the More Leaders You Need

Zig Ziglar says, "Success is the maximum utilization of the ability that you have." I believe a leader's success can be defined as *the maximum utilization of the abilities of those under him.* Andrew Carnegie explained it like this: "I wish to have as my epitaph: 'Here lies a man who was wise enough to bring into his service men who knew more than he.'" That is a worthy goal for any leader.

4

What Does a Potential Leader Look Like?

Great leaders seek out and find potential leaders,
then transform them into good leaders.

There is something much more important and scarce than ability: it is the ability to recognize ability. One of the primary responsibilities of a successful leader is to identify potential leaders. These are the people in whom you will want to invest your time equipping. Identifying them is not always an easy job, but it is critical.

Andrew Carnegie was a master at identifying potential leaders. Once asked by a reporter how he had managed to hire forty-three millionaires, Carnegie responded that the men had not been millionaires when they started working for him. They had become millionaires as a result. The reporter next wanted to know how he had developed these men to become such valuable leaders. Carnegie replied, "Men are developed the same way gold is mined. Several tons of dirt must be moved to get an ounce of gold. But you don't go into the mine looking for dirt," he added. "You go in looking for the gold." That's exactly the way to develop positive, successful people. Look for the gold, not the dirt; the good, not the bad. The more positive qualities you look for, the more you are going to find.

SELECTING THE RIGHT PLAYERS

Professional sports organizations recognize the importance of selecting the right players. Every year, coaches and owners of professional baseball, basketball, and football teams look forward to the draft. To prepare for it, sports franchises spend much time and energy scouting new prospects. For instance, scouts from pro football organizations travel to regular-season college games, bowl games, senior-only bowl games, and camps to gain knowledge about prospective players. All of this enables the scouts to bring plenty of information back to the owners and head coaches so that when draft day arrives, the teams can pick the most promising players. Team owners and coaches know that the future success of their teams depends largely on their ability to draft effectively.

It's no different in business. You must select the right players in your organization. If you select well, the benefits are multiplied and seem nearly endless. If you select poorly, the problems are multiplied and seem endless.

The key to making the right choice depends on two things: (1) your ability to see the big picture, and (2) your ability to judge potential employees during the selection process.

It is a good idea to start with an inventory. I use this one because I always want to look inside as well as outside the organization to find candidates. I call this list the Five A's:

Assessment of needs:	*What is needed?*
Assets on hand:	*Who in the organization is available?*
Ability of candidates:	*Who is able?*
Attitude of candidates:	*Who is willing?*
Accomplishments of candidates:	*Who gets things done?*

Notice that the inventory begins with an assessment of needs. The leader of the organization must base that assessment on the big picture. While he was manager of the Chicago Cubs, Charlie Grimm reportedly received a phone call from one of his scouts. The man was excited and began to shout over the telephone, "Charlie, I've landed the greatest young pitcher in the land! He struck out every man who came to bat. Twenty-seven in a row. Nobody even hit a foul until the ninth inning. The pitcher is right here with me. What shall I do?" Charlie replied, "Sign up the guy who got the foul. We're looking for hitters." Charlie knew what the team needed.

There is one situation that supersedes a needs analysis: When a truly exceptional person is available but doesn't necessarily match the current need, do whatever you can to hire him or her anyway. In the long run, that person will positively impact the organization. You see this kind of decision making in sports. Football coaches generally draft players to fill specific needs. If they lack a strong running back, they draft the best running back available. But sometimes they get an opportunity to draft an "impact player," a superstar who can instantly change the whole complexion of the team. Incidentally, impact players usually possess not only athletic ability but also leadership skills. Even as rookies, they have all the qualities to be team captains. When I have an opportunity to hire someone who is exceptional—a superstar—I do it. Then I find a place for him or her. Good people are hard to find, and there is always room for one more productive person in an organization.

Qualities to Look for in a Leader

To find leaders to equip, you first need to know what they look like. Here are ten leadership qualities to seek in anyone you hire:

1. Character
The first thing to look for in any kind of leader or potential leader is strength of character. I have found nothing more important than this

quality. Serious character flaws cannot be ignored. They will eventually make a leader ineffective—every time.

Character flaws should not be confused with weaknesses. We all have weaknesses. They can be overcome through training or experience. Character flaws cannot be changed overnight. Change usually takes a long period of time and involves significant relational investment and dedication on the part of the leader. Any person that you hire who has character flaws will be the weak link in your organization. Depending on the nature of the character flaw, the person has the potential to destroy the organization.

Some of the qualities that make up good character include: honesty, integrity, self-discipline, teachability, dependability, perseverance, conscientiousness, and a strong work ethic. The words of a person with right character match the deeds. His reputation is solid. His manner is straightforward.

The assessment of character can be difficult. Warning signs to watch for include:

- A person's failure to take responsibility for his actions or circumstances

- Unfulfilled promises or obligations

- Failure to meet deadlines

You can tell much about a person's ability to lead others from how well he manages his own life. Look at his interaction with others too. You can tell much about a person's character from his relationships. Examine his relationships with superiors, colleagues, and subordinates. Talk to your employees to find out how the potential leader treats them. This will give you additional insight.

LEADERSHIP IS INFLUENCE.

---

2. Influence

Leadership is influence. Every leader has these two characteristics: (A) he is going somewhere; and (B) he is able to persuade others to go with him. Influence by itself is not enough. That influence must be measured to determine its *quality*. When looking at a potential leader's influence, examine the following:

What is the leader's level of influence? Does that person have followers due to position (he uses the power of his job title); permission (he has developed relationships which motivate); production (he and his followers consistently produce results); personnel development (he has developed others around him); or personhood (he transcends the organization and develops people on a world-class scale)?

Who influences the leader? Who is she following? People become like their models. Is her model ethical? Does her model have the right priorities?

Whom does he influence? Likewise, the quality of the follower will indicate the quality of the leader. Are his followers positive producers or a bunch of mediocre yes-men?

Stuart Briscoe, in *Discipleship for Ordinary People*, tells the story of a young clergyman who officiated at the funeral of a war veteran. The veteran's military friends wanted to participate in the service to honor their comrade, so they requested that the young pastor lead them down to the casket for a moment of remembrance and then out through a side door. The occasion failed to have the desired effect when the clergyman led them through the wrong door. In full view of the other mourners, the men marched with military precision into a broom closet and had to beat a hasty and confused retreat. Every leader must know where he is going. And every follower had better be sure he's behind a leader who knows what he's doing.

3. Positive Attitude

A positive attitude is one of the most valuable assets a person can have in life. My belief in this is so strong that I wrote an entire book on the subject, *The Winning Attitude: Your Key to Personal Success*. So often, what people say their problem is really isn't their problem. Their problem is the attitude that causes them to handle life's obstacles poorly.

The individual whose attitude causes him to approach life from an entirely positive perspective is someone who can be called a no-limit person. In other words, the person doesn't accept the normal limitations of life as most people do. He is determined to walk to the very edge of his potential, or his product's potential, before he accepts defeat. People with positive attitudes are able to go places where others can't. They do things that others can't. They are not restricted by self-imposed limitations.

A person with a positive attitude is like a bumblebee. The bumblebee should not be able to fly, because the size, weight, and shape of its body in relationship to its wingspread makes flying aerodynamically impossible. But the bumblebee, being ignorant of scientific theory, flies anyway and makes honey every day.

This no-limit mind-set allows a person to start each day with a positive disposition, as did an elevator operator I once read about. One Monday morning, in a full elevator, the man began humming a tune. One passenger, irritated by the man's mood, snapped, "What are you so happy about?" "Well, sir," replied the operator happily, "I ain't never lived this day before." Not only does the future look bright when the attitude is right, but the present is much more enjoyable too. The positive person understands that the journey is as enjoyable as the destination.

Think of the attitude like this:

> It is the "advance man" of our true selves.
> Its roots are inward but its fruit is outward.
> It is our best friend or our worst enemy.
> It is more honest and more consistent than our words.
> It is an outward look based on past experiences.
> It is a thing which draws people to us or repels them.
> It is never content until it is expressed.
> It is the librarian of our past.

It is the speaker of our present.

It is the prophet of our future.[1]

Attitude sets the tone, not only for the leader with the attitude, but for the people following him or her.

4. Excellent People Skills

A leader without people skills soon has no followers. Andrew Carnegie, a fantastic leader, is reported to have paid Charles Schwab a salary of $1 million a year simply because of his excellent people skills. Carnegie had other leaders who understood the job better and whose experience and training were better suited to the work. But they lacked the essential human quality of being able to get others to help them, and Schwab could get the best out of his fellow workers. People may admire a person who has only talent and ability, but they will not follow him—not for long.

Excellent people skills involve a genuine concern for others, the ability to understand people, and the decision to make positive interaction with others a primary concern. Our behavior toward others determines their behavior toward us. A successful leader knows this.

5. Evident Gifts

Every person God creates has gifts. One of our jobs as leaders is to make an assessment of those gifts when considering a person for employment or for equipping. I think of every job candidate as a "wannabe" leader. My observation is that there are four types of wannabes:

Never be. Some people simply lack the ability to do a particular job. They simply are not gifted for the particular task at hand. A *never be* who is directed into an area where he is not gifted becomes frustrated, often blames others for his lack of success, and eventually burns out. Redirected, he has a chance of reaching his potential.

Could be. A *could be* is a person with the right gifts and abilities but lacking self-discipline. She may even be a person with superstar abilities who just can't get herself to perform. This person needs to develop the self-discipline to "just do it."

Should be. A *should be* is someone with raw talent (gifts) but few skills for harnessing that ability. He needs training. Once he is given help in developing those skills, he will begin to become the person he was created to be.

Must be. The only thing a *must be* lacks is opportunity. She has the right gifts, the right skills, and the right attitude. She has the drive to be the person she was created to be. It is up to you to be the leader who gives her that opportunity. If you don't, she will find someone else who will.

God creates all people with natural gifts. But He also makes them with two ends, one to sit on and one to think with. Success in life is dependent on which one of these ends is used the most, and it's a toss-up: Heads you win, and tails you lose!

6. PROVEN TRACK RECORD

Poet Archibald MacLeish once said, "There is only one thing more painful than learning from experience, and that is not learning from experience." Leaders who learn this truth develop successful track records over time. Everyone who breaks new ground, who strives to do something, makes mistakes. People without proven track records either haven't learned from their mistakes or haven't tried.

I've worked with many talented people who've established tremendous track records. When I first started my organization, one man stood out as a first-rate leader capable of the highest quality of leadership: Dick Peterson. He had worked with IBM for years, and he quickly demonstrated that experience had not been wasted on him. Dick already had a proven track record when I asked him to team with me in 1985 to start one of my companies, INJOY. In the beginning, we were long on potential and short on resources. Dick's hard work, planning, and insight turned a shoestring business operating out of his garage into an enterprise producing materials and influencing tens of thousands of leaders nationally and internationally every year. For fifteen years Dick served as the president of INJOY and helped get the company off the ground.

Management expert Robert Townsend notes, "Leaders come in all sizes, ages, shapes, and conditions. Some are poor administrators, some not overly bright. But there is one clue for spotting them. Since most people *per se* are mediocre, the true leader can be recognized because somehow or other, his people consistently turn in superior performances." Always check a candidate's past performance. A proven leader always has a proven track record.

7. CONFIDENCE

People will not follow a leader who does not have confidence in himself. In fact, people are naturally attracted to people who convey confidence. An excellent example can be seen in an incident in Russia during an attempted coup. Army tanks had surrounded the government building housing President Boris Yeltsin and his pro-democracy supporters. High-level military leaders had ordered the tank commander to open fire and kill Yeltsin. As the army rolled into position, Yeltsin strode from the building, climbed up on a tank, looked the commander in the eye, and thanked him for coming over to the side of democracy. Later the commander admitted that they had not intended to go over to his side. Yeltsin had appeared so confident and commanding that the soldiers talked after he left and decided to join him.

Confidence is characteristic of a positive attitude. The greatest achievers and leaders remain confident regardless of circumstances. Confidence is not simply for show. Confidence empowers. A *good* leader has the ability to instill within his people confidence in himself. A *great* leader has the ability to instill within his people confidence in themselves.

8. SELF-DISCIPLINE

Great leaders always have self-discipline—without exception. Unfortunately, our society seeks instant gratification rather than self-discipline. We want instant breakfast, fast food, movies on demand, and quick cash from ATMs. But success doesn't come instantly. Neither does the ability to lead. As General Dwight D. Eisenhower said, "There are no victories at bargain prices."

Because we live in a society of instant gratification, we cannot take for granted that the potential leaders we interview will have self-discipline—that they will be willing to pay the price of great leadership. When it comes to self-discipline, people choose one of two things: the pain of discipline that comes from sacrifice and growth, or the pain of regret that comes from the easy road and missed opportunities. Each person in life chooses. In *Adventures in Achievement*, F. James Rohn says that the pain of discipline weighs ounces. Regret weighs tons.

There are two areas of self-discipline we must look for in potential leaders we are considering equipping. The first is in the emotions. Effective leaders recognize that their emotional reactions are their own responsibility. A leader who decides not to allow other people's actions to dictate his reactions experiences an empowering freedom. As the Greek philosopher Epictetus said, "No person is free who is not master of himself."

The second area concerns time. Every person on the planet is given the same allotment of minutes in a day. But each person's level of self-discipline dictates how effectively those minutes are used. Disciplined people are always growing, always striving for improvement, and they maximize the use of their time. I have found three things that characterize disciplined leaders:

- They have identified specific long- and short-term goals for themselves.

- They have a plan for achieving those goals.

- They have a desire that motivates them to continue working to accomplish those goals.

Progress comes at a price. When you interview a potential leader, determine whether he or she is willing to pay the price. The author of the popular cartoon comic strip *Ziggy* recognized this when he drew the following scene:

As our friend Ziggy, in his little automobile, drove down a road, he saw two signs. The first stated in bold letters, THE ROAD TO SUCCESS. Farther down the road stood the second sign. It read, PREPARE TO STOP FOR TOLLS.

9. EFFECTIVE COMMUNICATION SKILLS

Never underestimate the importance of communication. It consumes enormous amounts of our time. One study, reported by D. K. Burlow in *The Process of Communication,* states that the average American spends 70 percent of his active hours each day communicating verbally. Without the ability to communicate, a leader cannot effectively cast his vision and call his people to act on that vision.

A leader's ability to convey confidence and his ability to communicate effectively are similar. Both require action on his part and a response from the follower. Communication is positive *interaction.* When communication is one-sided, it can be comical. You may have heard the story of the frustrated judge preparing to hear a divorce case:

"Why do you want a divorce?" the judge asked. "On what grounds?"

"All over. We have an acre and a half," responded the woman.

"No, no," said the judge. "Do you have a grudge?"

"Yes, sir. Fits two cars."

"I need a reason for the divorce," said the judge impatiently. "Does he beat you up?"

"Oh, no. I'm up at six every day to do my exercises. He gets up later."

"Please," said the exasperated judge. "What is the reason you want a divorce?"

"Oh," she replied. "We can't seem to communicate with each other."

When I look at a potential leader's communication skills, I look for the following:

A genuine concern for the person he's talking to. When people sense that you have a concern for them, they are willing to listen to what you have to say. Liking people is the beginning of the ability to communicate.

The ability to focus on the responder. Poor communicators are focused on themselves and their own opinions. Good communicators focus on the response of the person they're talking to. Good communicators also read body language.

The ability to communicate with all kinds of people. A good communicator has the ability to set a person at ease. She can find a way to relate to nearly anyone of any background.

Eye contact with the person he's speaking to. Most people who are being straight with you are willing to look you in the eye.

A warm smile. The fastest way to open the lines of communication is to smile. A smile overcomes innumerable communication barriers, crossing the boundaries of culture, race, age, class, gender, education, and economic status.

If I expect a person to lead, I must also expect him to be able to communicate.

10. DISCONTENT WITH THE STATUS QUO

I've told my staff before that *status quo* is Latin for "the mess we're in." Leaders see what is, but more important, they have vision for what could be. They are never content with things as they are. To be leading, by definition, is to be in front, breaking new ground, conquering new worlds, moving away from the status quo. Donna Harrison states, "Great leaders are never satisfied with current levels of performance. They constantly strive for higher and higher levels of achievement." They move beyond the status quo themselves, and they ask the same of those around them.

Dissatisfaction with the status quo does not mean a negative attitude or grumbling. It has to do with willingness to be different and take risks.

A person who refuses to risk change fails to grow. A leader who loves the status quo soon becomes a follower. Raymond Smith, former CEO and Chairman of the Bell Atlantic Corporation, once remarked, "Taking the safe road, doing your job, and not making any waves may not get you fired (right away, at least), but it sure won't do much for your career or your company over the long haul. We're not dumb. We know that administrators are easy to find and cheap to keep. Leaders—risk takers—are in very short supply. And ones with vision are pure gold."

Risk seems dangerous to people more comfortable with old problems than new solutions. The difference between the energy and time that it takes to put up with the old problems and the energy and time it takes to come up with new solutions is surprisingly small. The difference is attitude. When seeking potential leaders, seek people who seek solutions.

Good leaders deliberately seek out and find potential leaders. Great leaders not only find them, but transform them into other great leaders. They have an ability to recognize ability and a strategy for finding leaders who make it happen. That's what takes their organizations to the next level.

5

WHAT DOES IT TAKE TO EQUIP A LEADER?

Equipping, like nurturing, is an ongoing process.

Equipping is similar to training. But I prefer the term "equipping" because it more accurately describes the process potential leaders must go through. Training is generally focused on specific job tasks; for instance, you train a person to use a copy machine or to answer a phone in a particular way. Training is only a part of the equipping process that prepares a person for leadership.

When I think of equipping a potential leader, I think of preparing an unskilled person to scale a tall mountain peak. His preparation is a process. Certainly he needs to be outfitted with equipment, such as cold-weather clothing, ropes, picks, and spikes. He also needs to be trained how to use that equipment.

A mountain climber's preparation, though, involves much more than simply having the correct equipment and knowing how to use it. The person must be conditioned physically to prepare him for the difficult climb. He must be trained to be a part of a team. Most important, he must be taught to *think* like a mountain climber. He needs to be able to look at a peak and *see* how it is to be conquered. Without going through the complete equipping process, he not only won't make it to the top of the mountain, but he also might find himself stranded on the side of the mountain, freezing to death.

Equipping, like nurturing, is an ongoing process. You don't equip a person in a few hours or a day. And it can't be done using a formula or a videotape. Equipping must be tailored to each potential leader.

EQUIPPING IS AN ONGOING PROCESS.

YOUR ROLE AS EQUIPPER

The ideal equipper is a person who can impart the vision of the work, evaluate the potential leader, give him the tools he needs, and then help him along the way at the beginning of his journey.

The equipper is a *model*—a leader who does the job, does it well, does it right, and does it with consistency.

The equipper is a *mentor*—an advisor who has the vision of the organization and can communicate it to others. He or she has experience to draw upon.

The equipper is an *empowerer*—one who can instill in the potential leader the desire and ability to do the work. He or she is able to lead, teach, and assess the progress of the person being equipped.

The steps that follow will take you through the whole process. They begin with building a relationship with your potential leaders. From that foundation, you can build a program for their development, supervise their progress, empower them to do the job, and finally get them to pass on the legacy.

DEVELOP A PERSONAL RELATIONSHIP WITH THE PEOPLE YOU EQUIP

All good mentoring relationships begin with personal relationships. As your people get to know and like you, their desire to follow your direction and learn from you will increase. If they don't like you, they will not want to learn from you, and the equipping process slows down or even stops.

To build relationships, begin by listening to people's life stories, their journeys so far. Your genuine interest in them will mean a lot to them. It will also help you to know their personal strengths and weaknesses. Ask them about their goals and what motivates them. Find out what kind of temperament they have. If you first find their hearts, they'll be glad to give you their hands.

ALL GOOD MENTORING RELATIONSHIPS BEGIN WITH PERSONAL RELATIONSHIPS.

SHARE YOUR DREAM

While getting to know your people, share your dream. It helps them to know you and where you're going. There's no act that will better show them your heart and your motivation.

Woodrow Wilson once said, "We grow by dreams. All big individuals are dreamers. They see things in the soft haze of a spring day, or in the red fire on a long winter's evening. Some of us let those great dreams die, but others nourish and protect them; nourish them through bad days until they bring them to the sunshine and light which comes always to those who sincerely hope that their dreams will come true." I have often wondered, "Does the person make the dream or does the dream make the person?" My conclusion is both are equally true.

All good leaders have a dream. All great leaders share their dream with others who can help them make it a reality. As Florence Littauer suggests, we must:

Dare to dream: Have the desire to do something bigger than yourself.

Prepare the dream: Do your homework; be ready when the opportunity comes.

Wear the dream: Do it.

Share the dream: Make others a part of the dream, and it will become even greater than you had hoped.

ASK FOR COMMITMENT

In his book *The One Minute Manager*, Ken Blanchard says, "There's a difference between interest and commitment. When you are interested in doing something, you do it only when it is convenient. When you are committed to something, you accept no excuses." Don't equip people who are merely interested. Equip the ones who are committed.

To determine whether your people are committed, first you must make sure they know what it will cost them to become leaders. That means that you must be sure not to undersell the job—let them know what it's going to take. If they won't commit, don't go any further in the equipping process. Don't waste your time.

SET GOALS FOR GROWTH

People need clear objectives set before them if they are to achieve anything of value. Success never comes instantaneously. It comes from taking many small steps. A set of goals becomes a map a potential leader can follow in order to grow. As Shad Helmsetter states in *You Can Excel in Time of Change*, "It is the goal that shapes the plan; it is the plan that sets the action; it is the action that achieves the result; and it is the result that brings the success. And it all begins with the simple word *goal.*" We, as equipping leaders, must introduce our people to the practice of setting and achieving goals.

When you help your people set goals, use the following guidelines:

Make the goals appropriate. Always keep in mind the job you want the people to do and the desired result: the development of your people into effective leaders. Identify goals that will contribute to that larger goal.

Make the goals attainable. Nothing will make people want to quit faster than facing unachievable goals. I like the comment made by Ian MacGregor, former AMAX Corporation chairman of the board: "I work on the same principle as people who train horses. You start with low fences, easily achieved goals, and work up. It's important in management never to ask people to try to accomplish goals they can't accept."

Make the goals measurable. Your potential leaders will never know when they have achieved their goals if they aren't measurable. When they are measurable, the knowledge that they have been attained will give them a sense of accomplishment. It will also free them to set new goals in place of the old ones.

Clearly state the goal. When goals have no clear focus, neither will the actions of the people trying to achieve them.

Make the goals require a "stretch." As I mentioned before, goals have to be achievable. On the other hand, when goals don't require a stretch, the people achieving them won't grow. The leader must know his people well enough to identify attainable goals that require a stretch.

Put the goals in writing. When people write down their goals, it makes them more accountable for those goals. A study of a Yale University graduating class showed that the small percentage of graduates who had written down their goals accomplished more than all of the other graduates combined. Putting goals in writing works.

Communicate the Fundamentals

For people to be productive and satisfied professionally, they have to know what their fundamental responsibilities are. It sounds so simple, but Peter Drucker says one of the critical problems in the workplace today is that there is a lack of understanding between the employer and employee as to what the employee is to do. Often employees are made to feel they are vaguely responsible for everything. It paralyzes them. Instead, we need to make clear to them what they *are* and *are not* responsible for. Then they will be able to focus their efforts on what we want, and they will succeed.

Look again at how a basketball team works. Each of the five players has a particular job. There is a shooting guard whose job is to score points. The other guard is a point guard. His job is to pass the ball to people who can score. Another player is a power forward who is expected to get rebounds.

The small forward's job is to score. The center is supposed to rebound, block shots, and score. Each person on the team knows what his job is, what his unique contribution to the team must be. When each concentrates on his particular responsibilities, the team can win.

Finally, a leader must communicate to his or her people that their work has value to the organization and to the individual leader. To the employee, this often is the most important fundamental of all.

Perform the Five-Step Process of Training People

Part of the equipping process includes training people to perform the specific tasks of the jobs they are to do. The approach the leader takes to training will largely determine his people's success or failure. If he takes a dry, academic approach, the potential leaders will remember little of what's taught.

The best type of training takes advantage of the way people learn. Researchers tell us that we remember 10 percent of what we hear, 50 percent of what we see, 70 percent of what we say, and 90 percent of what we hear, see, say, and do. Knowing that, we have to develop an approach to how we will train. I have found the best training method to be a five-step process:

Step 1: I model. The process begins with my doing the tasks while the people being trained watch. When I do this, I try to give them an opportunity to see me go through the whole process.

Step 2: I mentor. During this next step, I continue to perform the task, but this time the person I'm training comes alongside me and assists in the process. I also take time to explain not only the *how* but also the *why* of each step.

Step 3: I monitor. We exchange places this time. The trainee performs the task and I assist and correct. It's especially important during this phase to be positive and encouraging to the trainee. It keeps him trying and it makes him want to improve rather than give up. Work with him until he develops consistency. Once he's gotten down the process, ask him to explain it to you. It will help him to understand and remember.

Step 4: I motivate. I take myself out of the task at this point and let the trainee go. My task is to make sure he knows how to do it without help and to keep encouraging him so he will continue to improve. It is important for me to stay with him until he senses success. It's a great motivator. At this time the trainee may want to make improvements to the process. Encourage him to do it, and at the same time learn from him.

Step 5: I multiply. This is my favorite part of the whole process. Once the new leaders do the job well, it becomes their turn to teach others how to do it. As teachers know, the best way to learn something is to teach it. And the beauty of this is it frees me to do other important developmental tasks while others carry on the training.

GIVE THE "BIG THREE"

All the training in the world will provide limited success if you don't turn your people loose to do the job. I believe that if I get the best people, give them my vision, train them in the basics, and then let go, I will get a high return from them. As General George S. Patton once remarked, "Never tell people how to do things. Tell them what to do and they will surprise you with their ingenuity."

You can't turn people loose without structure, but you also want to give them enough freedom to be creative. The way to do that is to give them the big three: *responsibility, authority,* and *accountability.*

What is difficult for some leaders is allowing their people to keep the responsibility after it's been given. Poor managers want to control every detail of their people's work. When that happens, the potential leaders who work for them become frustrated and don't develop. Rather than desiring more responsibility, they become indifferent or avoid responsibility altogether. If you want your people to take responsibility, truly give it to them.

With responsibility must go authority. Progress does not come unless they are given together. Winston Churchill, while addressing the House of Commons during the Second World War, said, "I am your servant. You have the right to dismiss me when you please. What you have no right to do is ask me to bear responsibility without the power of action." When responsibility and authority come together, people become genuinely empowered.

There's an important aspect of authority that needs to be noted. When we first give authority to new leaders, we are actually *giving them permission* to have authority rather than *giving them authority* itself. True authority has to be earned.

We must give our people permission to develop authority. That is our responsibility. They, in turn, must take responsibility for earning it.

I have found there are different levels of authority:

Position. The most basic kind of authority comes from a person's position on the organizational chart. This type of authority does not extend beyond the parameters of the job description. This is where all new leaders start. From here they may either earn greater authority, or they can minimize what little authority they have been given. It's up to them.

Competence. This type of authority is based on a person's professional capabilities, the ability to do a job. Followers give competent leaders authority within their area of expertise.

Personality. Followers will also give authority to people based on their personal characteristics, such as personality, appearance, and charisma. Authority based on personality is a little broader than competence-based authority, but it is not really more advanced because it tends to be superficial.

Integrity. Authority based on integrity comes from a person's core. It is based on character. When new leaders gain authority based on their integrity, they have crossed into a new stage of their development.

Spirituality. In secular circles, people rarely consider the power of spiritual-based authority. It comes from people's individual experiences with God and from His power working through them. It is the highest form of authority.

Leaders must earn authority with each new group of people. However, I have found that once leaders have gained authority on a particular level, it takes very little time for them to establish that level of authority with another group of people. The higher the level of authority, the more quickly it happens.

Once responsibility and authority have been given to people, they are empowered to make things happen. But we also have to be sure they are making the right things happen. That's where accountability comes into the picture. If we are providing them the right climate, our people will not fear accountability. They will admit mistakes and see them as a part of the learning process.

The leader's part of accountability involves taking the time to review the new leader's work and give honest, constructive criticism. It is crucial that the leader be supportive but honest. It's been said that when Harry Truman was thrust into the presidency upon the death of President Franklin D. Roosevelt, Speaker of the House Sam Rayburn gave him some fatherly advice: "From here on out you're going to have lots of people around you. They'll try to put a wall around you and cut you off from any ideas but theirs. They'll tell you what a great man you are, Harry. But you and I both know you ain't." Rayburn was holding President Truman accountable.

GIVE THEM THE TOOLS THEY NEED

Giving responsibility without resources is ridiculous; it is incredibly limiting. Abraham Maslow said, "If the only tool you have is a hammer, you tend to see every problem as a nail." If we want our people to be creative and resourceful, we need to provide resources.

Obviously, the most basic tools are pieces of equipment, such as copying machines, computers, and whatever else simplifies someone's work. We must be sure not only to provide everything necessary for a job to be done, but also equipment that will allow jobs, especially "B" priorities, to be done more quickly and efficiently. Always work toward freeing people's time for important things.

Tools, however, include much more than equipment. It is important to provide developmental tools. Spend time mentoring people in specific areas of need. Be willing to spend money on things like books, tapes, seminars, and professional conferences. There is a wealth of good information out there, and fresh ideas from outside an organization can stimulate growth. Be creative in providing tools. It will keep your people growing and equip them to do the job well.

Check on Them Systematically

I believe in touching base with people frequently. I like to give mini-evaluations all the time. Leaders who wait to give feedback only during annual formal evaluations are asking for trouble. People need the encouragement of being told they're doing well on a regular basis. They also need to hear as soon as possible when they are not doing well. It prevents a lot of problems with the organization, and it improves the leader.

How often I check on people is determined by a number of factors:

The importance of the task. When something is critical to the success of the organization, I touch base often.

The demands of the work. I find that if the work is very demanding, the person performing it needs encouragement more often.

The newness of the work. Some leaders have no problem tackling a new task, no matter how different it is from previous work. Others have great difficulty adapting. I check often on the people who are less flexible or creative.

The newness of the worker. I want to give new leaders every possible chance to succeed. So I check on newer people more often. That way I can help them anticipate problems and make sure that they have a series of successes. By that they gain confidence.

The responsibility of the worker. When I know I can give a person a task and it will always get done, I may not check on that person until the task is complete. With less responsible people, I can't afford to do that.

My approach to checking on people also varies from person to person. For instance, rookies and veterans should be treated differently. But no matter how long people have been with me, there are some things I always do: discuss feelings, measure progress, give feedback, and give encouragement.

Though it doesn't happen very often, I occasionally have a person whose progress is repeatedly poor. When that happens, I try to determine what's gone wrong. Usually poor performance is a result of one of three things: (1) a mismatch between the job and the person; (2) inadequate training or leadership; or (3) deficiencies in the person performing the work. Before I take any action, I always try to determine what the issues are. I line up my facts to be sure there really is a deficiency in performance and not just a problem with my perception. Next I define as precisely as possible what the deficiency is. Finally, I check with the person who is not performing to get the other side of the story.

Once I've done my homework, I try to determine where the deficiency is. If it's a mismatch, I explain the problem to the person, move him to a place that fits, and reassure him of my confidence in him.

If the problem involves training or leadership issues, I back up and redo whatever step hasn't been performed properly. Once again, I let the person know what the problem was and give him plenty of encouragement.

If the problem is with the person, I sit down with him and let him know about it. I make it clear where his failures are and what he must do to overcome them. Then I give him another chance. But I also begin the documentation process in case I have to fire him. I want him to succeed, but I will waste no time letting him go if he doesn't do what it takes to improve.

CONDUCT PERIODIC EQUIPPING MEETINGS

Even after you've completed most of your people's training and are preparing to take them into their next growth phase—development—continue to conduct periodic equipping meetings. It helps your people stay on track, helps them keep growing, and encourages them to begin taking responsibility for equipping themselves.

When I prepare an equipping meeting, I include the following:

Good news. I always start on a positive note. I review the good things that are happening in the organization and pay particular attention to their areas of interest and responsibility.

Vision. People can get so caught up in their day-to-day responsibilities that they lose sight of the vision that drives the organization. Use the opportunity of an equipping meeting to recast that vision.

Content. Content will depend on their needs. Try to focus training on areas that will help them in the priority areas, and orient the training on the people, not the lesson.

Administration. Cover any organizational items that give the people a sense of security and encourage their leadership.

Empowerment. Take time to connect with the people you equip. Encourage them personally. And show them how the equipping session empowers them to perform their jobs better. They will leave the meeting feeling positive and ready to work.

The entire equipping process takes a lot of time and attention. It requires more time and dedication from the equipping leader than mere training. But its focus is long term, not short term. Rather than creating followers or even adding new leaders, it *multiplies* leaders. As I explained earlier, it is not complete until the equipper and the new leader select someone for the new leader to train. It is only then that the equipping process has come full circle. Without a successor, there can be no success.

PART III

EQUIPPING FOR THE NEXT LEVEL

6

How Can a Leader
Inspire Others to Excel?

Adding value is really the essence of equipping others.

In 1296, King Edward I of England assembled a large army and crossed the border of his own nation into Scotland. Edward was a skilled leader and fierce warrior. A tall, strong man, he had gained his first real combat experience beginning at age twenty-five. In the following years, he became a seasoned veteran while fighting in the Crusades in the Holy Lands.

At age fifty-seven, he was fresh from victories in Wales, whose people he'd crushed and whose land he'd annexed. In that conflict, his purpose had been clear: He said it was "to check the impetuous rashness of the Welsh, to punish their presumption, and to wage war against them to their extermination."[1]

Edward's invasion of Scotland was intended to break the will of the Scottish people once and for all. Previously, he had managed to make himself overlord of the territory and then placed a weak king over it, a man the people of Scotland called Toom Tabard, meaning "empty coat." Then Edward bullied the straw king until he rebelled, thus giving the English monarch a reason to invade the country. The Scottish people crumpled.

A BOLD LEADER EMERGED

Edward sacked the castle of Berwick and massacred its inhabitants. Other castles surrendered in quick succession. The Scottish king was stripped of power, and many believed that the fate of the Scots would be the same as that of the Welsh. But they didn't take into account the efforts of one man: Sir William Wallace, who is still revered as a national hero in Scotland even though he has been dead for nearly seven hundred years.

If you saw the movie *Braveheart*, then you have an image of William Wallace as a fierce and determined fighter who valued freedom above all else. His older brother, Malcolm, as the firstborn son, was expected to follow in the footsteps of their father as a warrior. William, as many second sons of the day, was instead groomed for the clergy. He was taught to value ideas, including freedom. But Wallace grew to resent the oppressive English rulers after his father was killed in an ambush and his mother was forced to live in exile. At age nineteen, he became a fighter when a group of Englishmen tried to bully him. By his early twenties, William Wallace was a highly skilled warrior.

THE PEOPLE WENT TO A HIGHER LEVEL

During the time of William Wallace and Edward I, warfare was usually conducted by trained knights, professional soldiers, and sometimes hired mercenaries. The larger and more seasoned the army, the greater their power. When Edward faced the smaller Welsh army, they didn't stand a chance. And the same was expected of the Scots. But Wallace had an unusual ability. He drew the common people of Scotland to him, he made them believe in the cause of freedom, and he inspired and equipped them to fight against the professional war machine of England. He enlarged their vision and their abilities.

William Wallace was ultimately unable to defeat the English and gain Scotland's independence. At age thirty-three, he was brutally executed. (His treatment was actually worse than that portrayed in the movie

Braveheart.) But his legacy of enlargement carried on. The next year, inspired by Wallace's example, nobleman Robert Bruce claimed the throne of Scotland and rallied not only the peasants but also the nobility. And in 1314, Scotland finally gained its hard-fought independence.

Characteristics of Enlarging Leaders

Team members always love and admire a player who is able to help them go to another level, someone who enlarges them and empowers them to be successful. Those kinds of people are like the Boston Celtics Hall of Fame center Bill Russell, who said, "The most important measure of how good a game I played was how much better I'd made my teammates play."

Leaders who enlarge their teammates have several things in common:

They Value Their Team Members

Industrialist Charles Schwab observed, "I have yet to find the man, however exalted his station, who did not do better work and put forth greater effort under a spirit of approval than under a spirit of criticism." Your team members can tell whether you believe in them. People's performances usually reflect the expectations of those they respect.

"The most important measure of how good a game I played was how much better I'd made my teammates play."—Bill Russell

---

They Value What Their Team Members Value

Players who enlarge others do more than value their fellow team members; they understand what their team members value. They listen to discover what they talk about and watch to see what they spend their money on. That kind of knowledge, along with a desire to relate to their fellow players, creates a strong connection between them. And it makes possible an enlarger's next characteristic.

THEY ADD VALUE TO THEIR TEAM MEMBERS

Adding value is really the essence of enlarging others. It's finding ways to help others improve their abilities and attitudes. A leader who equips and enlarges others looks for the gifts, talents, and uniqueness in other people and then helps them to increase those abilities for their benefit and for that of the entire team. An enlarging leader is able to take others to a whole new level.

THEY MAKE THEMSELVES MORE VALUABLE

Enlargers work to make themselves better, not only because it benefits them personally, but also because it helps them to help others. You cannot give what you do not have. If you want to increase the ability of your team members, make yourself better.

HOW TO BECOME AN ENLARGER

If you want to be an enlarging team leader, then do the following:

1. BELIEVE IN OTHERS BEFORE THEY BELIEVE IN YOU

If you want to help people become better, you need to become an initiator. You can't hold back. Ask yourself, *What is special, unique, and wonderful about that team member?* Then share your observations with the person and with others. If you believe in others and give them a positive reputation to uphold, you can help them to become better than they think they are.

2. SERVE OTHERS BEFORE THEY SERVE YOU

One of the most beneficial services you can perform is helping other human beings to reach their potential. In your family, serve your spouse. In business, help your colleagues to shine. And whenever possible, give credit to others for the team's success.

3. ADD VALUE TO OTHERS BEFORE THEY ADD VALUE TO YOU

A basic truth of life is that people will always move toward anyone who increases them and away from others who devalue them. You can enlarge others by pointing out their strengths and helping them to focus on improvement.

For as long as he could remember, a boy named Chris Greicius dreamed of someday becoming a police officer. But there was a major obstacle standing in his way. He had leukemia, and he was not expected to make it to adulthood. When he was seven years old, Chris's battle with the disease took a turn for the worse, and that's when a family friend, who was a U.S. customs officer, arranged for Chris to come as close as he could to living his dream. He made a call to Officer Ron Cox in Phoenix and arranged for Chris to spend the day with officers from the Arizona Department of Public Safety.

A BASIC TRUTH OF LIFE IS THAT PEOPLE WILL ALWAYS MOVE TOWARD ANYONE WHO INCREASES THEM AND AWAY FROM OTHERS WHO DEVALUE THEM.

When the day arrived, Chris was welcomed by three squad cars and a police motorcycle ridden by Frank Shankwitz. Then he was treated to a ride in a police helicopter. They finished the day by swearing Chris in as the first—and only—honorary state trooper. The next day, Cox enlisted the assistance of the company that manufactured the uniforms for the Arizona Highway Patrol, and within twenty-four hours, their people presented Chris with an official patrolman's uniform. He was ecstatic.

Two days later, Chris died in the hospital, his uniform close at hand. Officer Shankwitz was saddened by his little friend's death, but he was grateful that he had experienced the opportunity to help Chris. And he also realized that there were many children in circumstances similar to Chris's. That prompted Shankwitz to cofound the Make-A-Wish Foundation. In twenty years since then, he and his organization have enlarged the experiences of more than eighty thousand children.

There is nothing as valuable—or rewarding—as adding value to the lives of others. When you help others to go to another level, you go to another level yourself.

How Can I Help Others Fulfill Their Potential?

Having the right people
in the right places is essential to
individual and team success.

If you succeed in developing people in your organization and equipping them to lead, you will be successful. If you enlarge them and motivate them to achieve, they will be grateful to you as their leader. And to be honest, you will have done more than many other leaders do. However, you can take yet another step that will help someone you equip to fulfill their potential. You can help them to find their niche in life. Good things happen when a player takes the place where he or she adds the most value. Great things happen when all the players on the team take the roles that maximize their strengths—their talent, skill, and experience. It takes every individual—and the whole team—to a whole new level.

When People Are in the Wrong Place

Just about everyone has experienced being on some kind of team where people had to take on roles that didn't suit them: an accountant forced to work with people all day, a basketball forward forced to play center, a guitarist filling in on keyboard, a teacher stuck doing paperwork, a spouse who hates the kitchen taking on the role of cook.

What happens to a team when one or more of its members constantly play "out of position"? First, morale erodes because the team isn't playing up to its capability. Then people become resentful. The people working in an area of weakness resent that their best is untapped. And other people on the team who know that they could better fill a mismatched position on the team resent that their skills are being overlooked. Before long, people become unwilling to work as a team. Then everyone's confidence begins to erode. And the situation just keeps getting worse. The team stops progressing, and the competition takes advantage of the team's obvious weaknesses. As a result, the team never realizes its potential. When people aren't where they do things well, things don't turn out well—for the individual or for the team.

Having the right people in the right places is essential to individual and team success. Take a look at how a team's dynamic changes according to the placement of people:

The Wrong Person in the Wrong Place   =   Regression

The Wrong Person in the Right Place   =   Frustration

The Right Person in the Wrong Place   =   Confusion

The Right Person in the Right Place   =   Progression

The Right People in the Right Places   =   Multiplication

It doesn't matter what kind of team you're dealing with: the principles are the same. David Ogilvy was right when he said, "A well-run restaurant is like a winning baseball team. It makes the most of every crew member's talent and takes advantage of every split-second opportunity to speed up service."

A few years ago I was asked to write a chapter for a book called *Destiny and Deliverance,* which was tied to the Dreamworks movie *The Prince of Egypt.* It was a wonderful experience, which I greatly enjoyed. During the writing process, I was invited to go to California and view parts of the movie while it was still in production. That made me want to do something I had never done before: attend a movie premiere in Hollywood.

My publisher managed to get me a pair of tickets for the premiere, and when the time arrived, my wife, Margaret, and I went out for the event. It was a blast. It was a high-energy event filled with movie stars and moviemakers. Margaret and I enjoyed the movie—and the whole experience—immensely.

Now, anybody who's gone to a movie, show, or sporting event with me knows my pattern. As soon as I am pretty certain about the outcome of a ball game, I hit the exit to beat the crowds. When the Broadway audience is giving the ovation, I'm gone. And the second the credits begin to roll in a movie, I'm out of my seat. As *The Prince of Egypt* came to a close, I started to get ready to get up, but not a person in the theater moved. And then something really surprising happened. As the credits rolled, people began to applaud the lesser known individuals whose names appeared on the screen: the costume designer, the gaffer, the key grip, the assistant director. It was a moment I'll never forget—and a great reminder that all players have a place where they add the most value. That not only helps people to reach their potential, but it builds the team. When each person does the job that's best for him or her, everybody wins.

TO PUT PEOPLE IN THEIR PLACE

NFL champion coach Vince Lombardi observed, "The achievements of an organization are the results of the combined effort of each individual." That is true, but creating a winning team doesn't come just from having the right individuals. Even if you have a great group of talented individuals, if each person is not doing what adds the most value to the team, you won't achieve your potential as a team. That's the art of leading a team. You've got to put people in their place—and I mean that in the most positive way!

To take people to the next level by putting them in the places that utilize their talents and maximize the team's potential, you need three things. You must . . .

1. Know the Team

You cannot build a winning team or organization if you don't know its vision, purpose, culture, or history. If you don't know where the team is trying to go—and why it's trying to get there—you cannot bring the team to the height of its potential. You've got to start where the team actually is; only then can you take it somewhere.

2. Know the Situation

Even though the vision or purpose of an organization may be fairly constant, its situation changes constantly. Good team builders know where the team is and what the situation requires. For example, when a team is young and just getting started, the greatest priority is often to just get good people. But as a team matures and the level of talent increases, then fine-tuning becomes more important. It's at that time that a leader must spend more time matching the person to the position.

3. Know the Player

It sounds obvious, but you must know the person you are trying to position in the right niche. I mention it because leaders tend to want to make everyone else conform to their image, to approach their work using the same skills and problem-solving methods. But team building is not working on an assembly line.

Mother Teresa, who worked with people her whole life, observed, "I can do what you can't do, and you can do what I can't do; together we can do great things." As you work to build a team, look at each person's experience, skills, temperament, attitude, passion, people skills, discipline, emotional strength, and potential. Only then will you be ready to help a team member to find his or her proper place.

"I CAN DO WHAT YOU CAN'T DO, AND YOU CAN DO WHAT
I CAN'T DO; TOGETHER WE CAN DO GREAT THINGS."
—MOTHER TERESA

START BY FINDING THE RIGHT PLACE FOR YOU

Right now you may not be in a position to place others on your team. In fact, you may be thinking to yourself, *How do I find my own niche?* If that's the case, then follow these guidelines:

- BE SECURE: My friend Wayne Schmidt says, "No amount of personal competency compensates for personal insecurity." If you allow your insecurities to get the better of you, you'll be inflexible and reluctant to change. And you cannot grow without change.

- GET TO KNOW YOURSELF: You won't be able to find your niche if you don't know your strengths and weaknesses. Spend time reflecting and exploring your gifts. Ask others to give you feedback. Do what it takes to remove personal blind spots.

- TRUST YOUR LEADER: A good leader will help you to start moving in the right direction. If you don't trust your leader, look to another mentor for help. Or get on another team.

- SEE THE BIG PICTURE: Your place on the team only makes sense in the context of the big picture. If your only motivation for finding your niche is personal gain, your poor motives may prevent you from discovering what you desire.

- RELY ON YOUR EXPERIENCE: When it comes down to it, the only way to know that you've discovered your niche is to try what seems right and learn from your failures and successes. When you discover what you were made for, your heart sings. It says, *There's no place like this place anywhere near this place, so this must be the place!*

A Place for Everyone,
and Everyone in His Place

One organization that strives to match its people to the right place is the U.S. military. That is particularly true now that it employs an all-volunteer force. If each of the various functions in a military command don't work at top efficiency (and interact well with all the other parts), then terrible breakdowns occur.

When you discover your place,
you will say, "There's no place like this
place anywhere near this place,
so this must be the place!"

Nobody is more keenly aware of that than a combat pilot. Take for example Charlie Plumb, who retired as a captain of the U.S. Navy. A graduate of Annapolis, he served in Vietnam in the mid-sixties, flying seventy-five missions from the aircraft carrier USS *Kitty Hawk*.

An aircraft carrier is a place where you can readily observe how all the pieces of the military "puzzle" come together to support each other. A carrier is often described as being like a floating city. It contains a crew of 5,500 people, a population greater than that of some of the towns in which its crew members grew up. It must be self-sustaining, and each of its seventeen departments must function as a team accomplishing its mission. And those teams must work together as a team.

Every pilot is acutely aware of the team effort required to put a jet in the air. It takes hundreds of people utilizing dozens of technical specialties to launch, monitor, support, land, and maintain an aircraft. Even more people are involved if that plane is armed for combat. Charlie Plumb was undoubtedly aware that many people worked tirelessly to keep him flying. But despite the efforts of the best-trained air support group in the world, Plumb found himself in a North Vietnamese prison as a POW after his F-4 Phantom jet was shot down on May 19, 1967, during his seventy-fifth mission.

Plumb was held prisoner for nearly six grueling years, part of the time in the infamous Hanoi Hilton. During those years he and his fellow prisoners were humiliated, starved, tortured, and forced to live in squalid conditions. Yet he didn't let the experience break him. He now says, "Our unity through our faith in God and in our love for Country were the great strength which kept us going through some very difficult times."

TURNING POINT

Plumb was released from his imprisonment on February 18, 1973, and continued his career in the navy. But an incident years after his return to the United States marked his life as surely as his imprisonment. One day he and his wife, Cathy, were eating in a restaurant, when a man came to the table and said, "You're Plumb. You flew jet fighters in Vietnam."

"That's right," answered Plumb, "I did."

"It was fighter squadron 114 on the *Kitty Hawk*. You were shot down. You were parachuted into enemy hands," the man continued. "You spent six years as a prisoner of war."

The former pilot was taken aback. He looked at the man, trying to identify him, but couldn't. "How in the world did you know that?" Plumb finally asked.

"I packed your parachute."

Plumb was staggered. All he could do was struggle to his feet and shake the man's hand. "I must tell you," Plumb finally said, "I've said a lot of prayers of thanks for your nimble fingers, but I didn't realize I'd have the opportunity of saying thanks in person."[1]

What if the navy had put the wrong person in the position of parachute rigger, the anonymous and the rarely thanked job that man performed during the Vietnam War? Charlie Plumb wouldn't have known about it until it was too late. And we wouldn't even know where the breakdown had occurred, because Plumb wouldn't have lived to tell the tale.

Today, Charlie Plumb is a motivational speaker to Fortune 500 companies, government agencies, and other organizations. He often tells the story of the man who packed his parachute, and he uses it to deliver a message on teamwork. He says, "In a world where downsizing forces us to do more with less, we must empower the team. 'Packing others' parachutes' can mean the difference in survival. Yours and your team's!"[2]

If you desire to pack the parachutes of your people, after you equip them, find the niche where they will flourish. That is the best way to empower them. They will grow to their potential, and your team will go to a whole new level.

MENTORING

101

WHAT EVERY LEADER NEEDS TO KNOW

Published in Nashville, Tennessee, by Thomas Nelson. Thomas Nelson is a registered trademark of Thomas Nelson, Inc.

Published in association with Yates & Yates, www.yates2.com

Thomas Nelson, Inc., titles may be purchased in bulk for educational, business, fund-raising, or sales promotional use. For information, please e-mail SpecialMarkets@ThomasNelson.com.

Portions of this book have been previously published in *Your Road Map for Success*, *The 21 Irrefutable Laws of Leadership*, *Developing the Leaders Around You*, *The 360° Leader*, and *Winning with People* by John C. Maxwell.

Library of Congress Cataloging-in-Publication Data

Maxwell, John C., 1947–
Mentoring 101 : what every leader needs to know / John C. Maxwell.
p. cm.
ISBN 978-1-4002-8022-3
1. Mentoring in business--Handbooks, manuals, etc. I. Title.
HF5385.M39 2008
658.3'124--dc22
2008026081

CONTENTS

PART 1

GETTING READY TO MENTOR OTHERS

What Do I Need to Know Before I Start?

*If you want to succeed as a mentor, first seek
to understand yourself and others.*

Most people who desire success focus almost entirely on themselves, not others, when they start to make the journey. They usually think in terms of what they can get—in position, power, prestige, money, and perks. But that's not the way to become truly successful. To do that, you have to give to others. As Douglas M. Lawson said, "We exist temporarily through what we take, but we live forever through what we give."

That's why it's so essential to focus on raising others to a higher level. And we can do that with people from every area of our lives—at work and home, in church and the clubhouse. That's evidently what Texas representative Wright Patman did, according to a story told by Senator Paul Simon. He said that Patman died at age eighty-two while serving in the U.S. House of Representatives. At his funeral, an older woman who lived in his district was heard to have said, "He rose up mighty high, but he brung us all up with him."

WHY MANY PEOPLE DON'T
MENTOR OTHERS

If mentoring others is such a rewarding calling, why doesn't everyone do it? One reason is that it takes work. But there are also many others. Here are a few of the most common ones.

INSECURITY

Virginia Arcastle commented, "When people are made to feel secure and important and appreciated, it will no longer be necessary for them to whittle down others in order to seem bigger in comparison." That's what insecure people tend to do—make themselves look better at others' expense.

Truly successful people, on the other hand, raise others up. And they don't feel threatened by the thought of having others become more successful and move to a higher level. They are growing and striving for their potential; they aren't worried about having someone replace them. They're nothing like the executive who wrote a memo to the personnel director saying, "Search the organization for an alert, aggressive young man who could step into my shoes—and when you find him, fire him." Raising up others is a successful person's joy.

EGO

Some people's egos are so huge that they have to be either the bride at the wedding or the corpse at the funeral. They think other people exist only to serve them in some way or another. Adolf Hitler was like that. According to Robert Waite, when Hitler was searching for a chauffeur, he interviewed thirty candidates for the job. He selected the shortest man in the group and kept him as his personal driver for the rest of his life—even though the man required special blocks under the driver's seat so that he could see over the steering wheel.[1] Hitler used others to make himself appear bigger and better than he really was. A person consumed with himself never considers spending time raising others up.

Inability to Discern People's "Success Seeds"

I believe every person has the seed of success inside. Too many people can't find it in themselves, let alone in others, and as a result, they don't reach their potential. But many do find that seed, and chances are, you are one of those people. The good news is that once you are able to find it in yourself, you're better able to do the same with others. When you do, it benefits both of you because you and the person you help will be able to fulfill the purposes for which each was born.

The ability to find another's seed of success takes commitment, diligence, and a genuine desire to focus on others. You have to look at the person's gifts, temperament, passions, successes, joys, and opportunities. And once you find that seed, you need to fertilize it with encouragement and water it with opportunity. If you do, the person will blossom before your eyes.

Wrong Concept of Success

True success is knowing your purpose, growing to reach your maximum potential, and sowing seeds to benefit others. The average person doesn't know that. He or she is scrambling to arrive at a destination or acquire more possessions than the next-door neighbors.

Fred Smith said: "Some of us tend to think, *I could have been a success, but I never had the opportunity. I wasn't born into the right family, or I didn't have the money to go to the best school.* But when we measure success by the extent we're using what we've received, it eliminates that frustration." And one of the most vital aspects of how we're using what we received comes in the area of helping others. As Cullen Hightower remarked, "A true measure of your worth includes all the benefits others have gained from your success."

Lack of Training

The final reason many people don't raise up the people around them is that they don't know how to do it. Mentoring others isn't something most people learn in school. Even if you went to college to become a teacher, you were probably trained to disseminate information to a group, not to come alongside a single person, pour into her life, and raise her to a higher level.

WHAT YOU NEED TO KNOW AS YOU START

Raising people to a higher level and helping them be successful involve more than giving them information or skills. If that were not the case, every new employee would go from trainee to success as soon as he understood how to do his job; every child would be successful whenever she learned something new at school. But success doesn't automatically follow knowledge. The process is complicated because you're working with people. However, understanding some basic concepts about people opens the door to your ability to develop others. For example, remind yourself that:

EVERYONE WANTS TO FEEL WORTHWHILE

Donald Laird said, "Always help people increase their own self-esteem. Develop your skill in making other people feel important. There is hardly a higher compliment you can pay an individual than helping him be useful and to find satisfaction from his usefulness." When a person doesn't feel good about himself, he will never believe he is successful, no matter what he accomplishes. But a person who feels worthwhile is ripe for success.

EVERYONE NEEDS AND RESPONDS TO ENCOURAGEMENT

One of my favorite quotes comes from industrialist Charles Schwab, who said, "I have yet to find the man, however exalted his station, who did not do better work and put forth greater effort under a spirit of approval than under a spirit of criticism." If you desire to raise another person up, then you need to become one of her staunchest supporters. People can tell when you don't believe in them.

PEOPLE ARE NATURALLY MOTIVATED

I've found that people are naturally motivated. If you doubt that, just watch toddlers soon after they learn to walk. They're into everything. They have natural curiosity, and you can't get them to stay still. I believe that innate sense of motivation continues to exist in adults, but for too many people it has been beaten down by lack of support, busyness, stress, bad attitudes, lack of appreciation, scarce resources, poor training, or faulty communication. To get people excited about growing to their potential, you need to remotivate them. Once you help them overcome the old things that knocked them down, they often motivate themselves.

PEOPLE BUY INTO THE PERSON BEFORE BUYING INTO THEIR LEADERSHIP

Many unsuccessful people who try to lead others have the mistaken belief that people will follow them because their cause is good. But that's not the way leadership works. People will follow you only when they believe in you. That principle applies even when you're offering to develop other people and raise them to a higher level.

The more you understand people, the greater your chance of success in mentoring. And if you have highly developed people skills and genuinely care about others, the process will probably come to you naturally.

How Do I Adopt a Mentor's Mind-set?

Mentoring is who you are
as much as what you do.

Whether you have a natural gift for interacting positively with people or you have to really work at it, you are capable of mentoring others and lifting them to a higher level. You can help them develop a road map for success and go on the journey with you as long as you keep growing as a person and a leader.

Think Like a Mentor

Here are the steps you will need to take in order to become the kind of mentor you are capable of being:

1. Make People Development Your Top Priority

If you want to succeed in developing people, you have to make it a top priority. It's always easier to dismiss people than to develop them. If you don't believe it, just ask any employer or divorce attorney. But many people don't realize that while dismissing others is easy, it also has a high price. In business, the costs come from lost productivity, administrative costs of firing and hiring, and low morale. In marriage, the cost is often broken lives.

I learned this lesson when I was in my first pastorate. My desire was to build a large church. I thought I would be a success if I did. And I accomplished that goal. I took that small congregation from 3 people to more than 250, and I did it in a tiny rural community. But I did most things myself—with my wife, Margaret's, help. I didn't develop anyone else. As a result, we had success only in the places I touched; we had complaints in all the places I didn't touch; and many things fell apart after I left.

I learned a lot from that experience, and in my second position, I made it a priority to develop others. Over an eight-year period, I developed thirty-five people, and they built up that church and made it successful. And after I left, the church was just as successful as when I was there because those other leaders were able to carry on without me. If you want to make a difference in the lives of others, do the same. Commit yourself to developing people.

2. Limit Who You Take Along

As you begin to develop people, think of it as being similar to a trip in a small private plane. If you try to take too many people along, you'll never get off the ground. Besides, your time is limited.

When I teach leadership seminars, I always teach what's known as the Pareto (80/20) Principle: In a nutshell, it says that if you focus your attention on the top 20 percent in anything you do, you will get an 80 percent return. In the case of developing people, you should spend 80 percent of your time developing only the top 20 percent of the people around you. That would include the most important people in your life, such as your family, and the people who have the most potential. If you try to mentor and develop more people than that, you're going to be spreading yourself too thin.

3. DEVELOP RELATIONSHIPS BEFORE STARTING OUT

The best leaders understand the important role of relationships when it comes to success. For example, Lee Iacocca once asked legendary Green Bay Packers coach Vince Lombardi what it took to make a winning team. Here's how Lombardi answered:

> There are a lot of coaches with good ball clubs who know the fundamentals and have plenty of discipline but still don't win the game. Then you come to the third ingredient: if you're going to play together as a team, you've got to care for one another. You've got to love each other. Each player has to be thinking about the next guy and saying to himself: "If I don't block that man, Paul is going to get his legs broken. I have to do my job well in order that he can do his."
>
> The difference between mediocrity and greatness is the feeling these guys have for each other.[1]

That concept doesn't apply only to football. It also applies to individuals traveling together for a season as mentor and mentee. If the personal relationships aren't there first, people won't travel far together.

As you prepare to develop other people, take time to get to know each other. Ask them to share their story with you—their journey so far. Find out what makes them tick, their strengths and weaknesses, their temperaments. And spend some time with them outside the environment where you typically see them. If you work together, then play sports together. If you know each other from church, meet with them at their workplace. If you go to school together, then spend some time together at home. You can even use this principle with your family. For example, if you spend time with your children outside your everyday environment, you'll learn a lot more about them. It will develop your relationship in ways it hasn't before, and it will help you grow.

Another advantage to building relationships with people before starting on the journey together is that you find out what kind of "traveling companions" you're going to have. As you bring others alongside you for the success journey, pick people you expect to like. Then get to know them to verify your choice. It's the best way to be effective—and enjoy the trip.

4. Give Help Unconditionally

When you start developing people, you should never go into it with the idea of getting something out of it. That attitude will almost certainly backfire on you. If you expect to get something in return and you don't, you will become bitter. And if you get back less than you expect, you'll resent the time you spent. No, you have to go into the process expecting nothing but personal satisfaction. Give for the sake of giving—just for the joy of seeing another person learn to fly. When you approach it that way, your attitude will always remain positive. And the times you do get something in return, it's a wonderful win-win situation.

5. Let Them Fly with You for a While

I want to share a secret with you. It guarantees success in mentoring. Are you ready? Here it is: never work alone. I know that sounds too simple, but it is truly the secret to developing others. Whenever you do anything that you want to pass along to others, take someone with you.

This isn't necessarily a natural practice for many of us. The learning model that's used in America by most people for teaching others was passed down to us from the Greeks. It's a cognitive "classroom" approach, like the one used by Socrates to teach Plato, and Plato to teach Aristotle. The leader stands and speaks, asking questions or lecturing. The follower sits at his feet, listening. His goal is to comprehend the instructor's ideas.

But that's not the only model available for developing others. We also have one used by another ancient culture: the Hebrews. Their method was more like on-the-job training. It was built on relationships and common experience. It's what craftspeople have done for centuries. They take apprentices who work alongside them until they master their craft and are able to pass it along to others. Their model looks something like this:

- *I do it.* First I learn to do the job. I have to understand the why as well as the how, and I try to perfect my craft.
- *I do it—and you watch.* I demonstrate it while you observe, and during the process, I explain what I'm doing and why.
- *You do it—and I watch.* As soon as possible, we exchange roles. I give you permission and authority to take over the job, but I stay with you to offer advice, correction, and encouragement.
- *You do it.* Once you're proficient, I step back and let you work alone. The learner is drawn up to a higher level. And as soon as he is on that higher level, the teacher is free to move on to higher things.

In all the years I've been equipping and developing others, I've never found a better way to do it than this. And for a long time, whenever I got ready to perform one of my duties, I made it a practice to take along the person I wanted to equip for the task. Before we did it, we talked about what was going to happen. And afterward, we'd discuss what we did.

Maybe you've already done this with people. If you haven't, try it, because it really works. Just remember to make including others part of the planning process. You don't want to find yourself going alone, nor do you want to just grab anybody who is available. Your goal is to spend your time with the people you've targeted to develop. And always select people and match them to tasks according to their strengths. Anyone who spends most of her time working in an area of weakness for a prolonged period of time will get frustrated and burned-out. But a person developed in an area of strength will be catapulted toward her potential.

6. PUT FUEL IN THEIR TANK

People won't get far without fuel—and that means resources for their continuing personal growth. Any mentor can give that valuable gift to someone he is developing. Many people don't know where to find good resources or what kinds of materials to select, especially when they're just starting out.

I regularly share books, CDs, and DVDs with the people I'm developing and equipping. And I also enjoy sending them to seminars. My goal is always to "bring something to the table" when I spend time with someone, whether it's an employee, a colleague, or a friend. You can do the same thing for others. There are few greater thrills than putting into others' hands a resource that can help take them to the next level.

7. Stay with Them Until They Can Solo Successfully

I've been told that every student pilot looks forward to the first solo flight with anticipation—and a certain amount of fear. But a good flight instructor wouldn't allow a student to take that solo flight until he is ready, nor would he let a student avoid her solo once she is ready. I guess you could say that's the difference between a true mentor and a wannabe. It's kind of like the difference between a flight instructor and a travel agent. The one stays with you, guiding you through the entire process until you're ready to fly. The other hands you a ticket and says, "I hope you have a good flight."

As you develop people, remember that you are taking them on the journey toward success with you, not sending them. Stay with them until they're ready to fly. And when they are ready, get them on their way.

8. Clear the Flight Path

Even after teaching people to fly, providing them with fuel, and giving them permission to take the controls, some mentors don't take the last step required to make their people successful.

They don't give them an unencumbered flight path. They usually don't intentionally restrict the people they're developing, but it still happens.

Here are several common obstacles created by mentors for potential leaders:

- *Lack of clear direction:* Many times a potential leader gets mentored and learns how to do a job, then he is left adrift, without any direction from his leader.

- *Bureaucracy:* Or she learns how her leader works and thinks, and then she is put into a bureaucratic system that stifles the innovative spirit that the mentor just engendered.
- *Isolation:* Everyone needs a community of people with whom to share and from whom to draw support. Often if the mentor does not provide it, the new leader won't have it.
- *Busywork:* Work with no perceived value demoralizes and demotivates people.
- *Poor or dishonest communication:* An agenda that isn't communicated honestly to the person being developed hinders the relationship and confuses the potential leader.

Once you begin to develop others, check to see that you're not leaving obstacles in their path. Give them clear direction, positive support, and the freedom to fly. What you do can make the difference between their failure and success. And when they succeed, so do you.

9. Help Them Repeat the Process

After you've done everything you can to help your people, and they have taken off and are soaring, you may think you're finished. But you're not. There is still one more step you must take to complete the process. You should help them learn to repeat the development process and mentor others. You see, there is no success without a successor.

A great joy in my life has been to see how leaders I've developed and equipped have turned around and repeated the process with others. It must be similar to the joy a great-grandfather feels as he looks at the generations that have been raised up in his family. With each successive generation, the success continues.

This process of reproduction has become a pattern in my life. For example, when I got to San Diego in 1981, I hired an assistant named Barbara Brumagin. I trained her, teaching her everything she needed to know to maximize my time and talents. She stayed with me for eleven years. But before she left me, she equipped Linda Eggers, who is my assistant today.

Perhaps the most remarkable example of development has been Dan Reiland, who was my executive pastor for many years. During the first eight years he worked for me, I spent a great deal of time developing him. Then for the next six years, he took over the responsibility of mentoring and equipping my entire staff. In addition, he has also personally developed well over one hundred people on his own. Many of those people are continuing the process by producing yet another generation of successful leaders. Dan now develops the staff at 12Stone Church in Georgia.

Lift Others Higher

The positive effects of developing others are remarkable. But you don't have to be a remarkable or unusually talented person to mentor others. You can raise up people around you and teach them to fly. It does take desire and a commitment to the process, but it is the most rewarding part of success. Raising up others is the greatest joy in the world. You see, once people learn to fly, they're capable of going just about anywhere. And sometimes when they're flying high, they help you along too.

Take others with you and help them change their lives for the better. Nothing in life is more fun—or has a greater return. You'll never regret the time you invest in people.

Part II

Engaging in the Mentoring Process

3

Whom Should I Mentor?

Invest your time in people
who will give the greatest return.

Over time I've learned this meaningful lesson: The people closest to me determine my level of success or failure. The better they are, the better I am. And if I want to go to the highest level, I can do it only with the help of other people. We have to take each other higher.

I discovered this truth about twenty years ago as I approached my fortieth birthday. At that time I already felt very successful. I was the leader of the largest church in my denomination. I had published five books. I was recognized as an authority on leadership, and I was teaching the subject live in conferences and via audio lessons every month. I was fulfilling the purpose for which I was created, daily growing to my potential, and sowing seeds that benefited others. But my desire was to make an even greater impact on others. I wanted to go to a whole new level.

My problem was that I had hit a wall. I was running a large organization that required much of my time. I had a family. I was writing books, leadership lessons, and sermons continually. And on top of that, my travel schedule was packed. I couldn't squeeze another thing into my schedule with a shoehorn and a bucket of axle grease. That's when I made the amazing discovery. The only places where my influence and productivity were growing were where I had identified potential leaders and developed them.

My intention in developing leaders had been to help them improve themselves, but I found I was also benefiting. Spending time with them had been like investing money. They had grown, and at the same time I had reaped incredible dividends. That's when I realized that if I was to make it to the next level, I was going to have to extend myself through others. I would find leaders and pour my life into them, doing my best to bring them up to a new level. And as they improved, so would I.

FINDING THE RIGHT PEOPLE
FOR THE JOURNEY

Over the years, I've narrowed down what I look for in a potential leader that I want to mentor to only ten things, and I want to share them with you. Here they are in order of importance. The people I want to mentor . . .

1. MAKE THINGS HAPPEN

Millionaire philanthropist Andrew Carnegie said, "As I grow older, I pay less attention to what men say. I just watch what they do." I've found that to be sound advice. And as I've watched what people do, I've discovered that the ones I want with me are people who make things happen. These people discover resources in places you thought were barren. They find prospects where you believed there weren't any. They create opportunities where you thought none existed. They take something average and make it exceptional. They never make excuses—they always find a way to make things happen.

About twenty years ago, I saw a piece in a magazine and cut it out because it's a great example of how someone with a lot of potential really knows how to make things happen. It was called "Sel Not Spel." It said that a recently hired salesman wrote his first sales report to the home office after working in his territory the first week. It shocked the sales manager because he suddenly realized that he had hired someone who was illiterate. Here's what the report said: "I went and seen this outfit which ain't never bot nothin from us befour and I sole em a good order. Now I'm movin on to Nu Yourk."

The manager was in a panic. But before he could get hold of the salesman to fire him, he received a second report. It said, "I done been hear fer too days and sole them haff a millyon."

Then the manager was really confused. He couldn't keep an illiterate salesman, but he couldn't fire a salesman who had outsold everyone else on the sales force. So he did what every good middle manager does: he dumped the problem in the lap of the company's president.

The next morning, everyone in the sales department was amazed to see the salesman's two letters on the bulletin board along with the following memo from the president: "We bin spendin weigh two much time tryin to spel in stead of tryin to sel. Lets all try to get our sails up. Reed these too letters from hour best salsman. He's doin a grate job and all you shud go out and do like he done."

Even under the worst of circumstances—or with major disabilities—people with potential make things happen. Dr. George W. Crane observed, "There is no future in any job. The future lies in the person who holds the job." If you want to go far on the success journey, partner with others who know how to make things happen.

2. SEE AND SEIZE OPPORTUNITIES

Many people are able to recognize an opportunity after it has already passed them by. But seeing opportunities coming, that's a different matter. Opportunities are seldom labeled. That's why you have to learn what they look like and how to seize them.

The best people to mentor don't sit back and wait for opportunities to come to them. They make it their responsibility to go out and find them. It's similar to the two ways you can go about picking up someone you don't know from the airport. One way is to make a sign with the name of the person you're expecting, stand near the baggage claim area, hold up the sign, and wait for the person to find you. If he sees you, great. If he doesn't, you keep waiting. The other way is to find out what the person looks like, position yourself strategically near the right gate, and search for him until you find him. There is a world of difference between the two approaches.

Ellen Metcalf said, "I would like to amend the idea of being in the right place at the right time. There are many people who were in the right place but didn't know it. You have to recognize when the right place and the right time fuse and take advantage of that opportunity. There are plenty of opportunities out there. You can't sit back and wait." Good potential leaders know that, and they don't rely on luck either. According to Walter P. Chrysler, founder of the automotive corporation that bears his name, "The reason so many people never get anywhere in life is because when opportunity knocks, they are out in the backyard looking for four-leaf clovers."

Ask yourself, of the people around you, who always seems able to recognize opportunities and grab hold of them? The people with these qualities are the ones you're probably going to want to spend time with mentoring.

3. INFLUENCE OTHERS

Everything rises and falls on leadership. That's true because a person's ability to make things happen in and through others depends entirely on her ability to lead them. Without leadership, there is no teamwork, and people go their own way. If your dream is big and will require the teamwork of a group of people, then any potential leaders you select to go with you on the journey will need to be people of influence. After all, that's what leadership is—influence. And when you think about it, all leaders have two things in common: they're going somewhere, and they're able to persuade others to go with them.

As you look at the people around you, consider the following:

- *Who influences them?* You can tell a lot about whom they will influence and how they will go about doing it by knowing who their heroes and mentors are.
- *Whom do they influence?* You'll be able to judge their current level of leadership effectiveness by whom they influence.
- *Is their influence increasing or decreasing?* You can tell whether a person is a past leader or a potential leader by examining which direction the level of influence is going.

To be a good judge of potential leaders, don't just see the person—see all the people that person influences. The greater the influence, the greater the leadership potential and the ability to get others to work together.

4. Add Value

Every person around you has an effect on you and your ability to fulfill your vision. You've probably noticed this before. Some people seem to hinder you, always taking more from you than they give in return. Others add value to you, improving everything you do. When they come alongside you, synergy develops that takes both of you to a new level.

Lots of wonderful people have added value to me through the years. Many of them have made it their main goal in life to help me. They complement my weaknesses and encourage my strengths. Their presence with me on the journey actually expands my vision. Alone, maybe I could have achieved some success. But they have truly made me much better than I could have been without them. And in response, I have always given them my best, trusted them implicitly, given them opportunities to make a difference, and added value to their lives.

There are probably people in your life with whom you experience synergy. You inspire and take each other to higher levels. Can you think of anybody better to take on the success journey? Not only would they help you go far, but they would make the journey of life more fun.

5. Attract Other Leaders

As you look for potential leaders to develop, you need to realize that there are really two kinds of leaders: those who attract followers and those who attract other leaders. People who attract and team up only with followers will never be able to do anything beyond what they can personally touch or supervise. For each person they interact with, they're influencing only one person—a follower. But people who attract leaders influence many other people through their interaction. Their team can be incredible, especially if the leaders they recruit also attract other leaders.

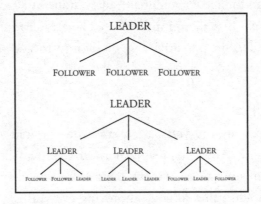

Besides the obvious factor of influence, there are other significant differences between people who attract followers and people who attract leaders. Here are a few:

LEADERS WHO ATTRACT FOLLOWERS . . .	LEADERS WHO ATTRACT LEADERS . . .
Need to be needed.	Want to be succeeded.
Want recognition.	Want to reproduce themselves.
Focus on others' weaknesses.	Focus on others' strengths.
Want to hold on to power.	Want to share power.
Spend their time with others.	Invest their time in others.
Are good leaders.	Are great leaders.
Experience some success.	Experience incredible success.

As you look for people to join you on the journey toward success, look for leaders who attract other leaders. They will be able to multiply your success. But also know this—in the long run, you can only lead people whose leadership ability is less than or equal to your own. To keep attracting better and better leaders, you will have to keep developing your leadership ability. In that way, you and your team will continue growing not only in potential, but also in effectiveness.

6. EQUIP OTHERS

It's one thing to attract other people to you and have them join you as you journey toward success. It's another to equip them with a road map for the trip. The best people always give others more than an invitation—they provide the means to get them there.

Think about this as you search for potential leaders: A person with charisma alone can draw others to her, yet she may not be able to persuade them to join her in pursuit of a dream. However, a leader who is an equipper can empower an army of successful people capable of going anywhere and accomplishing almost anything. As Harvey Firestone said, "It is only as we develop others that we permanently succeed."

7. PROVIDE INSPIRING IDEAS

Nineteenth-century author-playwright Victor Hugo observed, "There's nothing more powerful than an idea whose time has come." Ideas are the greatest resource a successful person could ever have. And when you surround yourself with creative people, you're never at a loss for inspiring ideas.

If you and the people around you continually generate good ideas, all of you have a better opportunity to reach your potential. According to Art Cornwell, author of *Freeing the Corporate Mind: How to Spur Innovation in Business*, creative thinking is what generates ideas. And the better you understand how to generate ideas, the better off you'll be. He suggests:

- The only truly bad ideas are those that die without giving rise to other ideas.

- If you want good ideas, you need a lot of ideas.
- It doesn't matter if "it ain't broke." It probably still can use fixing.
- Great ideas are nothing more than the restructuring of what you already know.
- When all your ideas are added together, the sum should represent your breakthrough.[1]

You are capable of generating good ideas—probably better able than you think. But you can never have too many ideas. That would be like saying you have too much money or too many resources when you're working on a project. That's why you would do well to get people around you who will continue to inspire you with their ideas. And when you find someone with whom you have natural chemistry, the kind that inspires each of you to greatness, you'll find that you always have more ideas than time to carry them out.

8. POSSESS UNCOMMONLY POSITIVE ATTITUDES

A good attitude is important to success. It often determines how far you will be able to go. But don't underestimate the importance of a positive attitude in the people around you either. When you travel with others, you can go only as fast as the slowest person and as far as the weakest one can travel. Having people around you with negative attitudes is like running a race with a ball and chain on your ankle. You may be able to run for a while, but you're going to get tired fast, and you certainly won't be able to run as far as you'd like.

9. LIVE UP TO THEIR COMMITMENTS

It's been said that commitment is another name for success. And that's really true. Newsman Walter Cronkite declared, "I can't imagine a person becoming a success who doesn't give this game of life everything he's got."

Commitment takes a person to a whole new level when it comes to success. Look at the advantages of commitment as described by motivational speaker Joe Griffith:

You cannot keep a committed person from success. Place stumbling blocks in his way, and he takes them for stepping-stones, and on them he will climb to greatness. Take away his money, and he makes spurs of his poverty to urge him on. The person who succeeds has a program; he fixes his course and adheres to it; he lays his plans and executes them; he goes straight to his goal. He is not pushed this side and that every time a difficulty is thrust in his way. If he can't go over it, he goes through it.[2]

When the people on your team share your level of commitment, success is inevitable. Commitment helps you overcome obstacles and continue moving forward on the success journey no matter how tough the going gets. It is the key to success in every aspect of life: marriage, business, personal development, hobbies, sports—you name it. Commitment can carry you a very long way.

10. HAVE LOYALTY

The last quality you should look for in people to join you on your journey is loyalty. Although this alone does not ensure success in another person, a lack of loyalty is sure to ruin your relationship with him or her. Think of it this way: When you're looking for potential leaders, if someone you're considering lacks loyalty, he is disqualified. Don't even consider trying to develop him, because in the end, he'll hurt you more than help you.

So what does it mean for others to be loyal to you?

- *They love you unconditionally.* They accept you with your strengths and weaknesses intact. They genuinely care for you, not just for what you can do for them. And they are neither trying to make you into someone you're not nor putting you on a pedestal.
- *They represent you well to others.* Loyal people always paint a positive picture of you with others. They may take you to task privately or hold you accountable, but they never criticize you to others.

- *They are able to laugh and cry with you as you travel together.* Loyal people are willing and able to share your joys and sorrows. They make the trip less lonely.
- *They make your dream their dream.* Some people will undoubtedly share the journey with you only briefly. You help one another for a while and then go your separate ways. But a few—a special few—will want to come alongside you and help you for the rest of the journey. These people make your dream their dream. They will be loyal unto death, and when they combine that loyalty with other talents and abilities, they can be some of your most valuable assets. If you find people like that, take good care of them.

The funny thing about loyalty is that the more successful you are, the more of an issue it becomes.

PASS IT ON

I've been very fortunate as I've traveled through life. Not only have I had wonderful people come alongside me and take the journey with me, but I've also had others take me along when I couldn't make it on my own. And that's what life is all about—people helping people and adding value to others.

As you pick people to mentor, focus on people who will not only make the most of what you give and help you. Pick people who will pass it on. Mentoring is meant to be shared.

4

HOW CAN I SET THEM UP
FOR SUCCESS?

See everyone you mentor as a "10."

I want to ask you a question: Who is your favorite teacher of all time? Think back through all your years in school, from kindergarten to the last year of your education. Who stands out? Is there a teacher who changed your life? Most of us have one. Mine was actually a Sunday school teacher named Glen Leatherwood. Who was yours?

What made that teacher different? Was it subject knowledge? Was it teaching technique? Though your teacher may have possessed great knowledge and mastered outstanding technique, I'm willing to bet that what separated that teacher from all of the others was his or her belief in you. That teacher probably saw you as a 10. The teacher who browbeats you and tells you how ignorant or undisciplined you are isn't the one who inspires you to learn and grow. It's the one who thinks you're wonderful and tells you so.

Now I'd like you to think about your working life and the leaders you've worked for over the years. As you think about them, ask yourself the following questions:

- *Who gets my best effort?* The leader who believes I'm a 10 or the leader who believes I'm a 2?
- *Whom do I enjoy working with?* The leader who believes I'm a 10 or the leader who believes I'm a 2?
- *Who is the easiest for me to approach?* The leader who believes I'm a 10 or the leader who believes I'm a 2?
- *Who wants the best for me?* The leader who believes I'm a 10 or the leader who believes I'm a 2?
- *Whom will I learn the most from?* The leader who believes I'm a 10 or the leader who believes I'm a 2?

Mentoring leaders get more out of their people because they think more of their people. They respect and value them, and as a result, their people want to follow them. The positive, uplifting attitude that they bring to leadership creates a positive working environment where everyone on the team has a place and purpose—and where everyone shares in the win.

For some leaders, this is easy and natural, especially if they have positive personalities. I find that people who were greatly encouraged and valued as children often build up others almost instinctively. But it is a skill that can be learned by anyone, and it is a must for anyone who desires to become a successful person.

How to Treat Others Like a 10

If you want to really shine in this area, apply the following suggestions when working with your people:

1. See Them as Who They Can Become

Author Bennett Cerf wrote that J. William Stanton, who served many years as a representative from Ohio in the United States Congress, treasured a letter he received from the Chamber of Commerce in Painesville, Ohio, dated 1949. The letter declined Stanton's offer to bring a new congressman as the featured speaker for a fund-raising dinner. The missive reads: "We feel that this year we really need a big-name speaker who'll be a drawing card so we're hoping to bag the head football coach at John Carroll University. Thanks anyhow for suggesting Representative John F. Kennedy."[1] Do you have any idea who that coach might have been? I certainly don't.

Do you have a potential JFK in your midst? Or a Jack Welch? Or a Mother Teresa? It's easy to recognize great leadership and great talent once people have already blossomed, but how about before they come into their own?

Look for the great potential that is within each person you lead. When you find it, do your best to draw it out. Some leaders are so insecure that when they see a potential all-star, they try to push that person down because they worry that his or her high performance will make them look bad. But successful leaders reach down to lift those people up. They recognize that people with huge potential are going to be successful anyway. The best role they can assume is that of discoverer and encourager. In that way, they add value to them and get to be a positive part of the process of their emergence as leaders.

2. Let Them "Borrow" Your Belief in Them

In 1989, Kevin Myers moved from Grand Rapids, Michigan, to Lawrenceville, Georgia, to plant a church. Kevin was a sharp young leader whose future looked bright, and his sponsoring organization, Kentwood Community Church, was glad to support his efforts.

Kevin did all the right things as he prepared for the first service of Crossroads Community Church. He spent weeks talking to people in the community, he selected a good location, and he got his volunteers ready. When he opened the doors for the first time, his hopes were crushed as only about ninety people showed up—about a third of what he had expected. It was a major disappointment, because Kevin had been on staff at a large, dynamic, growing church, and he had little desire to lead a small congregation. He was determined to persevere, however, figuring that in a year or two, he would get over the hump and build the kind of church that matched his vision.

After three years of struggle and little growth, Kevin was ready to throw in the towel. He made a trip to Michigan to meet with Wayne Schmidt, his former boss at Kentwood and the original sponsor of Kevin's church-planting endeavor. Feeling like a failure, Kevin explained to Wayne that he needed a job, because he was planning to close down the church in Georgia. Wayne's response changed Kevin's life. He said, "Kevin, if you've lost faith, borrow mine."

Uncertain about his future, but grateful to Wayne for his faith in him, Kevin returned to Georgia and didn't give up. Slowly, as Kevin grew in his leadership, so did his congregation. As I write this, Kevin leads 3,400 people every week, putting his congregation in the top 1 percent in the United States.

When the people you lead don't believe in themselves, you can help them believe in themselves, just as Wayne did for Kevin. Think of it as a loan, something you are giving freely, but that will later return with dividends as that person succeeds.

3. Catch Them Doing Something Right

If you desire to see everyone as a 10 and help them believe in themselves, you need to encourage them by catching them doing something right. And that is really countercultural. We are trained our whole lives to catch people doing something wrong. If our parents and teachers caught us doing something, you can bet it was something wrong. So we tend to think in those same terms.

When you focus on the negative and catch people doing something wrong, it has no real power to make them any better. When we catch people doing something wrong, they become defensive. They make excuses. They evade. On the other hand, if we catch people doing something right, it gives them positive reinforcement. It helps them tap into their potential. It makes them want to do better.

Make it part of your daily agenda to look for things going right. They don't have to be big things, though of course you want to praise those things as well. It can be almost anything, as long as you are sincere in your praise.

4. Believe the Best—Give Others the Benefit of the Doubt

When we examine ourselves, we naturally give ourselves the benefit of the doubt. Why? Because we see ourselves in the light of our intentions. On the other hand, when we look at others, we usually judge them according to their actions. Think about how much more positive our interaction with others would be if we believed the best in them and gave them the benefit of the doubt, just as we do for ourselves.

Many people are reluctant to adopt this attitude because they fear that others will consider them naive or will take advantage of them. The reality is that trustful people are not weaker than distrustful ones; they are actually stronger. As evidence, I offer the following trust fallacies and the facts that refute them, researched by sociology professor Morton Hunt.

Fallacy: Trustful people are more gullible.

Fact: Trustful people are no more likely to be fooled than mistrustful ones.

Fallacy: Trustful people are less perceptive than mistrustful people of what others are really feeling.

Fact: People who scored high on trust are actually better than others at reading people.

Fallacy: People with a poor opinion of themselves are more trustful than people with a good opinion of themselves.

Fact: The opposite is true. People with high self-esteem are more willing to take emotional risks.

Fallacy: Stupid people are trustful; smart people are mistrustful.

Fact: People with high aptitude or scholastic scores are no more mistrustful or skeptical than people judged to be less intelligent.

Fallacy: Trustful people rely on others to direct their lives for them; mistrustful people rely on themselves.

Fact: The opposite is true. People who feel controlled by outside persons and forces are more mistrustful, while those who feel in charge of their lives are more trustful.

Fallacy: Trustful people are no more trustworthy than mistrustful people.

Fact: Mistrustful people are less trustworthy. Research validates what the ancient Greeks used to say: "He who mistrusts most should be trusted least."[2]

I'm not saying that you should become like an ostrich and stick your head in the sand. All I'm suggesting is that you give others the same consideration you give yourself. It's not a lot to ask, and the dividends it will pay you relationally can be huge.

5. REALIZE THAT "10" HAS MANY DEFINITIONS

What does it mean to be a 10? When you started reading this chapter and I suggested that you see everyone as a 10, did a certain image of a 10 come to mind? And did you immediately start comparing the people who work for you to that image and find them coming up short? I wouldn't be surprised if that were the case, because I think most of us have a pretty narrow view of what constitutes a 10.

When it comes to improving in skills, I believe that most people cannot increase their ability beyond about two points on a scale of 1 to 10. So, for example, if you were born a 4 when it comes to math, no matter how hard you work at it, you will probably never become better than a 6. But here's the good news. Everybody is exceptional at something, and a 10 doesn't always look the same.

In their book *Now, Discover Your Strengths* (Free Press, 2001), Marcus Buckingham and Donald O. Clifton identify thirty-four areas of strength that they believe people exhibit—anything from responsibility to woo (the ability to win over others). And the authors assert that everyone has at least one skill they can perform better than the next ten thousand others. That means they believe everyone can be a 10 in some area. You can always focus on that area when encouraging one of your employees.

But let's say you employ someone who does not have any skill that is a 10 or could be developed into a 10. Does that mean you write him off as hopeless? No. You see, there are other non-skill areas where a person can grow into a 10 no matter what his or her starting point is—areas such as attitude, desire, discipline, and perseverance. If you don't see 10 potential anywhere else, look for it there.

6. Place People in Their Strength Zones

If it's in your power, help people find their best place in their careers. As you think about the people you mentor, try to do the following for each individual:

- *Discover Their True Strengths.* Most people do not discover their strengths on their own. They often get drawn into the routine of day-to-day living and simply get busy. They rarely explore their strengths or reflect on their successes or failures. That's why it is so valuable for them to have a mentoring leader who is genuinely interested in helping them recognize their strengths.

    There are many helpful tools available that you can use to aid people in the process of self-discovery, but often the most valuable help you can give will be based on your personal observations.

- *Give Them the Right Job.* Moving someone from a job he hates to the right job can be life changing. One executive I interviewed said he moved a person on his staff to four different places in the organization, trying to find the right fit. Because he'd placed her wrong so many times, he was almost ready to give up on her. But he knew she had great potential, and she was right for the organization. Finally, after he found the right job for her, she was a star!

    Trying to get the right person in the right job can take a lot of time and energy. Let's face it. Isn't it easier for a leader to just put people where it is most convenient and get on with the work? Once again, this is an area where leaders' desire for action works against them. Fight against your natural tendency to make a decision and move on. Don't be afraid to move people around if they're not shining the way you think they could.

- *Identify the Skills They'll Need, and Provide World-Class Training.* Every job requires a particular set of skills that employees must possess in order to be really successful. Even someone with great personal strengths and a great "fit" will not truly be working in his strength zone if he doesn't have these skills. As a mentoring leader, it is your job to make sure your people acquire what they need to win.

In *The 17 Indisputable Laws of Teamwork*, the Law of the Niche says, "All players have a place where they add the most value." Whatever that niche is determines the best role that person should assume on your team. And it really does make a difference. When leaders really get this, the teams they lead perform at an incredible level. And it reflects positively on those leaders. I don't think it is an exaggeration to say that the success of a leader is determined more by putting people into their strength zones than by anything else.

7. GIVE THEM THE "10" TREATMENT

Most leaders treat people according to the number that they place on them. If employees are performing at an average level—let's say as a 5— then the boss gives them the 5 treatment. But I believe people always deserve their leader's best, even when they are not giving their best. I say that because I believe every person has value as a human being and deserves to be treated with respect and dignity. That doesn't mean you reward bad performance. It just means that you treat people well and take the high road with them, even if they don't do the same for you.

It's been my observation that people usually rise to the leader's expectations—if they like the leader. If you have built solid relationships with your employees and they genuinely like and respect you, they will work hard and give their best.

ALWAYS SET PEOPLE UP FOR SUCCESS

I've learned a lot of things about leadership from many leaders over the years, but the one I still admire most is my father, Melvin Maxwell. In December 2004, I visited my parents in the Orlando area, and while I was there, I was scheduled to participate in a conference call. Because I needed a quiet place to do it, my dad graciously let me use his office.

As I sat at his desk, I noticed a card next to the phone, with the following words written in my father's hand:

#1 Build people up by encouragement.
#2 Give people credit by acknowledgment.
#3 Give people recognition by gratitude.

I knew in a second why it was there. My father had written it to remind him of how he was to treat people as he spoke on the phone with them. And I was instantly reminded that Dad, more than anyone else, taught me to see everyone as a 10.

Begin today to see and lead people as they can be, not as they are, and you will be amazed by how they respond to you. Not only will your relationship with them improve and their productivity increase, but you also will help them rise to their potential and become who they were created to be.

5

How Do I Help Them
Do Better Work?

Equip the people you mentor
for professional success.

At this point you know how to identify potential leaders, build relationships with them, create an environment in which they'll grow, and encourage them. It is time to look more specifically at how to prepare them for leadership in their work. That preparation process is called equipping.

Remember, all good mentoring relationships begin with a personal relationship. As your people get to know and like you, their desire to follow your direction and learn from you will increase. If they don't like you, they will not want to learn from you, and the equipping process slows down or even stops.

EQUIP FOR EXCELLENCE

Once you've gotten to know the person you desire to mentor, it's time to get started on the equipping process. Here's how to proceed:

SHARE YOUR DREAM

Sharing your dream helps people to know you and where you're going. There's no act that will better show them your heart and your motivation. Woodrow Wilson once said:

> We grow by dreams. All big individuals are dreamers. They see things in the soft haze of a spring day, or in the red fire on a long winter's evening. Some of us let those great dreams die, but others nourish and protect them; nourish them through bad days until they bring them to the sunshine and light which comes always to those who sincerely hope that their dreams will come true.

I have often wondered, "Does the person make the dream or does the dream make the person?" My conclusion is both are equally true. All good leaders have a dream. All great leaders share their dream with others who can help them make it a reality. As Florence Littauer suggests, you must:

> *Dare to dream:* Have the desire to do something bigger than yourself.
> *Prepare the dream:* Do your homework; be ready when the opportunity comes.
> *Wear the dream:* Do it.
> *Share the dream:* Make others a part of the dream, and it will become even greater than you had hoped.

ASK FOR COMMITMENT

In his book *The One Minute Manager*, Ken Blanchard says, "There's a difference between interest and commitment. When you are interested in doing something, you do it only when it is convenient. When you are committed to something, you accept no excuses." Don't equip people who are merely interested. Equip the ones who are committed.

Commitment is the one quality above all others that enables a potential leader to become a successful leader. Without commitment, there can be no success. Football coach Lou Holtz recognized the difference between being merely involved and being truly committed. He pointed out, "The kamikaze pilot that was able to fly 50 missions was involved—but never committed."

To determine whether your people are committed, first you must make sure they know what it will cost them to become leaders. That means that you must be sure not to undersell the job—let them know what it's going to take. Only then will they know what they are committing to. If they won't commit, don't go any further in the equipping process. Don't waste your time.

SET GOALS FOR GROWTH

People need clear objectives set before them if they are to achieve anything of value. Success never comes instantaneously. It comes from taking many small steps. A set of goals becomes a map a potential leader can follow in order to grow. As Shad Helmstetter states in *You Can Excel in Times of Change*, "It is the goal that shapes the plan; it is the plan that sets the action; it is the action that achieves the result; and it is the result that brings the success. And it all begins with the simple word *goal*." We, as equipping leaders, must introduce our people to the practice of setting and achieving goals.

Comic and actress Lily Tomlin once said, "I always wanted to be somebody, but I should have been more specific." Many people today find themselves in the same situation. They have some vague idea of what success is, and they know they want to achieve it. But they haven't worked out any kind of plan to get there. I have found that the greatest achievers in life are people who set goals for themselves and then work hard to reach them. What they *get* by reaching the goals is not nearly as important as what they *become* by reaching them.

When you help your people set goals, use the following guidelines:

Make the goals appropriate. Always keep in mind the job you want the people to do and the desired result: the development of your people into effective leaders. Identify goals that will contribute to that larger goal.

Make the goals attainable. Nothing will make people want to quit faster than facing unachievable goals. I like the comment made by Ian MacGregor, former AMAX Corporation chairman of the board: "I work on the same principle as people who train horses. You start with low fences, easily achieved goals, and work up. It's important in management never to ask people to try to accomplish goals they can't accept."

Make the goals measurable. Your potential leaders will never know when they have achieved their goals if they aren't measurable. When they are measurable, the knowledge that they have been attained will give them a sense of accomplishment. It will also free them to set new goals in place of the old ones.

Clearly state the goals. When goals have no clear focus, neither will the actions of the people trying to achieve them.

Make the goals require a "stretch." As I mentioned before, goals have to be achievable. On the other hand, when goals don't require a stretch, the people achieving them won't grow. The leader must know his people well enough to identify attainable goals that require a stretch.

Put the goals in writing. When people write down their goals, it makes them more accountable for those goals. A study of a Yale University graduating class showed that the small percentage of graduates who had written down their goals accomplished more than all of the other graduates combined. Putting goals in writing works.

It is also important to encourage your potential leaders to review their goals and progress frequently. Ben Franklin set aside time every day to review two questions. In the morning he asked himself, "What good shall I do today?" In the evening he asked, "What good have I done today?"

COMMUNICATE THE FUNDAMENTALS

For people to be productive and satisfied professionally, they have to know what their fundamental responsibilities are. It sounds so simple, but Peter Drucker says one of the critical problems in the workplace today is that there is a lack of understanding between the employer and employee as to what the employee is to do. Often employees are made to feel they are vaguely responsible for everything. It paralyzes them. Instead, we need to make clear to them what they *are* and *are not* responsible for. Then they will be able to focus their efforts on what we want, and they will succeed.

Look at how a basketball team works. Each of the five players has a particular job. There is a shooting guard whose job is to score points. The other guard is a point guard. His job is to pass the ball to people who can score. Another player is a power forward who is expected to get rebounds. The small forward's job is to score. The center is supposed to rebound, block shots, and score. Each person on the team knows what his job is, what his unique contribution to the team must be. When each concentrates on his particular responsibilities, the team can win.

One of the best ways to clarify expectations is to provide your people with job descriptions. In the description, identify the four to six primary functions you want the person to perform. Avoid long laundry lists of responsibilities. If the job description can't be summarized, the job is probably too broad. Also try to make clear what authority they have, the working parameters for each function they are to perform, and what the chain of authority is within the organization.

Finally, a leader must communicate to his or her people that their work has value to the organization and to the individual leader. To the employee, this often is the most important fundamental of all.

PERFORM THE FIVE-STEP PROCESS OF TRAINING PEOPLE

Part of the equipping process includes training people to perform the specific tasks of the jobs they are to do. The approach the leader takes to training will largely determine his people's success or failure. If he takes a dry, academic approach, the potential leaders will remember little of what's taught. If he simply throws the people into the job without any direction, they will likely feel overwhelmed and unsure of what to do.

The best type of training takes advantage of the way people learn. Researchers tell us that we remember 10 percent of what we hear, 50 percent of what we see, 70 percent of what we say, and 90 percent of what we hear, see, say, and do. Knowing that, we have to develop an approach to how we will train. I have found the best training method to be a five-step process:

Step 1: I model. The process begins with my doing the tasks while the person being trained watches. When I do this, I try to give the person an opportunity to see me go through the whole process. Too often when leaders train, they begin in the middle of the task and confuse the people they're trying to teach. When people see the task performed correctly and completely, it gives them something to try to duplicate.

Step 2: I mentor. During this next step, I continue to perform the task, but this time the person I'm training comes alongside me and assists in the process. I also take time to explain not only the *how* but also the *why* of each step.

Step 3: I monitor. We exchange places this time. The trainee performs the task, and I assist and correct. It's especially important during this phase to be positive and encouraging to the trainee. It keeps him trying, and it makes him want to improve rather than give up. Work with him until he develops consistency. Once he's gotten down the process, ask him to explain it to you. It will help him to understand and remember.

Step 4: I motivate. I take myself out of the task at this point and let the trainee go. My task is to make sure he knows how to do it without help and to keep encouraging him so he will continue to improve. It is important for me to stay with him until he senses success. It's a great moti-vator. At this time the trainee may want to make improvements to the process. Encourage him to do it, and at the same time learn from him.

Step 5: I multiply. This is my favorite part of the whole process. Once the new leaders do the job well, it becomes their turn to teach others how to do it. As teachers know, the best way to learn something is to teach it. And the beauty of this is it frees me to do other important developmen-tal tasks while others carry on the training.

GIVE THE "BIG THREE"

All the training in the world will provide limited success if you don't turn your people loose to do the job. I believe that if I get the best people, give them my vision, train them in the basics, and then let go, I will get a high return from them. As General George S. Patton once remarked, "Never tell people how to do things. Tell them what to do and they will surprise you with their ingenuity."

You can't turn people loose without structure, but you also want to give them enough freedom to be creative. The way to do that is to give them the big three: *responsibility, authority,* and *accountability.*

For some people, responsibility is the easiest of the three to give. We all want the people around us to be responsible. We know how important it is. As author/editor Michael Korda said, "Success on any major scale requires you to accept responsibility. . . . In the final analysis, the one quality that all successful people have . . . is the ability to take on responsibility."

What is more difficult for some leaders is allowing their people to keep the responsibility after it's been given. Poor managers want to control every detail of their people's work. When that happens, the potential leaders who work for them become frustrated and don't develop. Rather than desiring more responsibility, they become indifferent or avoid responsibility altogether. If you want your people to take responsibility, truly give it to them.

With responsibility must go authority. Progress does not come unless they are given together. Winston Churchill, while addressing the House of Commons during the Second World War, said, "I am your servant. You have the right to dismiss me when you please. What you have no right to do is ask me to bear responsibility without the power of action." When responsibility and authority come together, people become genuinely empowered.

There's an important aspect of authority that needs to be noted. When we first give authority to new leaders, we are actually *giving them permission* to have authority rather than *giving them authority* itself. True authority has to be earned.

Leaders must earn authority with each new group of people. However, I have found that once leaders have gained authority on a particular level, it takes very little time for them to establish that level of authority with another group of people. The higher the level of authority, the more quickly it happens.

Once responsibility and authority have been given to people, they are empowered to make things happen. But we also have to be sure they are making the right things happen. That's where accountability comes into the picture. True responsibility on the part of new leaders includes a willingness to be held accountable. If we are providing them the right climate, our people will not fear accountability. They will admit mistakes and see them as a part of the learning process.

The leader's part of accountability involves taking the time to review the new leader's work and give honest, constructive criticism. It is crucial that the leader be supportive but honest. It's been said that when Harry Truman was thrust into the presidency upon the death of President Franklin D. Roosevelt, Speaker of the House Sam Rayburn gave him some fatherly advice: "From here on out you're going to have lots of people around you. They'll try to put a wall around you and cut you off from any ideas but theirs. They'll tell you what a great man you are, Harry. But you and I both know you ain't." Rayburn was holding President Truman accountable.

Check on Them Systematically

I believe in touching base with people frequently. I like to give mini-evaluations all the time. Leaders who wait to give feedback only during annual formal evaluations are asking for trouble. People need the encouragement of being told they're doing well on a regular basis. They also need to hear as soon as possible when they are not doing well. It prevents a lot of problems with the organization, and it improves the leader.

How often I check on people is determined by a number of factors:

The importance of the task. When something is critical to the success of the organization, I touch base often.

The demands of the work. I find that if the work is very demanding, the person performing it needs encouragement more often. He may also need questions answered or need help solving difficult problems. Occasionally, when the job is really tough, I tell the person to take a break—demanding work can lead a person to burnout.

The newness of the work. Some leaders have no problem tackling a new task, no matter how different it is from previous work. Others have great difficulty adapting. I check often on the people who are less flexible or creative.

The newness of the worker. I want to give new leaders every possible chance to succeed. So I check on newer people more often. That way I can help them anticipate problems and make sure that they have a series of successes. By that they gain confidence.

The responsibility of the worker. When I know I can give a person a task and it will always get done, I may not check on that person until the task is complete. With less responsible people, I can't afford to do that.

My approach to checking on people also varies from person to person. For instance, rookies and veterans should be treated differently. But no matter how long people have been with me, there are some things I always do:

Discuss feelings. I always give my people an opportunity to tell me how they feel. I also tell them how I'm feeling. It clears the air and makes it possible for us to get down to business.

Measure progress. Together, we try to determine their progress. I often ask questions to find out what I need to know. If people are hitting obstacles, I remove the ones I can.

Give feedback. This is a critical part of the process. I always give them some kind of evaluation. I'm honest, and I do my homework to make sure I'm accurate. I give constructive criticism. This lets them know how they're doing, corrects problems, encourages improvements, and speeds the work.

Give encouragement. Whether the person is doing well or poorly, I always give encouragement. I encourage poor performers to do better. I encourage peak performers. I praise milestones. I try to give hope and encouragement when people are experiencing personal issues. Encouragement keeps people going.

CONDUCT PERIODIC EQUIPPING MEETINGS

Even after you've completed most of your people's training and are preparing to take them into their next growth phase—development—continue to conduct periodic equipping meetings. It helps your people stay on track, helps them keep growing, and encourages them to begin taking responsibility for equipping themselves.

When I prepare an equipping meeting, I include the following:

Good news. I always start on a positive note. I review the good things that are happening in the organization and pay particular attention to their areas of interest and responsibility.

Vision. People can get so caught up in their day-to-day responsibilities that they lose sight of the vision that drives the organization. Use the opportunity of an equipping meeting to recast that vision. It will also give them the appropriate context for the training you are about to give.

Content. Content will depend on their needs. Try to focus training on areas that will help them in the "A" priority areas, and orient the training on the people, not the lesson.

Administration. Cover any organizational items that give the people a sense of security and encourage their leadership.

Empowerment. Take time to connect with the people you equip. Encourage them personally. And show them how the equipping session empowers them to perform their jobs better. They will leave the meeting feeling positive and ready to work.

IMPROVING A LEADER IMPROVES THE ORGANIZATION

The entire equipping process takes a lot of time and attention. But its focus is long-term, not short-term. Rather than creating followers or even adding new leaders, it multiplies leaders. As I explained in the section on the five-step process of equipping, it is not complete until the equipper and the new leader select someone for the new leader to train. It is only then that the equipping process has come full circle. Without a successor, there can be no success.

Leaders who are equipping others have the greatest possibility of success, no matter what type of organization they're in. When a mentoring leader is dedicated to the equipping process, the whole level of performance within the organization rises dramatically. Everyone is better prepared to get the work done. More important, the best-equipped people will be ready for the final growth stage that creates the very best leaders—development. As Fred A. Manske Jr. said, "The greatest leader is willing to train people and develop them to the point that they eventually surpass him or her in knowledge and ability."

6

How Do I Create the Right Environment?

Mentoring leaders understand that it takes one
to know one, show one, and grow one.

Many organizations today fail to tap into their potential. Why? Because the only reward they give their employees is a paycheck. Successful organizations have leaders who do more than just give people a paycheck. They create an environment of encouragement that has the ability to transform people's lives.

Once you have identified potential leaders, you need to begin the work of building them into the leaders they can become. To do this you need a strategy. I use the *BEST* acronym as a reminder of what people need when they get started with my organization. They need me to:

> B *elieve in them.*
> E *ncourage them.*
> S *hare with them.*
> T *rust them.*

The *BEST* mentoring leaders are encouragers.

Encouraging benefits everyone. Who wouldn't be more secure and motivated when his leader *believes* in him, *encourages* him, *shares* with him, and *trusts* him? People are more productive when encouraged. Even more important, giving encouragement creates a strong emotional and professional foundation within workers who have leadership potential. Later, using training and development, a leader can be built on that foundation.

The process of building up leaders involves more than just encouragement. It also includes modeling. In fact, the leader's major responsibility in encouraging those around him is modeling leadership, a strong work ethic, responsibility, character, openness, consistency, communication, and a belief in people. As eighteenth-century writer Oliver Goldsmith once said, "People seldom improve when they have no other model but themselves to copy." We leaders must provide ourselves as models to copy.

Mark Twain once joked, "To do right is wonderful. To teach others to do right is even more wonderful—and much easier." I have a corollary to Twain's idea: "To lead others to do right is wonderful. To do right and then lead them is more wonderful—and harder." Like Twain, I recognize that the self-disciplines of doing right and then teaching others to do right are made difficult by human nature. Everyone can find excuses for not giving to those around them. Great leaders know the difficulties and encourage their people anyway. They know that there are people who will respond positively to what they give, and they focus on those positive results.

CREATE AN ENVIRONMENT OF GROWTH

Here are the things I have found a mentoring leader must do to encourage the potential leaders around him.

CHOOSE A LEADERSHIP MODEL FOR YOURSELF

As mentors, you and I are first responsible for finding good models for ourselves. Give careful thought to which leaders you will follow because they will determine your course. I have developed six questions to ask myself before picking a model to follow:

Does My Model's Life Deserve a Following? This question relates to quality of character. If the answer is not a clear yes, I have to be very careful. I will become like the people I follow, and I don't want models with flawed character.

Does My Model's Life Have a Following? This question looks at credibility. It is possible to be the very first person to discover a leader worth following, but it doesn't happen very often. If the person has no following, he or she may not be worth following.

If my answer to either of the first two questions is no, I don't have to bother with the other four. I need to look for another model.

What Is the Main Strength That Influences Others to Follow My Model? What does the model have to offer me? What is his best? Also note that strong leaders have weaknesses as well as strengths. I don't want to inadvertently emulate the weaknesses.

Does My Model Produce Other Leaders? The answer to this question will tell me whether the model's leadership priorities match mine in regard to developing new leaders.

Is My Model's Strength Reproducible in My Life? If I can't reproduce his strength in my life, his modeling will not benefit me. For instance, if you admire Shaquille O'Neil's ability as a basketball center, but you're only 5 feet, 9 inches tall and weigh 170 pounds, you are not going to be able to reproduce his strengths in the basketball arena. Find appropriate models . . . but strive for improvement. Don't be too quick to say that a strength is not reproducible. Most are. Don't limit your potential.

If My Model's Strength Is Reproducible in My Life, What Steps Must I Take to Develop and Demonstrate That Strength? You must develop a plan of action. If you only answer the questions and never implement a plan to develop those strengths in yourself, you are only performing an intellectual exercise.

The models we choose may or may not be accessible to us in a personal way. Some may be national figures, such as a president. Or they may be people from history. They can certainly benefit you, but not the way a personal mentor can.

Build Trust

I have learned that trust is the single most important factor in building personal and professional relationships. Warren Bennis and Burt Nanus call trust "the glue that binds followers and leaders together." Trust implies accountability, predictability, and reliability. More than anything else, followers want to believe in and trust their leaders. They want to be able to say, "Someday I want to be like him or her." If they don't trust you, they cannot say it. People first must believe in you before they will follow your leadership.

Trust must be built day by day. It calls for consistency. Some of the ways a leader can betray trust include: breaking promises, gossiping, withholding information, and being two-faced. These actions destroy the environment of trust necessary for the growth of potential leaders. And when a leader breaks trust, he must work twice as hard to regain it. As Christian leader Cheryl Biehl once said, "One of the realities of life is that if you can't trust a person at all points, you can't truly trust him or her at any point."

People will not follow a leader they do not trust. It is the leader's responsibility to actively develop that trust in him from the people around him. Trust is built on many things:

T *ime*. Take time to listen and give feedback on performance.
R *espect*. Give the potential leader respect, and he will return it with trust.
U *nconditional Positive Regard*. Show acceptance of the person.
S *ensitivity*. Anticipate the feelings and needs of the potential leader.
T *ouch*. Give encouragement—a handshake, high five, or pat on the back.

Once people trust their leader as a person, they become able to trust his leadership.

Show Transparency

All leaders make mistakes. That's simply part of life. Successful leaders recognize their errors, learn from them, and work to correct their faults. A study of 105 executives determined many of the characteristics shared by successful executives. One particular trait was identified as the most valuable: they admitted their mistakes and accepted the consequences rather than trying to blame others.

We live among people who try to make someone else responsible for their actions or circumstances. People don't want to reap the consequences of their actions. You can see this attitude everywhere. Television advertisements invite us daily to sue "even if you were at fault in an accident" or "declare bankruptcy" to avoid creditors. A leader who is willing to take responsibility for his actions and be honest and transparent with his people is someone they will admire, respect, and trust. That leader is also someone they can learn from.

Offer Time

People cannot be encouraged from a distance or by infrequent, short spurts of attention. They need you to spend time with them—planned time, not just a few words on the way to a meeting. I make it a priority to stay in touch with the leaders I'm developing in my organization. I plan and perform training sessions for my staff, I schedule one-on-one time for mentoring, and I schedule meetings where team members can share information. Often I'll take a potential leader to lunch. I frequently check with my people to see how their areas of responsibility are progressing and give assistance if needed.

We live in a fast-paced, demanding world, and time is a difficult thing to give. It is a leader's most valuable commodity. Peter Drucker wrote, "Nothing else, perhaps, distinguishes effective executives as much as their tender loving care of time." Time is valuable, but time spent with a potential leader is an investment. When you give of yourself, it benefits you, the organization, and the receiver.

BELIEVE IN PEOPLE

When you believe in people, you motivate them and release their potential. And people can sense intuitively when a person really believes in them. Anyone can see people as they are. It takes a leader to see what they can become, encourage them to grow in that direction, and believe that they will do it. People always grow toward a leader's expectations, not his criticism and examinations. Examinations merely *gauge* progress. Expectations *promote* progress. You can hire people to work for you, but you must win their hearts by believing in them in order to have them work with you.

GIVE ENCOURAGEMENT

Too many leaders expect their people to encourage themselves. But most people require outside encouragement to propel them forward. It is vital to their growth. Physician George Adams found encouragement to be so vital to a person's existence that he called it "oxygen to the soul."

New leaders especially need to be encouraged. When they arrive in a new situation, they encounter many changes and undergo many changes themselves. Encouragement helps them reach their potential; it empowers them by giving them energy to continue when they make mistakes.

Use lots of positive reinforcement with your people. Don't take acceptable work for granted; thank people for it. Praise a person every time you see improvement. And personalize your encouragement any time you can. Remember, what motivates one person may leave another cold or even irritated. Find out what works with each of your people and use it.

UCLA basketball coach John Wooden told players who scored to give a smile, wink, or nod to the player who gave them a good pass. "What if he's not looking?" asked a team member. Wooden replied, "I guarantee he'll look." Everyone values encouragement and looks for it.

EXHIBIT CONSISTENCY

Consistency is a crucial part of developing potential leaders. When we are consistent, our people learn to trust us. They are able to grow and develop because they know what to expect from us. They can answer the question, "What would my leader do in this situation?" when they face difficult decisions. They become secure because they know what our response to them will be, regardless of circumstances.

Hold Hope High

Hope is one of the greatest gifts mentors can give to those around them. Its power should never be underestimated. It takes a great leader to give hope to people when they can't find it within themselves. Winston Churchill recognized the value of hope. He was prime minister of England during some of the darkest hours of World War II. He was once asked by a reporter what his country's greatest weapon had been against Hitler's Nazi regime. Without pausing for a moment he said: "It was what England's greatest weapon has always been—hope."

People will continue working, struggling, and trying if they have hope. Hope lifts morale. It improves self-image. It reenergizes people. It raises their expectations. It is the leader's job to hold hope high, to instill it in the people he leads. Our people will have hope only if we give it to them. And we will have hope to give if we maintain the right attitude. Clare Boothe Luce, in *Europe in the Spring*, quotes Battle of Verdun hero Marshal Foch as saying, "There are no hopeless situations: there are only men who have grown hopeless about them."

Add Significance

No one wants to spend his time doing work that is unimportant. People want to do work that matters. Workers often say things like, "I want to feel that I've achieved, that I've accomplished, that I've made a difference. I want excellence. I want what I do to be important work. I want to make an impact." People want significance.

It is the job of a mentoring leader to add significance to the lives of the people he leads: One of the ways we can do this is to make them a part of something worthwhile. Too many people simply fall into a comfortable niche in life and stay there rather than pursue goals of significance.

Leaders can't afford to do that. Every leader must ask himself, "Do I want survival, success, or significance?" The best leaders desire significance and expend their time and energy in pursuit of their dreams. As former *Washington Post* CEO Katharine Graham said, "To love what you do and feel that it matters—how could anything be more fun?"

One way to add significance to the lives of the people you lead is to show them the big picture and let them know how they contribute to it. Many people get so caught up in the task of the moment that they cannot see the importance of what they do.

A member of my staff who was once dean of a vocational college told me about a day he was showing around a new employee. As he introduced each person and described each person's position, the receptionist overheard him say that hers was a very important position. The receptionist commented, "I'm not important. The most important thing I do each day is fill out a report."

"Without you," the dean replied, "this school wouldn't exist. Every new student who comes here talks to you first. If they don't like you, they won't like the school. If they don't like the school, they won't attend here, and we would soon run out of students. We would have to close our doors."

"Wow! I never thought of it that way," she replied. The dean immediately saw her appear more confident, and she sat up taller behind her desk as she answered the phone. The leader of her department had never explained to her the significance of her job. He had never explained her value to the organization. By seeing the big picture, she had significance added to her life.

PROVIDE SECURITY

Norman Cousins said, "People are never more insecure than when they become obsessed with their fears at the expense of their dreams." People who focus on their fears don't grow. They become paralyzed. Leaders are in a position to provide followers with an environment of security in which they can grow and develop. A potential leader who feels secure is more likely to take risks, try to excel, break new ground, and succeed. Mentoring leaders make their followers feel bigger than they are. Soon the followers begin to think, act, and produce bigger than they are. Finally, they become what they think they are.

Henry Ford once said, "One of the great discoveries a man makes, one of his great surprises, is to find he can do what he was afraid he couldn't do." A mentoring leader provides the security a potential leader needs to make that discovery.

Reward Production

People rise to our level of expectations. They try to give us what we reward. If you want your people to produce, then you must reward production.

Thomas J. Watson Sr., the founder of IBM, was famous for carrying a checkbook as he walked through offices and plants. Whenever he saw somebody doing an exceptional job, he wrote out a check to that person. It may have been for $5, $10, or $25. The amounts were small, but the impact of his action was tremendous. In many cases, people never cashed the checks. They framed them and put them on their walls. They found their reward not in the money, but in the personal recognition of their production. That's what gives significance and leads a person to give his personal best.

We must give positive acknowledgment and encouragement to the producers, and we must be careful not to reward the idle. Take a hard look at your organization. What are you rewarding?

Establish a Support System

Develop a support system for employees. Nothing hurts morale more than asking people to do something and not giving them resources to accomplish it. I believe every potential leader needs support in five areas:

Emotional Support. Provide a "yes, you can" atmosphere. Even when support is lacking in other areas, a person can forge ahead when given emotional support. This support costs the least and yields an incredible return.

Skills Training. One of the fastest ways to build people up is to train them. People receiving training perceive that the organization believes in them. And they are more productive because they are more highly skilled.

Money. It is difficult for people to give of themselves when their leaders and mentors do not give of themselves. If you pay peanuts, expect to get monkeys. Invest money in people; it always yields the highest return on your investment.

Equipment. To do the job right, you need the right tools. Too often a poor leader looks at things from a short-term perspective. Investing in the right equipment will give your people the time to be more productive, and it will keep up their morale.

Personnel. If you are in a position to do so, provide the people needed to get the job done. And provide good people. Personnel problems can eat up the time and energy of a potential leader, leaving little time for production.

Create a support system for all the people around you. But increase it for any individual only as he grows and is successful. I have found the familiar 80/20 principle holds especially true here. The top 20 percent of the people in the organization will perform 80 percent of the organization's production. So when structuring your support system, provide the top 20 percent producers with 80 percent of the total support.

Never Underestimate the Power of a Great Environment

People who live in a supportive and encouraging environment are more likely to succeed. Tom Geddie, of Central and Southwest Services, gives a wonderful illustration of what can happen in a such an environment where everyone desires to succeed:

Draw an imaginary line on the floor, and put one person on each side. The purpose is to get one person to convince the other, without force, to cross the line. U.S. players almost never convince one another, says Geddie, but Japanese workers do. They simply say, "If you'll cross the line, so will I." They exchange places, and they both win.

They recognize the importance of cooperation and mutual support. It has been a key to their success in the last fifty years. It can be a key to your success and to that of the leaders you mentor.

PART III

TAKING PEOPLE HIGHER

How Do I Help Them Become Better People?

Focus on improving the person,
not just the work he gets done.

When you equip people, you teach them how to do a job. Development is different. When you develop people, you are helping them improve as individuals. You are helping them acquire personal qualities that will benefit them in many areas of life, not just their jobs. When you help someone to cultivate discipline or a positive attitude, that's development. When you teach someone to manage his time more effectively or improve his people skills, that's development. When you teach leadership, that's development. What I've found is that many leaders don't have a developmental mind-set. They expect their employees to take care of their developmental needs on their own. What they fail to realize, however, is that development always pays higher dividends than equipping because it helps the whole person and lifts him to a higher level.

DEDICATE YOURSELF TO
DEVELOPING OTHERS

Personal development of your people is one of the most important things a mentoring leader will ever do. Though development is harder to do than equipping, it is well worth the price. Here's what you need to do as you get started:

1. SEE DEVELOPMENT AS A LONG-TERM PROCESS

Equipping is usually a fairly quick and straightforward process. Most people can learn the mechanics of their job very rapidly—in a matter of hours, days, or months, depending on the type of work. But development always takes time. Why? Because it requires change on the part of the person being developed, and you just can't rush that. Like the old saying goes, it takes nine months to produce a baby—no matter how many people you put on the job.

As you approach the development of your people, think of it as an ongoing process, not something you can do once and then be done. When I led Skyline Church in the San Diego area, I made the development of my staff one of my highest priorities. Some of it I did one-on-one.

But I also scheduled a time of teaching for the entire staff every month on topics that would grow them as leaders. It's something I did consistently for a decade.

I recommend that you plan to develop the people who work for you. Make it a consistent, regularly scheduled activity. You can ask your staff to read a book every month or two and discuss it together. You can teach a lesson. You can take them to conferences or seminars. Approach the task with your own unique spin. But know this: you cannot give what you do not have. In order to develop your staff, you must keep growing yourself.

2. DISCOVER EACH PERSON'S DREAMS AND DESIRES

When you equip people, you base what you do on your needs or those of the organization. You teach people what you want them to know so that they can do a job for you. On the other hand, development is based on their needs. You give them what they need in order to become better people. To do that well, you need to know people's dreams and desires.

Walter Lippmann, founder of *The New Republic*, said, "Ignore what a man desires and you ignore the very source of his power." Dreams are the generators of energy with your people. If they have high passion for their dreams, they have high energy. If you know what those dreams are and you develop them in a way that brings those dreams within reach, you not only harness that energy, but you also fuel it.

Unfortunately, some leaders don't like to see others pursuing their dreams because it reminds them of how far they are from living their dreams. As a result, these types of leaders try to talk people out of reaching for their dreams, and they often do it using the same excuses and rationalizations they give themselves.

If you have found yourself resenting the dreams of others and trying to talk them out of pursuing them, then you need to rekindle the fire you have for your own dreams and start pursuing them again. When a leader is learning, growing, and pursuing his own dreams, he is more likely to help others pursue their own.

3. Lead Everyone Differently

One of the mistakes rookie leaders often make is that they try to lead everyone the same way. But let's face it. Everyone doesn't respond to the same kind of leadership. You should try to be consistent with everyone. You should treat everyone with kindness and respect. But don't expect to use the same strategies and methods with everyone.

You have to figure out what leadership buttons to push with each individual person on your team. One person will respond well to being challenged; another will want to be nurtured. One will need the game plan drawn up for him; another will be more passionate if she can create the game plan herself. One will require consistent, frequent follow-up; another will want breathing room. If you desire to be a successful person, you need to take responsibility for conforming your leadership style to what your people need, not expecting them to adapt to you.

4. Use Organizational Goals for Individual Development

If you have to build a mechanism that is entirely separate from the actual work that needs to get done in order to develop your people, it's probably going to wear you out and frustrate you. The way to avoid that is to use organizational goals as much as possible for people's individual development. It's really the best way to go.

- When it's bad for the individual and bad for the organization—everyone loses.
- When it's good for the individual but bad for the organization—the organization loses.
- When it's bad for the individual but good for the organization—the individual loses.
- When it's good for the individual and good for the organization—everyone wins.

I know this may seem a little simplistic, but I want you to notice one thing. The only scenario where there are no losses is when something is good for the organization *and* the individual. That's a recipe for long-term success.

The way to create this kind of win is to match up three things:

- *A Goal:* Find a need or function within the organization that would bring value to the organization.
- *A Strength:* Find an individual on your team with a strength that needs developing that will help achieve that organizational goal.
- *An Opportunity:* Provide the time, money, and resources the individual needs to achieve the goal.

The more often you can create alignments like this, the more often you will create wins for everyone—the organization, the individual to be developed, and you.

5. Help Them Know Themselves

I always operate on the basic principle that people don't know themselves. A person can't be realistic about his potential until he is realistic about his position. In other words, you have to know where you are before you can figure out how to get someplace else.

Max DePree, chairman emeritus of Herman Miller, Inc. and a member of *Fortune* magazine's National Business Hall of Fame, said that it is the first responsibility of a leader to define reality. I believe it is the first responsibility of a leader who develops others to help them define the reality of who they are. Leaders help them recognize their strengths and weaknesses. That is critical if we want to help others.

6. Be Ready to Have a Hard Conversation

There is no development without hard lessons. Almost all growth comes when we have positive responses to negative things. The more difficult the thing is to deal with, the more we need to push in order to grow. The process is often not very pleasant, but you always have to pay a price for growth.

Good leaders are willing to have hard conversations to start the growth process for the people under their care. A friend told me the story of a former U.S. Army officer who was working in a Fortune 500 company. The man was repeatedly passed over when the organization's leaders were seeking and recruiting employees with leadership potential to advance in the organization, and he couldn't understand why. His performance record was good, his attitude was positive, and he possessed experience. So what was the problem?

The former officer possessed some peculiar personal habits that made others uncomfortable around him. When he became stressed, he hummed. When he became especially agitated, he sat on his hands. He wasn't aware that he did these things, and nobody ever pointed out the distracting and unprofessional nature of these peculiar habits. People simply wrote him off as being odd.

Fortunately, the man finally worked for a leader who was willing to have a hard conversation with him. The leader made him aware of the problem, he broke the habit, and today he is a senior leader in that organization.

When you don't want to have a difficult conversation, you need to ask yourself: *Is it because it will hurt them or hurt me?* If it is because it will hurt you, then you're being selfish. Good leaders get past the discomfort of having difficult conversations for the sake of the people they lead and the organization. The thing you need to remember is that people will work through difficult things if they believe you want to work with them.

7. Celebrate the Right Wins

Leaders who develop others always want to help their people get wins under their belts, especially when they are just starting out. But a strategic win always has greatest value. Try to target wins based on where you want people to grow and how you want them to grow. That will give them extra incentive and encouragement to go after the things that will help them improve.

It really does matter how you set up these wins. A good win is one that is not only achieved but also approached in the right way. If someone you're leading goes about an activity all wrong but somehow gets the right results—and you celebrate it—you're setting up that person to fail. Experience alone isn't a good enough teacher—evaluated experience is. As the leader, you need to evaluate what looks like a win to make sure it is actually teaching what your employee needs to learn in order to grow and develop.

8. Prepare Them for Leadership

In an organizational context, no development process would be complete without the inclusion of leadership development. The better your people are at leading, the greater potential impact they will have on and for the organization. But that means more than just teaching leadership lessons or asking people to read leadership books. It means taking them through a process that gets them ready to step in and lead.

WATCH THEM FLY HIGHER

If you dedicate yourself to the development of people and commit to it as a long-term process, you will notice a change in your relationships with the people who work with you. They will develop a strong loyalty to you because they know that you have their best interests at heart and you have proven it with your actions. And the longer you develop them, the longer they are likely to stay with you.

Knowing this, don't hold on to your people too tightly. Sometimes the best thing you can do for people is to let them spread their wings and fly. But if you have been diligent in the development process—and helped them to pass on what they've learned—someone else will step up and take their place. When you continually develop people, there is never a shortage of leaders to build the organization and help you carry the load.

8

WHAT SHOULD I DO
IF THEY PASS ME BY?

There is no greater accomplishment for mentors
than when people they develop pass them by!

I was very fortunate early in my career. I've known since I was four
years old what I wanted to do in life. And I grew up in a home with
a father who was experienced and successful in the profession in which I
would follow him. The situation is similar to that of the Manning family in football. Successful NFL quarterbacks Peyton and Eli Manning
grew up in the home of Archie Manning, who played for the New
Orleans Saints. As a result, they had a jump-start in football that 99 percent of other kids didn't.

In addition to the experiences and exposure I received from just being
around my father, I benefited from his strong leadership and mentoring.
He was very strategic in my development, identifying and encouraging
my strengths early. He sent me to several Dale Carnegie seminars before
I graduated from high school, directed my growth through extensive
reading, and took me to see and meet some of the great preachers of the
era. The advantages I received are too many to list. I am truly grateful for
all of them.

The result of my upbringing was that I saw success early in my career. I achieved a lot of firsts in my denomination. I was the youngest person to be elected to a national office. I was the first pastor to change the name of the church to better reach the community. I was the youngest to write his first book. And I had the first church that averaged more than one thousand in attendance every Sunday.

Unfortunately, during those early years, I might have also been the loneliest pastor in my denomination. The good news was that when I failed, plenty of people were glad to commiserate with me. But when I succeeded, few celebrated. I thought my colleagues and I were on the same team, but evidently they didn't see it that way. Many times Margaret and I celebrated alone.

GOOD MENTORS LEARN
THE CELEBRATION PRINCIPLE

Those early experiences taught us a lot. From them we learned the Celebration Principle: the true test of relationships is not only how loyal we are when friends fail, but how thrilled we are when they succeed. We also learned some things that you may find valuable:

THE JOY OF THE ACCOMPLISHMENT IS DIMINISHED WHEN NO ONE CELEBRATES WITH YOU

When I went to my denomination's conference following my first year as a pastor, I was excited about the things that were happening in my church. I was helping people, and I thought I was really making a difference in my community. My enthusiasm was unbounded. Much to my surprise, nobody shared my excitement! People seemed to look at me with skepticism or disdain. It really deflated me emotionally. The words of playwright Oscar Wilde were true: "Anybody can sympathize with the sufferings of a friend, but it requires a very fine nature to sympathize with a friend's success."

After Margaret and I talked about it, we decided that we would never let others' lack of enthusiasm hinder our own. And we also became determined to celebrate with friends when they succeeded—and to be even more enthusiastic when they surpassed us!

That's one reason I love doing conferences for young leaders. It gives me a chance to celebrate with them—and to champion their successes. I want them to feel encouraged and keep pursuing their dreams. There's no telling what they might accomplish with the knowledge that others want them to succeed.

MANY PEOPLE IDENTIFY WITH FAILURE; FEWER PEOPLE IDENTIFY WITH SUCCESS

Several years ago, I wrote a book called *Failing Forward*. As I was preparing to work on it, I lectured on the subject around the country. And what I found is that *everyone* identifies with failure. In fact, when I told people that they needed to learn how to use their mistakes as stepping-stones for success by *failing forward*, the reaction of the audience was audible. They wanted to learn how to fail forward.

What I've discovered over the years of working with people is the following: you may be able to impress people with your successes, but if you want to influence them, share your failures. Everybody has failed, so it's a great way to connect.

The problem is that because people so readily identify with failure, they sometimes have a hard time connecting with success. And if they don't identify with success, they may resent it.

WHAT HINDERS PEOPLE FROM SUCCESS OFTEN KEEPS THEM FROM CELEBRATING OTHERS' SUCCESS

Frequently the very same qualities that prevent people from achieving success—emotional insecurity, a scarcity mind-set, petty jealousy, etc.—prevent them from celebrating others' successes. They constantly compare themselves to others and find themselves wanting. As a result, they have a hard time getting beyond themselves.

Professional speaker Joe Larson once said, "My friends didn't believe that I could become a successful speaker. So I did something about it. I went out and found me some new friends!" It's sad, but sometimes that's what it takes.

The People Who Celebrate with You Become Lifelong Friends

Back during the first years of my career, two people outside my family who celebrated with us when we succeeded were Dave and Mary Vaughn. Dave was a few years ahead of me in his career, and he was always ready to cheer me on when I achieved a goal or passed a milestone. Even when my church grew to be larger than his and I gained more notoriety, he never held back. And thirty-five years later, he and Mary still celebrate with us!

Beware of the Green-Eyed Monster

In October 2003 at *Catalyst,* a conference for young leaders put on by Maximum Impact, Andy Stanley spoke. Andy is an effective and authentic communicator. He leads Northpoint Community Church, one of the top churches in the country with an attendance of more than fifteen thousand people every weekend. (Just in case you are unfamiliar with the church world, that puts Northpoint's attendance in the top 1 percent of all churches in America.)

Andy's second session was about four negative characteristics that can trip up a leader: guilt, anger, greed, and jealousy. Andy confessed that he sometimes experiences moments of professional jealousy when hearing other successful people speak. He said, "I have to make an extra effort to celebrate the success of other people who do what I do."

That potential for jealousy extends even to Andy's closest friends, including Louie Giglio, who directs Choice Resources. Andy explained,

> Louie and I have been friends since the sixth grade . . . We met at youth camp under a bunk bed while seniors battled it out above our heads. Louie is just a phenomenal communicator. When I

announce at our church that Louie Giglio is going to be speaking next week, they all start clapping and we have high attendance Sunday. And then for four or five days the rest of the week everyone's going, "Oh, Louie, Louie, Louie."

Andy went on to tell how Louie always teaches to capacity crowds at his events and delivers outstanding material. And every time Andy hears him speak, tiny pangs of jealousy threaten to rear their ugly heads.

Such feelings could destroy Andy and Louie's relationship, and that relationship is deep. Not only do they sometimes work together, but their families are close, and they even go on vacations together. How does Andy handle the envy he feels? By celebrating Louie's accomplishments. When Louie delivers a great message, Andy goes out of his way to praise him and celebrate with him. And Louie does the same with him. Andy said, "It's not enough to think it. I have to say it because that's how I cleanse my heart. Celebration is how you defeat jealousy."

BECOME A PARTY STARTER

Andy isn't alone. If most people were honest, they would admit to feelings of jealousy or envy when they witness others' success—even when the people succeeding are close friends or individuals they've mentored. I know I've fought feelings of jealousy. Haven't you? So how do you learn to celebrate with others instead of ignoring or undermining them? Start by doing these four things:

1. REALIZE IT'S NOT A COMPETITION

It's impossible to do anything of real significance on your own. It's very difficult to achieve success without help. And even if you do become successful, you won't enjoy it without friends. Life is better in a community of people you love and who also love you.

When I reflect on the value of community, many thoughts come to mind:

My success can be achieved only with others.
My lessons can be learned only from others.
My weaknesses can be strengthened only by others.
My servanthood can be tested only under others' leadership.
My influence can be compounded only through others.
My leadership can be focused only on others.
My best can be given only to others.
My legacy can be left only for others.
So I should commit myself to and celebrate with *others!*

Other people have an impact on every aspect of life. Most of the time, I choose with my attitude whether that impact is positive or negative.

Entertainer Bette Midler said, "The worst part of success is trying to find someone who is happy for you." Don't look at your friends, family, and teammates as competition. Be the rare kind of person who is happy when others succeed.

2. Celebrate When Others See Success

Not everyone views success the way you do. When it comes to the Celebration Principle, you must be willing to look at things from other people's point of view. What are their dreams? What goals have they set? What battles are they fighting? When they achieve something that is important to *them,* then celebrate! And be especially careful when a friend accomplishes something that you've already achieved and perhaps find to be old hat. Be sure to celebrate with enthusiasm. Never steal another person's thunder.

3. Celebrate Successes Others Don't Yet See

Sometimes people make great strides and aren't even aware of it. Have you ever started to diet or exercise and after a while felt that you were struggling, only to have a friend tell you how good you look? Or haven't you worked on a project and felt discouraged by your progress, but had someone else marvel at what you accomplished? It is inspiring and makes you want to work that much harder. If you *haven't* had a friend do that for you, then you may need some new friends—people who practice the Celebration Principle. And you should definitely celebrate the successes of the people you mentor that may be unseen by others.

4. Celebrate Most with Those Closest to You

The closer people are to you and the more important the relationship, the more you ought to celebrate. Celebrate early and often with those closest to you—especially with your spouse and children if you have a family. It's usually easy to celebrate victories on the job or in a hobby or sport. But the greatest victories in life are the ones that occur at home.

My friend Dan Reiland says, "A genuine friend encourages and challenges us to live out our best thoughts, honor our purest motives, and achieve our most significant dreams." That's what we need to do with the important people in our lives.

I have a confession to make. I haven't always been a practicer of the Celebration Principle at work. I've always done fairly well celebrating at home, but in the early years of my career, I was very competitive. I was driven to achieve, and I was very aware of where I was ranked in comparison to my colleagues. I took secret joy in watching my progress as I rose in those ranks. But as I progressed toward the top, something happened. The achievement of my goals wasn't as rewarding as I expected it to be. I felt that something was missing.

In the late 1980s and early 1990s, I finally began to change. When I turned forty, I realized that to accomplish my goals, I would need the help of others. I began to more aggressively develop my employees to lead. At first, my motives were somewhat selfish. But as I helped others to succeed, I found that it brought me great joy, regardless of whether it benefited me personally.

What I discovered is that the journey is a lot more fun if you take somebody with you. It's hard to have that perspective if your own success is the only thing you celebrate. If you want others to succeed alongside you, then you must encourage them, mentor them, and celebrate their successes. Not only does it give them the incentive to keep striving for their dreams, but it also helps them enjoy the journey along the way. As I began reaching out and celebrating others' successes, I found that the success of others brought me more joy than my success.

Now I try to celebrate with as many people as I can—not just my family, friends, and closest colleagues, but also the people farther outside my circle. The more people I can encourage and help to succeed, the better I like it. If you help enough people, the party never stops.

NOTES

ATTITUDE 101

Chapter 1
1. John C. Maxwell, *The Winning Attitude* (Nashville: Thomas Nelson, 1993), 24.
2. Denis Waitley, *The Winner's Edge* (New York: Berkley Publishing Group, 1994).
3. Pat Riley, *The Winner Within* (New York: Berkley Publishing Group, 1994), 41, 52.

Chapter 2
1. Galatians 6:7 NKJV.
2. J. Sidlow Baxter, *Awake, My Heart* (Grand Rapids: Kregal Publications, 1996).
3. See Luke 15:29–30 NKJV.

Chapter 4
1. Proverbs 23:7 NKJV.
2. Philippians 4:8 NKJV.

Chapter 5
1. David Bayles and Ted Orland, *Art and Fear: Observations on the Perils (and Rewards) of Artmaking* (Santa Barbara: Capra Press, 1993), 29.
2. Patricia Sellers, "Now Bounce Back!" *Fortune*, May 1, 1995, 49.
3. Lloyd Ogilvie, *Falling into Greatness* (Nashville: Thomas Nelson, 1984).
4. Genesis 40:14–15 NIV.

Chapter 6
1. Andy Andrews, ed., "Erma Bombeck" in *Storms of Perfection 2* (Nashville: Lightning Crown Publishers, 1994), 51.
2. Brodin, "The Key to Bouncing Back," *Discipleship Journal*, issue 109, 1999, 67.
3. "Where Failures Get Fixed," *Fortune*, May 1, 1995, 64.

Chapter 8
1. David Wallechinsky, *The Twentieth Century* (Boston: Little, Brown, 1995), 155.

SELF-IMPROVEMENT 101

Chapter 1
1. John C. Maxwell, *Breakthrough Parenting* (Colorado Springs: Focus on the Family, 1996), 116.
2. Denis E. Waitley and Robert B. Tucker, *Winning the Innovation Game* (Grand Rapids: Revell, 1986).

Chapter 2
1. Warren Bennis and Bert Nanus, *Leaders: The Strategies for Taking Charge* (New York: Harper Business, 2003), 56.
2. Longfellow, http://www.blupete.com/Literature/Poetry/Psalm.htm.
3. Jack Welch with Suzy Welch, *Winning* (New York: Harper Business, 2005), 61.

Chapter 4
1. Philip B. Crosby, *Quality Is Free: The Art of Making Quality Certain* (New York: Mentor Books, 1992), 68.

Chapter 5
1. Marcus Buckingham and Donald O. Clifton, *Now Discover Your Strengths* (New York: The Free Press, 2001), 6.

Chapter 6
1. Harry Golden, *The Right Time: An Autobiography* (New York: Putnam, 1969).

LEADERSHIP 101

Chapter 1
1. John F. Love, *McDonald's: Behind the Arches* (New York: Bantam Books, 1986).

Chapter 2
1. "The Champ," *Reader's Digest*, January 1972, 109.

Chapter 4
1. R. Earl Allen, *Let It Begin in Me* (Nashville: Broadman Press, 1985).

Chapter 5
1. E. M. Swift, "Odd Man Out," *Sports Illustrated*, 92–96.
2. Robert Shaw, "Tough Trust," *Leader to Leader* (Winter 1997), 46–54.

Chapter 7
1. Quoted at www.abcnews.com on February 4, 1998.
2. Thomas A. Stewart, "Brain Power: Who Owns It . . . How They Profit from It," *Fortune*, March 17, 1997, 105–6.

Chapter 8
1. Robert Dilenschneider, *Power and Influence: Mastering the Art of Persuasion* (New York: Prentice Hall, 1990).
2. E. C. McKenzie, *Quips and Quotes* (Grand Rapids: Baker, 1980).
3. Fred Smith, *Learning to Lead* (Waco: Word, 1986), 117.
4. John C. Maxwell, *Be a People Person* (Wheaton: Victor, 1989).

Chapter 10
1. Mickey H. Gramig, *Atlanta Constitution*, November 10, 1997.

RELATIONSHIPS 101

Chapter 1
1. Michael K. Deaver, "The Ronald Reagan I Knew," *Parade*, April 22, 2001, 12.
2. Ibid., 10.
3. "Thirty Years with Reagan: A Chat with Author, Former Reagan Aide Michael Deaver," April 20, 2001, www.abcnews.com.
4. Ibid.

Chapter 2
1. Art Mortell, "How to Master the Inner Game of Selling," vol. 10, no. 7.
2. Ecclesiastes 4:9–12 NIV.

Chapter 3
1. 1 Samuel 17:33–37 NIV.

Chapter 4
1. H. Norman Schwarzkopf, "Lessons in Leadership," vol. 12, no. 5.
2. Kevin and Jackie Freiberg, *Nuts! Southwest Airlines' Crazy Recipe for Business* (New York: Broadway Books, 1996), 224.

Chapter 6
1. Stephen R. Covey, *The Seven Habits of Highly Effective People: Restoring the Character Ethic* (New York: Simon and Schuster, 1989).
2. Proverbs 22:1 NIV.
3. Donald T. Phillips, *Lincoln on Leadership: Executive Strategies for Tough Times* (New York: Warner Books, 1992), 66–67.

Chapter 7
1. Gary Bauer, "American Family Life," *Focus on the Family*, July 1994, 2.
2. William Kirkpatrick, *Why Johnny Can't Tell Right from Wrong* (New York: Simon and Schuster, 1992).
3. Quoted in *Christianity Today*, October 4, 1993.

SUCCESS 101

Chapter 3
1. Robert M. McMath and Thom Forbes, *What Were They Thinking?* (New York: Random House, 1998).
2. Patricia Sellers, "Now Bounce Back!" *Fortune*, May 1, 1995, 50–51.

Chapter 4
1. Tommy Franks and Malcolm McConnell, *American Soldier* (New York: Regan Books, 2004), 99.
2. Jim Collins, *Good to Great* (New York: Harper Business, 2001), 139.

Chapter 5
1. Ella Wheeler Wilcox, "Which Are You?" *Custer, and Other Poems* (Chicago: W. B. Conkey Company, 1896), 134.
2. Anonymous.

Chapter 10
1. John C. Maxwell, *Developing the Leader Within You* (Nashville: Thomas Nelson, 1993), 75–76.

TEAMWORK 101

Chapter 2
1. Lt. Commander Smith's description was so complex and detailed that I asked him to e-mail it to me so that I could describe it accurately in this book.
2. Michael Jordan and Mark Vancil, *I Can't Accept Not Trying* (San Francisco: Harper, 1994).

Chapter 3
1. "Mount Everest History/Facts," www.mnteverst.com.
2. James Ramsey Ullman, *Man of Everest: The Autobiography of Tenzing* (London: George G. Harrap and Co., 1955), 250.
3. Ibid., 255.

Chapter 4
1. Tommy Franks and Malcolm McConnell, *American Soldier* (New York: Regan Books, 2004), 99.

Chapter 6
1. Peter N. Davies, *The Man Behind the Bridge: Colonel Toosey and the River Kwai* (London: Athlone Press, 1991), 56.
2. Ibid., 107–8.
3. Ibid., 99.
4. "A Tale of Two Rivers," *Electronic Recorder*, March 1998, www.livgrad.co.uk.

Chapter 8
1. Danny Cox with John Hoover, *Leadership When the Heat's On* (New York: McGraw-Hill, 1992), 69–70.

EQUIPPING 101

Chapter 2
1. Don Banks, "Teacher First, Seldom Second, Wootten Has Built Monument to Excellence at Maryland's DeMatha High," *St. Petersburg Times*, April 3, 1987, www.dematha.org.
2. John Feinstein, "A Down-to-Earth Coach Brings DeMatha to New Heights," *Washington Post*, February 27, 1984, www.dematha.org.
3. Morgan Wootten and Bill Gilbert, *From Orphans to Champions: The Story of DeMatha's Morgan Wootten* (New York: Atheneum, 1979), 24–25.
4. William Plummer, "Wootten's Way," *People*, November 20, 2000, 166.
5. Wootten and Gilbert, *From Orphans to Champions*, 12–13.

Chapter 4
1. John C. Maxwell, *The Winning Attitude: Your Key to Personal Success* (Nashville, Tennessee: Thomas Nelson, 1993).

Chapter 6
1. "Edwardian Conquest," June 14, 2001, www.britannia.com/wales.

Chapter 7
1. "Packing Parachutes," audiotape excerpt, www.charlieplumb.com.
2. "Charlie Plumb's Speech Content," www.charlieplumb.com.

MENTORING 101

Chapter 1
1. Robert G. C. Waite, *The Psychopathic God: Adolph Hitler* (New York: Basic Books, 1977), 244–45.

Chapter 2
1. Lee Iacocca and William Novak, *Iacocca* (New York: Bantam, 1986).

Chapter 3
1. Quoted in Ted J. Rakstis, "Creativity at Work," *Kiwanis Magazine*.
2. Joe Griffith, *Speaker's Library of Business* (Englewood Cliffs: Prentice-Hall, 1990), 55.

Chapter 4
1. Bennet Cerf, *The Sound of Laughter* (Garden City, NY: Doubleday and Company, 1970), 54.
2. Morton Hunt, "Are You Mistrustful?" *Parade*, March 6, 1988.